LEGAL TRADITIONS in *LOUISIANA* and the *FLORIDAS* 1763-1848

The Spanish forces led by ***Bernardo de Gálvez*** *at the battle of Pensacola*
Oil on canvas, Augusto Ferrer-Dalmau, 2015

LEGAL TRADITIONS in LOUISIANA and the FLORIDAS 1763-1848

SEÁN PATRICK DONLAN &
VERNON VALENTINE PALMER
Editors

TALBOT
PUBLISHING
Clark, New Jersey

ISBN 978-1-61619-584-7

TALBOT PUBLISHING

AN IMPRINT OF

THE LAWBOOK EXCHANGE, LTD.

33 Terminal Avenue

Clark, New Jersey 07066-1321

Please see our website for a selection of our other publications and fine facsimile reprints of classic works of legal history:
www.lawbookexchange.com

Library of Congress Cataloging-in-Publication Data

Names: Donlan, Sean Patrick, editor. | Palmer, Vernon Valentine, editor.
Title: Legal traditions in Louisiana and the Floridas 1763-1848 / Sean Patrick Donlan, Vernon Valentine Palmer, editors.
Description: Clark, NJ : Talbot Publishing, an imprint of The Lawbook Exchange, Ltd., 2019. | Includes bibliographical references and index.
Identifiers: LCCN 2018057427 | ISBN 9781616195847 (hardcover : alk. paper)
Subjects: LCSH: Law--Gulf States--History. | Law--Florida--History. | Law--West Florida--History. | Law--Louisiana--History. | Law--Gulf States--Spanish influences. | Law--Gulf States--French influences.
Classification: LCC KF358 .L44 2019 | DDC 349.7609/034--dc23
LC record available at https://lccn.loc.gov/2018057427

Printed in the United States of America on acid-free paper

TABLE OF CONTENTS

CONTRIBUTORS

Ken Aslakson is Associate Professor of History at *Union College* (Schenectady, NY). His research interests include Early American History and the intersections of Law and Race. His book, *Making Race in the Courtroom: The Legal Construction of Three Races in Early New Orleans,* was published by NYU Press in 2014. His most recent research project is examining how admiralty courts in British colonial North America dealt with slaves and slavery.

John W. Cairns is Professor of Civil Law at the *University of Edinburgh* (United Kingdom). His research interests cover Scottish legal history, slavery, law and the Enlightenment, and the early territorial history of Louisiana. He is the author of *Codification, Transplants and History: Law Reform in Louisiana (1808) and Quebec (1866)* (Talbot Publishing, 2015) and "The Early Historiography of the Lex Aquilia in Britain: Introducing Students to the Digest" in Paul du Plessis (ed.) *Wrongful Damage to Property in Roman Law* (Edinburgh University Press, 2018), 3-45.

Seán Patrick Donlan is Associate Dean of the *Thompson Rivers University* Faculty of Law (Canada). His research interests include Irish history, comparative law, and legal history. Most recently, he edited *Comparative Legal History* (Hart/Taylor & Francis (UK), 2013-2016) and (with D Heirbaut), *The Law's Many Bodies: Studies in Legal Hybridity and Jurisdictional Complexity, c1600-1900* (Duncker & Humblot (Germany), 2015).

Eberhard L. "Lo" Faber is Extraordinary Assistant Professor of Music Industry Studies at Loyola University New Orleans. His research focuses on politics in the Early National and Jacksonian periods as well as the history of early New Orleans. His first book, *Building the Land of Dreams: The American Transformation of New Orleans*, won the 2015 Williams Prize for best book in the field of Louisiana history.

Paul E. Hoffman is Professor Emeritus of History at *Louisiana State University* (Baton Rouge), he has been awarded a *Cruz de Oficial de la Orden de Isabela la Católica* (Spain) and is a Fellow, *Louisiana Historical Association*. His research interests cover the Spanish Empire in the greater Caribbean area, 16th to 18th centuries. His publications include *A New Andalucia and a Way to the Orient* (1990; Paperback, 2004); *Florida's Frontiers* (2002); and *Luisiana* (Spain, 1992).

Samuel C. Hyde, Jr. is Leon Ford Endowed Chair, Professor of History, and Director of the *Center for Southeast Louisiana Studies* at *Southeastern Louisiana University*. He is the screen writer and director of numerous films highlighting Louisiana history and the author or editor of nine books on southern history including the award winning *Pistols and Politics: Feuds, Factions, and the Struggle for Order in Louisiana's Florida Parishes, 1810-1935* (LSU Press, 2018).

Keagan LeJeune is Head of Department of English and Foreign Languages at McNeese State University, former president of Louisiana Folklore Society, and former editor of *Louisiana Folklore Miscellany*. His publications include *Always for the Underdog* (*Texas* Folklore Society, 2012) and *Legendary Louisiana Outlaws: The Heroes and Villains of Folk Justice* (LSU Press, 2016), which won the 2017 Louisiana Literary Award and the 2016 Brian McConnell Book Award presented by International Society for Contemporary Legend Research.

M.C. Mirow is Professor of Law at *Florida International University*, Miami, Florida. He writes on Latin American and Florida legal history. He is the author of *Latin American Constitutions: The Constitution of Cádiz and its Legacy in Spanish America* (Cambridge University Press, 2015) and "The Court of Common Pleas of East Florida 1763-1783", *Tijdschrift voor Rechtsgeschiedenis* 85:540 (2017).

Vernon Valentine Palmer is Thomas Pickles Professor of Law and Director of the *Eason Weinmann Center for International and Comparative Law*, Tulane University. He is a titular member of the *International Academy of Comparative Law*, recipient of the Légion d'Honneur, and the founder and president of the *World Society of Mixed Jurisdictions*. His research interests mainly concern comparative law, civil law, and legal history. His recent publications include *Mixed Jurisdictions Worldwide: The Third Legal Family* (CUP 2ed 2012) and *Through the Codes Darkly: Slave Law and Civil Law in Louisiana* (Lawbook Exchange 2012).

Susan Richbourg Parker specializes in the history of the Spanish presence in the colonial Southeast. Her recent publications appear in *The Yamasee Indians; From Florida to South Carolina, Signposts: New Directions in Southern Legal History,* and *From La Florida to La California: Franciscan Evangelization in the Spanish Borderlands.* She is writing a book on tri-racial Spanish St. Augustine.

LEGAL HISTORY, LOUISIANA, AND THE FLORIDAS

Seán Patrick Donlan and Vernon Valentine Palmer

INTRODUCTION

This collection looks at the legal traditions and contexts of Louisiana and the Floridas. Like all traditions, each was strongly marked by its time and place. The focus of the contributors is largely on the period between 1763-1843, with many chapters concentrating on the first decade of the nineteenth century. The eighty or so years covered here were a time of significant, complex shifts in national and imperial boundaries across the West, as well as in our region. It was a period, too, in which both modern nations or cultures and states and political institutions were crystalizing. These changes are, we suggest, best understood through a mix of different historiographical methods, a broad understanding of legal history, and a wide comparative context.

In this period, 'Louisiana', as the French and Spanish knew it, extended from the Gulf of Mexico throughout the present Midwest of the United States. And the Floridas, East and West, stretched all the way from the Mississippi River at Baton Rouge to include the entire modern state of Florida. Eventually, parts of the former West Florida were absorbed into present day Louisiana, Mississippi, Alabama and Florida. Throughout, there was a necessary struggle to balance the legal and normative desires of their populations – free and unfree, native and newcomer – with changing economic, political, and social realities. Understanding the entangled histories of these territories and traditions tells us much about continuity and change in a critical transition period for the modern nation-state and its increasingly common laws.

Our collection is the result of a conscious attempt to encourage dialogue among legal historians, professional historians, and others working in the areas of law and history. The contributions here reflect a range of complementary approaches to this subject. Some adopt a traditional, necessary focus on legal doctrine, on lawyers and judges, and on the courts. Others attempt to set those developments within a wider social context. Still others look beyond for wider comparative perspectives. Most combine these different approaches. And as editors, we have embraced this diversity of methods. If historical truth is not merely a matter of perspective, it is only through perspectives that we will arrive at truth.

LEGAL HISTORY AND HISTORIOGRAPHY

For most of their histories, European legal traditions, including those of Britain and Ireland, consisted of overlapping and competing plural legal orders. The law was only slowly monopolized by the state, with increasingly homogenous laws and unitary institutions. And a wide variety of non-legal norms, from custom to religion to dueling, remained essential aspects to social life. These could be *intra legem* (within or consistent with law), *praeter legum* (outside the law, but not illegal), or *contra legem* (against the law).[1] Even in the period examined here, continental legal practice – a legacy of far more than Roman law – was dominated by the complex balancing of legal texts, reason, and *équité* in adjudication of the *ius commune*, and *ancien régime*, traditions.

---

1. William Claiborne, the American Governor of the Orleans Territory and later the new state, participated in a duel in 1807, though he slipped into Spanish territory to do it. He was shot, but survived. See Elizabeth Urban Alexander, 'Daniel Clark: Merchant Prince of New Orleans' in Gene Allen Smith and Sylvia L Hilton (eds), *Nexus of Empire: Negotiating Loyalty and Identity in the Revolutionary Borderlands, 1760s-1820s* 261-262 (2010).

For its part, the legal ideas and institutions of Anglo-American law still included more than the doctrines and courts of 'common law', or indeed even of Equity. And the systems reflecting its tradition lacked a consistently-applied binding rule of precedent. In England, this was true, in part, because there was still no united and formally hierarchical court structure. But even in the United States, the Federal Supreme Court had a theoretical power that was rarely exercised. Much was decided within the states themselves. It would take decades, and Union armies, to establish meaningful centralization throughout the Republic.[2]

But things were changing. In the aftermath of the French Revolution, a series of related developments – nationalism, political centralism and monism, and state legal positivism – would establish many of the legal concepts still with us. Modern state legal systems of the nineteenth century were able to make claims of authority comparatively more meaningful than in the past, grounded in a slowly expanding notion of popular sovereignty, while threading together the diverse existing legal regimes into a single body of law. Earlier ideas and institutions continued within reformed structures and substantive laws. The doctrines of 'Equity', for example, in the sense of the English Courts of Chancery, continue to have a meaningful, subterranean existence in English law. But such changes did not happen overnight.

Many of the chapters that follow examine the laws and cultures of the region under Spanish rule.[3] As a result, they inevitably engage with both the history and historiography of Spanish rule in the Americas. In particular, they engage with or elide the so-called 'black legend' (*la leyenda negra*) of American historical scholarship. That tradition painted Spanish colonialism as

---

2. See Seán Patrick Donlan and Dirk Heirbaut, "A Patchwork of Accommodations": Reflections on European Legal Hybridity and Jurisdictional Complexity' in Donlan and Heirbaut (eds), *The Law's Many Bodies: Studies in Legal Hybridity and Jurisdictional Complexity, c1600-1900* (2015).
3. This was, in fact, the theme of the conference from which this collection developed. For a wide variety of earlier articles on the subject, see Gilbert C. Din (ed), *The Louisiana Purchase Bicentennial Series in Louisiana History: Volume II – The Spanish Presence in Louisiana* (1996).

inherently tyrannical, corrupt and inefficient.[4] But that perspective has been criticized for being simplistic, too often a product of assumptions about Anglo-American exceptionalism, rather than historical fact. And historians of the last generation have been far kinder to the Spanish. Their laws and legal institutions were not, it's suggested, particularly corrupt, inefficient, or unsophisticated by contemporary standards.[5] And as Matthew Mirow has recently written in the context of East Florida from 1783-1821, "constitutional law and civil proceedings [there] indicate a complex, and at times sophisticated, legal world."[6]

As throughout the West, Spain's formal laws co-existed with other social practices, especially away from the metropole and in its many colonies. In addition, Spanish legal traditions, both home and abroad, provided considerable accommodation to local practices. As was the pan-European inheritance of the time, its formal laws frequently underscored a non-legalistic equity in which both legal and local norms were important. Indeed, writing about New Spain for the period of 1700-1801, Charles Cutter wrote that

> In general terms colonial magistrates were to exercise their experience, knowledge, and prudence in meting out justice. More specifically, they drew from a system that sought justice somewhere in the convergence of written law, *doctrina* (the opinion of jurists), custom, and *equidad* (a community defined sense of fairness).[7]

This is a constant theme in legal history of the period. Stuart Banner, for example, noted much the same thing about the upper part of Louisiana. This territory became the District of Louisiana

---

4. David J. Weber, 'The Spanish Legacy in North American and the Historical Imagination' in 23 Western Historical Q. 5 (1992).
5. Derek N. Kerr, *Petty Felony, Slave Defiance, and Frontier Villainy. Crime and Justice in Spanish Louisiana, 1770-1803* 198 (1993). Kerr's study included West Florida.
6. Matthew C. Mirow, 'Testamentary Proceedings in Spanish East Florida, 1783-1821' in T.L. Harris (ed), *Studies in Canon Law and Common Law in Honor of R.H. Helmholz* 301 (2015).
7. Charles R. Cutter, *The legal culture of Northern New Spain, 1700-1810* 34 (1995).

(1804), the Territory of Louisiana (1804-1812), the Missouri Territory (1812-1819), and eventually many American states.[8] There, French laws that preceded Spanish rule continued to be important as custom under Spanish law.[9] Andrew McMichael's work on Spanish West Florida also echoes this sentiment. There, Spanish subjects were overwhelming Anglophones.[10] Spanish law, especially with respect to property and slavery, was important, but there remained considerable play in the joints.

For example, forty years ago Hans Baade asked if "French marriage contracts, surviving under Spanish rule outside of New Orleans, [rose] to the level of the customary law prevailing at the posts, to the exclusion of Castilian law formally applicable?"[11] But this is more complicated than it first appears. French rule had introduced the *Coutume de Paris* or *Customs of Paris*, a redacted collection of norms with rich Romano-Germanic roots. In France, these 'customs' of Paris competed with numerous other local regimes. In the colonies, where greater clarity was required, they were treated as a kind of common law, applying to settled subjects whatever their origins in France. They are also best seen, as Dirk Heirbaut has noted of German law history, as 'legal customs' rather than genuinely 'customary law' or merely customary practices.[12] And there were numerous ways in which these familiar laws, rooted in some manner in custom, could interact with the new Spanish regime. Were they *infra legem*, *praetor legem*, or *contra legem*? In the end, Baade concluded that

> the French legal folkways with respect to marriage contracts persisted in Spanish *Luisiana*, outside of New Orleans after

---

8. Stuart Banner, *Legal Systems in Conflict: Property and Sovereignty in Missouri, 1750-1860* (1996) [hereinafter Banner, *Legal Systems*].
9. Banner argues that it was Anglophone lawyers who were most positivistic. Banner, *Legal Systems, supra*, note 8, at 128. See also Idem., 'Written Law and Unwritten Norms in Colonial St Louis' 14 Law & Hist. Rev. 33 (1996).
10. See Andrew McMichael, *Atlantic Loyalties: Americans in Spanish West Florida, 1783-1810* 38 (2008) [hereinafter McMichael, *Atlantic Loyalties*].
11. Hans Baade, 'Marriage Contracts in French and Spanish Louisiana: A Study in Notraial Jurisprudence' 53 Tul. L. Rev. 1, 75 (1979).
12. Dirk Heirbaut, 'An Unknown Treasure for Historians of Early Medieval Europe: the Deebate of German Legal Historians on the Nature of Medieval Law' 27 Rechtsgeschichte 87 (2010).

> 1769 not only because they were so deeply entrenched, but also because there was no ready means of ascertaining to what extent their substantive dispositions might have been contrary to Castilian *ius cogens* (imperative law). There was, in all likelihood, the hope that such conflicts would not materialize, but if they did it seems equally clear that in the contemporary view, Castilian law would have prevailed.[13]

That is, they continued to exist *de facto* without the sanction of the new state and despite falling within an area clearly regulated by Spanish laws and legal customs. But lacking *de jure* status, they could only operate until some conflict with those Spanish laws and customs arose.

Another problem within legal-historical scholarship is the frequent belief, or prejudice, that involvement in a legal tradition necessitates a deep cultural attachment. One consequence of this is to see debates about legal ideas and institutions as profound cultural clashes or conflicts, rather than more superficial – but deeply meaningful – contests of divergent interests: economic, imperial, and cultural. If such views are now very much a minority opinion, especially among comparative legal histories, they can still represent the views of a sizable body of jurists. Another result of prejudice is that scholars looking for difference will miss equally significant continuities and confluences between traditions.

Indeed, much of the contemporary writing on this period is critical of any narrowly nationalistic interpretations of the peoples who occupied its spaces. It suggests, instead, that loyalty and identity were negotiable or nested in the times and places discussed here. Indeed, as Light Townsend Cummins has suggested, culture and identity here "should not be confused with nationalism because it was significantly more subtle and operated independently from any individual relationship to the concept of nation. It was instead cultural and social."[14] In fact, loyalty and

---

13. Baade, *supra* note 11 at 77. "[I]n all likelihood it was impossible for customary law *contra legem* to develop.' *Id.*, 76.
14. Light Townsend Cummins, 'Oliver Pollock and the Creation of an American Identity in Spanish Colonial Louisiana' in Smith and Hilton, *supra* note 1, at 208.

identity was easily altered when required to secure property and privilege. Sylia L. Hilton puts it succinctly: "Many Americans clearly thought that their loyalty could be legitimately transferred to whichever power best protected their interests."[15]

There are, of course, real differences in legal consciousness across different communities: in conceptions of the state and the judiciary, marital regimes and successions, etc. For example, Sara Sundburg has discussed the legal differences in a geographical and ideological intersection in the early years of the nineteenth century. The Territory of Orleans, the lower part of the vast Louisiana Purchase, was culturally French and had been ruled by continental private laws. The Mississippi Territory was also American. But it was culturally Anglophone with Anglo-American laws. Conceptually in-between, was Spanish West Florida. As will be explained below, it was culturally Anglophone, but governed – at least with respect to property – by Spanish laws. Sundberg suggests that in this situation, women fared best in Orleans and worst in Mississippi. But West Florida "demonstrates the encroachment of Anglo common law principles among male testators. These Anglo will writers often sought to circumvent the law, by reducing women's share of marital property."[16] Even here, however, this preference appears as much a practical positioning (resulting in greater shares of property, or greater control of property, for men) as a cultural attachment (a bias towards the familiar).[17]

---

15. Sylvia L. Hilton, 'Loyalty and Patriotism on North American Frontiers: Being and Becoming Spanish in the Mississippi Valley, 1776-1803' in Smith and Hilton, *supra* note 1, at 15. See also David Narrett, *Adventurism and Empire: The Struggle for Mastery in the Louisiana-Florida Borderlands, 1762-1803* (2015).

16. Sara Brooks Sundberg, *Women and the Law of Property Under Louisiana Civil Law, 1782-18 35* (Ph.D. dissertation, Louisiana State University, 2001), 195. She actually focuses on 'West Feliciana', the westernmost part of West Florida that straddled both the Orleans and Mississippi Territories. See Idem, 'Women and Property in Early Louisiana: Legal Systems at Odds' (2012) J. the Early Republic 633 (2012).

17. Cf. Banner, *Legal Systems*, *supra*, note 8 at 4 and David Langum, *Law and Community on the Mexican California Frontier: Anglo-American Expatriates and the Clash of Legal Traditions, 1821-1846* (1989).

With this in mind, our collection attempts to broaden the focus of Louisiana's legal history beyond narrow doctrinal research. We do so without insisting on any single perspective and, insofar as we recommend anything, we modestly consul a plurality of approaches. Taking into account the best of the work of its legal historians and recent critiques, this book and the event that proceeded it are explicit attempts to encourage dialogues between historians and legal historians of different perspectives. In this sense, we wish, with others, to pull scholars working on Louisiana into a more conscious engagement with the mainstream of both American and comparative legal history.[18] If American legal historians too seldom look abroad to other traditions, they have for much of the last half-century sought to place law within wider economic, political, and social contexts. But Louisiana's legal historians have frequently focused on ongoing internal debates about the character of its legal tradition, past and present. This was arguably made worse by the neglect of legal history by Louisiana's professional historians.[19]

But if Louisiana's legal historians should engage with American and Southern perspectives, they cannot stop there. The colonization of Louisiana and the Floridas created complex legal and social orders. As a result, as Cécile Vidal recently wrote, "[i]t is impossible to confine oneself to a strictly national or imperial approach when studying Louisiana over a lengthy period of time; one is compelled to engage transnational, connected, and/or comparative history."[20] And in one of the best recent collections on Southern legal history, Sally Hadden and Patricia Hagler Minter argue persuasively that "southern experiences need more frequently to be placed into comparative

18. See Mark F. Fernandez, *A Law Unto Itself? Essays in the New Louisiana Legal History* (2001) (suggesting deeper socio-cultural scholarship, especially in American comparisons).
19. Seán Patrick Donlan, 'Clashes and Continuities: Brief Reflections on the "New Louisiana Legal History"' 5 J. Civ. L. Stud. 67 (2012) [hereinafter Donlan, 'Clashes and Continuities'].
20. Cécile Vidal, 'Louisiana in Atlantic Perspective' in Vidal (ed), *Louisiana: Crossroads of the Atlantic World* 4 (2014).

context."[21] Louisiana and the Floridas were entangled with external developments, both in North America and beyond: military threats, economic competition, and colonial contests. The region was a 'crossroads', a 'frontier', and 'borderlands'.[22] It warrants multiple approaches and perspectives – American, Atlantic, and Caribbean, etc – all at once.

LOUISIANA AND THE FLORIDAS

In her colonization of the Americas, the Spanish claimed large swathes of southeastern North America as early as the sixteenth century, as *La Florida*. They did not, however, permanently settle much of the territory. And in 1682, Robert de La Salle (1643-87) claimed significant sections of North America, west and south of the British colonies, for the French. The Perdido—or lost—River, now dividing the American states of Alabama and Florida, was eventually agreed to be the boundary between French and Spanish territories. In the expanses of French *Louisiane*, the most important settlement in the early eighteenth century was the so-called *Isle* of Orleans, present-day New Orleans and the surrounding area. As noted, the French introduced the *Coutume de Paris* there, and throughout their territories. But again, both at home and abroad, social regulation was a *métis*, a complex hybrid of legality and normativity. French rule ended in *Louisiane* in 1763 with the end of the 'French and Indian War' (1756-63, aka the 'Seven Years War'). That conflict had pitted, among others, Britain against France and Spain.

The *Treaty of Paris* (1763) ceded French territories east of the Mississippi, excluding the Isle of Orleans, to Britain. Spain also ceded Florida to Britain in exchange for Cuba. And under the secret *Treaty of Fontainebleau* (1762, made public in 1764), French territories west of the Mississippi, including the Isle of

---

21. Sally E. Hadden and Patricia Hagler Minter, 'Introduction' to Hadden and Minter (eds), *Signposts: New Directions in Southern Legal History* 8 (2013).
22. On 'frontiers' and 'borderlands', see Jeremy Adelman and Stephen Aron, 'From Borderlands to Borders: Empires, Nation-States, and the Peoples in Between in North American History' 104 Am. Historical Rev. 814, 840 (1999).

Orleans, were transferred to Spain. Actual possession of Louisiana by the Spanish, however, took several years, in part due to the resistance of French Louisianans. Spanish colonial law or the '*derecho indiano*', no less complex than the French norms that preceded it, was ultimately imposed, along with other administrative alterations, though its unique detail shared similarities with French colonial law through the Roman influence on both.[23] The population and culture of Spanish *Luisiana* remained Francophone, as did much of its administration and judiciary. As a result, there was inevitably what Paul E. Hoffman calls here "A Confusion of Institutions". He concludes that

> the imposition of the Spanish institutions of the Cabildo, *comercio libre*, and different slave laws initially produced varying degrees of confusion as both the Spanish governors and their new subjects – especially the socially and economically powerful planters of the area around New Orleans – tried to square them with existing customs and practices, that is, with existing institutions.

Indeed, despite no intention to highlight it in this collection, the theme of dominant social orders attempting to weather social, political, and legal change is seen throughout.[24]

As a result of these different treaties, there were also a sometimes-disorienting series of inter-colonial transfers. Louisiana in the period covered here moved from France (1718-1763) to Spain (1763-1800) to France (1800-1803 *de jure*, only briefly *de facto* in 1803) to the United States (from 1803-). In the Floridas, leaving aside early French claims, the territories moved from Spain to Britain (1763-1783) to Spain (1783-1810 and following years) to the United States (from 1810 and following). As noted below, the distinction between legal and actual control over the Floridas was particularly complex in the decade after the American seizure of parts of West Florida. Jack Greene has suggested

---

23. On 'Spanish colonial law', see M.C. Mirow, 'Pre-Constitutional Law and Constitutions: Spanish Colonial Law and the Constitution of Cadiz' 12 Wash. U. Global. Stud. L. Rev. 313 (2013).
24. This theme is also central to Eberhard L. Faber, *Building the Land of Dreams: New Orleans and the Transformation of Early America* (2015).

how fruitful the study of such intercolonial transfers can be. He argued that

> we should focus not on those few cases in which old settlers managed to retain some of their old ways, but on the vastly greater number of cases in which old settlers suffered loss of control not just over their territory and instruments of government, but, more important, over the cultures they had constructed in those spaces.[25]

Indeed, in her chapter here, Susan Richbourg Parker continues her research on the impact of shifting sovereignties in East Florida from 1763-1821, and the related attempt to settle lands claims.[26] On the whole, she concludes that

> But what is truly notable about the three nations is the similarities of their performance, not the differences in laws and systems. None of the three nations truly endeavored to fulfill their promises made in the treaties to their own subjects/citizens or to their new, holdover citizens.

Indeed, each power was instead guilty of delays intended to force the holdovers out so that the new sovereign could better control the lands.

For its part, Britain divided Florida in two. 'West Florida' and 'East Florida' were split along the Apalachicola River, to the east of the Perdido and the earlier French-Spanish boundary. The northern border was set at the 31st Parallel, but remained fluid and contentious, subsequently extending north (32° 22′ north) from the Yazoo River to the Chattahoochee River. Many Anglophones moved into the Territory in the first decade or so of British rule. In fact, as the American War of Independence (1776-83) approached, the settler population of the Floridas was

---

25. Jack P. Greene, 'The cultural dimensions of Political Transfers: An Aspect of the European Occupation of the Americas' 6 Early Am. Stud. 1, 25-26 (2008).
26. See, eg, Susan Richbourg Parker, 'In My Mother's House: Dowry Property and Female Inheritance Patterns in Spanish Florida' in Hadden and Minter, *supra* note 21.

primarily loyalist, perhaps as a consequence of their less established and more precarious position. But after Spain entered the war on the side of the Americans in 1779, the Spanish Governor of *Luisiana* Bernardo de Gálvez successfully captured the whole of British West Florida in 1781, in a campaign that lasted a mere two months. After the war, Britain ceded both Floridas to Spain in another a second *Treaty of Paris* (1783).[27]

Settlement patterns in Spanish West Florida were not very different than they had been under British rule.[28] Spain struggled to attract colonists and instead developed the territory largely as a buffer against American expansion. But Anglophones continued to be attracted to the area by low taxes, generous land grants, and *de facto* religious tolerance. As noted, Spanish colonial laws applied, though they were administered separately from Louisiana and with local variation. In the Natchez District, for example, the English language was used and English customs followed.[29] But the lack of clear boundaries between American and Spanish territories led to persistent disputes between the former allies. The *Treaty of San Lorenzo* (1795) eventually established the 31st parallel (North) as the border between them. This required Spain to surrender, among other places, Natchez itself. Isaac Joslin Cox noted a century ago that the loss of "the Natchez district served as a prototype for West Florida, as that region in turn did for Texas and California."[30]

In West Florida, as later in Texas and California, Anglophone settlement would be used – with or without the participation of the settlers – as a pretext for American annexation, often on the basis of the vague provisions of earlier treaties. But at the turn of the nineteenth century, Spanish North America was still vast. *Luisiana* extended from the Gulf of Mexico, including New Orleans, north

---

27. Robin F.A. Fabel, 'British Rule in the Floridas' in Michael Gannon (ed), *The New History of Florida* (1996).
28. William S. Coker and Susan R. Parker, 'The Second Spanish Period in the Two Floridas' in Gannon, *supra*, note 27.
29. Jack D.L. Holmes, 'Law and Order in Spanish Natchez, 1781-1798' 25 J. Miss. Hist. 186 (1963). See Idem, 'Spanish Religious Policy in West Florida: Enlightened or Expedient?' 15 J. Church & State 259 (1973).
30. Isaac Joslin Cox, *The West Florida Controversy, 1798-1813: A Study in American Diplomacy* (1918).

into present-day Canada. 'West Florida' extended from the Mississippi River, through the present-day states of Mississippi and Alabama, to present-day Florida. 'East Florida' comprised most of present-day Florida. Within little more than two decades, all of this would be American.

In 1800, the secret *Treaty of San Ildefonso* formally returned *Luisiana* to France, on condition that it would not be ceded to a third, rival nation. Spain retained both East and West Florida. For its part, the United States Government was keen to secure New Orleans for commerce and the Floridas for security. They sought to buy both to expand all the way to the Gulf of Mexico. Instead, American negotiators found that they were able to obtain, through the *Louisiana Purchase* (1803), the immense Territory of French *Louisiane*. Despite earlier French assurances to the Spanish that there would be no transfers to third nations, the sale doubled the size of the United States (by expansion westward rather than southward). Boundary disputes in the Floridas would continue for two decades. The Spanish claimed West Florida as theirs and retained possession of it. But the curiously-worded *Treaty of San Ildefonso* permitted the Americans to claim that it had not been transferred to Spain, but retained by France. They argued that the Purchase included *all* French territory prior to 1763. Indeed, this was important not only in West Florida, but to the western edge of *Louisiane*. Continuing disputes over territories there would lead to the creation of a large, lawless 'neutral strip', 'neutral ground', or 'No Man's Land' (1806) between Spain and the United States.

But the Spanish continued to govern in *Louisiane* for almost three years until the arrival of French Prefect Pierre Clément de Laussat in 1803, shortly before transferring the Purchase territory to the United States. In the brief period of French rule, Laussat eliminated the Cabildo and hence all existing judicial structures, but left the laws unaltered. He was also very critical of the Spanish. As Eberhard (Lo) Faber suggests in his chapter,

> French newcomers to Louisiana ... frequently exhibited many of the virulent prejudices against Spanish America often attribute to Anglo-Americans under the rubric of the 'Black Legend,' including the belief that Spanish rule was corrupt, venal, violent, and prone to atrocities, and the belief that Span-

> ish-descended creoles were racially and morally compromised because of their alleged proclivity for intimate contact with Africans and Indians.[31]

Faber notes that Anglo-Americans entering the Orleans Territory often moderated their views on Spanish laws after their arrival. But he recognizes, too, the influence that was played by the wider political context on the continent. American "hostility to Spain and a darker view of Spanish colonial America ... had much in common with the ethnic prejudice of the Bonapartists, but also added a dimension of naked territorial aggression."[32]

When the Americans gained control of Louisiana, they divided the area into two regions. The Territory of Orleans – created formally in 1805 – was largely again the modern state of Louisiana, minus West Florida between the Mississippi and Pearl rivers. The remaining northern District of Louisiana (1804) spread across the continent; it would become the Territory of Louisiana (1804-1812), then the Territory of Missouri (1812-1819) to avoid confusion with the new State of Louisiana, and subsequently many states. It had always, however, been very thinly populated under French and Spanish rule. Written law had only exceptionally made it to the populations there.[33] While Banner has shown how the unwritten norms that dominated can be recovered, he has also noted the difficulty of that work. "To the extent those conventions remained unwritten," he writes,

> there is no direct way of knowing what they were. To the extent they were embodied in written rules ... they are no longer unwritten custom but, instead, written law. One can thus get at the norms of the past only indirectly, by trying to infer them from whatever written or physical evidence one has.[34]

---

31. Citing Gilbert Din and John Harkins, Vernon Palmer makes a similar suggestion in his contribution to this collection. See Din and Harkins, *The New Orleans Cabildo: Colonial Louisiana's First City Government 1769-1803* (1996).
32. See also Faber, *supra*, note 24.
33. Joseph W. McKnight, 'Law Books on the Hispanic Frontier' 27 J. the West 74 (1988).
34. Banner, *Legal Systems*, *supra*, note 8, at 53.

There, Anglophone settlers would relatively easily envelop the existing French-speaking populations. And their laws, in written texts the earlier inhabitants had lacked and interpreted by the judges only newly arrived, would relatively easily replace what had governed before.[35]

In any event, American control of the Orleans Territory brought its existing laws into close contact with Anglo-American laws. An Act of Congress in March of 1804 initially maintained the established laws of Orleans where they were consistent with the Act itself. Over the course of the decade after the Purchase, however, what we now call a 'mixed jurisdiction' would be established. That concept is easily misunderstood. It differs from the plurality of earlier Western legal traditions, where diverse laws and institutions competed with one another, distinct from other social norms. And it is different, too, from so-called 'legal pluralism', which means to embrace both laws and other law-like norms (ie, normative pluralism), especially in colonial and post-colonial contexts.[36] What we now call 'mixed jurisdictions' or 'mixed legal systems' are *unitary* legal systems whose different sections (private or civil law, criminal law, and public law) originate from diverse legal traditions. In the Orleans Territory, and subsequently the state of Louisiana, this would include Spanish and French private or civil law, Anglo-American criminal law, and American public law (already distinct from England).[37] That the legal system of the Territory was 'mixed' in this way was obvious and arguably problematic, both for contemporaries – especially the Americans – and some subsequent historians. If the exact shape may be, and has been, disputed, the fact of accommodation between the laws before the Purchase and those of the Americans afterwards cannot.

Indeed, American influence was no less obvious, immediate, and unavoidable. Their judges and advocates flooded into the

---

35. See Banner, *Legal Systems, supra*, note 8, and Morris S Arnold, *Savage Race: European Legal Traditions in Arkansas, 1686-1836* (1985).
36. See, eg, Seán Patrick Donlan and Lukas Heckendorn Urscheler, 'Concepts of Law: An Introduction' in Donlan and Heckendorn-Urscheler (eds), *Concepts of Law: Comparative, Jurisprudential, and Social Science Perspectives* (2014).
37. See Vernon V. Palmer, *Mixed Jurisdictions Worldwide: The Third Legal Family* ((2nd edn) 2012).

new Territory. Even where local law applied, it was often interpreted by outsiders untrained in its nuances. Like locals, these jurists were also cut off from the texts that might have made interpretation more accurate, and that were so important to the *ius commune* tradition that still dominated continental jurisdictions. But as Kenneth Aslakson notes, these new lawyers did not necessarily herald change. As he suggests, they were, in fact, critical to the defense of the status quo and, in particular, to the institution of slavery. Indeed,

> Immigrant lawyers from both the civil law and common law traditions were willing to compromise in their creation of New Orleans' legal system so that they could combine forces in an effort to maintain local control in the face of national government attempts to place restrictions in slavery in the newly acquired territories. Such was the institution's importance in building and shaping the profession.

Citing George Dargo's *Jefferson's Louisiana: Politics and the Clash of Legal Traditions* (1975), Aslakson stresses that the "controversies" of the period "were, for the most part, personal or political in nature, and it would be a mistake to read them as a clash of legal cultures." There was less a clash of traditions, that is, than of interests. And, as in other contexts, property trumped principle.

Dargo himself later moderated his thesis of a 'clash of legal traditions'. In revising his earlier work, he adopted the 'post-colonial' understanding of 'hybridity'. In this view, a hybrid is a complexity singularity that falls in-between, and draws from, other – nominally pure – forms. Dargo wrote that "[h]ybridity produced a rich interaction – call it conflict, contestation, or negotiation – from within the mix of languages, cultures and legal traditions that the American found in their first colony."[38] This gentler, more complex and accommodating idea of negotiation appears more consistent with the evidence than the earlier

---

38. George Dargo, 'The Digest of 1808: Historical Perspectives' 24 Tul. Eur. & Civ. L.F 30 (2009). See Idem, *Jefferson's Louisiana: Politics and the Clash of Legal Traditions* (a revised reprint of the 1975 text, 2010).

stark imagery of a clash. Some amount of low-grade competition and anxiety was articulated in the period, at least with regard to private law regulating land, matrimonial regimes, successions, etc. But Louisiana Creoles and their allies likely had mixed motives, including the stability of property and politics and the possibility of expediting statehood. Culture may not have been central. As Richard Kilbourne noted three decades ago:

> Louisianians' primary concern during that period was federal validation of their land grants, and the survival of the traditional legal institutions whereby landholding was structured must have been a secondary consideration, of prominence only because their removal might result in a divestiture of property rights.[39]

Indeed, Kilbourne denied that President Thomas Jefferson or William C. C. Claiborne, the Territorial Governor of Orleans, sought to suppress the local laws and replace them with Anglo-American law. This doesn't mean that there was no concern about the substance of the law and the culture to which it was attached. But historians must be cautious not to confuse rhetoric for reality.[40] Perhaps the more important point is that conflict and consensus, like clashes and continuities, are not mutually exclusive.[41]

Indeed, this idea of a sharp confrontation between legal cultures is frequently the result of anachronism, of projecting subsequent distinctions between legal traditions into a very different past. The utility of comparative legal history to the history of Louisiana and the Floridas is especially obvious here. And a similar distinction can be made between the nascent legal positivism of the early nineteenth century and the mature state legal positivism of the mid- and late century. Robert A. Pascal is, along with his adversary Rodolfo Batiza, one of the great champions of Louisiana legal history. The latter's argument that Louisiana law immediately before and after statehood reflected

---

39. Richard H. Kilbourne, Jr, *A History of the Louisiana Civil Code: The Formative Years, 1803-1839* 10 (1987).
40. See Seán Patrick Donlan, 'Entangled up in red, white, and blue: Spanish West Florida and the American Territory of Orleans, c1803-1810' in Thomas Duve (ed), *Entanglements in Legal History: Conceptual Approaches* (2014).
41. See Donlan, 'Clashes and Continuities', *supra*, note 19, at 76-78.

its Spanish, rather than French, nature, has been forcefully challenged in recent decades.[42] But Pascal also made a parallel argument – taken up most clearly by Kilbourne – that Louisiana law of the period was far less positivistic than contemporary France was or was becoming (ie, the mature state legal pluralism of the future). As he noted in comparing the law of the Orleans Territory and France, the former was

> much closer in thought and method to the Anglo-American law of the time. The Romanist-Spanish law certainly contained much more legislation than the Anglo-American, but the opinions of the commentators on the Roman and Spanish legislation occupied a position similar to that of the judge in Anglo American law.[43]

Judges of the continental *ius commune* and Anglo-American common law were not unbounded in their decisions, though the types of texts that limited each was different. If the constraints involved would not be enough to satisfy the critics and jurists of the later nineteenth century, judges believed themselves meaningfully constrained by their traditions.[44]

Of course, real change was occurring in Louisiana's laws. In this collection, Vernon Palmer shows how Spanish law was "dismembered" from 1803-1808. Indeed, he notes that this begins with Laussat's "dismantlement of the Cabildo" in 1803. But it continued with the Practice Act of 1805 which "was fundamentally incompatible with the Spanish civil procedure set forth in Governor O'Reilly's Instructions of 1769." This was followed by "the Crimes Act of 1805 drafted by James Workman. In a single stroke, it repealed and replaced the Spanish

---

42. See especially John W. Cairns, *Codification, Transplants and History: Law Reform in Louisiana (1808) and Quebec (1866)* (2015).
43. Robert A. Pascal, 'Louisiana's Mixed Legal System' 15 Revue Générale de Droit 341 (1984), 353. See Kilbourne, *supra*, note 39, at 42, 93.
44. Even Pascal's critics have now made similar arguments, while deemphasizing both a strong French connection and an exaggerated Spanish perception. See Cairns' discussion of natural law and positivism in Cairns, *supra*, note 42, at 441-444. See more generally Vernon Valentine Palmer. 'The French Connection and The Spanish Perception: Historical Debates and Contemporary Evaluation of French Influence on Louisiana Civil Law' 63 La. L. Rev. 1067 (2003).

criminal law with the English law of crimes." Such changes were linked, too, to extra-legal factors, not least to Anglo-American criticisms – whether or not justified – of Spanish law. Similarly, the new slave Code passed in 1806-1807 "suppressed Spanish slave law and replaced it with a repressive, security-conscious law of the Creoles' own devising that was drawn from American sources." This was a meaningful change from the earlier Spanish regime, at the same time that it protected the established interests of the Creoles and brought Louisiana closer to American laws on slavery.[45] And in the same period, American commercial law quickly began to displace its Spanish equivalent, though this would assist both native and newcomer alike. Finally, Palmer notes that the Marriage Act of 1807 borrowed from French sources in advance of more considerable borrowing that would take place in the *Digest of 1808*, or *A Digest of the Civil Laws Now in Force in the Territory of Orleans* (1808).[46]

Perhaps no one has done more to clarify the status of the *Digest*, and the law of the period, than legal historian John Cairns.[47] In his contribution here, Cairns stresses the uniqueness of the *Digest*. Referring to Pascal, he notes "[t]hat the Digest is not Spanish law in French dress does not mean … that it is entirely French. The issue is much more complicated. The Digest is a

---

45. Jennifer M. Spear, '"Using the Faculties Conceded to Her by Law": Slavery, Law, and Agency in Spanish New Orleans, 1763-1803' in Hadden and Hagler Minter (eds), *supra* note 21.

46. The *Digest of 1808* has long held a special position in Louisiana legal history and historiography. The text has served as a lightning rod for a number of ongoing debates, including those between Professors Pascal and Batiza. Jurists have debated its status, ie is the *Digest of 1808* a lightly-ordered collection that redacts existing law without necessarily altering them? Is it instead a modern code akin to the contemporary French *Code Civil* (1804), the result of a process of deep revision and a concomitant repeal of the laws of different subject areas (here private or civil law)? Was its substance primarily Spanish, reflecting the long period of Spanish rule, or French, reflecting the culture of Louisiana creoles, the French language in which it was written, and developments in France? What was the role of the redactors, who put it together? What was the significance of the "De La Vergne volume" of the *Digest*? And, again, entangled in these questions is the question of whether the law reflected natural law or modern positivism?

47. See Cairns, *supra*, note 42.

unique and fascinating civil code." It is instead "unique and different in all kinds of ways." Its redactors would not have understood their role as simply capturing, as if such a thing were simple, pre-existing Castilian law. The sources of the *Digest* resemble the hermeneutically open norms of the period. These were rooted in natural law and fluid legal norms more than a closed system of positive norms. Indeed, even in France that latter idea was only slowly taking hold. The revolutionary possibilities of the *Code Civil* were not yet clear, not least in the Orleans Territory. Cairns also examines a bill vetoed by the Governor in advance of the passage of the Digest which listed "an unusual mix of primary and secondary sources, though this perhaps could be justified given the state of legal science in the Territory." Cairns reiterates that the Act "emphasized that the law in the Territory of Orleans was the civil law in the sense of laws based on the Roman law. The Spanish law was represented as just a modern variation." The private law of Orleans was neither simply Spanish nor French.

As the Spanish crown was threatened in Europe by Napoléon and his armies, changes were inevitable, too, in its colonies. Spanish West Florida still consisted of a population that was overwhelmingly Anglophone. Largely content under Spanish rule, the West Floridians of the extreme westernmost part of the territory became increasingly anxious about the machinations of the Americans, British, and French. As in other Spanish colonies across the Americas, the West Floridians sought to secure their peace and property in the face of imperial insecurity. This was about careful and cultured self-interest more than self-identity and culture. Indeed, it is additional evidence of

> the multifaceted nature, as well as the mutability, of national loyalty and identity on the Gulf Coast borderlands and the degree to which political nationalism – inasmuch as it existed – relied on local issues and the promise of prosperity rather than loyalty to any single political entity.[48]

---

48. Andrew McMichael, 'William Dunbar, William Claiborne, and Daniel Clark: Intersections of Loyalty and National Identity on the Florida Frontier' in

West Floridian loyalty only flagged as instability intensified. Fearful of Spanish regulars being raised and supplemented—or so they believed—by Choctaws and slaves, they could wait no longer. By late September of 1810, they had taken the Spanish Fort at Baton Rouge. Similar actions occurred throughout Spain's American possessions.

If West Florida's *Declaration* recognised their "legitimate sovereign" and their "upright intentions and inviolable fidelity to our King and parent country", it also called labelled them "a free and independent State".[49] But the rebellion was limited in both its aim and impact. The West Florida text explicitly mirrored the American *Declaration of Independence* (1776), which declared the colonies "Free and Independent States". And the *Constitution or Form of Government of the State of Florida ...* (1810) was based on both the Federal *Constitution* (1789) and that of the State of Kentucky (1799). This "State of Florida", complete with a Governor, never formally extended beyond the Pearl River; real control didn't extend even that far.[50] Earlier in 1810, the Territory of Orleans had already sought admission as a state. And as J. C. A. Stagg has written of West Florida,

> Considered as a whole ... the actions of the delegates ... were not the preliminaries to the establishment of a new nation but rather a series of hastily improvised expedients to force the United States to settle the West Florida problem – on West Floridian terms ....[51]

Smith and Hilton, *supra* note 1. See McMichael, *Atlantic Loyalties*, *supra*, note 10, at 101.

49. Stanley Clisby Arthur, *The Story of the West Florida Rebellion* (1934), 113, 113, 114. The entity is frequently referred to anachronistically as the 'Republic of West Florida'.

50. See the 'Constitution of West Florida 1801' in Horst Dippel (ed), *Constitutional Documents of the United States of America, 1776-1860, Part 7* 143-153 (2009).

See, eg, the letters from John Rhea, President of the Convention, in Henry S. Marks (ed), 'Boundary Disputes in the Republic of West Florida in 1810' 12 La. Hist. 355 (1971).

51. J.C.A. Stagg, *Borderlines in Borderlands: James Madison and the Spanish-American Frontier, 1776-1821* 69 (2009). Indeed, West Florida's constitution was modelled on the American and Kentucky (1799) constitutions, complete with a 'Governor'.

Rather than reflecting any deeper cultural or political loyalties, their actions suggested the preservation of their properties and place. Had statehood been achieved on their terms, the West Florida Constitution suggests that the result might have been another 'mixed' legal system, though one in which Spanish influence was likely limited to property and slave law.

In any event, the West Floridians were ignored. President James Madison saw the same opportunity that they did. On the same day the West Floridian constitution was approved, Madison issued a proclamation annexing West Florida, from the Mississippi to the Perdido River (rather than the Apalachicola River to its east). American troops seized the hopeful state only seventy-one days after its break from Spain. Samuel C. Hyde, Jr argues, however, that the light touch of Spanish governance would lead to future problems. Rather than the repression of the 'black legend', Spanish authorities and laws in West Florida were weak and ineffective. The consequence was violence not only in the final months of 1810 – between American, pro-Spanish, and independent factions – but long after American annexation. Spanish weakness left a "bitter legacy" into the modern period. Indeed

> Spanish policies and jurisprudence including land grant regulations and loosely enumerated title surveys, toleration of suspect residents including known deserters from multiple armies, lack of resources, especially troops, to enforce the necessary mechanisms of governance and timid, if not ineffective, leadership doomed their authority in West Florida.[52]

As Hyde has suggested elsewhere, American control of what had been West Florida, and shortly became part of Louisiana, did not mean an end to extra-legal violence.[53]

The movement towards statehood for the Territory of Orleans continued somewhat fitfully in Washington. The inclusion of Francophone catholics raised a number of problems about the expansion of the nation, the dilution of power among the estab-

---

52. See also Samuel C. Hyde, Jr., 'Consolidating the Revolution: Factionalism and Finesse in the West Florida Revolt, 1810' 51 La. Hist. 261 (2010).
53. See Samuel C. Hyde, Jr, *Pistols and Politics: The Dilemma of Democracy in Louisiana's Florida Parishes, 1810-1899* (1998).

lished states, the boundaries of the new state and nation, and the inclusion of a territory without democratic traditions. Louisiana law wasn't rooted in English law. Its slave law was distinct, too, from existing American law. What's more, the Territory had a large population of free people of color. Congressional approval of statehood only came after agreement that these black citizens were prohibited from voting. A Convention in New Orleans agreed to a constitution, again modelled on that of Kentucky, though in the French language and with special provisions to protect the Territory's private law. The western end of West Florida, between the Mississippi and the Pearl Rivers, was also added to the new state in 1812. This served American purposes well. It provided a significant injection of Anglo-Americans broadly versed in continental law and who diluted the power of the established Creoles.

As James C. Cusick has suggested, "the Spanish Floridas … typified problems that are common in border zones across time."[54] Changes here also occurred with considerable speed. The Americans added West Florida's Mobile District to the Mississippi Territory in 1812, as Louisiana achieved statehood. Indeed, in the same year, filibusters from Georgia unsuccessfully sought to overthrow the government of East Florida. While Spain still held legal title, the United States continued to expand and intervene in Spanish territory. In addition, in the context of the *War of 1812* (1812-1815), the Americans faced native American attacks throughout the South (1813-1814), including West Florida. And under Andrew Jackson, they would successfully repel the British in the Battle of New Orleans (1815). The United States also had effective control of East Florida as a consequence of the *First Seminole War* (1817-1818). Spain finally acquiesced to the inevitable and ceded the Floridas formally to the United States in the *Adams-Onís Treaty* (1819). That treaty took effect in 1821. The following year, most of East Florida and a small

---

54. James C. Cusick, 'Some Thoughts on Spanish East and West Florida as Borderlands' 90 Fla. Historical Q. 133 (2011).

portion of the former West Florida, was admitted as the Territory of Florida.[55]

In his contribution here, extending beyond the period of the other chapters, Matthew Mirow looks at the American Supreme Court's role in determining private land ownership in the territory finally under its control. This necessarily meant that the court "was confronted with different legal systems and terminology. Other aspects of Florida land grants presented deeper questions of Spanish law." Mirow shows how, whatever its motivations, the court

> took Spanish law and Spanish documents seriously determining title to large tracts of land under its jurisdiction. The Court made reasonable efforts to understand and to apply *derecho indiano* to resolve petitioner's claims and appears to have dealt fairly with petitioners, though different justices brought approaches that may have been more favorable … of less favorable to claimants under Spanish grants.

Especially important in this were the writings of Joseph M. White. White's materials on land law were used throughout the 1830s. They were published commercially as *A New Collection of Laws, Charters and Local Ordinances of the Governments of Great Britain, France, and Spain Relating to the Concessions of Land* (1839). Litigants, or rather their lawyers, played on ambiguities and differences in the laws involved in attempting to win their cases.

Bringing the collection to a close, Keagan Lejeune discusses the importance of legend and place, of folklore and folk laws, and of "outlawry" to popular understandings of law in the past and present. His focus is, in particular, on Louisiana's western "neutral strip" and the legacy of Spanish rule there. [56] As he notes, extra-legal or extra-state boundaries and notions of justice at once threaten and confirm institutionalized law as

---

55. See W.S. Belko, 'The Origins of the Monroe Doctrine Revisited: The Madison Administration, the West Florida Revolt, and the No Transfer Policy' 90 Fla. Historical Q. 157, 192 (2011).
56. See Keagan LeJeune, *Legendary Louisiana Outlaws: The Villians and Heroes of Folk Justice* (2016).

> the outlaw in legend for a time outwits the law, avoids capture, and escapes punishment, which demonstrates the limits of the official system of justice and the power of the folk; however, the outlaw never lasts. Living outside the law comes with a heavy price. Once the community's tolerance and perhaps even celebration of violence and outlawry end, the outlaw is brought to justice, but not by the power and might of the official legal system.

With respect to the neutral strip, Spain had largely "governed the region with a blind eye, allowing squatters and all manner of self-directed settlers, such as American Indians who lost land during the French-Indian War, to settle there in order to thwart American expansion." The suspicion was not, that is, of a domineering state, but of a weak one that could not guarantee either its norms or those of the local population. As a result, the felt need for vigilantism, or "vigilance committees for protection," was not insignificant where the state –the American nation-state or the state of Louisiana – could not easily enforce its authority. As Lejeune illustrates, these views resulted in a belief both that lost gold remained after the Spanish, as well as a cursed or 'voodooed' landscape that served as "a metaphorical scapegoat for the region's history."

CONCLUSION

This collection has looked at the legal traditions and contexts of Louisiana and the Floridas from a mix of perspectives. The contributions have revealed the importance of both legal institutions and extra-legal influences, not least abstract notions of nation/state identity and the practical demands of imperial politics. As editors, we have encouraged open, respectful communication between those engaged. The result has been an expanded sense of contexts that are not mutually exclusive, but rather necessary to a richer understanding of law and history in this time and place.

LEGAL TRADITIONS in *LOUISIANA* and the *FLORIDAS* 1763-1848

Portrait of Charles III of Spain
Anton Raphael Mengs, 1765

CHAPTER 1

A CONFUSION OF INSTITUTIONS

Spanish Law and Practice in a Francophone Colony, Louisiana, 1763-circa 1798

Paul E. Hoffman[*]

INTRODUCTION

French Louisiana had been a thorn in the flank of Spain's Atlantic Empire from its founding in 1699. Failure to remove that thorn in 1699 and again in 1716, when doing so would have been comparatively easy and Spanish naval forces were positioned to do so, meant that by 1762 the wound had festered, so that the colony had become what La Salle, Iberville, Bienville, and their royal masters had envisioned: a smuggling station through which French goods reached New Spain and Cuba and their goods—dye stuffs and silver mostly—reached France and helped to pay the costs of a colony that consumed more than it produced, at least so far as the French crown's finances were concerned.[1]

---

* © 2017 Paul E Hoffman. Professor Emeritus of History, Louisiana State University.

1. I have borrowed the "thorn" from Robert S. Weddle, *The French Thorn: Rival Explorers in the Spanish Sea, 1682-1762* (1991); Robert S. Weddle, *Changing Tides: Twilight and Dawn in the Spanish Sea, 1763-1803* (1995) (carries the story of explorations). The most detailed history of the French colony to 1731 is the five volumes of *A History of French Louisiana*: Marcel Giraud, 1-4 *Histoire de le Louisiana Française* (1953-74); 1 *A History of French Louisiana: The Reign of Louis XIV*, 1698-1715 (Joseph C. Lambert trans., LSU Press, 1974); 5 *A History of French Louisiana: The Company of the Indies, 1723-31* (Brian Pearce trans., 1991) (not previously published). For

In the early 1760s, Spain's government determined to cauterize that wound by acquiring the province, if possible, as part of its general alliance with France (the third Family Compact) initiated in the last years of the Seven Years' War. The disastrous outcome of that war, which forced Spain to accept the cession of all of the Gulf South east of the Mississippi River[2] to Great Britain and the right of that power's subjects to use the Mississippi River through the Isle of Orleans (which became Spanish) in order to reach the Natchez district and points north and east on the great river, made acquisition even more important because it gave the world's leading trading and naval nation access to the same flanking position, the same opportunities for smuggling. France willingly gave Spain what was left of its expansive, and largely unbounded, claim over the Mississippi drainage, being careful to preserve the economic heart of the colony, the Isle of Orleans (whose center was New Orleans) for Spain and, thus for French economic interests.

La Louisiane was a colony like no other that Spain had acquired in the Americas, save possibly what we know as Uruguay. Although slightly more than half of its population was enslaved, by the standards of the time it was a European, not a Native American province.[3] Fitting it into Spain's American

---

a general economic history, John Clark, *New Orleans, 1718-1812: An Economic History* (1970) is still the best work although it lacks notes (a decision of the Press, not the author).

2. What is today Bayou Manchac was thought to be the easternmost distributary of the Mississippi's lower delta. It was a high water overflow channel whose appearance on maps when the peace treaty was being drafted made it appear to be more navigable than it actually was. Also by using it as the northeastern boundary of the Isle of Orleans, France preserved the economic heart of its Louisiana for Spain.

3. Spanish census documents generally did not count Native Americans living in Lower Louisiana, the most densely settled part. They were, in any case, a small minority compared to the African and European inhabitants. Regarding race, Gwendolyn Midlo Hall, *Africans in Colonial Louisiana: The Development of Afro-Creole Culture in the Eighteenth Century* 239 (1992), notes that Spanish administrators relied on local officials, who tended to classify free persons of mixed-race as "white," distorting the White-African ratios in those censuses and blunting the Spanish system of classifying on the basis of actual or imagined genealogical degrees of race-mixture. For the slave/free ratios of particular Posts based on those censuses, see Antonio Acosta Rodriguez, *La Poblaciòn de Luisiana Española* (1763-1803) (1979) (especially tbls.1.8 B (Proporción de

empire was thus not a matter of using that empire's traditional combination of Spanish towns and missions and presidios. Moreover, the acquisition of Louisiana occurred when the Spanish government was beginning to reform its colonial administration in an attempt to gain greater control and revenue.

Captain Antonio de Ulloa, well known as an investigator of colonial societies[4] and a fluent speaker of French and then without assignment, was designated as Spain's first governor of Louisiana. His charge was to discover and report how the colony actually ran, thus allowing Madrid to formulate policies for its incorporation into the empire should Charles III and his Minister of State—The Marquis of Grimaldi, who was given charge of the operation because he had helped to negotiate the French cession and the Peace Treaty of 1763—decide to treat it as other than an entirely separate colony governed by its own laws and customary government but allowed to trade with the Spanish colonies. That is, would it become a province incorporated into the empire in the way that the Hapsburgs had done—one King but many semi-autonomous kingdoms? That seemed to be what Ulloa's initial instructions indicated. But such an initial situation was unlikely to continue. And indeed Louisiana's unique situation in 1763-1768 did not continue, whatever assurances the French Naval Minister, the Duc de Choiseul, had sent to the colonists on the basis of what he knew of Ulloa's initial orders.[5]

Esclavos/Libres, 1763-1777), 2.8 B (Proporción Número Esclavos/Número Libres, 2o Período, 1778-1788) & 3.8 B (Proporción entre Número de Esclavos y Número de Libres (1791-1803)).

4. He had done so in 1734-1736 with Jorge Juan when they had accompanied La Condamine's French scientific expedition to Ecuador to measure the arc of the meridian as part of an effort to accurately determine the shape of the Earth, and again, less successfully, as Governor of Huancavelica, Upper Peru (Bolivia), 1758-1764. The first investigation had produced the originally secret but now famous *Noticias Secretas de América*, the second, various reports on the corruption of the local establishment and frustration when they successfully resisted changes not only in their system of exploiting the mine but also in technical aspects of the mining. John Preston Moore, *Revolt in Louisiana* 3-8 (1976).

5. Moore, *supra* note 4, at 42-44 (quoting Letter from Charles III to Ulloa (May 1, 1765) and Letter from Charles III to Council of Indies (May 22, 1765): "I

A confusion of institutions was almost bound to happen as both the new rulers and their new subjects defended their own institutions and traditions. Let me add that I am using "institution" in a broad and general sense as denoting significant patterned behaviors defined in part by laws, not just "an established corporation of a public character," the usual restrictive definition.[6]

I want to focus briefly on what seems to me the three principal institutions where Spanish law and practice came into conflict with the local French institutions, laws, and practices. These are the economic system, the nature and thus the role of the council governing at New Orleans, and slavery. For analytical purposes, these institutions could be treated separately, but that does violence to the overlaps between them, as will become clear below.

THE ECONOMIC SYSTEM AND LOCAL LAW AND ORDER

Ulloa found that French Louisiana had developed trade not only with France, but also Cap Français (Cape Haitian), Martinique, Guadalupe, the Gulf of Campeche, the east coast of central Mexico (other than Veracruz) and Cuba. In 1765-1768 those trades and the local economy were in disarray, or so the New Orleans merchants claimed. Untaxed importation of all manner of goods was routine and fairly open. Too, the English and Anglo-Americans had arrived on the Mississippi in force, building on smuggling begun decades earlier and offering slaves on credit as well as other goods and also shipping for Louisiana's bulky exports (timber, bricks, grains).[7]

---

have resolved that in this new acquisition no changes in its government will be made for the moment." Moore italicized "for the moment.").

6. *Institution*, *Webster's Seventh New Collegiate Dictionary* 438 definitions 3a & 3b (1963).

7. Clark, *supra* note 1, at 90-91 (early English trade), 159-62, 166-67; Moore, *supra* note 4, at 104. While these merchants were usually called "English," it is evident that some were Anglo-American, from the thirteen colonies.

Ulloa also found that the Superior Council, in form and judicial function somewhat like a Spanish Cabildo or city council, was in fact, as French Director General (i.e., Governor & Commissaire-Ordonnateur) Jean Jacques Blaise d'Abbadie had reported to his ministers in June 1764, the center of corruption, notably for speculation in the French Crown's funds and supplies and colonial currency and in the administration of probates.[8] It was also failing to repress what he called the "spirit of insubordination and independence which has manifest itself" and had almost since the colony's founding.[9] D'Abbadie's reference was to social conditions in New Orleans as well as trade, but the same could be said of the social situation in the countryside with regard to the treatment of slaves and generally with regard to trade. In both spheres laws were routinely ignored, especially by the powerful.

The Superior Council had been created in 1716 to enforce law and social order by detecting and punishing crimes and as a mechanism for the resolution of civil law disputes. Its authority extended over all of the settlements in lower Louisiana. That is, it was a provincial, not simply an urban institution. For

---

8. Carl A. Brasseaux, *Denis-Nicolas Foucault and the New Orleans Rebellion of 1768*, at 32 (1987) (d'Abbadie's titles); Moore, *supra* note 4, at 114-15 (as much as 10,000,000 livre in various forms of heavily discounted paper money were in circulation or in the hands of speculators; Ulloa claimed Foucault had a "considerable quantity of these notes" (*id.* at 115), but Brasseaux's discussion of Foucault's calling in of a million plus livre in treasury notes in 1762 does not indicate any speculation by him (Brasseaux, *supra* at 23-25)); James D. Hardy, Probate Racketeering in Colonial Louisiana, 9 La. Hist. 109 (1968).

9. Letter from D'Abbadie to the French Ministry (June 7, 1764), *in* Charles Gayarré, 2 *History of Louisiana* 104-06 (Pelican Publishing Co. 1965) (1903); also in Moore, *supra* note 4, at 39 n.34. Charles Aubry, D'Abbadie's successor after the latter's death on February 4, 1765, wrote much the same thing, but indicated the problem was at least a decade old (*id.* at 41). While I do not agree with all of her ideas, Shannon Lee Dawdy, *Building the Devil's Empire: French Colonial New Orleans* (2008) describes the general "disorder" as European administrators and religious figures saw it, to 1763. Lawrence N. Powell, *The Accidental City: Improvising New Orleans* (2012) provides a more balanced account, while acknowledging the wide-open nature of Louisiana's economic system and the social "disorders" of New Orleans's multi-ethnic society, disorders common to port cities in most of the Atlantic world.

example, marriage contracts and wills had to be registered with its notaries to be valid, regardless of where the parties resided.

However, because some of the same men held offices in each body (the overlap was not total) during the Company of the Indies period (1718-1731) the Superior Council became overlaid with administrative and even some legislative functions that belonged to the Company's Council of Administration. The royal governors and the commissaire-ordonnateurs, or Commissaries (that is, the Crown's chief fiscal officials) seem to have been content after 1731 to govern through the Superior Council, allowing the continuation of the mixing of its original judicial functions with the administrative, commercial, and legislative ones of the Company's Council of Administration. They and long-term Attorney General François Fleuriau (1722-1752) also did not challenge the Council's assumption of a right to refuse to obey royal orders that were at odds with local custom and/or existing local law. In that regard, the Superior Council acted like one of the thirteen Parlements of France.[10] That is, by historical precedent more than by law, the Superior Council saw itself as the government of the colony, able to mediate between the French crown and its local subjects in all matters, but especially regarding commerce, a topic on which it allowed great liberty, the more so if doing so touched the interests of the planter class.

---

10. As of 1748, the governor, *ordonnateur*, commandant, procurator-general, counselors, and ranking military officers (when present) were members, in some cases ex-officio as befitted their rank in the socio-political hierarchy. Its staff included notaries and clerks. Its judges (assessors) were those of first instance in New Orleans while the body as a whole served as an appeals court from those judges and the district commandants' courts. Jerry A. Micelle, *From Law Court to Local Government: Metamorphosis of the Superior Council of French Louisiana*, 9 La. Hist. 85 (1968) (discussing its evolution); *cf.* Moore, *supra* note 4, at 30 n.13 (disputing Micelle's views, especially regarding the Council's legislative role, which Moore thinks was quite limited). Giraud's *Histoire* provides many details of its early years. *See also* Donald J. LeMeux, *The Office of 'Commissaire Ordonnateur' in French Louisiana, 1731-1769: A Study in French Colonial Administration* (1972) (unpublished Ph.D. Dissertation, Louisiana State University), 7228360 PQDT 302605641.

By Ulloa's time six of the nine members—the three councilors and three assessors—were planters or merchant-planters of note, some of whom often stayed on their plantations rather than attend meetings.[11] The winter social season in New Orleans that Governor Pierre de Rigaud, Marquis de Vaudreuil, had enhanced provided the opportunity for these men and others like them to gather and informally agree on how Louisiana was to be run. The social season thus supplemented meetings with each other around dining tables on the plantations.[12]

Ulloa's first trade decree, dated September 6, 1766, brought to the surface the Superior Council's claims to power. The decree allowed Louisiana's customary trades with France, St. Domingue, and Martinique but required ship captains to come to Louisiana with passports issued by the Spanish consuls resident in France and French West Indian ports. Too, the Superior Council's "commissioners"—that is, some of the members who normally monitored market conditions—had to obtain Ulloa's approval of the prices at which the imported goods would be sold before they could enter the market. And at least a third of the value of imports were to be paid for with Louisiana products. Ulloa's intention was to mollify the general populace, which was complaining about the high costs of imports, especially wine.[13]

---

11. Moore, *supra* note 4, at 51-52. Ulloa noted the lack of any legal training among its members, except, possibly, for the attorney general, and that the councilors normally resided on their plantations outside of the city and did not attend its meetings. Injustices resulted. *See also* Gilbert Din & John E. Harkins, *The New Orleans Cabildo: Colonial Louisiana's First City Government*, 1769-1803, at 42 (1996).

12. Powell, *supra* note 9, at 110-12. Francisco Bouligny commented in his Memoria of 1776 that the planters "often dine together, and their conversation is always directed toward the condition of the crop and the progress that each is making in the cultivation of his land" (per copy in Alcée Fortier, 2 *A History of Louisiana*: *The Spanish Dominion and the Cession to the United States, 1769-1893*, at 34 (2nd ed. by Jo Ann Carrigan, 1972)).

13. Moore, *supra* note 4, at 105-06 (quoting the decree). On May 6, 1766, the Crown had authorized trade with the French West Indies and certain Spanish colonial ports from which agents for Louisiana's French government (so long as it lasted) could export beef and grain, paying a 5% duty, and complying with

Immediately the merchants of New Orleans asked the Superior Council to stop the issuance of the decree until the Attorney General, Nicolas Chauvin de Lafrenière, a local man recently (1763) returned from France with a law degree, could study it and rule on its legality. They also enlisted Denis-Nicolas Foucault, the acting Commissary.[14] By French law, the Commissary regulated commerce (because it was taxed) and also controlled the use of the King's subvention that supported the soldiers and officials stationed in the colony, powers that Foucault and his predecessors used to favor merchants who reciprocated, although in Foucault's case, Ulloa charged, he was more interested in speculating in the depreciated paper of the French regime, expecting Spain to redeem it at face value.[15] Shortly, Ulloa went to the Balize at the mouth of the Mississippi River to superintend the works he had ordered—for defense and to improve navigation—and to await the arrival of his Peruvian bride.[16] In effect, he allowed the local interests to protest a royal order, although the mechanism they used was not the one customary in the Spanish empire.[17] The established system of trade continued with minimal interference.[18]

---

certain paperwork requirements. The export of Louisiana products to pay for those imports was allowed (*id.* at 105).

14. Foucault had been named the commissary for Mobile, but the temporary detention of Jean-Jacques-Blaise d'Abbadie, the appointed *Commissaire Ordonnateur* for La Louisiane, while a British prisoner of war in 1762-1763 made Foucault, the next ranking fiscal agent, the acting Commissary (Brasseaux, *supra* note 8, at 17).

15. Brasseaux, *supra* note 8, at 14-15; Moore, *supra* note 4, at 115.

16. Moore, *supra* note 4, at 70, 139-40.

17. The merchants' appeal to the Superior Council to rule on the legality of the decree was based on the Council's unlawful but long-standing practice of exercising a sort of veto over royal decrees if they were thought inconsistent with established local privileges and law. Foucault's protest was a defense of his office's right to locally issue and enforce royal orders on matters of trade and economic life generally. In the Spanish empire, royal officials and cabildos could refuse to carry out a royal decree by invoking the "obedezco pero no cumplo" rule—I obey, that is recognize that this is a lawful order of my sovereign, but "do not carry out" because the royal intent is to do good but this order is based on incorrect, incomplete, or incompetent advice and so is not what the sovereign intended. This was a formal process, done before a notary. More often, decrees that conflicted with local interests were simply ignored. For an explanation of the philosophical basis of this Spanish practice, see Colin M.

Ulloa did not let this challenge to Spanish authority pass. He wrote to Madrid identifying the Superior Council as a body that had to be abolished, while acknowledging its judicial role. Madrid responded with two plans to replace it with purely judicial bodies, neither implemented before the Revolt of 1768. In March 1767, Grimaldi prepared a decree suppressing the Superior Council except, temporarily, as the Governor's court, effective when Spain assumed full formal control of Louisiana.[19] Then in early 1768 Grimaldi ordered Ulloa to establish a small Spanish law court, one Ulloa expanded to include three Spaniards and four locally prominent men who were friendly to the Spanish regime.[20]

As is well known, while Ulloa was away from New Orleans, La Frenière and others who foresaw yet more Spanish interference with their power and customs began to plot. Rumors about and then the arrival in the colony of the trade decree of March 23, 1768, brought the stew of discontent to a

---

MacLachlan, *Spain's Empire in the New World: The Role of Ideas in Institutional and Social Change* 21-23 (1988).

18. Ulloa did enforce Spanish law when *Nuestra Señora de La Luz* arrived at Balize in October 1766, claiming stress of weather on a voyage from the Bay of Campeche to Havana. The intention was to sell a cargo of dyewood at New Orleans, as had been done before. The Superior Council helped with the sale and repairs. Moore, *supra* note 4, at 107-08.

19. Memo to Grimaldi (Jan. 1767), in Moore, *supra* note 4, at 51-53. Grimaldi signed a decree on March 22, 1767, suppressing the Superior Council as of the date that Spain took formal possession of Louisiana while allowing its members to continue to draw salaries and judge cases already in process, but under the governor's authority as presiding judge. Criminal matters would be judged by the customs of the land, but all other laws would be those of Spain and its empire. The small court Grimaldi ordered reflected Spanish practice. Spanish governors had superior jurisdiction in the towns as well as the provinces where they resided. Almost never trained in law, they nominally presided over a court whose actual operations were directed by an *asesor letrado*, a trained legal expert, who also advised the governor on what to rule. Grimaldi's order forbade the Commissary from interfering, whatever the instructions he had from France or had been the custom.

20. The court order was to consist of the governor, an *asesor* (legal adviser), and a French and a Spanish notary. To them, Ulloa added three Spaniards and four Frenchmen, but left the Superior Council intact. Din & Harkins, *supra* note 11, at 43.

full boil.[21] Based on the new comercio libre or "free trade" regulations being implemented for Cuba and Spanish Hispaniola, the decree authorized point-to-point trade with six, later nine, ports in Spain in ships of Spanish construction and ownership with crews that were two-thirds Spanish subjects. Goods shipped from Spain paid no tariffs on either end of the voyage; Louisiana goods entering Spain were to pay 4% there, but export from Spain to another country rebated that tariff, although not the additional shipping costs.[22] Ulloa and later O'Reilly and the Spanish Crown ruled that ships owned in Louisiana were Spanish; the rule on crews was, as always, largely ignored.

Invoking the authority of the Superior Council on which many of the plotters sat, the conspirators had the Superior Council order Ulloa to leave the colony on a claim that he had no legal authority to issue his decrees. They backed this with the threat of a drunken Acadian/German Coast mob brought to New Orleans for the purpose. With a pregnant wife and no reliable nor numerous military forces to suppress the insurrection, Spain's first governor boarded ship and sailed to Havana.[23]

Field Marshall Alejandro de O'Reilly's landed at New Orleans on August 18, 1769, with a force of two thousand soldiers and authority to fully implement Spanish rule. This event signaled a coming shift in the management of Louisiana from the Minister of State, Grimaldi, to the Ministry of the Indies and the full Spanish colonial system.[24]

---

21. There were other factors such as Ulloa's forced reliance on the French administration, his lack of Spanish soldiers and funds, and his private life. Moore and Brasseaux explore these factors and the historiography of the rebellion.

22. Moore, *supra* note 4, at 111-13. For *comercio libre*, see Clark, *supra* note 1, at 171-72.

23. Moore, *supra* note 4, at 124-64, *passim*; *see also* Brasseaux, *supra* note 8.

24. Bibiano Torres Ramirez, *Alejandro O'Reilly en las Indias* 97-105 (1969); Moore, *supra* note 4, at 185-98, 216-17 (Cabildo and integration); Din & Harkins, *supra* note 11, at 46-47. The formal integration of Louisiana into the Spanish empire was done with a decree of November 24, 1770.

O'Reilly quickly abolished the Superior Council, replacing it with a nine-member city council (ayuntamiento), which had the same functions of maintaining law and order and mediating civil law disputes, but only in the city of New Orleans and its district (partido), a district which was understood to include not just the city but also the plantation zone extending from below New Orleans up to, but not including, the German coast. A seeming exception to this limited jurisdiction was that the Alcalde Mayor Provincial (one of the councilors) was to investigate crimes, fires, and certain other matters that took place in the countryside where there was no villa or lugar, smaller subordinate settlements that could exist within a municipal district and that sometime had their own judicial officials.[25] None existed within the partido of New Orleans, effectively making the Alcalde Mayor Provincial the face of the law in rural areas much as the alcaldes ordinarios were in the city.

Until the 1790s, the Cabildo (to use its popular name) consisted of six proprietary regidores or councilors (each with specified duties) who annually elected two alcaldes ordinarios (local judges), a síndico procurador general de la republica (defender of the public interest or attorney general) and a keeper of the ayuntamiento's incomes (mayordomo de proprios). Most of the holders of these offices were wealthy francophone planters, although in time Spaniards also acquired some of them. Gilbert Din and John Harkins have shown that the alcaldes handled most criminal and civil matters not involving fueros (legal privileges such as those of soldiers) unless the Governor chose to remove a case to his own court. Appeals from both sorts of court went to Havana where a special tribunal was created and, in some rare cases, all the way to the Council of the Indies at Madrid. Commandants in the countryside (aided by syndics who reported local events) and, after 1779, alcaldes de barrio (neighborhood judges) in the city, served as (investigating) judges of first instance for limited kinds of cases in their areas, cases that then went to the

25. Torres Ramirez, *supra* note 24, at 115-18, 188-96.

governor's court.[26] The governor or his lieutenant normally presided over the Cabildo's Friday meetings, making it clear where the real political and legal authority lay; that is, not with the Cabildo.

Because none of the initial regidores knew how Spanish town councils operated as courts of law much less in the limited administrative and legislative areas allowed, General O'Reilly had his legal advisors prepare comprehensive regulations that followed the Laws of the Indies, the so called Code O'Reilly of November 25, 1769. O'Reilly also ordered a number of annual fees and various taxes to give the new municipal government income with which to pay its officials and provide for (limited) city services.[27]

O'Reilly not only reformed the government of the city of New Orleans, he also enforced the trade decree of 1768 but with exceptions that marked the beginning of the Spanish retreat from its terms. His order of September 22, 1769, expelled seventeen British merchants from New Orleans and made it clear that British smuggling along the Mississippi would not be tolerated. However, he allowed Oliver Pollock and William Moore, British subjects who had provided flour from British North America, to remain and to continue to trade in that commodity (and others) via the French West Indies. He also allowed the owners of five ships based at New Orleans to go there with Louisiana products, in effect recognizing a trade

---

26. Din & Harkins, *supra* note 11, following 100 fig.2, 101-26 (see 57 tbl.1, 60-61 tbl.2, 69 tbl.3, 72 tbl.4 for lists of incumbents). The *alcaldes de barrio* were somewhat like justices of the peace in the Anglo-American system. Two at first, in 1792 Carondolet created an additional two (*id.* at 121).

27. Torres Ramirez, *supra* note 24, at 125 (initial officials only); Din & Harkins, *supra* note 11, at 60-61 tbl.2 (listing the offices and the men who held them). Of the men elected, only Francisco María Reggio (royal standard bearer) had also been on Ulloa's court. Torres Ramirez, *supra* note 24, at 126 (citing the various salaries, taxes, and fees), app. at [1], [187]-202 (citing the full Spanish text of O'Reilly's *Reglamento*, defining the duties of each office and procedures), app. at [2], 203-25 (citing a second *reglamento* dealing with judicial standards and processes. Din & Harkins, *supra* note 11, discusses the details, with examples. See chapters 8-11 for the growth of limited city services in the last decades of the 18th century.

pattern of long-standing and supporting the French merchants trading with the colony. Looking to the future, O'Reilly suggested that the decree be modified to allow a three-legged trade with Havana in which Catalan wines (and a few other products) would be brought to Louisiana, exchanged for Louisiana products (except tobacco) to the extent that the local demand allowed, after which the rest of the wine and the Louisiana goods would be shipped to Cuba, where the Catalans could obtain cargos of sugar to return to Catalonia. Spanish manufactures brought to Havana by licensed trade and Cuban aguardiente would flow back to Louisiana to pay for the lumber, rice, indigo, cotton and peltry thus supplied. Both legs of the Havana-New Orleans trade should be tariff free. The Crown approved this arrangement on an interim basis on January 26, 1770, except for the permission for Louisiana-owned ships to trade with the French West Indies. Only trade with Spain and Havana was allowed; unofficially, the favored Anglo-Americans continued their commerce. In August 1772, a duty (almojarifazgo) of 2.5% was imposed on goods (legally) entering the colony and O'Reilly's preliminary regulations were made final.[28]

O'Reilly's disruption of the British trade, the decree of January 1770, and then an Anglo-Spanish crisis over ownership of the Falkland/Malvinas Islands in 1770-1771 and difficulties initiating the Havana trade produced a sharp fall in Louisiana's commerce and reports that the French merchants (who had driven the indigo trade, Louisiana's most valuable export) were leaving New Orleans.[29] However, Governor Luis de Unzaga's toleration of British trading out of sight of New Orleans produced a reversal. Ship traffic at the Balize, where a pilotage

---

28. Clark, *supra* note 1, at 173-76; Ruth King, *Social and Economic Life in Spanish Louisiana, 1763-1783* (1931) (unpublished Ph.D. Dissertation, University of Illinois), 01224265 PQDT 301837351 (providing a detailed account); see also Charles Gayarré, 4 *History of Louisiana* (Pelican Publishing Co. 1965) (1903); Charles Gayarré, 3 *History of Louisiana*: *The Spanish Domination* 26-28, 49 (Pelican Publishing Co. 1965) (1903) [hereinafter Gayarré, 3 *History of Louisiana*] (commenting that the decree of August 17, 1772, "did not prove of much importance to the welfare of the colony").
29. Clark, *supra* note 1, at 176-78.

fee was required of all ships entering or leaving the Mississippi, rose steadily from 58 passages in 1770 to a peak of 161 in 1775, with a decline thereafter to the outbreak of the Anglo-Spanish war of 1779-1783. Fragmentary evidence shows that the majority of these ships were British, not Spanish or ships owned at New Orleans. Spanish tax records and Francisco Bouligny's Memoria of 1776 indicate that Louisiana's legal commerce was about 600,000 pesos a year by 1775. Of that, 50,000 pesos involved trade with Havana but only 15,000 pesos was with Spain. The remaining 535,000 pesos evidently was with France and the French West Indies and English North America. Trade with the first two had again been authorized in 1774, in response to the Cabildo's petitions of 1771 decrying the loss of the French markets for peltry, indigo, and tobacco, although the direct trade with France was a one-off experiment at the time.[30]

Spain's preparations for its war with Great Britain over control of the Caribbean (1779-1783) led Governor Bernardo de Gálvez to seize eleven British "floating warehouses" anchored at various places along the Mississippi and to order British merchants to leave the colony, both measures with little effect. To replace British trade and shipping, on November 21, 1777, Gálvez announced a continuation of trade with the French West Indies for ten years in Spanish and Louisiana ships. French ships coming from the West Indies could bring slaves, coins, or bills of exchange to the colony and take away its exports. Both sorts of ships required consular clearance in the West Indies. The import duty was lowered to 2%. This was followed in April 1778 with a decree authorizing trade directly with France in colonial goods carried by Spanish ships and subject to a 6% export duty; goods brought from France also paid 6%. These arrangements allowed indigo and peltry to return to their traditional French markets while favoring Spanish (and

---

30. Pilotage fee: Archivo General de Indias, Santo Domingo 2628; King, *supra* note 28, 163-69 (almojarifazgo receipts); Francisco Bouligny, *Memoria* (1776), in Fortier, *supra* note 12, at 38; Paul E. Hoffman, *A History of Louisiana Before 1813*, at 133-34, 137-47 (1996) (a general overview of the shifting trade decrees and situation).

Louisiana-owned) shipping and maintaining a tariff differential that favored the direct trade with Spain. In short, unable to bend Louisiana's economy to the commercio libre model, as a wartime measure Spain allowed the colony's commerce to return to its pre-Spanish pattern.[31]

As the end of the war came into view, Spain ratified these arrangements with a decree of 1782 that was a mercantilist solution to the problem of Louisiana's trade: commerce carried in nominally Spanish ships to and from Spain under favorable tariff treatment; commerce with French ports where a Spanish Consul resided in nominally Spanish ships paying 6% duties on goods exported thence and imported hence, and trade with the French West Indies under similar stipulations. As John Clark observed: "If Spain could derive no direct commercial benefits from Louisiana, at least the colony could be strengthened in its role as a buffer by diverting its commerce to an ally of Spain."[32] In the end, most of the commerce authorized in 1782 returned to the French West Indies because French merchants preferred to send their goods and ships to Cap Français (Cape Haitian), St. Domingue's great free port where return cargos of high value were available. Louisiana's relatively small market and export trade were more efficiently serviced in this way, at least until the wars of the French Revolution interrupted this commerce.[33]

---

31. Clark, *supra* note 1, at 222-24. Spain did arrange for the royal tobacco monopoly to purchase Louisiana tobacco, providing an outlet for that product and a boom of a few years' duration in its production. Brian E. Coutts, *Boom and Bust: The Rise and Fall of the Tobacco Industry in Spanish Louisiana, 1770-1790*, 42 Americas 289-309 (Jan. 1986).

32. Clark, *supra* note 1, at 224.

33. *Id.* at 224-29; Gayarré, 3 *History of Louisiana*, *supra* note 28, at 153-56. The terms of the 1782 decree were in part set to benefit Gilbert St. Maxent, Bernardo de Gálvez' father-in-law, who aspired to monopolize Louisiana's Indian trade and thus force out the English companies (Panton Leslie & Co., John Forbes, James Mather) that controlled it east of the Mississippi, an area now once again Spanish because of the Anglo-Spanish treaty of 1783, although also claimed by the United States under its treaty of 1782 with Great Britain. For the British companies, see William S. Coker & Thomas D. Watson, *Indian Traders of the Southeastern Spanish Borderlands: Panton, Leslie & Company and John Forbes & Company, 1783-1847* (1986).

All of which is to say that the French Louisiana's commercial "institution" (patterned behavior sanctioned in part by laws) was too economically logical to be transformed to fit even the new Spanish "free trade" institution that the Spanish Crown was creating for its Atlantic empire between 1765 and 1789. In this confusion of institutions, the older French economic pattern won out, forcing Spain to change its laws so that they more nearly described the economic reality of La Luisiana.

SLAVERY[34]

When Spain acquired Louisiana in 1763, its officials found a slave system (or institution) with one law, the Code Noir of 1724, but at least two regimes of practice that roughly corresponded to how many enslaved Africans and Native Americans were held by each owner. Owners who held one to perhaps five slaves seem generally to have treated them as lesser members of the household, more or less in line with the paternalistic provisions of the Code Noir of 1724, the legal framework that supported slavery. The other regime was the harsh disciplinary one of the staple-oriented plantations where gangs of fifteen or more slaves often labored under overseers, and masters who did as they pleased in terms of providing for the physical needs of their chattels, demanding labor, and disciplining them; that is, the Code was often ignored, especially when market conditions worsened as they had in the early 1760s. Although encouraging slave couples to have children, both sorts of masters did not allow parents to marry in

---

34. Powell, *supra* note 9, at 224-58, 274-76 (covering the ground sketched in this part of the essay). Powell sees a three-sided struggle between slaves defending what had become their customary rights to work and gather on Sundays and holidays and otherwise look to their own interests and then those rights that Spanish laws conveyed and the great planters who wished near absolute power over the slave institution (but sometimes contradicted themselves when responding to particular situations) and the career bureaucrats sent to govern Louisiana, men who supported slavery and would overlook some abuses by masters but never fully ignored Spanish laws.

the Catholic church and were willing to break up common-law families if it suited a whim or financial need. Carl Brasseaux has argued that the French colony's attorneys general treated the master-slave relationship as a domestic matter (that is private law), only intervening when harm was done to the chattel of third parties or abuses provoked scandal or rebellion that could not be overlooked. The result was that flight because of abuses—that is, marronage—(as well as passive forms of resistance) was common, especially in the New Orleans area where the larger plantations and slave gangs were found. Brasseaux argues further that an unusually strong episode of marronage in 1748 frightened the larger slave holders into tightening disciplinary practices after a decade and a half when discipline had been relatively less severe because no slaves could be imported to replace losses. Governor Pierre de Rigaud, Marquis de Vaudreuil's regulations of 1751 embodied that tightening. A second outburst of marronage, coupled with thefts, produced another crackdown in 1764.[35] In the law, flight as well as violence directed at white persons were punishable by heavy flogging and even execution, as the Superior Council might decide. No owner wanted to lose a slave, but the larger holders seem to have been willing to inflict the most savage punishments against marronage, and other forms of resistance, because they believed that terror was the most effective way to manage slaves for maximum productivity. Small holders, especially if outside of the plantation zone around New Orleans, seem to have tried to avoid reporting their slaves to the authorities lest judicial process result in the loss of valuable assets. All of which is to say that the institution of slavery in French Louisiana was another site of the French "freedom," that is license, that D'Abbadie and Ulloa and other Spaniards observed in the mid-1760s. It was also an institution that had no answer to the problem of marronage except to continue to tighten laws that restricted slave movements off the plantations and punishments when they did, a strategy that made slavery

---

35. Carl A. Brasseaux, *The Administration of Slave Regulations in Louisiana, 1724-1766*, 21 La. Hist. 147-51 (Spring 1980); Powell, *supra* note 9, at 224-25 (for 1764).

even less tolerable as customary rights of nocturnal assembly and weekend dances, self-employment, and the right to sell goods slaves produced during their "free time" were withdrawn, usually temporarily.[36]

After at first allowing a continuation of the existing slave regime while he dealt with the leaders of the insurrection and other matters, O'Reilly decreed the abolition of the Code Noir and its replacement with Spanish slave laws (November 25, 1769). Like the Code, Spanish laws stipulated minimal allowances of clothing and food, restricted flogging and other punishments (ideally only inflicted via legal process, a change from the Code), required baptism, and made limited provisions for families. However, the two systems differed sharply in their views of the slave. The Code Noir did not recognize the slave as anything more than animated or movable property. The Spanish laws affirmed a legal and spiritual personality, if of lesser status and value than those of Europeans. Informed by Roman Catholic reforms from the 16th century Council of Trent, the Spanish code also ordered baptism and religious instruction and that slave couples, especially those with children, should be married in the Church and not separated thereafter. Families were to be kept together until the children reached teenaged years, after which they might be sold apart from their parents. Slaves had the right to take "cruel" masters to court and limited rights to testify against them; a slave accused of a crime could have an attorney (a white representative, usually not a trained lawyer) for his/her defense, provisions not found in the Code Noir. Manumissions, restricted in the Code Noir by the requirement that each case had to be approved by the Superior Council (even for testamentary manumissions), were more readily available under

---

36. Gilbert C. Din, *Spaniards, Planters, and Slaves: The Spanish Regulation of Slavery in Louisiana, 1763-1803*, at 4-39 (1999) [hereinafter Din, *Slavery*]. Each crackdown seems to have lasted only briefly because slave owners took different approaches to their slaves or had an economic interest in allowing them to work on Sundays and holidays or realized that taking away these privileges might provoke rebellion. Too, those days were used to raise crops in the gardens most planters provided, saving the planter money on food for his chattel.

the Spanish code by simple notarial act. Famously, Spanish law allowed self-purchase (coartación) and the purchase and freeing of other slaves by enslaved persons, who had property rights never recognized in the Code Noir. The laws also outlawed Indian slavery, a potential issue in a colony where some slaves were Native Americans and others were descendants in the maternal line. Finally, Spanish law required that the buying and selling of slaves be done by notarial act, evidently not a legal requirement in French Louisiana. However, punishments for violence against whites, rebellion, and marronage were no less severe than they were in the Code Noir, if now mediated by the requirement of court proceedings that offered the slave limited protection against arbitrary action.[37] Subsequent Spanish governors all supported and inflicted strong punishments except for a brief aberration under Bernardo de Gálvez (below).

Gilbert Din's study of slavery under the Spanish regime shows that from 1770 onwards, the Cabildo and the owners of large numbers of slaves (represented by the regidores) repeatedly tried to get the restoration of the Code Noir, primarily via police regulations aimed at restricting the customary freedoms of slaves and preventing runaways while increasing the power of masters.

Their first and almost successful attempt took place in 1773-1778. Concerned about fugitive slaves, the Cabildo wanted to create a fund to support a slave-hunting patrol and compensate masters whose chattel might be maimed, killed, or executed because they had deserted their plantations. Governor Luís de Unzaga insisted that the Cabildo call a meeting of "notables" before approving the creation of that fund and

---

37. Hans W. Baade, The Law of Slavery in Spanish Louisiana, 1769-1803, in *An Uncommon Experience: Law and Judicial Institutions in Louisiana, 1803-2003*, at 280-304 (Judith Kelleher Shafer & Warren M Billings eds., 1997) (showing that Spanish slave law embraced those aspects of Roman law that favored the slave (as noted here), whereas French Code Noir favored the master (*id.* at 284), clarifies O'Reilly's allowing and then revocation of the Code Noir (*id.* at 285-86), and by citing cases shows that Spanish emancipation law was applied in New Orleans); Din, *Slavery*, *supra* note 36, at 43; Hall, *supra* note 3, *passim* (painting a more favorable picture of French-slave relations and the Code Noir and argues that the Spanish regime was not more favorable to the slave).

passing ordinances for the fund and for finding runaways. The "notables" approved both, and the proposition was sent to Madrid for approval because it involved a tax.[38] Then Bernardo de Gálvez became governor, quickly not only marrying into the slave-holding elite but also, apparently, adopting its attitude toward blacks in general. Din suggests that he may have prodded Madrid to reply to the overture of 1773 with a decree of May 14, 1777, approving the proposed compensation fund, but only if contributions were voluntary. The decree also allowed the colony's residents to draft new rules for the discipline of slaves and free blacks, supposedly to reduce the causes of marronage.[39] This was the opening that the planters seized. The Cabildo instructed two of its members to prepare regulations that restored the rights that Spanish law had taken from masters. The drafters took as their model the 1724 Code Noir, even naming their handiwork the "Code Noir ou Loi Municipale" and added a few provisions from the 1751 police regulations that had marked the previous height of the reaction to the lax regulation of slavery that had arisen prior to the indigo boom of the 1740s. Under the proposed rules, manumissions could only be with judicial approval, and self-purchase was to end. Virtually all of the ameliorative aspects of Spanish slave law were removed so that masters would again enjoy essentially unlimited rights over the bodies of their chattels. Presented to the Cabildo on October 16, 1778, the draft was circulated for comment in the district and then revised. The revision in turn was the subject of a meeting at which twenty-five of the largest planters were present. This

---

38. While waiting for a reply, Unzaga created a fugitive-hunting patrol of free persons of color under his own authority, in effect taking over the project, even to the point of trying to collect money to compensate owners whose slaves died as a result of the patrol's activities. The next year he supported the local custom that allowed slaves to hire themselves out on Sundays without their owner's permission, something that large planters opposed. And he supported slave property rights as well as *coartación*, which was just beginning to catch on among slaves in and near New Orleans. Din, *Slavery*, *supra* note 36, at 58-61, 64 (property rights, the case of horses confiscated at Pointe Coupée in 1775), 65. For how the compensation fund worked, see *id.* at 62-65.
39. *Id.* at 71-75.

body approved asking the Cabildo, the Governor, and then the Crown to respect the laws of the province and approve the revised draft. Thirty-three persons, including Governor Gálvez, signed the minutes of that meeting on March 1, 1779. But Governor Gálvez did not forward the document to Spain and the initiative died.[40]

For the next sixteen years, the great planters had to be content with seeking to regain their powers by trying to deal with the problem of marronage, which grew during Spain's war against Great Britain (1779-1783) and the subsequent economic booms. Repeatedly the Cabildo and planters tried to create a compensation fund and implement restrictions on slaves' customary practices and privileges.[41] And although they identified Spanish "leniency" as a cause of slave unrest, they were not able to prevent the growth of emancipation by notarial acts, wills, and self-purchases; the protection of slaves' rights to property they accumulated by work on Sundays and holidays; and the rights of slaves when in court, including to seek sale away from abusive masters.[42] Nor could the planters persuade

---

40. *Id.* at 76 (citing all the provisions), 76-79 (denoting the politics and why Gálvez did not send it to Spain). Din believes that Bernardo cooperated with the planter interests until the planter members of the Cabildo, thinking that power was shifting to that body, tried to assert control over the charity hospital as their counterparts on the Superior Council had done. But that was one of the Governor's powers. *Id.* at 88 (Din's summary: "In the end, Gálvez did little either to fulfill royal instructions or to satisfy the major slaveholders."); *see also* Powell, *supra* note 9, at 234-36 (following Baade in describing the Loi Municipale project as "a slaveholder's Fronde, a transparent effort . . . to wrest back the slave owner power that O'Reilly had taken from them ten years earlier."); Baade, *supra* note 37, at 290-93 (reviewing Gálvez' ruling in Suriray v. Jenkins (where he seemed to side with the argument that the Code Noir remained in force), his possible motives (or excuses) and the Cabildo's project, drafted by one of the men, Joseph Ducros, who had been given authority to enforce existing law (including the Code Noir) during the first months of O'Reilly's administration).

41. Din, *Slavery*, *supra* note 36, at 79-80 (1779), 85-87 (c. 1781-82), 89-94, 99-100, 116-18 (1780s), 141-45 (1792).

42. Kimberly S. Hanger, *Bounded Lives, Bounded Places: Free Black Society in Colonial New Orleans, 1769-1803*, at 17-51 (1997) (discussing the various methods of emancipation and their temporal and other patterns) (see especially 28, fig.1.2, Type of Manumission by Sex, New Orleans, 1771-1803); Hall,

governors Gálvez, Esteban Miró, or Francisco Louis Héctor, Baron de Carondelet to consistently use the police regulations they favored. Owners of few slaves, mostly in the outlying districts upriver from New Orleans, did not willingly pay into the fund, whose primary beneficiaries were the planters of the New Orleans area whose slaves, labor, and disciplinary practices, and paranoia, were the central problem. So while some aspects of Spanish slave law were being followed in the city and for those slaves bold enough to claim their rights under it, slavery on the great plantations and to a degree in the city continued to be controlled by the masters, whose attitudes toward their chattel and discipline followed the French institution as it had developed in Louisiana before 1769. That is, the confusion of slave institutions continued.

On two occasions—November 25, 1776, and May 31, 1789—the Spanish government issued orders for the good treatment for slaves while affirming some of the restrictions that planters wanted. In both decrees, adherence to the Catholic Church's views about marriage was enjoined along with mild treatment of slaves and respect for Sundays and holidays as days of rest. At the same time, strong punishments were ordered for anyone selling liquor, guns, and gunpowder to slaves or buying stolen goods from them.[43] And governors Miró and Carondelet both issued decrees that attempted yet again to

---

supra note 3, at 266-74 (discussing the high rate of emancipations in Pointe Coupée during the Spanish period and the probable destruction of additional documentation by persons wishing to hide African ancestors).

43. Din, *Slavery*, *supra* note 36, at 68-69, 125-30. The instructions were dated November 25, 1776, but not delivered to Gálvez until April 1, 1777. He did not publish it. The decree of 1789 was published in 1790, provoking a protest from the Cabildo, especially its provisions that every plantation of a certain size have a chaplain, that single slaves be segregated by sex in work and in living arrangements, and that marriages take place in the Church, not just by consent of the masters and parties. While continuing to favor "mild" treatment of slaves, Governor Carondolet allowed most of the decree's provisions to remain unenforced. The Cabildo chose not to comment on the severe punishments also contained in the decree. See also Gayarré, 3 *History of Louisiana*, *supra* note 28, at 301-05.

regulate slavery by repeating the need for good treatment and by ordering stern punishments for infractions.[44]

The Pointe Coupée conspiracy of 1795[45] revealed that the memory of the Superior Council had not vanished. Although the authorities in Pointe Coupée arrested the plotters before they could act, fear of a Haitian-style uprising caused the Cabildo's Francophone members to try to extend their authority into the countryside as if the body were still the Superior Council. Although opposed by a Spanish regidor, they followed the lead of the procurador general (general prosecutor) in appointing four assisting witnesses (testigos de asistencia) to go to Pointe Coupée to take part in the investigation of the plot and the summary punishment of those involved, and eight other men to more generally investigate who among slaves and free persons of color was insubordinate and ungovernable and should be expelled from Louisiana. Compensation to masters for slaves imprisoned or executed or expelled was left for another day. Asked to approve these initiatives (the planters had learned that much about their place in Spanish colonial government), Governor Carondelet refused to allow them. Instead, he sent the Intendent's legal advisor (asesor), Manuel

---

44. Miró's decree upheld some of the traditional rights of slaves such as the right to work for themselves on Sundays and holidays and hold dances but tried to impose sumptuary laws and an end to concubinage on free women of color (Din, *Slavery*, *supra* note 36, at 124-25). Carondelet's slave regulations of July 11, 1792, enjoined proper food and clothing and generally mild treatment for slaves. His earlier *bando de buen gobierno* continued bans on importing slaves from the French West Indies or Jamaica (both places where revolutionary ideas might be spread). His *bando* of 1795 (issued after the Pointe Coupée conspiracy was put down) prohibited the customary slave gatherings that Miró had allowed and required plantation slaves to leave New Orleans by sundown, even if traveling with their owners' permissions (*id.* at 135, 188). Powell, *supra* note 9, at 255-56 (seeing the bando of 1795 as a capitulation to the slave owners).

45. Juan José Andrew Ocariz, *Movimientos Rebeldes de Los Esclavos Negros Durante el Dominio Español en Luisiana* 117-77 (1977); Hall, *supra* note 3, at 344-74; Din, *Slavery*, *supra* note 36, at 154-76 (providing accounts of the plot, its discovery and investigation, and the sentences and circumstances), 174-75 (discussing what he sees as the errors of certain historians in evaluating what was, in fact, a serious but very local disturbance). Only the hysteria among some circles in New Orleans (notably the planters on the Cabildo) has made it seem more important than it was. Din, *Slavery*, *supra* note 36, at 174.

Serrano, and a small group of soldiers, who duly completed the investigations and carried out the sentences that he approved. He did not send his own legal advisor, Nicolas María Vidal, because, like the Governor himself, Vidal had a reputation among the planters as friendly toward blacks.[46]

Carondelet did follow up on another of the procurador's ideas. He ordered the Post commandants to conduct censuses of the slaves and free blacks in their districts who were known to be dangerous for public safety and to ask the slave owners if they would contribute to a compensation fund to cover the value of slaves expelled for that reason. Almost uniformly, the slave owners in the posts refused to pledge for a fund which was open-ended, and raised various objections to expelling slaves. The desire of the planters of Pointe Coupée for all the other planters of Louisiana to compensate them for slaves they were losing to execution and exile found no sympathy elsewhere.[47]

The limitations that Spanish law placed on the jurisdiction and power of cabildos had been upheld once again in the face of another effort of the Francophone great planters of the New Orleans area to claim for themselves the jurisdiction and powers that the Superior Council had exercised. The protections of Spanish slave law continued until French Prefect Pierre Clément de Laussat briefly restored the Code Noir on December 17, 1803, just days before the transfer to the United States. However, Spanish slave laws (like the rest of Spanish civil law) continued in force until replaced by Louisiana's own Code Noir of 1806 and the Digest of 1808.[48]

---

46. Din, *Slavery*, *supra* note 36, at 154-67, 159-60 (citing the Cabildo's actions). Vidal had a free mulata mistress by whom he had three acknowledged daughters. Carondolet was suspect because his *reglamento* of 1792 had warned the masters to properly feed and clothe their slaves and generally treat them with a degree of leniency.
47. *Id.* at 169-73.
48. *Id.* at 230 (quoting Laussat's lament about the pressure that the "members of the local government" put on him until he relented and had the law published on December 17, 1803).

CONCLUSION

In conclusion, it can be shown that the imposition of the Spanish institutions of the Cabildo, *comercio libre*, and different slave laws initially produced varying degrees of confusion as both the Spanish governors and their new subjects—especially the socially and economically powerful planters of the area around New Orleans—tried to square them with existing customs and practices, that is, with existing institutions. Of the three, "free commerce" failed almost immediately and completely. The other two, intertwined as they were with questions of social order, produced something of a compromise because Spanish governors supported strong disciplinary measures even as Spanish law and practice in the city of New Orleans, if nowhere else, granted slaves rights and supported local traditions that offered small areas of personal freedom that some slaves were able to use even in the face of the desires of the powerful to have the sort of absolute control over black bodies that they had attained through the French Code Noir of 1724 and the Superior Council.

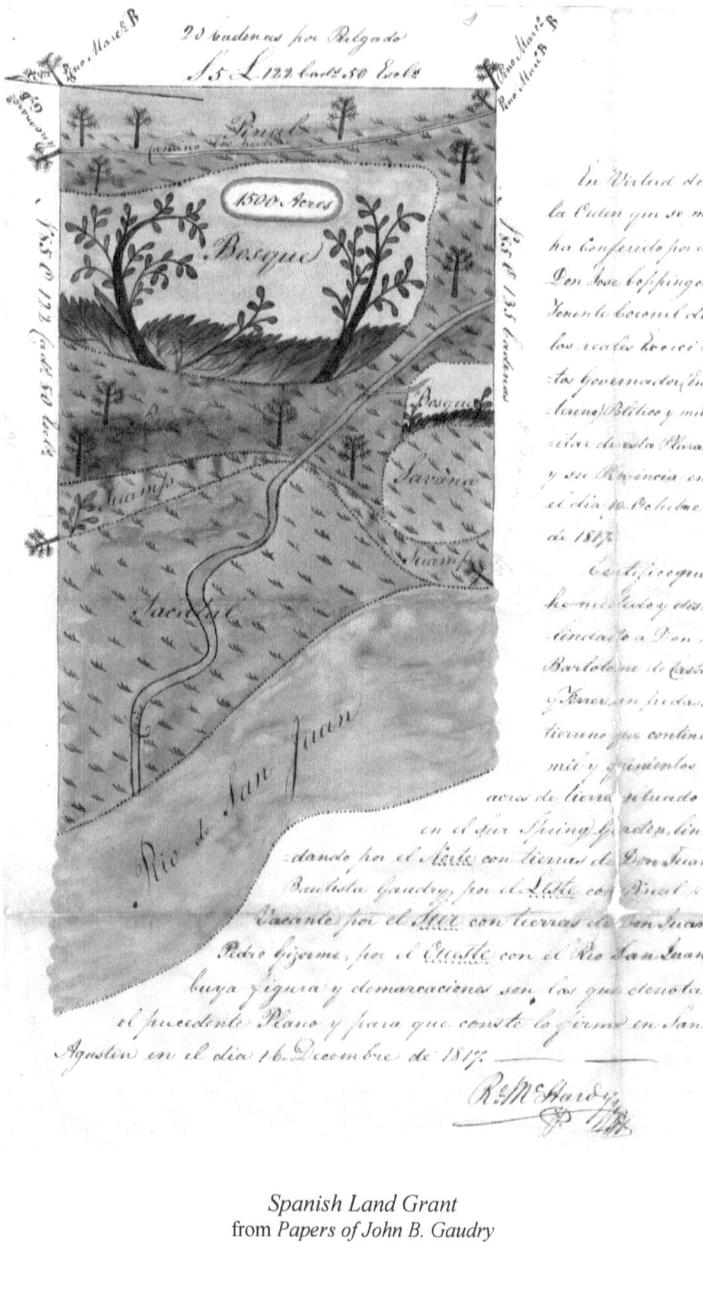

Spanish Land Grant
from *Papers of John B. Gaudry*

CHAPTER 2

CHANGING SOVEREIGNS AND SETTLING LAND CLAIMS IN FLORIDA

Susan Richbourg Parker

Over a span of six decades (1763-1821) the residents of Florida found themselves under a sequence of four sovereign nations—Spain, Great Britain, Spain again, and the United States. None of the three nations truly endeavored to fulfill their promises made in treaties to their own subjects or citizens or to their newly acquired, holdover citizens. Change swept across North America with the agreements set forth in the Treaties of Paris of 1763 and of 1783 and the Adams-Onís Treaty of 1820 as well as some secret arrangements. Each treaty redrew the map of North America and redrew the lives of ordinary persons.

In Florida (later East Florida) and its capital city of St. Augustine, each treaty uprooted residents and jeopardized their ownership of real property. The high-level negotiators did not forget colonial residents, for the diplomats included clauses in each of the aforementioned treaties to protect ownership of real property or at least mitigate losses. Verbiage in the treaties succinctly expressed the philosophical positions of the party nations that private ownership of land deserved consideration but did not offer any prescriptions for resolving owners' claims. Defeated and departing nations looked to protect their subjects, while it was the victorious and incoming regimes that handled the claims of the "conquered."

The Treaty of Paris ended the French and Indian War (Seven Years' War) and redrew the map of North America. France departed the North American continent. Great Britain acquired French Canada and La Florida. Spain changed its venue in the continent from *La Florida* to *Luisiana,* as agreed in the secret Treaty of Fontainebleau (November 1762) between France and Spain. Thus Great Britain came to control the entire Atlantic coast of North America. The Proclamation of 1763 issued by the Board of Trade declared that the king had issued letters patent to create the two colonies of East Florida and West Florida, divided at the Apalachicola River.[1]

Twenty years later, with the end of the War of the American Revolution, a nation not even imagined in 1763 or even in 1773, appeared on the continent—the United States of America. After the Treaty of Paris of 1783 Great Britain gave up its continental holdings south of Canada; Spain returned to a Florida that was smaller than its previous Florida colony. France gained no territory on the continent. For Great Britain the year 1783 marked the end of the Old Empire or First Empire that was focused on the Americas, and British leaders and diplomats changed their emphasis to the New Empire or Second Empire in Asia.[2] Later the Adams-Onís Treaty or Transcontinental Treaty of 1820 effectuated Spain's 1821 transfer of East Florida and West Florida to the United States.[3]

---

1. Charles Loch Mowat, *East Florida as a British Province, 1763-1784*, at 12 (photo. reprint 1964) (1943).
2. J. Leitch Wright, Jr., *Anglo-Spanish Rivalry in North America* 135 (1971). *The Oxford History of the British Empire* Series sets forth five British empires: the First Empire, 1651-1783, and the Second, 1783-1860, are pertinent here. 5 *The Oxford History of the British Empire* (Robin Winks ed., 2001).
3. U.S. sources usually use the year 1819 for the date of the treaty, while Spanish sources use the year 1820. Agreement was reached between negotiators John Quincy Adams and Luis de Onís in 1819. Political changes in Spain and the status of the Spanish Constitution delayed agreement by Ferdinand VII until October 24, 1820. Treaty of Amity, Settlement, and Limits Between the United States of American and His Catholic Majesty (Adams-Onís Treaty), U.S.-Spain, Feb. 22, 1819, Tex. A&M U., http://www.tamu.edu/faculty/ccbn/dewitt/adamonis.htm (last visited July 7, 2017). The version of the treaty in this link includes the "Spanish Instrument of Ratification" signed in Madrid by Spain's Secretary of Despatch of State Fernando Evaristo Pérez de Castro on behalf of

For the residents of East Florida and its capital of St. Augustine the pen was truly mightier than the sword, for there was no war-related conquering or occupation of colonial Florida that brought the transfers.[4] Diplomats faraway and often across the Atlantic Ocean made agreements for changes in the southeast that did not reflect the events or realities of the region. The forces that drove "the impermanence of boundaries" translated into impermanence of a home for residents ensnared by the international negotiations.[5] While diplomats thought in terms of thousands of square miles and about defining and defending international boundaries or navigational rights, ordinary persons in Florida worried about their own small pieces of property. Florida residents, whether Spanish or British, owned lots with shops, homes, and gardens in St. Augustine and Pensacola that were perhaps no larger than about fifty feet by seventy-five feet or fifteen by twenty-five Spanish *varas*. Land grantees in the countryside hoped to retain their several hundred acres. Preserving moveable property in the confusion of changes of sovereigns could be even more challenging than settling land claims, and personal property was often more valuable than land. Great Britain offered the possibility of restitution to its own citizens and the United States agreed in the Adams-Onís Treaty to compensate their new citizens in Florida for losses suffered from U.S. insurgency while the Floridians were still Spanish subjects. With valuations of lost personal property, such as enslaved workers, tools, or horses often exceeding the price of land, such claims were definitely worth the effort to pursue. Yes, treaty makers did attempt to protect ownership of private property as they ceded away colonies and the Treaties of Paris of 1763 and of

---

the king. The version of the treaty offered by Avalon Project of Yale Law School does not include the "Ratification": Treaty of Amity, Settlement, and Limits Between the United States of America and His Catholic Majesty, 1819, U.S.-Spain, Feb. 22, 1819, Yale L. Sch.: Avalon Project, http://avalon.law.yale.edu/19th_century/sp1819.asp (last visited July 7, 2017).

4. Events in West Florida did impact treaty-making. The 1781 Siege of British Pensacola by Spain's Bernardo de Gálvez was a pivotal battle during the War of the American Revolution.

5. For reference to the "impermanence of boundaries," see David Narrett, *Adventurism and Empire: The Struggle for Mastery in the Louisiana-Florida Borderlands, 1762-1803*, at 257 (2015).

1782 and the Adams-Onís Treaty did address the issue of land ownership. But the fate of ordinary residents was not the foremost issue for treaty makers, and once the transfers of sovereignty were completed, private property claimants had to look to their own efforts to defend their ownership. The previous sovereign did not assist with the claims.

The first group to deal with the transfer of sovereignty and thus the fate of their privately owned land were the Spanish residents of La Florida in 1763. Surely these *floridanos* (Floridians) were stunned when a representative of the British governor of South Carolina sailed into St. Augustine on March 16, 1763, bearing an account of the ratification of preliminary articles of peace.[6] After more than two centuries, Spain was relinquishing Florida. South Carolinians and Georgians had been trying to oust the Spanish from Florida for decades. How ironic that the victory came through no actions within the American southeast. Ink on treaties in Paris counted for more than cannon and muskets that might be fired in St. Augustine. Spain's King Charles III made a gross error when he joined France in the Seven Years' War in January of 1762. In the end there was no benefit of the war to Spain, and the invaluable harbor at Havana, Cuba, was captured by British forces, endangering the existing sea route for delivery of goods from the Americas to Spain. Florida was sacrificed in the treaty to regain Havana. By the time of the 1763 treaty Spain's effective claims to *La Florida* were much diminished from its sixteenth-century claims, which had stretched north to Newfoundland and far too vague limits in the west. In fact, British claims reached south of Spanish St. Augustine.[7]

St. Augustine was a presidio, a military town, thus the evacuation of 3100 persons proceeded in an orderly fashion. Spanish royal funds sustained most of the population of St. Augustine with the defense payroll—soldiers or support personnel and their families. Spanish schooners, brigantines, and sloops, as well as a few English vessels, evacuated the residents to Havana. The first evacuees composed of seventy-five persons with more than half of them children, sailed on April 12, 1763, only a month after the

---

6. Mowat, *supra* note 1, at 7.
7. Wright, Jr., *supra* note 2, at 70.

arrival of the initial news borne by a British agent.[8] But orderly did not mean it was not disruptive and costly for the evacuees. For example, in October of 1763, Juana Navarro, with a five-week-old baby in her arms, her husband, and as many as six other children boarded the brigantine *San Antonio* to evacuate St. Augustine and sailed for Havana. Two decades later the middle child of Juana Navarro would return to St. Augustine and delineate what properties the family had been forced to abandon.[9] By January 22, 1764, the last of the emigrants had sailed away.

Historian Robert L. Gold asserts in his study of the "Triple-Nation Transfer" that "Article 20 definitely stipulated that the Spanish residents of Florida could sell their estates to English subjects within an eighteen-month period." Regarding the property owned by the evacuees, a portion of Article XX of the 1763 treaty states:

> His Britannick Majesty farther agrees, that the Spanish inhabitants, or others who had been subjects of the Catholick King in the said countries, may retire, with all safety and freedom, wherever they think proper; and may sell their estates, provided it be to his Britannick Majesty's subjects, and bring away their effects, as well as their persons without being restrained

---

8. Letter from Melchor Feliú and Eligio de la Puente to Julián de Arriaga, *in* Robert L. Gold, *Borderland Empires in Transition: The Triple-Nation Transfer of Florida* 71-74 (1969). A few English ships were also hired for transportation. Thirty-three of the evacuees from St. Augustine were transported to Campeche.
9. Baptisms of Catalina Gerónima Rafaela de Porras (Jan. 9, 1753) and Génera Antonia de Porras (Sept. 9, 1763) (on file with St. Augustine Cathedral Parish Records); Claim of Juana Navarro (on file with Claims for Town Lots, Spanish Land Grant manuscripts [hereinafter SLG], Florida Department of State, Division of Historical Resources, Tallahassee, Bundle 320 [hereinafter Bnd.], Claims no.15, 80) (microfilm copies on file with St. Augustine Historical Society). Juan José Solana, Report on Conditions of St. Augustine (Apr. 9, 1760) (on file with Archivo General de Indias [hereinafter AGI] John B. Stetson Collection [hereinafter SC], P. K. Yonge Library of Florida History) (microfilm copies on file with St. Augustine Historical Society) stated that Porras was selling English dry goods and other things. Translations of the inventories of both of "Porras's" real properties appeared in Charles W. Arnade, 'The Architecture of Spanish St. Augustine', 18 Americas 149, 175-79 (Oct. 1961).

> in their emigration, under any pretence whatsoever, except that of debts, or of criminal prosecutions . . . .[10]

Officials of newly British East Florida had little to deal with regarding the properties of Spanish-era residents; Spanish officials had arranged for the handling of private property sales. Two men were appointed to deal as agents for the evacuees: Juan José Eligio de la Puente to be the man in Havana and Jesse Fish in St. Augustine.[11] Jesse Fish, a British subject, had been in St. Augustine intermittently since 1735. Fish was to hold properties as agent and make sales agreements for East Florida property, contact Eligio de la Puente in Cuba, and transfer the funds in gold, silver, or notes of exchange to Eligio after Fish withheld his agent's fees. Fish also intended to withhold what he claimed were debts of Spanish residents that he had absorbed as agent/purchaser of properties. Gold comments that this arrangement "encouraged" the Spanish-period proprietors to "anticipate later profits." Gold asserts that the Eligio de la Puente-Fish transactions were "clearly illegal and arbitrary." Fish engaged in treasonous activities, and Eligio disregarded the terms of the Treaty of Paris. Had Fish not purchased the property titles, they would have reverted to the British government. However hopeful the evacuees might have been, newly British St. Augustine was a buyers' market. British residents moved onto the former Spanish home sites with impunity and often without purchase. Eligio de la Puente and Fish accused each other of non-performance.[12] Floridanos who had moved to Cuba in 1763 would claim that they did not receive their money for purported sales.

---

10. Treaty of Paris 1763, art. XX, Yale L. Sch.: Avalon Project, http://avalon.law.yale.edu/18th_century/paris763.asp (last visited July 7, 2017).
11. Juan José Eligio de la Puente, El Presidio de San Agustín de la Florida . . . . (Jan. 22, 1764) (on file with Royal Depository of Hydrography, Madrid) (copies at St. Augustine Historical Society) (depicting representational buildings). A key that frames the map noted the apparent owner, lot dimensions, and building material for each parcel. Anglophone researchers called this the "Puente" map although the mapmaker referred to himself as "Eligio" or in full "Eligio de la Puente."
12. Gold, *supra* note 8, at 47.

In East Florida, British officials were exasperated to find that Fish and others claimed to hold titles to almost all of the lands, six million acres, which the officials had envisioned for plantation development. The officials refused to recognize the legitimacy of the titles claimed by Fish et al. British-era cartographer and surveyor Bernard Romans observed that "the crown would not allow the transfer of Spanish landed interest to be good, although mentioned in the articles of peace." Gold concludes that "[Great Britain's] new colony was settled, however, without particular regard to the treaty regulations." Adhering to the treaty was not always compatible with maximizing the land for profit.[13] "Florida fever" gripped entrepreneurs in England, and they did not intend to be hindered by the treaty. Foremost among the investor-enthusiasts was British East Florida's first governor, General James Grant. All participants ignored the treaty agreements regarding private property, except the evacuees whose property was in question.

Twenty-odd years later, in consequence of the Treaty of Paris of 1783, as Great Britain left East Florida and Spain returned to the peninsula, British subjects were given eighteen months beginning in March 1785 to leave or to remain in East Florida and become Spanish subjects, if they qualified. East Florida had become the new home to thousands of British loyalists, who had fled British colonies during the last years of the American Revolution. Loyalist refugees, especially those from South Carolina or Georgia, headed to other British colonies, such as East Florida or the Bahamas. In the last years of the war perhaps as many as 13,000 persons entered East Florida as loyalists or were the enslaved workers brought by the loyalists. Loyalist evacuee Hugh Rose lamented that he had believed that East Florida "offered a safe and not unpromising asylum for people in his unfortunate situation." Rose claimed that in Florida "he invested what little remains of fortune was left to him." Like other loyalists, Rose had believed that Great Britain would surely

---

13. Daniel L. Schafer, 'St. Augustine's British Years, 1763-1784', 38 El Escribano 1, 7-9 (2001); Gold, *supra* note 8, at 26; Bernard Romans, *A Concise Natural History of East and West Florida* 223 (New York, 1774), http://purl.flvc.org/fcla/dl/UF00000163.pdf.

maintain East Florida as a home for King George's loyal subjects.[14] Historian J. Leitch Wright observed that "the 1783 peace treated British subjects in the Floridas almost the same way as the 1763 treaty dealt with Spanish subjects"—as "conquered populations."[15]

Separate from the treaties' agreements, the departing governments, Spain in 1763 and Great Britain in 1784-1785, offered compensation to their own subjects for losses arising from departures brought by the changes of flags. In anticipation of the cession in 1763, two Spanish engineers were sent from Havana to St. Augustine to appraise both royal and private buildings in St. Augustine.[16] Two decades later British evacuees from East Florida were left on their own to make claims for losses to review boards in London or in the Bahamas and provide testimony of witnesses about the existence, condition, and value of the abandoned property. This study focuses on treaties and clarifying titles to land, but it is still important to include the process of claims for loss of personal property and the performance of the governments in handling and paying the claims as part of the analysis of officials and sovereigns. Departing loyalists filed for compensation for their chairs, tables, clocks, cooking utensils, and the timbers of their dismantled buildings left on the shore when there was no space on ships leaving East Florida or which washed overboard in bad weather.[17]

East Florida's Spanish officials after 1784 dealt with property claims by British loyalists who wished to remain in East Florida as

---

14. 2 Wilbur Henry Siebert, *Loyalists in East Florida, 1774-1785*, at vii-ix, 105 (1929).

15. J. Leitch Wright, Jr., *Florida in the American Revolution* 123 (1975).

16. Works Progress Admin., *Historical Records Survey, Spanish Land Grants in Florida* xiv n.28 (1941) [hereinafter Spanish Land Grants in Florida]. All five volumes of *Spanish Land Grants in Florida* have the same introduction in pages i through lxi. The five-volume set is translated abstracts of the claims for affirmation of Spanish Land Grants. The Claims for Town Lots are included in the Spanish Land Grants manuscript collection, but the Town Lots are not included in the volumes of abstracts.

Engineers Juan de Cotilla and Pablo Castelló relied on assistance by local masons and carpenters. Arnade, *supra* note 9, at 161-69.

17. Siebert, *supra* note 14, at vii-viii. Claims had to be filed in London by January 1, 1787, and in the Bahamas by May 1, 1787.

well as claims by Spanish families who had returned after evacuating to Cuba in 1763. *Floridano* evacuees now had some pragmatic recourse for their losses. With the return of East Florida to Spain, restitution of their lands, which was unavailable while Great Britain held the Floridas, was now a possibility. After Spain regained Florida, that nation was also eager to provide land to settlers. The initial requirement that Florida's residents adhere to Roman Catholicism delayed settling of claims made by British-era, mostly Protestant, residents. Some converted, at least nominally, others left East Florida, still others waited for clarification. The indecision contributed to the unsettledness and rancor in an already disturbed countryside, especially near the East Florida-Georgia border, which at that time was an international boundary with mostly loyalists living on the East Florida side and American Revolutionaries across the St. Mary's River in Georgia.

The absence of Spanish-period records complicated assessing the Floridanos' claims for town property. Local records for St. Augustine's first two centuries sailed away with the town's Spanish residents in 1763 and with only a few exceptions remain unavailable, still in Cuba today if they have not disappeared or deteriorated.[18] Notarial records, probate records, and legal cases were relocated to Cuba and not returned to St. Augustine with the Spanish regime in 1784. Records of St. Augustine's Roman Catholic parish that memorialized baptisms, marriages, and deaths, the vital-statistics records of their day and useful in establishing inheritance of property, were eventually returned to St. Augustine, but not until 1906—much too late to benefit colonial claimants.[19] Documents that were never recorded in official archives but remained with an interested party probably did not survive the dislocations of twenty years. Dowry agreements, account books "of the amounts I still owe, and those owed me," in the verbiage of a death-bed will, and other unrecorded

---

18. Pablo Castelló, Plano del presidio de San Agustín de la Florida y sus contornos . . . . (July 21, 1763) (on file with Library of Congress) (original in the Spanish Ministry of War, LM 8a-1a); Eligio de la Puente, *supra* note 11; Gold, *supra* note 8, ch.5.

19. Michael Gannon, *Rebel Bishop: Augustin Verot, Florida's Civil War Prelate* 235 (1964).

agreements were taken to Havana in chests or strong boxes. In the colonial era, testators described the location, usually within the residence, where such a chest might be found.[20] Worse yet for claimants, other agreements may have been only verbal over sequential generations and known to only family members and not to neighbors who might be able to offer other corroborating evidence. Commenting about family or personal agreements in the province of León in Spain, anthropologist Ruth Behar noted that personal records were considered as binding as those that were recorded. Castilian law prevailed in the Spanish America, but *peninsular (*Iberian*)* soldiers who had served in Florida before evacuating might have still followed some traditions of their native regions.[21]

With minimal judicial structure in the small colony of Spanish East Florida, the military governor judged the claims, sometimes with assistance of a legal officer (*auditor de guerra*). At times a returning Floridano and a loyalist who chose to remain in Spanish Florida made a claim for the same parcel of property. At times East Florida Governor Juan Nepomuceno de Quesada (1790-1795) took his inspiration from King Solomon's attempt to "split the baby," in one instance dividing property to accommodate, but probably not satisfy, either Floridano claimants or holdover British residents.[22] The attempt to regain the property of Floridana Victoria Escalona offers an informative example of procedures, problems, and unwritten dowry agreements. Victo-

---

20. Father Pedro Camps pointed out in his will where to find the chest that held his accounts. Estate of Pedro Camps (1790) (on file with East Florida Papers [hereinafter EFP], Library of Congress Manuscript Collection, Bnd. 308) (microfilm copies on file with St. Augustine Historical Society); Will of José Guillén (Dec. 17, 1743) in Claim of Antonia de Avero (on file with Bnd. 320, Claim no. 19, or Town Lots, SLG, Tallahassee); Will of Francisco Menéndez Marquez (Sept. 2, 1742) (on file with AGI, Seville, Spain, SC, P. K. Yonge Library of Florida History, 58-1-34/73).

21. Behar noted that many documents were not retained beyond a period of reasonable usefulness: "[M]ost villagers throw away records that involve people whom they no longer remember. . . . the records are mainly of interest if they have some bearing on the present." Ruth Behar, *Santa María del Monte: The Presence of the Past in a Spanish Village* 69 (1987).

22. *See* Claim of Juana Navarro, *supra* note 9 (including the claim of her daughter Catalina de Porras).

ria's family was quite proactive in reclaiming their property. The dossier for the claim contains a petition, a report of a search of archives in Havana, and a power of attorney all completed before the British had relinquished East Florida. The claims process could be expensive for persons who had little cash; each of these documents required a payment as noted by the four-*cuartillo* stamp at the top of the pages. A cuartillo was one-fourth of a real or two pesos or four days' pay of an artilleryman's funding. The initial petition was dated April 19,1783, five months before the final treaty had been was signed in September.[23] In the petition Victoria's children, Rosalía and Joaquín Martínez, asserted that the lot of their mother Victoria had never been sold. (Women kept their own surnames after marriage; the children usually used the surname of the father.) In marginal notes on the petition, a typical manner of response, the Intendant of Cuba Juan Ignacio de Urriza affirmed that among archives of the *Tribunal y Real Audiencia de Cuentas* (Exchequer) there was indeed no record by the Floridanos' property agent, Eligio de la Puente, that he had received money for Victoria's lot. Rosalía and Joaquín designated Aunt Lucía Escalona (their mother's sister) to be their attorney-in-fact to pursue affirmation of ownership in Florida. Aunt Lucía appeared at the St. Augustine property of her deceased sister Victoria (d. 1743) and claimed it for Victoria's children. This rather brash aunt verbally evicted the astounded British-period occupant, a man who had been paying rent for years to some self-proclaimed owner. She ordered him to vacate immediately—and apparently he did. Victoria's masonry house had not survived the intervening years, and a wooden house built by the British occupant now sat upon the lot.

The claims process moved slowly. In 1800, sixteen years after submitting the petition, three witnesses testified, in the absence of paper evidence, that Victoria's family had possessed the property in the prior Spanish period and that they knew of

23. Support for soldiers is listed in Don José Antonio Gelabert to the Crown, General List of All Who Serve and Are Paid by the King at the Presidio of San Agustín (1752) (on file with AGI SC 87-1-14/2, Havana). Perhaps Victoria's family was aware of the Preliminary Articles of Peace between Spain and England, signed January 20, 1783, at Versailles.

"no other residents or owner" than Victoria and her family. The term "no other . . . owner" suggests that this was dowry property. There is no mention of Victoria's widower, Martín Martínez Gallegos, and his children of his subsequent marriage. The dowry property reverted to Victoria's children as the heirs of her body when her widowed husband no longer needed it. The practice in St. Augustine of residential properties' serving as dowry further complicated the claims. Residences passed from mothers to daughters over several generations without documents, or so the absence of such evidence suggests. The claim on behalf of Victoria's children was affirmed, and Lucia moved into the house on the lot confirmed to Victoria's children.[24] Other claimants for real estate in St. Augustine were able to submit copies made in Havana of deeds, wills, or other documents to support the claims. The earliest date cited of a conveyance of property was February 17, 1717, as an item in deraignment of a title.[25]

A number of the potential claims for lots in St. Augustine was resolved when the town lots reverted to the sovereign for delinquent taxes. The lots had been claimed by Jesse Fish, the agent on the mainland side of the Florida Straits. Governor Quesada held tax sales and conveyed them to new owners.

In the summer of 1821 the cession of the Spanish Floridas, agreed in the Adams-Onís Treaty, took place. On July 10, 1821, the Spanish flag was lowered for the final time at St. Augustine as the United States took control of East Florida, and the ceremony was repeated in West Florida the following week. With the transfer of St. Augustine to the United States, most of the residents of St. Augustine and Spanish East Florida remained. Spanish soldiers and government employees, their dependents, and prisoners

---

24. Claim of Joaquín Martínez and Rosalía Martínez [children of Victoria Escalona] and Lucía de Escalona (on file with SLG, Claim 79, Bnd. 320). For a discussion and other examples of dowry practice in St Augustine, see Susan Richbourg Parker, 'In My Mother's House: Dowry Property and Female Inheritance Patterns in Spanish Florida', *in* Signposts: New Directions in Southern Legal History 19-44 (Sally E. Hadden & Patricia Hagler Minter eds., 2013). Page 27 deals with the claim of the Martínez siblings.
25. Deed from Juan Méndez and Micaela González to José de Escalona (Feb. 17, 1717) (on file with Towns Lots, Claim of Juan Bautista de los Ríos on behalf of his wife, María Marcelina de la Rosa, Bnd. 320, claim no. 75).

departed for Cuba on the day of the change of flags. Spanish East Florida Governor José Coppinger had encouraged relocation to other Spanish lands and informed Florida residents of "the immunities, favors and protection" offered to those who wished to move to other locations in the Spanish realm. During the remainder of the year 1821 more left St. Augustine for new lands and opportunities in Spanish America.[26]

Florida's U.S. Territorial Governor Andrew Jackson initially seemed conciliatory toward the holdover residents from the Spanish period, concurring with the suggestion of Governor Coppinger that St. Augustine's municipal representatives be retained under U.S. sovereignty. Jackson's beneficence lasted about six weeks, when St. Augustine's city councilmen were required to abjure Spanish citizenship on August 22. Four of the five aldermen refused to take the oath and resigned. They were replaced with recently arrived Americans.[27] Persons from outside of Florida were appointed to top Territorial Government positions. The holdover residents were being supplanted. Geographer Richard Campanella's description of New Orleanians after the 1803 transfer of Louisiana to the United States probably well describes Spanish Floridians two decades later:

> Compared to their new compatriots, they spoke a different language, practiced a different religion, and followed distinct legal philosophies. They perceived race and managed slavery differently. . . . They ate different foods, celebrated different festivals, and honored different heroes. . . . [They] fretted, then resented, then resisted the onslaught of [in the case of Louisiana] les Amèricains.[28]

---

26. L. David Norris, 'The Squeeze: Spain Cedes Floridas to the United States', 20 El Escribano 127-29 (1988) (quoting Jose Coppinger's Proclamation of 7 July 1821 on page 127). There were also some civilian residents who moved to Cuba at the time of the transfer.

27. Letter from Acting Governor of East Florida W.G.D. Worthington to Andrew Jackson (Aug. 1821), *in* 22 Territorial Papers of the United States, Florida Territory 193 (Clarence E. Carter, ed., 1956-1962) [hereinafter 22 Territorial Papers].

28. Richard Campanella, *Bourbon Street: A History* 30 (2014).

The tenured Floridians faced another unexpected disappointment and burden—proving ownership of their private properties when the Board of Land Commissioners for East Florida was appointed on August 4, 1823.[29] After more than two years since the transfer of flags and of property owners' believing that their private land claims were accepted at face value, property owners in St. Augustine and Fernandina became disgruntled when they learned that they would have to submit their land claims to the Land Commission's scrutiny. Property owners held that Article II of the treaty implied that all private claims in those towns were accepted as valid. Article VIII of the Adams-Onís Treaty stated that Spanish grants made prior to January 24, 1818, were to be "ratified and confirmed to the persons in possession of the lands, to the same extent that the said grants would be valid if the territories had remained under the domain of His Catholic Majesty."[30] Floridians expected that only public (formerly royal or crown) properties would have to be examined.

The treaty also offered other hope to former Spanish subjects. In Article Nine the United States committed to "cause satisfaction to be made for the injuries, if any, which by process of Law, shall be established to have been suffered by the Spanish Officers, and individual Spanish inhabitants, by the late operations of the American Army in Florida." In 1812 American troops and insurgents invaded Spanish East Florida attempting to annex the colony into the United States. Known as the Patriot War, American troops and adventurers occupied northeast Florida from the spring of 1812 until 1814, except the city of St. Augustine, and destroyed the Spanish Floridians' crops, buildings, and possessions, and slaughtered cattle.

Newly American claimants for real property held mass meetings and petitioned Congress to exempt them from exhibiting their titles.[31] Appointed officials for East Florida initially held the same opinion as the residents. Colonel Alexander Hamilton, Jr.,

---

29. Land Commissioners for West Florida had been appointed more than a year before the examiners for East Florida.
30. Spanish Land Grants in Florida, *supra* note 16, at xxxii.
31. *Id.* at xlii.

District Attorney for East Florida, wrote to Secretary of State John Quincy Adams in December of 1822 about the hardships that the Florida residents would suffer from delays, which were "a source of positive sacrifice." The experience of the late 1700s under the returned Spanish regime was to be repeated for a subsequent generation "whose claims [would] most probably be confirmed [could] not sell and dare[d] not cultivate." Hamilton asserted that the "present law" would cause unexpected hardship upon the heirs and representatives of such persons who have held their lands "by descent for centuries, particularly in the Cities . . . ." The individuals would be "put to great expense and exposed in the deraignment of their titles, to much subsequent vexatious litigation."[32]

The East Florida Land Commissioners faced a severe lack of resources of evidence and information. The Commission did have second-Spanish-period documents to consult. At the time of East Florida's transfer to the United States, U.S. officials had broken the lock on the Spanish governor's office and confiscated every document in the room.[33] All documents for claims had to be submitted in the English language, but there was insufficient funding or personnel to translate papers. Congress did not supply the commissioners with published copies of Spain's land laws, and such copies were difficult to acquire in the United States. Finally Joseph M. White compiled information from his own research and from published works finally obtained from Spain in his *Spanish And French Ordinances Affecting Land Titles in Florida and Other Territories of France and Spain*. This would serve as an "adequate guide" for adjudicating land titles in Florida. Secretary of State Adams had provided to Governor Jackson the Laws of Congress enacted for the Louisiana Territories, which might provide information and precedents. Among them was an act passed in March of 1805 "for ascertaining and

---

32. Letter from Alexander Hamilton [Jr.] to Secretary of State John Q. Adams (Dec. 15, 1822), *in* 22 Territorial Papers, *supra* note 27, at 580-82.
33. Norris, *supra* note 26, at 131-32.

adjusting the titles & claims to Land within the Territory of Orleans and the District of Louisiana."[34]

Holdover Florida residents feared for the ownership of the St. Augustine parish church, so essential to the spiritual and social life of the community. Hamilton had written so supportively of the plight of the Spanish title holders, yet earned their animus with his opinion that property of the Roman Catholic Church during Spanish rule had been property of the Spanish crown and that with the cession of Florida Church property passed to the United States—from sovereign to sovereign.

Electoral politics entered the land claims process. Hamilton, in his capacity of a land commissioner in addition to district attorney, had threatened to look unfavorably upon the land claims of anyone who he might learn had voted for his opponents during his campaign for Territorial Delegate in 1823. Fearful and irate former Spanish residents petitioned Secretary of State John Quincy Adams to resolve the problem with Hamilton. In addition to sending the petition to Secretary Adams, the document was published in the St. Augustine newspaper, *The East-Florida Herald*, in English and Spanish, listing the petitioners who signed.[35]

For the Land Commissioners rural lands did not present the same problem of missing documents as did city lots, for few claims were made to affirm first Spanish period titles for lands in the countryside. Only a few originally British grants for thousands of acres were submitted to the Commission. Most of the rural claims arose from headrights grants made by Spanish governors during the second Spanish period.

Disappointment and frustration plagued claims made for personal property. The claims by British loyalists were an "internal" matter as the dynamic of the claim involved the British government dealing with British subject-claimant. Claimants received about one-fourth, £170 million, of the total amount claimed of

---

34. Spanish Land Grants in Florida, *supra* note 16, at xxxvi; Letter from Secretary of State John Q. Adams to Andrew Jackson (Aug. 20, 1821), *in* 22 Territorial Papers, *supra* note 27, at 172-73 (Acts listed in correspondence).
35. Letter from Bernard Segui et al., to Secretary of State John Q. Adams (June 23, 1823), *in* 22 Territorial Papers, *supra* note 27, at 702-04.

£647 million. As for the Patriot War claims, Congress initially attempted to renege in the 1820s on Article Nine of treaty. Finally more than a quarter of a century after the invasion, the claims, made by almost the entire free population of East Florida in 1812, were reviewed between 1836 and 1842 by the U.S. Treasury Department and judges in Jacksonville, Florida. James Cusick comments that "the claims cases reflected almost as poorly on American justice as the conflict [the Patriot War] itself." Cusick reveals that "impoverished families received little in the way of restitution while . . . the richest inhabitants ate up the lion's share."[36]

Assessing the succession of these three nations in handling the matter of private real property ownership or its loss would seem to allow us to compare and contrast the philosophies of laws and legal systems. But what is truly notable about the three nations is the similarity of their performance, not the differences in laws and systems. None of the three nations truly endeavored to fulfill their promises made in the treaties to their own subjects/citizens or to their new, holdover citizens.

Comparisons between Spanish and British legal systems and practices emphasize the role of an individual's ability in Spanish colonies to appeal for justice to the King or the Council of the Indies in the face of the actions of colonial officials. In contrast, as Richard Ross comments that "the English empire preferred regulating government structures rather than assuring individual justice."[37] Studies have also contrasted the intentional centralization of Spain as a colonial power while noting the individuality of the laws among the British American colonies. Historian Marylynn Salmon contends that the pervasive problem with studying property rights in early British America is the remarkable diversity in the laws because of the diverse situation in the home islands. Yet in the Iberian peninsula too, laws varied among

---

36. James G. Cusick, *The Other War of 1812: The Patriot War and the American Invasion of Spanish East Floridas* 305-06 (2003).
37. Richard J. Ross, 'Legal Communications and Imperial Governance: British North America and Spanish America Compared', *in* 1 *The Cambridge History of Law in America, Early America* (1580-1815) 104-42, quote at 142 (Michael Grossberg & Christopher Tomlins eds., 2008).

the old kingdoms that formed the nation of Spain, but the laws of Castile applied in the Indies and offered, at least ideally, a consistency throughout the colonies.[38] The acquisition of the Floridas by the United States would seem to be a more peaceful action that would result in a more considered treaty than the treaties of 1763 and 1783, which were the products of post-war negotiations. Yet the U.S. Government seemed surprisingly unprepared to review land claims although Florida was not the first territory to be transferred to the United States.

Perhaps Spain did the most to compensate its Florida evacuees, but doing so was a happenstance. The return of Spain to the Florida peninsula after the War of the American Revolution offered the possibility for Spain to make good on compensation for the losses arising from the 1763 evacuation with the very land abandoned two decades before. Compensation by restoring property ownership from 1763 took place after more than two decades and even then not quickly; the beneficiaries were the children or even grandchildren of the "owners" of 1763. Spanish Florida officials, no doubt, preferred restoration of lands to cash compensation, for the former made no demand on the funds in the Spanish colonial treasury.

Incoming governments looked as well to resolve property owner-ship issues so that the respective government could discern what land was available for granting to individuals or for use by the government itself. Great Britain's Board of Trade was eager to turn East Florida into a "plantation" and granted large tracts to (usually absentee) investors.[39] Later, when the United States took possession of the Floridas in 1821, the demand for live oak for building ships pressured the U.S. Government to move quickly to resolve the ownership of timber stands so the U.S. Navy could exploit timber lands that were without valid claims as soon as possible. But the U.S. Navy began cutting timber or contracting for timber on land it viewed as "public"

---

38. Marylynn Salmon, *Women and the Law of Property in Early America* 1157 (1986); José María Ots y Capdequí, *Manual de historia del derecho español en las indias y del derecho propiamente indiano* 112-77 (1945).
39. Schafer, *supra* note 13, ch. 3.

before the claims process was begun.[40] Once again claims of private citizens were subordinated to the needs of the sovereign nation and the private citizens were holdover residents of the departed regime, their reluctant or undeveloped loyalty to the new sovereign making them expendable.

Departing nations were reticent to compensate and equivocated about doing so. Arriving nations dawdled and did not follow through quickly on commitments to "the conquered." The U.S. Congress tried to renege on its treaty commitment to compensate for Patriot War damages.[41]

All three sovereign governments—Great Britain, Spain, and the United States—followed some sort of a delaying strategy, hoping holdover claimants would weary of the delays and move out of Florida. Their departure would open up lands and lots to the subjects/citizens of the now occupying nation and would encourage immigration of the supposedly like-minded into Florida.

---

40. Letter from Louis McLane to the Secretary of the Navy, Washington D.C. (Mar. 1, 1822), *in* 22 Territorial Papers, *supra* note 27, at 370; Letter from Worthington to U.S. Marshall James G. Forbes, St. Augustine (Mar. 5, 1822), *in* 22 Territorial Papers, *supra* note 27, at 375-76; Letter from John H. Elton, U.S.N. to Secretary of the Navy, U.S. Brig *Spark* at Sea (May 16, 1822), *in* 22 Territorial Papers, *supra* note 27, at 430-42.
41. Siebert, *supra* note 14, at viii; Cusick, *supra* note 36, at 305.

Hoisting of American Colors over Louisiana
Painting by Thure de Thulstrup, 1904

CHAPTER 3

THE SPANISH SPIRIT IN THIS COUNTRY

Newcomers to Louisiana in 1803-1805, and their Perceptions of the Spanish Regime

Eberhard L. Faber

The summer of 1803, like many New Orleans summers, was hot, sticky, and miserable, and Pierre Clément de Laussat, the French Prefect sent by Napoléon Bonaparte to take possession of Louisiana, was having a terrible time. His dream of presiding over a modernized, Bonapartist regime in the onetime French colony had been undermined by war with Britain and the failure of the French occupying force to reach the colony. At the same time, he was humiliated by the insubordination of members of his own entourage and infuriated by persistent rumors that Louisiana was to be sold to the United States. Mid-June brought stifling, hundred-degree days, interspersed with fierce tropical storms; then on July 1, Laussat fell victim to the region's most dreaded disease: yellow fever.[1]

As he spent the next twenty-five days confined to bed, seeing his remaining hopes for Louisiana wither away, Laussat's bitterest words were reserved not for the vulgar Americans who were taking away his colony, nor for his arrogant subordinates with whom he feuded continuously—but for his Spanish hosts, a

1. Pierre Clément de Laussat, *Memoirs of My Life to My Son During the Years 1803 and After* [...] 41-42, 48 (1978); Letter from Laussat to Decrès (July 21, 1803) (on file with Laussat Papers, Historic New Orleans Collection [hereinafter LP-HNOC], no. 227).

group of officials who had initially received him with ostentatious courtesy and good will. He considered the governor, Manuel de Salcedo, a witless dotard, and the special commissioner for the cession, the Marquis de Casa Calvo, an intemperate bully. But his harshest judgment was reserved for Nicolás Maria Vidal, the lieutenant governor and judge-advocate, widely rumored to be corrupt, described by the Prefect as "an old stager of justice, who sells his judgments almost openly."[2]

Laussat's further description of Vidal is revealing for the intertwined racial and sexual tropes used to evoke Spanish colonial rule:

> There was not a more diseased heart, a more twisted mind, a more mealymouthed disposition hidden behind a yellow countenance shaded by black ... he had as his mistress a foul-smelling mulatto ... his weakness for African blood was displayed on festival days; his doorstep was a gathering place for Negro dancing. He had two splendid Negro males. In the wintertime, instead of using a warming pan in his bed, he had them get into bed first to warm it up, and then he would get in between them. Sometimes, ... he fell to his knees and cried out, "For God's sake, don't kill me, for I am in the state of mortal sin." I would call this man Vidal the personification of the Spanish spirit in this country . ...[3]

The "Spanish spirit," in Laussat's view, thus combined senility, corruption, racial weakness, and effeminate degeneracy—in contrast, of course, with Bonapartist austerity, efficiency, and

---

2. Letter from Laussat to Decrès (July 18, 1803), in 2 *Louisiana Under the Rule of Spain, France, and the United States, 1785-1807: Social, Economic, and Political Conditions of the Territory Represented in the Louisiana Purchase* 42-43 (James Alexander Robertson ed., 1911) [hereinafter 2 Louisiana Under the Rule]; Laussat, supra note 1, at 102. Eventually Laussat began to complain about the Spanish to the French minister in Madrid, asking that they be punished by the King; Letters from Laussat to Beurnonville (July 27 & July 30, 1803) (on file with LP-HNOC, nos. 231, 232); Letter from Laussat to Decrès (Oct. 6, 1803) (on file with LP-HNOC, no. 274); see also Letter from Laussat to Beurnonville (Nov. 5, 1803) (on file with LP-HNOC, no. 306) (complaining of Casa Calvo's ill will).

3. Letter from Laussat to Decrès (July 18, 1803), in 2 *Louisiana Under the Rule*, *supra* note 2, at 42-43.

virility. And his contempt for the Spanish regime had a lasting impact when, during his brief twenty days in power in December 1803, before turning Louisiana over to the Americans, he abolished the New Orleans Cabildo, reorganized its militia, and reinstated a law of slave control long desired by the region's wealthiest planters. The incoming American governor, William Claiborne, frequently complained that his job had been made more difficult by these hasty innovations.[4]

Nor was Laussat the only French newcomer to offer severe strictures on Spanish rule in Louisiana. Jacques Pitot, a French merchant whom Laussat appointed to his new-designed Municipal Council, and who eventually became the city's Mayor, had arrived in the late 1790s and in 1802 published a scathing critique of the local regime—touching on everything from corruption to trade restrictions to local officials' alleged indifference to law and order. He lamented the fact that the half million pesos sent annually by Spain to subsidize the colony wound up in the hands of "a thieving treasury, indifferent to the welfare of the country." And, striking a chord among New Orleans's merchant class, Pitot dilated at length on the cumbersome regulations the Spanish regime imposed on commerce, condemning the "excessive covetousness" and "annoying pettiness" of Spanish officials, and "the humiliation and discouragement in which [they] can hold the commerce of a country."[5]

Uninterested in the problems of groups such as slaves, free people of color, or poor whites, Pitot equated Louisiana's welfare with "the often humiliated and vexed businessman" and "the planters ignored in misery" under Spanish rule. And tellingly, on what would become a contentious issue after 1803, Pitot condemned restrictions on the slave trade, which "left agriculture

---

4. *See, e.g.*, Letter from Claiborne to Jefferson (Nov. 25, 1804), *in* 9 *Territorial Papers of the United States: Orleans Territory* 338-41 (Clarence Edwin Carter ed., 1934); Jared William Bradley, *Interim Appointment: W. C. C. Claiborne Letter Book, 1804-1805*, at 100-02 (2002). For a further discussion of Laussat's innovations and their destabilizing effects, see Mark Fernandez, *From Chaos to Continuity: The Evolution of Louisiana's Judicial System, 1712-1862*, at 18-19 (2001).

5. James Pitot, *Observations on the Colony of Louisiana, from 1796 to 1802*, at 21, 37-41 (Robert D. Bush ed., 1979).

without an increase in laborers when other Spanish colonies were receiving ... the slaves necessary for their prosperity."[6]

Above all, Pitot condemned the absence of law and order, wrapping drinking, gambling, racial mixing, and lawlessness into a synthetic portrait of urban disorder:

> The patrols are insignificant; the garrison is inconsequential; the militia not in uniform ... it must have been seen in order to describe to what extremes they have carried the laxity and neglect of the police. The patrols in town are so poorly organized that nighttime burglaries in the warehouses are frequent, as are murders .... Hundreds of licensed taverns openly sell to slaves, and, in making them drunk, become ... the receivers of goods stolen from their masters .... A public ball ... organized by the free people of color, is each week the gathering place for the scum of such people and of those slaves who, eluding their owner's surveillance, go there to bring their plunder ... and as a crowning infamy one finds even some white people who repeatedly battle with the slaves for places in the quadrilles, and for their share of the household pilferage which they decide by a throw of the dice.[7]

Pitot's racially tinged call for increased law enforcement was echoed by still another newcomer from France, Dr. Paul Alliot—which was ironic, since Dr. Alliot had been imprisoned for medical fraud. From his prison cell he wrote a long missive to Laussat, full of practical and ideological suggestions for the administration of Napoleonic Louisiana—and complaints about being lodged "pele-mele" alongside black prisoners, a practice which he believed showed why French blood remained pure while Spanish was weakened by mixture with "barbarians and savages."[8]

In fact, French newcomers to Louisiana—many of whom, like Alliot and Pitot, arrived there by way of St. Domingue—

---

6. *Id.* at 2, 55. Dr. Alliot agreed that Spanish restrictions on the slave trade had "entirely paralyzed the progress of agriculture"; Paul Alliot, 'Reflexions Historiques et Politiques sur la Louysiane', *reprinted in* 2 *Louisiana Under the Rule*, *supra* note 2, at 29-232.

7. Pitot, *supra* note 5, at 29.

8. Letter from Alliot to Laussat (Apr. 14, 1803) (on file with LP-HNOC, no. 128).

frequently exhibited many of the virulent prejudices against Spanish America often attributed to Anglo-Americans under the rubric of the "Black Legend," including the belief that Spanish rule was corrupt, venal, violent, and prone to atrocities, and the belief that Spanish-descended creoles were racially and morally compromised because of their alleged proclivity for intimate contact with Africans and Indians. They also characterized Spanish rule as effeminate and impotent in contrast with French masculinity. Finally, many like Pitot believed that Spain's on-again, off-again restrictions on the slave trade had kept Louisiana from reaching her rightful degree of colonial prosperity.[9]

By contrast, the views of many American newcomers—who began to arrive in New Orleans immediately following its acquisition by the United States—were considerably milder than those of Laussat or Pitot. To be sure, Americans had their own criticisms of the Spanish regime. But they tended to be abstract, impersonal, and legalistic. Extensive reading in the letters and published writings of these American newcomers reveals little evidence of the kind of ethnic prejudice against the Spanish that Laussat and Alliot indulged in, none of the metaphors of impotence and effeminacy, no indignant rants against Spanish "atrocities," and certainly no complaints about Spain's regulation of the slave trade.[10]

One of the best-known American critiques of Spanish rule in Louisiana took the form not of a pamphlet or book but of a play—and a slapstick comedy at that—by the gifted Irish-born jurist and polemicist, James Workman. Workman was a onetime British Army quartermaster whose first published work, in 1797, advocated a plan to conquer and liberate Spanish America with the use of Irish soldier-settlers. As Catholics, Workman argued,

---

9. A third francophone travel account containing similar views, in addition to Pitot's *Observations* and Alliot's *Reflexions*, was Pierre Berquin-Duvallon, *Travels in Louisiana and the Floridas, in the Year 1802 Giving a Correct Picture of Those Countries* (N.Y., I. Riley & Co 1806).

10. In addition to the sources mentioned in the text, the letters read include the complete manuscript papers of Edward Livingston, now held by Princeton University's Rare Books and Special Collections, and the published Claiborne Letter Books; both contain extensive correspondence with a wide range of "Anglo-Americans" in and around early New Orleans.

these soldiers would be opposed "with less fury and acrimony" than Protestant settlers—while at the same time, the venture would provide an outlet for simmering discontent back home in Ireland. Finally, the mission would also emancipate Spain's African slaves—a goal Workman called "just and glorious," citing Pennsylvania's 1780 emancipation law as a model. For Workman, this was win-win-win.[11]

Discouragingly, however, the Portland ministry showed no interest whatsoever in Workman's visionary scheme—which may have been why he decided to migrate across the Atlantic, and pitch the plan to Thomas Jefferson instead. Workman's 1801 letter to Jefferson emphasized the way his plan could dovetail with American national abolition of slavery—or as Workman called it, "an Establishment by which [the United States] is enfeebled, Endangered, contaminated & disgraced"—and suggested the use of Louisiana as a territory for the resettlement of freed slaves.[12]

By 1803 Workman had moved to Charleston, where he continued to advocate for the liberation of Louisiana—now with less emphasis on the liberation of Africans and more on the overthrow of Spanish despotism. His next major literary production, celebrating the Louisiana Purchase, was the stage comedy *Liberty in Louisiana*—which ran for several months and garnered enthusiastic support from Charleston theatergoers. The play is often cited as an instance of anti-Spanish "propaganda"—George Dargo called it "an American caricature of the Spanish system," and Workman himself in a Preface declared that his intention was

---

11. James Workman, 'A Memorial, Proposing a Plan, for the Conquest and Emancipation of Spanish America [...]', *in Political Essays, Relative to the War of the French Revolution* 144-74 (Alexandria, Va., Cottam & Stewart 1801) [hereinafter Political Essays]; a mention of the scheme also occurs in *A Letter to the Duke of Portland, in* Political Essays, *supra*, at 138-41. It is also noteworthy that in Workman's plan, the first step called for the taking of strategically crucial New Orleans, as a base for further operations to the south. *See also* Ernesto de la Torre Villar, 'Dos Proyectos Para La Independencia de Hispano-America: James Workman y Aaron Burr', 49 Revista de Historia de America 1 (1960).

12. Letter from Workman to Thomas Jefferson (Nov. 15, 1801), *in* 35 *The Papers of Thomas Jefferson* 669-70 (Barbara Oberg et al. eds., 1950), http://founders.archives.gov/documents/Jefferson/01-35-02-0511.

to show "the great principles of general and genuine liberty, and [hold] up despotism to alternate derision and abhorrence." Notably, Workman did not say "Spanish" despotism—and he did go out of his way to explain, in a preface, that his major characters "belong[ed] rather to general than to local nature."[13]

Perhaps an insufficiently mentioned aspect of *Liberty in Louisiana*, among historians preoccupied with its geopolitical significance, is its quality. The play was, after all, a popular success on the Charleston stage. Workman's style is deft, witty, and good-natured, and remains passably entertaining today; it is also somewhat formulaically Shakespearean, with its parallel plotlines involving disparate social classes, its farcical misunderstandings and conventional episodes of mistaken identity, and its multiple love stories with their joyous final resolution. The light bits of ethnic humor it does contain are aimed mainly at Irish targets, not Spanish.[14]

But at the play's climax—which coincides with the entry of American troops into New Orleans—Workman does veer away from light farce into somewhat heavy-handed political moralizing. Throughout the story he personifies the corruption of the Spanish regime through the character of the scoundrel Don Bertholdo, a Spanish judge who uses his position to extort bribes from hapless petitioners—much as the real judge-advocate, Vidal, was widely believed to be doing at the same time. Bertholdo also comically plots to abduct the lovely heiress Donna Laura to Havana, away from her beloved American Captain O'Brien, to torment her with his lecherous attentions. At the play's climax, when Bertholdo's nefarious schemes are exposed, Captain O'Brien presses him to answer the charges against him—but the Don arrogantly replies, "Do you not know that I am a person of the first rank in the province? That alone is a sufficient answer to the calumny of those wretches." Here

---

13. James Workman, *Liberty in Louisiana: A Comedy, Performed at the Charleston Theatre* iv, vi (Charleston, S.C., Query & Evans 1804); George Dargo, *Jefferson's Louisiana: Politics and the Clash of Legal Traditions* 211-12 (1975).
14. For a discussion focused on the play's characterization of Spanish rule, see Charles S. Watson, 'A Denunciation on the Stage of Spanish Rule: James Workman's Liberty in Louisiana (1804)', 11 La. Hist. 245 (1970).

Workman showed himself to be either an instinctive sharer or a rapid adopter of Jeffersonian values, stressing Bertholdo's "rank" and assumption of hereditary privilege in lieu of equality before the law.[15]

In response, the virtuous O'Brien, speaking for Workman (both as a republican and an Irishman) sternly informs Bertholdo that the era of arbitrary rule is at an end:

> Not so, Señor—LIBERTY IS NOW IN LOUISIANA!—The government which now rules here will not admit your rank as the testimony of your innocence; nor suffer it to shelter you if you have acted wrong. Our laws confer no privilege ... the humblest are shielded by their protection—the proudest oppressor is not beyond the reach of their avenging power.[16]

In an essay written in 1804—after he had moved to New Orleans and started a long career as a jurist and legislator—Workman clarified the nature of his judgments on the Spanish system. Spanish rule could be venal, arbitrary, and oppressive, he wrote, not because of any essential underlying racial or cultural quality—but because of the quality of the men who administered it, the predominance of military interests, and the laxness of imperial oversight. In fact, Workman insisted, "[t]he laws of Spain are generally excellent in themselves; for they are founded on the Roman Code, one of the most perfect and elegant systems of jurisprudence ever promulgated to the globe."[17]

Workman's views—that Spanish laws were unexceptionable, and Spanish rule was essentially mild, but prone to corruption because of antiquated practices and insufficient oversight, which had been particularly prevalent in the circumstances of pre-1803 Louisiana—generally prevailed among the American lawyers and

---

15. Workman, *supra* note 13, at 94. The widespread and potent Jeffersonian antipathy to "aristocratic" privilege, if it was in any way a cultural prejudice at all, was more an anti-European prejudice than an anti-Spanish one, and applied, of course, to hereditary rank of the English variety above all.
16. *Id.* at 94-95.
17. *Letter from LAELIUS*, Miss. Messenger, Nov. 30, 1804, *quoted in* Dargo, *supra* note 13, at 217-18. According to Dargo, "Laelius" was an alias for Workman, who wrote the letter to support the position of Governor Claiborne.

jurists, like James Brown and Edward Livingston, who relocated to New Orleans soon after the Purchase. They were also shared by the young governor William C. C. Claiborne, whose main complaint was not the Spanish laws or systems that he was ordered to maintain in place, but the hasty innovations of Laussat, as well as the continued machinations of Laussat's cronies, like Etienne Boré and Jean Blanque, long after Laussat left the territory.[18]

Moreover, these views were developed and amplified by the Connecticut-born Army major, Amos Stoddard, whose 1812 *Sketches of Louisiana* became one of the best known works written from an American perspective on the Orleans Territory. Like Workman, Stoddard believed that the Spanish colonial laws comprised "a complete system of wise and unexceptionable rules, calculated to ensure justice, and to promote the happiness of the people." Going considerably beyond Workman, he continued that Spain's systems of government amounted to "an extraordinary and magnificent superstructure, duly proportioned in all its parts, and exhibiting the wisdom and ingenuity of the political artists of several centuries."[19]

The real problem with Louisiana's colonial governance, Stoddard insisted, was neither the legal system nor the actual laws, but the fact that "very few of the public officers ... were acquainted with them." The difficulty of finding printed laws

> made it necessary for many of the subordinate officers at a distance from the capital to decide according to their conceptions of equity .... No wonder, then, that the Spanish government in Louisiana was deemed arbitrary, and that it was put and kept in operation more by the military than by the civil power.

---

18. For Brown's views, see Letter from James Brown to John Breckinridge (Jan. 22, 1805), *in* 9 *Territorial Papers of the United States: Orleans Territory*, *supra* note 4, at 378-80; for Claiborne's views, see Letter from Claiborne to Jefferson (Nov. 25, 1804), *in* 9 *Territorial Papers of the United States: Orleans Territory*, *supra* note 4, at 338-41; Bradley, *supra* note 4, at 100-02.
19. Amos Stoddard, *Sketches, Historical and Descriptive, of Louisiana* 270 (Philadelphia, Mathew Carey 1812).

And Spain's governors, too, "neglected the great concerns of the province"; aside from Baron de Carondelet, whom Stoddard singled out for praise, "the accumulation of wealth was the predominant motive of their actions."[20]

On the whole, though, Stoddard had little but praise for Spain's colonial regime and its administrators, who he felt had built the best regime possible given Louisiana's particular circumstances. In a long chapter expounding on the evils of slavery, he credited the Spanish with a slave regime that was milder than most. He also admired the fact that Louisiana was remarkably free from crime, and freely admitted that the inhabitants' preference for "summary justice" could be reasonable—particularly when it came to commercial matters. Merchants, he wrote, disliked the delays and unpredictability involved with juries: "[t]hey preferred the judgment of one man to that of twelve; and it is but justice to observe, that their judicial officers were in most instances upright and impartial in their decisions." Finally, Stoddard concluded his discussion of Spanish government by admonishing his American readers not to "severely condemn the provincial systems of the Spaniards, [simply] because they differ from our own."[21]

There is no question that views like those of Stoddard and Workman were widely held among American newcomers, whose general impression of the Spanish regime was considerably more benign than that of Bonapartists like Laussat. Although they certainly criticized many aspects of Spanish governance, they usually saw its flaws as deriving more from contingent circumstances than essential qualities, and often expressed respect for its underlying system of laws. Even Thomas Jefferson, when he wrote his massive and deeply researched response to Edward Livingston's arguments in the batture case, showed his respect for the Spanish legal system, which in his view prevailed in Louisiana.[22]

---

20. *Id.* at 273, 333-34. The best scholarly analysis of actual Spanish governance in Louisiana appears in Gilbert C. Din & John E Harkins, *The New Orleans Cabildo: Colonial Louisiana's First City Government, 1769-1803* (1996).
21. Stoddard, *supra* note 19, at 281, 283.
22. In the absence of statutory law to the contrary, that is. Thomas Jefferson, *The Proceedings of the Government of the United States, in Maintaining the Public Right to the Beach of the Missisipi, Adjacent to New-Orleans, Against*

But perhaps it is wise to conclude by acknowledging the obvious: that this was not the whole story, that alongside this benign view, there also existed, among Americans in the Orleans Territory, a hostility to Spain and a darker view of Spanish colonial America that had much in common with the ethnic prejudice of the Bonapartists, but also added a dimension of naked territorial aggression. As the nineteenth century wore on, and many Americans in the West and East alike began to covet Spanish territory more openly, cultural prejudices of exactly the sort articulated by Laussat became a major ingredient in the complex array of ideological justifications that supported American expansion. But these attitudes crystallized decades later and gradually, and it would be a mistake to read them back into the century's earliest years—or to overlook the fact that anti-Spanish sentiments could produce division and chaos among Americans just as easily as they could support the early republic's territorial aggrandizement.[23]

In fact, even in the earliest years following the acquisition of Louisiana, rumors of an imminent war with Spain were a constant and destabilizing factor. Many Americans were infuriated by the continued residence in New Orleans of Spanish officials, like Casa Calvo, and believed—with some reason—that they harbored concealed hopes of retaking the colony. At the same time, Spanish agents on the Louisiana-Texas frontier were believed to be instigating slave rebellions; and the United States's top Army officer, General James Wilkinson, was accused of

---

the Intrusion of Edward Livingston (N.Y., Ezra Sargeant 1812). The present author's interpretation of the complex batture controversy, and Jefferson's role in it, can be found in Eberhard L. Faber, *Building the Land of Dreams: New Orleans and the Transformation of Early America* 246-81 (2015).

23. On a related note, Caitlyn Fitz, *Our Sister Republics: The United States in an Age of American Revolutions* (2016) argues that well into the Jacksonian period, American observers saw revolutions in Spanish America much more as affirmations of their republic than as threats to it—even when, as they often did, these revolutions overtly included slavery abolition in their agendas. There ought to be nothing surprising about this hemispheric republican solidarity, except for the understandable but misguided historiographical impulse to project later Yankee jingoism back into the early national period.

being secretly in the pay of the Spanish (an accusation historians have verified).[24]

It is important to stress that these controversies stemmed not from vague ethnocultural beliefs but from particular actions and provocations on the part of both sides in a moment of very real geopolitical tensions. The Louisiana Purchase's legitimacy had been questioned by the Spanish ambassador in Washington, imperial officials like Casa Calvo and Vicente Folch had strong reason to believe their machinations might succeed in regaining the territory on the west bank of the Mississippi, and international events seemed to be pushing inexorably toward war between Spain and the American republic. In this context, as Vernon Palmer has described, the 1806 attempt of the Orleans Territory's creole-dominated Legislative Council to establish Spanish law as the Orleans Territory's basic legal system met with derision and outrage from many Americans, and a rare veto from governor Claiborne. The outrage, and the veto, had nothing to do with any views, favorable or unfavorable, on Spain and its colonial system—and everything to do with concerns about Louisiana creoles and their questionable loyalties in the event of armed conflict.[25]

In fact, later the same year, divisions on "the Spanish question" were at the center of the controversy that fatally and permanently split American political unity in the Orleans territory: the famous Aaron Burr expedition of 1806, and the so-called

---

24. Daniel Clark, *Proofs of the Corruption of Gen. James Wilkinson and of His Connection with Aaron Burr: With a Full Refutation of His Slanderous Allegations* [...] (Philadelphia, Wm. Hall, Jr. & Geo. W. Pierie 1809); Andro Linklater, *An Artist in Treason: The Extraordinary Double Life of General James Wilkinson* (2009).

25. Vernon Valentine Palmer, *Louisiana: Microcosm of a Mixed Jurisdiction* 33-34 (1999). For various other views on the so-called "Manifesto of 1806," also sometimes styled as the Declaratory Act, see Elizabeth G. Brown, 'Legal Systems in Conflict: Orleans Territory, 1804-1812', 1 Am. J. Legal Hist. 35 (1957); Dargo, *supra* note 13, at 239-44; Mitchell Franklin, 'The Eighteenth Brumaire in Louisiana: Talleyrand and the Spanish Medieval Legal System of 1806', 16 Tul. L. Rev. 514 (1941), which rather intemperately declaimed against the Act as "not merely snobbish, pretentious, and insolent, but provocative, disruptive and counter-revolutionary." The document itself is printed in both French and English in 9 *Territorial Papers of the United States: Orleans Territory*, *supra* note 4, at 643-57.

"reign of terror" which followed. While some, notably including James Workman, allegedly embraced the idea of a filibustering project to "liberate" Spanish territory under the banner of the controversial ex-Vice President, others, like Claiborne and Wilkinson, opposed it with a degree of forceful repression that caused resentments and divisions in the American community for years thereafter.[26]

Nor did the question of aggression against Spanish territories end there, of course; nor did it remain a local issue; and nor did it lose any of its formidable capacity to divide Americans against each other. In West Florida in 1810, East Florida in 1817-1818, and Texas in the 1830s, Anglo adventurists conducted incursions of various kinds on Spanish and Mexican territory, in each case adding to the territory of the American nation but also bringing about bitter opposition in the arena of American politics—a process which only culminated with a war of unconcealed aggression against Mexico in the 1840s, a war whose architects and enthusiasts imagined it would strengthen American unity, yet whose aftermath, in turn, indirectly and ironically, precipitated the near-collapse of the American union itself in the cataclysm of the Civil War.

---

26. Among many Burr biographies, the most balanced and scholarly can be found in Nancy Isenberg, *Fallen Founder: A Life of Aaron Burr* (2007); the most comprehensive treatment of the "western adventure" and subsequent Burr trial, albeit somewhat prosecutorial, is Buckner F. Melton, *Aaron Burr: Conspiracy to Treason* (2001). On the "reign of terror" and its effects on local power struggles, two primary documents remain the best guide: James Workman, *A Letter to the Respectable Citizens, Inhabitants of the County of Orleans* [...] (New Orleans, Bradford & Anderson 1807); *A Faithful Picture of the Political Situation of New Orleans, at the Close of the Last and the Beginning of the Present Year 1807* (Boston, no pub. 1808).

Portrait of Edward Livingston
Thomas Sully, 1848

CHAPTER 4

IMMIGRANT LAWYERS AND SLAVERY IN TERRITORIAL NEW ORLEANS

Kenneth Aslakson

On March 20, 1804, six men appeared in the newly created Court of Pleas in New Orleans, the first court of the Territory of Orleans, to present their licenses from the Governor-General to practice law and to swear an oath. Nine years later, seven other men swore to "demean [themselves] honestly in the practice as counsellor or attorney" in the first meeting of the Louisiana State Supreme Court. In between, dozens of men practiced law in the various courts of territorial and early statehood New Orleans. Almost all of these men were immigrants and all but a few arrived after the Louisiana Purchase. They came from different countries, and different cultural, educational, and socio-economic backgrounds. They were mostly young, thirty-five or under, but a significant minority of them were middle-aged or older. They had different reasons for coming to New Orleans, different ambitions as lawyers, different expectations about how long they would stay, and met with different levels of success and notoriety. They debated among themselves, and some of them developed deep long-standing rivalries, which sometimes escalated into duels and more than once resulted in death.

Yet, despite of all these divisions and rivalries, the lawyers of early New Orleans shared one common trait—they were all white men. More than just an obvious statement, this is a reminder of the patriarchy and racism that buttressed the burgeoning slave society of the Lower Mississippi Valley in the early nineteenth century. New Orleans was a city of opportunity for white male immigrants from a variety places in both the Anglophone and Francophone Atlantic world, but this opportunity was created at the expense of the enslaved. The burgeoning commercial depot of an expanding plantation hinterland was an attractive place for both ambitious young men looking to start a career in the law and middle-aged men looking to start over and rebuild their fortunes. While these men were influential in shaping the region's legal system, the expanding slave economy ensured that such influence would be in support of the institution of slavery and help ensure its entrenchment and growth for several decades to follow.

This chapter examines lawyers practicing in New Orleans during the territorial period and early statehood. Its focus is not on codes, cases, or statutes, or even on the law per se, but on the men who made up the legal profession. First, it will provide a demographic overview of the national, ethnic, and socio-economic make-up of the early lawyers as well as their different visions, involvement, and levels of success in the profession. It will show that other than their race and sex, little else tied these men together. Then, it will briefly examine some specific sources of disagreement among the early lawyers—some personal, some professional, and some political—that occasionally became violent. Finally, it will broaden out again to examine the group of lawyers with respect to their attitudes toward and relationships with the institution of slavery. In the end, it will show that while the immigrant lawyers of New Orleans's territorial period came from a variety of backgrounds and vehemently disagreed on several topics, they remained unified on slavery, the issue that was soon to create national divisions. Among the sixty-plus men who made their living arguing in early New Orleans, not one of them argued against slavery.

The uniqueness of Louisiana's legal system within the United States has driven both legal scholars and historians to try to understand its origins. From the narrative histories of gentlemen scholars of the late nineteenth century (lawyers and judges among them) to the "New Louisiana Legal History" of the early twenty-first, the scholarship of the history of Louisiana law is rich and lively.[1] Early works either criticized or romanticized, but certainly exaggerated, the civilian influence on Louisiana law. By the mid-twentieth century, however, the focus had shifted to the so-called "clash of legal traditions" that ensued after the Louisiana Purchase, when a civil law territory abruptly became part of a common law country.[2] One of the more specific, long-standing, and involved scholarly debates concerns whether the civilian law of Louisiana had Spanish or French origins. The question was first raised by Rodolfo Batiza in 1972, when he argued that French Law accounted for 85% of the 1808 Code/Digest. Robert Pascal criticized Batiza's methodology, and as a result, a "tournament of scholars" evolved between some of the most notable names in the field.[3] More recently, a group of Louisiana legal historians has moved away from the "sui generis" approach to "root their work in the main themes of southern and legal history."[4] The legal history of slavery in Louisiana, especially, has benefitted from this approach.[5]

While the body of scholarship on the history of Louisiana law is impressive and growing, there is still a paucity of literature on the men who made up the legal profession in early New Orleans. To be sure, scholars have written books and articles about the most influential among them—men like Edward Livingston, Louis Moreau-Lislet, Pierre Derbigny, and Francois

---

1. For an excellent review of the literature on Louisiana legal history, see Mark F. Fernandez, 'Louisiana Legal History, Past, Present, and Future, Introduction' *to A Law Unto Itself? Essays in the New Louisiana Legal History* (Warren Billings & Mark F. Fernandez eds., 2001).
2. The thesis is most clearly stated in George Dargo, *Jefferson's Louisiana: Politics and the Clash of Legal Traditions* (1975).
3. *See* A.N. Yiannopoulos, 'The Early Sources of Louisiana Law: Critical Appraisal of a Controversy', *in Louisiana's Legal Heritage* (Edward F. Haas ed., 1983).
4. Fernandez, *supra* note 1, at 1.
5. The list of works on the history of slave law in Louisiana is long. Some of the best include Hans W. Baade, 'The Law of Slavery in Spanish Louisiana, 1769-1803', *in Louisiana's Legal Heritage, supra* note 3; Judith K. Schafer, *Becoming Free Remaining Free: Manumission and Enslavement in New Orleans, 1846-1862* (2003); and Vernon V. Palmer, *Through the Codes Darkly: Slave Law and Civil Law in Louisiana* (2012).

Xavier Martin.[6] Yet very little has been written on the history of the legal profession in general. Elizabeth Gaspard's *The Rise of the Louisiana Bar: The Early Period, 1813-1839* is one of the few exceptions. Gaspard covers what she calls the first period of growth of the Louisiana state bar. She claims that during this period, "There were few rules to control admission to the bar, and the question of what constituted adequate training was left open. Ambitious men were unfettered in their efforts to use the law as a springboard into other areas of Louisiana society."[7] Working from a database of 565 men, Gaspard provides a sound collective biography of the Louisiana Bar in the first twenty-five years of statehood.

The present chapter is, in part, a prequel to Gaspard's *The Rise of the Louisiana Bar, 1813-1829*. It covers the territorial period, before there was a State of Louisiana or a bar per se, and works from a smaller data set of sixty-four lawyers, some of whom are well-known while others have been obscured by history.[8] Yet, this chapter also differs conceptually from Gas-

---

6. *See* William B. Hatcher, *Edward Livingston: Jeffersonian Republican and Jacksonian Democrat* (1940); Alain Levasseur, *Moreau Lislet: The Man Behind the Digest of 1808* (2008); 'Derbigny, Pierre Augustin Bourguignon', *in* 1 *Dictionary of Louisiana Biography* (Glenn R. Conrad ed., 1988). Francois Xavier Martin, a member of the American Antiquarian Society, was a "gentleman scholar" himself writing several books on law and Louisiana history.

7. Elizabeth Gaspard, 'The Rise of the Louisiana Bar: The Early Period, 1813-1839', 28 La. Hist. 183 (1987); *see also* Warren Billings, 'Origins of the Louisiana State Bar Association', 41 La. Hist. 389 (2000).

8. The list of lawyers was (primarily) compiled from the names of lawyers who appeared in the New Orleans City Court and/or who were listed as members of the legal profession in the 1811 and/or 1822 City Directories. This certainly does not claim to be an exhaustive list of lawyers who practiced in any court in New Orleans during the period but is likely a representative sample. The information about the lawyers was taken from a variety of sources, including, but not limited to: *The Official Letter Books of W.C.C. Claiborne, 1801-1816* (Roland Dunbar ed., 1972) (1917); Jared Bradley, *Interim Appointment: W.C.C. Claiborne Letter Book, 1804-1805* (2002); 42 *National Cyclopaedia of American Biography* (James Terry White ed., 1958); Gwendolyn Midlo Hall, comp., 'Louisiana, Slave Records, 1719-1820', Ancestry (2009), http://search.ancestry.com/search/db.aspx?dbid=7383; Hunting For Bears, comp., 'Louisiana, Marriages, 1718-1925', Ancestry (2004), http://search.ancestry.com/search/db.aspx?dbid=7837; 'Race and Slavery Petitions Project', UNCG (2000-09), https://library.uncg.edu/slavery/petitions/.

pard's work in two important ways. First, it focuses on New Orleans lawyers as immigrants, examining where these men were from and what drew them to the city. Second, this chapter connects the men of the legal profession in territorial New Orleans to the institution of slavery. The Louisiana Purchase created opportunities for talented, ambitious men with a knowledge of the law to be very influential in shaping the young government and legal system. But the expanding slave economy played a role in who would get into these influential positions and how the government and legal system would be shaped.

One of the most striking aspects of the legal profession in the territorial period is that it is made up almost entirely of immigrants, and recent immigrants at that. Lawyers (and would-be lawyers) flocked to New Orleans in the era of the Louisiana Purchase from many areas of the Atlantic World. Only four of the fifty-four people for which there is sufficient data were born in Louisiana. Two of them, Alexander Dupuy and Jacques Philipe Ginault, were among the earliest to practice law in the American courts of New Orleans, but none of the four rose to any level of prominence in the profession. Moreover, only seven others had lived in New Orleans prior to the Purchase and, of these, only three for more than a decade.[9] Only one of these seven men, Pierre Derbigny, who arrived in New Orleans in 1797, went on to make a name for himself in the Louisiana Bar. In terms of both numbers and influence, therefore, the legal profession in territorial New Orleans was dominated by men who had just recently moved to the city.[10]

While the early New Orleans legal profession was clearly controlled by white male immigrants, it was not, at least not in the territorial period, dominated by any particular ethnicity or by men from any particular part of the Atlantic World. Among the immigrants, there was a good mixture of those from the United

---

9. The three immigrant men who had lived in New Orleans for over a decade at the time of the Louisiana Purchase were Joseph Henri De Mahy Desmontils, a Frenchman who was in New Orleans at least as early as 1792, Jean Rodriguez, who migrated from the Canary Islands as a young boy in the 1770s, and Pierre (Pedro) Pedesclaux, who migrated from the Basque country as a young man, also in the 1770s.

10. *See* sources cited *supra* note 8.

States North, the United States South, the British Isles, French-speaking Europe, the French Caribbean, Spain, and even one person from the Canary Islands. Of the people for whom there is sufficient information, English was the primary language for about 56%, French for 37%, and Spanish for 7%. If one were to assume ethnicity based on the names of the ten for which there is not sufficient information, then just over half of the lawyers (thirty-four out of sixty-four) were Anglophone. Four of the English speakers came from the British Isles, but the vast majority came from the Eastern Seaboard of the United States.[11]

The Northeastern United States sent sixteen men to practice law in New Orleans during the territorial period, which was more than any other region. Five came from Pennsylvania alone, with four coming from Massachusetts, two each from Connecticut, New York, and New Jersey, and one from Rhode Island. Some of the biggest names in early American Louisiana history were among this group. Edward Livingston, from New York, authored a provisional code of judicial procedure in 1805, shortly after he arrived, and later created a new code of criminal law and procedure known as the "Livingston Code." John Bartow Prevost, from Paramus, New Jersey, was appointed the first justice of the Superior Court of the Territory of Orleans, sitting alone on the bench for half of his four-year term. John Ward Gurley, from Connecticut, served as Attorney General for the Territory of Orleans before he met an early demise in a duel in 1808. Several others had very successful careers, both as lawyers and outside the profession.[12]

Ten more lawyers came from the Chesapeake region, four from Maryland and six from Virginia. Richard Raynal Keene left Maryland for New York City in 1801 to elope with Eleanora Martin, the fifteen-year-old daughter of one of the signers of the United States Constitution, Luther Martin, in whose Maryland law office Keene had been an apprentice. Martin never forgave Keene or Eleanora for this and published a scathing attack on Keene in 1802. The Keenes left for New Orleans shortly after the Purchase, where Keene was named the territory's first Attorney

---

11. *See* sources cited *supra* note 8.
12. *See* sources cited *supra* note 8.

General.[13] Virginia produced three very important political figures in early New Orleans: James Brown, John Randolph Grymes, and Henry Cox Carleton. Brown arrived in New Orleans in 1804 to serve as the Secretary of the Territory of Orleans, and, the following year, President Jefferson appointed him to be United States Attorney for the Territory. He was one of the authors of the 1808 Civil Digest and was later elected to the United States Senate and served as Minister to France. Grymes arrived in New Orleans in 1808 and quickly rose to become one of the most prominent members of the bar. He was appointed district attorney in 1811 and later served in the Louisiana state legislature. Before he died in 1854, he was involved in several famous cases in Louisiana history. He was well-respected and well-paid.[14] Carleton was a relative late comer to New Orleans, arriving in 1814, at which time he began reading law in the office of Edward Livingston, his brother-in-law. He went on to become the United States Attorney for Eastern District of Louisiana and then Justice on the Supreme Court of Louisiana. The Chesapeake region, therefore, supplied territorial New Orleans with talented and ambitious immigrant lawyers.[15]

The other Anglophone lawyers in territorial New Orleans came from the British Isles. At least three men born in Ireland and one born in England practiced law in the courts of territorial New Orleans. Two of the Irish-born men, James Workman and Lewis Kerr, were legal scholars educated and trained in the common law. They played key roles in shaping Louisiana's criminal law to make it better conform to the rest of the United States. Both men's careers were tarnished a couple of years later, however, when they became embroiled in the Burr conspiracy and the Wilkinson "reign of terror" that followed.[16]

---

13. Luther Martin, *Modern Gratitude in Five Numbers, Addressed to Richard Raynal Keene, Esq., Concerning a Family Marriage* (Baltimore, self-published 1801). Eleanora did not live long after, dying in 1807.
14. Grymes was part of the defense team in the case of *State v. Parker*, the subject of Judith Schafer's article 'The Murder of a "Lewd and Abandoned Woman"', 44 Am. J. Legal Hist. 19 (2000).
15. *See* sources cited *supra* note 8.
16. *See* sources cited *supra* note 8.

Francophone Europe sent many more lawyers to territorial New Orleans than Anglophone Europe. Thirteen lawyers in the database, for whom we have sufficient information, were born in France or Belgium, second only to the northeastern United States. Among them was the aforementioned Pierre Derbigny, for whom New Orleans was the last of many stops after leaving his country of birth. Born in Laon, France, in 1769, Derbigny was studying law in Paris when the French Revolution erupted. He left for St. Domingue in 1791, but found the conditions there even less conducive to establishing a legal career. In the next six years he lived in Pittsburg, the Illinois country, and Havana, among other places, before arriving in New Orleans, his final destination, in 1797. Derbigny was one of the most ardent defenders of both the civil law and the slave trade in the region. Another influential New Orleans lawyer from France was Eligius Fromentin. Born in France in 1767, Fromentin was studying to become a priest when the craftsmen and store owners of Paris attacked the Bastille. He fled during the reign of terror and went first to Pennsylvania and then to the Catholic-friendly Maryland, where he was a schoolteacher and a priest. After the Louisiana Purchase he left the priesthood and moved to New Orleans to become a lawyer. He later served in the territorial legislature and was a United States Senator from Louisiana from 1813 to 1819.[17] More than any other American city, New Orleans was welcoming to French immigrant lawyers, especially for those who may have lacked a solid command of the English language.

Just as the French Revolution drove some men from their homelands who eventually made their way to New Orleans to practice law, so too did the Haitian Revolution. A half dozen men in the database were immigrants from St. Domingue. Four were born there and two others were born in France but had been in the French colony many years prior to the slave uprising in 1791. While all six of these men fled the revolution, they came at different times and took different paths to New Orleans. Philadelphia, Charleston, Kingston, and Santiago all served as temporary homes for refugee lawyers before they arrived in the

---

17. *See* sources cited *supra* note 8.

Lower Mississippi Valley. All six St. Domingue refugee lawyers managed to rebuild their lives rather rapidly, with four of them transitioning into plantation life. The other two men, while perhaps not as rich, were certainly more famous. Auguste Davezac was born in Aux Cayes, St. Domingue, in 1780 to a wealthy planter. His father sent him as a young boy to be educated in France, which is where he was when the French and Haitian Revolutions broke out. Both of his brothers and his uncle died in the Haitian Revolution. The rest of his family fled to New Orleans, including two sisters who would later marry New Orleans lawyers. Davezac took a circuitous route to New Orleans. After studying medicine in North Carolina and opening a medical practice in Virginia, Davezac arrived in New Orleans sometime after 1805 to study law under his brother-in-law, Edward Livingston. Davezac made a name for himself in national politics, where he served in the Jackson and Van Buren administrations. Louis Moreau-Lislet was born in Cap Francais in 1766, studied law in Paris, and became an *avocat* just before the beginning of the French Revolution. He returned to Le Cap prior to its burning in 1793 and remained in the colony for most of the next decade, only leaving after the French army had surrendered to Jean Jacques Dessalines' forces in August of 1803. He went first to Cuba, but then sometime between August of 1804 and February of 1805, he arrived in New Orleans and quickly made an impact. He was the official interpreter in the colony, the first judge of the newly formed New Orleans City Court in 1806, and the primary author of the 1808 Civil Digest. Although not as numerous as the group from the northeastern United States, the Chesapeake, or France, the refugee lawyers from St. Domingue were very influential.[18]

While a variety of factors may have driven these men away from their homes, the promise of the Louisiana Purchase drew them to New Orleans. Two-thirds of the immigrant lawyers arrived in the years 1803-1805. The "Generation of 1804," as Eberhard "Lo" Faber has labeled them, "were not 'settlers' but educated, urbane professional men: doctors, engineers, and above

---

18. *See* sources cited *supra* note 8. Most of the biographical information on Moreau-Lislet comes from Levasseur, *supra* note 6.

all, lawyers."[19] New Orleans's burgeoning economy and the implementation of an Anglo-American style adversarial court system helped to create an explosion of the legal profession and new opportunities for aspiring lawyers.[20]

By and large, the immigrant lawyers were young men seeking to start a career in New Orleans. Nearly three-fourths of the lawyers were in their mid-thirties or younger at the time of the Louisiana Purchase. Many came fresh out of college, such as Charles Bushnell from Salisbury, Connecticut, who graduated from Harvard in 1803 at the age of twenty-one and went to New Orleans immediately afterwards. Bushnell spent several years building a practice and making connections before purchasing land near Baton Rouge in 1811. Later in the decade he served two different stints as District Attorney for the 3rd District of Louisiana. John Randolph Grymes and Alfred Hennen were still teenagers at the time of the Purchase. They waited until 1808 to come to New Orleans, both just twenty-two years old, after having received elite educations—Grymes at the University of Virginia and Hennen at Yale.[21]

Still, not all of the lawyer immigrants were young men pursuing their first careers. After the Purchase, some came to New Orleans seeking a new lease on life after a series of setbacks or a calamitous event. Both Moreau-Lislet and Jacques Pailette had successful careers in St. Domingue before the upheaval of the Haitian Revolution temporarily reversed their fortunes. Edward Livingston had been mayor of New York City and Congressional representative from New York before an embezzlement scandal ruined his finances and reputation. Others were escaping more personal crises. Fromentin left the priesthood in Maryland to become a lawyer in New Orleans. The oldest of the men was an immigrant from England, Edward Nicholls, who was in his late fifties at the time of the Purchase. He also had studied for the priesthood in France but the college closed in 1762. He then switched career paths to the chagrin of his family, studied law,

---

19. Eberhard L. Faber, *Building the Land of Dreams: New Orleans and the transformation of early America* 119 (2016).
20. *See* sources cited *supra* note 8.
21. *See* sources cited *supra* note 8.

and sailed to the British North American colonies before the American Revolution. He was a lawyer in Prince George's County, Maryland, and, briefly, in the newly created District of Columbia before coming to New Orleans in 1804, "where he was sure his knowledge of the French language would insure his success."[22] For a significant minority of the immigrants, the legal profession in New Orleans offered a chance to start anew.[23]

One of the attractive features of the legal profession in New Orleans at the time of the Purchase was that it offered a variety of paths to success for the ambitious, well-educated white men of the Atlantic world. The men in the database had different visions about what they could do for the law and what the law could do for them. For at least a dozen of the men, practicing law was just one of several, and not necessarily the most lucrative, means of making a living. In addition to being lawyers, they were also merchants, bankers, educators, translators, soldiers, clerks, wardens, speculators—in land and slaves—and, above all, planters. Knowledge of the law and the ability to navigate the legal system could, of course, assist in most, if not all, of these other vocations.[24]

Many of the lawyers in territorial New Orleans also doubled as notaries. Both jobs involved many of the same functions, especially in the civil law tradition. But the adversarial court system introduced after the Purchase was less familiar to the civilian notary. Michel D'Armas, Etienne De Quinones, Pedro Pedesclaux, and Pierre Francois Simon Godefroy are better known to historians as names in the archives of notaries during the late Spanish and territorial periods in New Orleans, but these men also practiced law. While Godefroy had some success, Pedesclaux and De Quinones, who were among the first to receive their licenses in the Court of Pleas, never fully immersed themselves in the changing legal system and soon left the profession altogether. D'Armas had an extensive law library and some success as a lawyer but was excluded from the Bar in 1818

22. Glen Conrad, comp., Biography of Edward Church Nicholls, *Dictionary of Louisiana Biography*, La. Hist. Ass'n (2008), http://www.lahistory.org/site31.php.
23. *See* sources cited *supra* note 8.
24. *See* sources cited *supra* note 8.

when the Louisiana Supreme Court ruled that speaking English was a requirement for admission.[25]

Some men fully immersed themselves in territorial New Orleans's legal profession, only to later leave the city, the profession, or both. Livingston, for example, may have stayed in New Orleans longer than he originally intended, but in the end he used the practice of law in the city as a way of rebuilding his reputation and helping to finance his retirement in New York. Several others retired in the places of their births after pursuing their fortunes in New Orleans. A few took their practices to smaller Louisiana towns or rural parishes. A handful of dispossessed planters from St. Dominque, moreover, used the legal profession in New Orleans as a platform to re-establish themselves as planters in Louisiana.[26] For all these men, the legal profession in New Orleans was a jumping off point rather than a final destination.[27]

Often, the immigrant lawyers used their law practices as platforms to build political careers. Over a quarter of the lawyers in the database held state or federal office at some point in their lives in Louisiana. As a group, the immigrant lawyers occupied many different offices at the state and national levels. At the state level, they comprised one governor, two secretaries of state, four attorneys general, one district attorney, four representatives, four justices of the state Supreme Court, and six judges of other courts. At the National government level, they made up two United States Attorneys, two representatives, three senators, and one secretary of state. Most of these influential lawyer/politicians were American, but five Francophone men represented more than a third of the offices and held some of the most important positions.[28]

Yet, not all of the immigrant lawyers were aspiring politicians or planters. More than a third of the men who practiced in

---

25. *See* sources cited *supra* note 8.
26. Three men were planters or sons of planters in St. Domingue before coming to New Orleans as refugees of the Haitian Revolution: Pierre Ambroise Cuvillier, Jean Baptiste Desdunes, fils, and Jacques Cesar Paillette. Each of them practiced law for a short time during the territorial period before accumulating enough money (either through the law or otherwise) to invest in a plantation.
27. *See* sources cited *supra* note 8.
28. *See* sources cited *supra* note 8.

the New Orleans courts were career lawyers with no seeming political ambitions or plans to leave the law after building a fund. About a third of these career lawyers were from French-speaking countries and one of them was Louisiana-born. The rest were English-speaking immigrants from the United States and Ireland. These men did not have codes named after them, hold political office, or otherwise become famous, but most of them had steady careers that were lucrative enough for them to buy real property and slaves.[29]

However loose were the rules in controlling admission to the bar during the territorial period, restrictions of race and gender were strictly enforced. This, in itself, is a reminder of the racist and patriarchal ideologies that dominated slave societies in the period—and Louisiana was rapidly becoming a slave society in the era of the Louisiana Purchase. The rest of this Chapter will focus on first, the specific controversies in the territorial period that divided the legal profession in New Orleans, and second, the ways in which the support for slavery united it.

The sudden influx in territorial New Orleans of dozens of immigrant lawyers from a variety of places and with different goals sometimes led to personal and political conflicts and contributed to existing cultural tensions. These conflicts and tensions are the subject of George Dargo's canonical study, *Jefferson's Louisiana: Politics and the Clash of Legal Traditions.* In two parts, the book addresses first, three "problems of colonial rule" and second, the general "clash" of the common law and civil law "traditions." This Part of this Chapter will discuss some of the immigrant lawyers in territorial Louisiana within the Dargo framework.[30]

The first "problem of colonial rule" addressed by Dargo centers on the reception of William C.C. Claiborne, Thomas Jefferson's appointed governor of the Orleans Territory who came to New Orleans from the Mississippi Territory. Claiborne brought several lawyers with him from Natchez and encouraged others to come, including Workman, Kerr, and Israel Trask, a Massachusetts-born lawyer purported to have opened the first law practice in

29. *See* sources cited *supra* note 8.
30. *See* Dargo, *supra* note 2.

American New Orleans. Claiborne gave some of these men positions in the territorial government, thereby gaining their loyalty. But Claiborne was not popular among the French (and Spanish) speaking Louisianans. He did not speak their language and was under instructions to introduce into the territory a foreign legal system. The few lawyers who had lived in New Orleans prior to the Purchase found it difficult to get a foothold in the new legal system except Pierre Derbigny. The Frenchman took up the cause of the "creole" opposition to Claiborne, even though he was not a true creole himself.[31] Claiborne had been in the territory less than six months before Derbigny published a scathing rebuke of the governor as incompetent, despotic, and out of touch with the local population. After Claiborne vetoed the Declaratory Act of 1806, which would have kept "Roman law" as the principal law of the land, Derbigny, again acting as the penman of the creoles, renewed his attacks on the governor in a manifesto published in the *Telegraph.* Several common law trained lawyers came to Claiborne's defense, none more aggressively than James Workman who engaged in a battle of words with Derbigny over the preferred future of Louisiana's legal system.[32]

Dargo's second controversy pitted some of New Orleans' most prominent attorneys against each other. If the Claiborne controversy tended to split Anglophone and Francophone lawyers, the Burr conspiracy caused divisions within the Anglophone ranks, with the French-speaking lawyers sitting on the sidelines for the most part. Historians are still uncertain what the former Vice President had planned when he leased land from the Spanish crown in the Texas territory, organized a small army of men, and established contacts in the Louisiana territory and New Orleans. His indictment for treason alleged that he had conspired to forcibly take New Orleans and create a new nation in the middle of North America. Burr answered that he was merely trying to take possession of the land he leased. One of the key figures in the Burr conspiracy was General James Wilkinson,

---

31. Creole is often used to describe the Francophone population in early New Orleans. A true Louisiana creole, however, would have been born in Louisiana.
32. Dargo, *supra* note 2, at 121; Faber, *supra* note 19, at 238; Bradley, *supra* note 8, at 396.

who had initially partnered with Burr but later turned him in to President Jefferson.[33]

The Burr affair and its aftermath created divisions within New Orleans's legal profession. Several New Orleans lawyers were implicated in a conspiracy with Burr, mostly by virtue of their connection to the Mexican Association, a group of American New Orleanians dedicated to "liberating" Mexico. In the so-called reign of terror that followed in the wake of the Burr conspiracy, Wilkinson had several local lawyers arrested, including Livingston, Kerr, Workman, and James Alexander, a young immigrant lawyer from Massachusetts. Meanwhile, Abner Duncan, John Ward Gurley, James Brown, and Ebenezer Bradish, all American-born lawyers, worked on behalf of Wilkinson. Claiborne named Alexander, Workman, Kerr, and Davezac as members of the "Society of 'Choice Spirits'" with "friendly dispositions towards the 'would be Emperor [Burr].'"[34] Alexander was sent to Baltimore to stand trial. Although he was acquitted of the charge, he committed suicide in 1811, having never recovered from his shame and humiliation.

Edward Livingston was at the center of Dargo's third controversy during the territorial period that saw him battle two of New Orleans finest Francophone attorneys on the opposite side of the docket. Officially called *Gravier v. City of New Orleans,* it is remembered simply as the "batture case" after the piece of land abutting the Mississippi River that was the subject of the suit.[35]

---

33. *See* Milton Lamask, *Aaron Burr, the Conspiracy and Years in Exile, 1805-1836* (1982).

34. Letter from W.C.C. Claiborne to James Madison (Mar. 17, 1808), *in* 4 *The Official Letter Books of W.C.C. Claiborne, 1801-1816, supra* note 8, at 167.

35. "Batture" comes from the French verb "to beat" and refers to the land beaten by the river. The batture in question in the *Gravier* case was upriver from the *Vieux Carre* in Faubourg St. Marie. In the late eighteenth century the land was part of Bertrand Gravier's plantation, but in 1788, he subdivided much of the land in establishing New Orleans's first suburb and sold parcels of this estate throughout the 1790s. When Bertrand died in 1797, his brother, Jean Gravier, inherited the land that had not been sold. The batture land bordering Faubourg St. Marie had been neither sold nor improved but was being used by the public. In 1803-1804, Jean Gravier attempted to move the levee on this batture closer to the river in order to claim more land, a practice that had developed throughout New Orleans's history because the batture was constantly

Jean Gravier claimed to have inherited the batture land from his brother Bertrand, and in the spring of 1806 he sued the city in the Superior Court to quiet title. Livingston agreed to represent Gravier on the condition that if he won, Gravier would grant him a part of the batture on which Livingston planned to construct a commercial dock. In the trial itself, Livingston took on two heavyweights—Pierre Derbigny and Louis Moreau-Lislet, who, together, represented the city. Livingston won the case in a court of law but lost in the court of public opinion. Crowds occupied the lands and obstructed construction of Livingston's improvements. Influential members of the community pressed Governor Claiborne to get the national government involved, and Thomas Jefferson, who had no warm feelings for Edward Livingston, claimed the land as federal government property. In the end, the batture controversy was only a temporary setback for Livingston who managed to win back the favor of his community.[36]

The conflicts among lawyers in territorial New Orleans sometimes spilled over into the dueling field. John Ward Gurley was the most notorious dueler of the group. In his short time in New Orleans, he managed to wage battles of honor with three different men. The first with Richard Raynal Keene in 1804 originated after Claiborne replaced Keene with Gurley as Attorney General for the Territory. Both men survived this duel, but Gurley did not learn his lesson. After that, he had a running two-year feud with Livingston that came close, but never resulted, in a duel. Finally, Gurley met his demise in a duel with Livingston's cousin, Philip Jones, in 1808.[37]

Dargo's "clash of legal traditions" thesis for the Orleans territory is part of the broader narrative of Creole-American conflict in early New Orleans. Yet, a brief review of the practicing lawyers suggest that the differences between common and civil law were not a big source of conflict among them. The controversies discussed above were, for the most part, personal or

---

widening by the build-up of soil. This time, however, since Gravier did not own any of the land bordering the batture, the public protested.

36. For a variety of interpretations of the batture controversy, see Dargo, *supra* note 2, ch. 4; Faber, *supra* note 19, at 273-75; and Ari Kelman, *A River and Its City: The Nature of Landscape in New Orleans* 40-47 (2003).

37. *See* sources cited *supra* note 8.

political in nature, and it would be a mistake to read them as a clash of legal cultures. Those trained in different legal traditions learned from each other and even practiced together. Knowledge of and training in both traditions, as well and multilingual skills, often distinguished the prestigious lawyers from the pack. Workman and Kerr, although trained in the common law, had broad knowledge of all legal systems. Workman was complimentary of civilian law in general, even if he was at times critical of the law of pre-Purchase Louisiana. Livingston studied civil law after arriving in Louisiana, not only to become a better lawyer, but also because he seemed genuinely interested in improving the Territory's legal system. He was well versed in French and Spanish law, and he based his arguments in the batture case on these traditions. He partnered with Mazureau, a French-born lawyer trained in civil law, and trained Davezac and Carleton, from St. Domingue and Virginia respectively. In his time on the City Court bench, Moreau-Lislet acted like a common law judge in his liberal interpretations of existing law and willingness to make decisions based on custom and precedent. Indeed, the respective careers in New Orleans of both Livingston and Moreau-Lislet suggest that each was more concerned with creating certainty in the territory's laws than in pushing for one tradition over the other. Even Derbigny accepted that some elements of the American legal system were unavoidable and perhaps preferable. Meanwhile, the law practitioners learned the hybrid system that the lawmakers were creating.[38]

More recent scholarship has interpreted the legal and political maneuvering of the territorial period differently. Instead of a "clash of legal traditions," the controversies of the period represented a clash of the local with the national government.[39] Faber argues, for example, that "The anti-Livingston arguments

---

38. *See supra* note 8; *see also* William B. Hatcher, *Edward Livingston: Jeffersonian Republican and Jacksonian Democrat* (1940); Levasseur, *supra* note 6.

39. *See* Peter Kastor, '"Motives of Peculiar Urgency": Local Diplomacy in Louisiana, 1803-1821', 58 Wm. & Mary Q. 819 (2001); John Craig Hammond, '"They Are Very Much Interested in Obtaining an Unlimited Slavery;" Rethinking the Expansion of Slavery in the Louisiana Purchase Territories, 1803-1805', 23 J. Early Republic 353 (2003); Faber, *supra* note 19.

[in the batture case] . . . share an underlying common denominator: an advocacy, as the terms of the city's attachment to the American nation were being negotiated, for the primacy of local culture, authority, and autonomy against national power and distant rule."[40] While Faber makes an important point about the republican struggle for local rule, John Craig Hammond shows the centrality of slavery to this clash. "By exploiting fears of disunion—not between northern and southern Atlantic states but between the East and West—white Louisianans destroyed congressional efforts to restrict growth of western slavery."[41] The fight for local rule in the territory, therefore, was, first and foremost, a fight to preserve slavery. New Orleans lawyers were united in this effort. Whatever differences existed between civil law and common law with regard to the issue of slavery, they paled in comparison to their similarities. Both legal traditions developed in the early modern era to support bourgeois values by naturalizing the individual's right to private property.[42] In New World slave societies, this meant the right to own enslaved people of African descent.

Indeed, despite all of the conflict among New Orleans's lawyers during the territorial period, they could all agree on one thing—their support of slavery. As lawmakers and jurists, lawyers in territorial New Orleans fought hard to re-open the transatlantic slave trade in the face of national government restrictions.[43] In the aftermath of the Louisiana Purchase, Congress dealt with several bills designed to eventually eliminate slavery in all of the Louisiana Purchase lands, including the Orleans Territory. First, the Louisiana Ordinance of March 26, 1804, prohibited the introduction of any slaves into the territory except by U.S. citizens who were "bona fide" settlers. In other

---

40. Faber, *supra* note 19, at 277.
41. Hammond, *supra* note 39, at 378.
42. Indeed, this is the common socialist law critique of both traditions.
43. Soon after the Louisiana Purchase, the lower Mississippi Valley became an early battle ground regarding the future of slavery in America. Several historians have recently done a good job of historicizing the spread of slavery to what became the Deep South, showing that it was not an inevitable process. *See*, among others, Adam Rothman, *Slave Country: American Expansion and the Origins of the Deep South* (2005); Hammond, *supra* note 39.

words, the act forbade the transatlantic and domestic slave trades in Orleans upon the penalty of such slaves being freed. The House introduced and passed a bill that would have prohibited the introduction of slaves altogether, but this bill failed to pass the Senate. Some members of Congress from states that had already abolished slavery saw the immediate post-Purchase period as an ideal time to set the entire nation on a course toward the peaceful abolition of slavery.[44]

While Congress was debating what to do about slavery in the newly acquired territory, local elites in New Orleans, from both the common law and civil law traditions, were united in their opposition to any national government restrictions on slavery in the region. Edward Livingston and Pierre Derbigny, who would later clash in the batture case, led the charge to protect local control of slavery. In the summer of 1804, Livingston drafted a *Remonstrance of the People of Louisiana against the Political System Adopted by Congress,* which was delivered to Congress by Derbigny and two other Francophone New Orleanians. The Remonstrance was an attack on the National government's policies in the territories in general, but its real focus was on the restrictions it had placed on slavery. Livingston was making his case to Congress and, as Faber puts it, "His client, in effect, was the New Orleans slaveholding planter elite." On July 4, 1804, the first time American independence was celebrated in New Orleans, Derbigny gave a rousing speech celebrating Louisiana's attachment to the American republic. He also argued for the reopening of the slave trade, tying this to American liberty.[45] These elite lawyers of different backgrounds were engaged in a form of unofficial nullification, and Congress learned that any laws it passed restricting slavery in the region were useless without the willingness of white Louisianans to enforce and abide by them. Thus, the battle for local control was a battle to preserve slavery and resembles the cries coming from the seceding states half a century later. In the face of strong protests

44. *See* Hammond, *supra* note 39, at 256 (referring to the collective action of some members of Congress in 1804 as "a bold measure designed to destroy the plantation revolution in the lower Mississippi Valley").
45. Faber, *supra* note 19, at 181.

from local elites in New Orleans, the law prohibiting the slave trade in Orleans, which expired by its own terms a year after it was enacted, was never renewed.[46]

Once in control, the local legislature took measures to increase the powers of the slaveholding class. In its first session in June 1806, the legislature passed a Black Code that reshaped the law of slavery in the region. Among other things, the laws of the Code deprived slaves of the ability to own property without the consent of their masters and ended the right of a slave to sue and demand to be sold to a new master for cruel treatment. Then, in March of 1807, the legislature amended the Black Code to make it much more difficult for a slave to obtain freedom by prohibiting a master from emancipating his or her slave unless the slave was at least thirty years old and had not tried to run away or commit any other crime in the four years prior to emancipation. It also officially ended *coartación,* the Spanish policy of allowing a slave to purchase his or her own freedom with or without the master's consent.[47] The increased powers granted to slaveholders over their slaves under the law was a victory for local lawyers from both legal traditions and their "planter elite clients" over National government attempts to place restrictions on the peculiar institution.

The lawyers, as a group, not only spoke out in favor of local rights to own and import slaves but also practiced what they preached. Every lawyer in territorial New Orleans for which there is sufficient information was a slave-owner, and at least eleven of the sixty-four men could be classified as planters. Of course one did not need to be a plantation owner to own slaves

---

46. An Act for the Government of Orleans Territory, Mar. 2, 1805, *in Territorial Papers of the United States. Volume IX. The Territory of Orleans 1803-1812*, at 406 (Clarence Edwin Carter ed., 1940).
47. Acts Passed at the First Session of the First Legislature of the Territory of Orleans, *in* Moreau-Lislet, General Digest of the Acts of the Legislature of Louisiana: Passed from the Year 1804, to 1827, Inclusive, and in Force at this Last Period, with an Appendix and General Index (New Orleans, 1828); An Act Prescribing the Rules and Conduct To Be Observed with Respect to Negroes and Other Slaves of this Territory, June 7, 1806, *in* Moreau-Lislet, *supra*; An Act To Regulate the Conditions and Forms of the Emancipation of Slaves, Mar. 9, 1807, *in* Moreau-Lislet, *supra*.

and otherwise profit from the institution. At least ten others, even though they were not planters, owned at least ten different slaves at points in their lives in New Orleans. Four engaged in the slave trade.[48] Whether slaves served as sources of wealth or signs of wealth, slave owning was an aspiration of the men who made up the legal profession of territorial New Orleans.

Even immigrant lawyers from places where slavery had been abolished seemingly had no moral qualms with the institution in the Lower Mississippi Valley. Three of the ten confirmed planters were from New England. Massachusetts-born Ebenezer Bradish was not a planter himself but his brother George, a merchant and sea captain by trade, partnered with William Johnson to buy the Magnolia sugar plantation in Terrebonne Parish. Abraham Ellery, from Newport, Rhode Island, was involved in slavery even before he even came to New Orleans. While his cousin, William Ellery, spoke out against the slave trade, a common feature of Newport, Rhode Island, during his childhood, Abraham bought and sold slaves in New Orleans and eventually inherited his father's Antigua plantation. He continued to practice law in the city for a while and remained an absentee planter. The immigrant lawyers from the Northern United States immersed themselves in the economy of the Lower Mississippi Valley culture and the slaveholding that came with it.[49] It is not surprising that northerners coming to New Orleans in this period would support slavery. Indeed, perhaps the opportunities for economic success that slavery offered to white men of ambition had been the reason they left the North in the first place. There was not yet a strong abolition movement anywhere in the United States, and the North was far from galvanized around an anti-slavery position.

French-born Etienne Mazureau, who came from a country that had abolished slavery in all its possessions for a period in the 1790s, explained to Alexis de Tocqueville how he came around on the issue of slavery. De Tocqueville asked, "Do you think that

---

48. Of the sixty-four lawyers in the data set, there is clear evidence that fifty-six of them were slave-owners. This does not mean that the other eight did not own slaves, simply that I could not find information on this topic. There is also no evidence that any of these eight men were adverse or opposed to slavery.
49. *See* sources cited *supra* note 8.

in Louisiana the whites could cultivate the land without slaves?" "I do not think so," replied Mr. Mazureau. "But I was born in Europe and arrived here with the ideas you seem to have on that point. But experience has seemed to me to contradict the theory. I do not think that Europeans can work the land, exposed to this tropical sun. Our sun is always unhealthy, often deadly." Mazureau ended by offering the example of whites from various districts of Louisiana who, unable to labor diligently in the local climate, eked out only marginal existences. "But might not their poverty be attributed to their laziness rather than to the climate?" de Tocqueville countered. The southerner's response was blunt: "In my view the climate is the chief reason."[50] Mazureau's interaction with de Tocqueville is an illustration of at least one rationalization for the exploitation of enslaved people of African descent.

Even reform-minded lawyers of the period, and there were a few, had no interest in anti-slavery causes. Alfred Hennen was by most accounts a pious, reform-minded, philanthropic man. He was born in Maryland, studied at Yale, and apprenticed with lawyers in New Haven and Nashville, before coming to New Orleans in 1808, still only twenty-two years old. A devoutly religious man, Hennen was purportedly "engaged in all the celebrated causes of his time." He never drank or smoked or wore glasses (all seen as moral weaknesses). He regularly visited orphanages in the city to share the gospel with the children. He was caring, giving, and honest—and by 1830 he had the third largest rice plantation in Louisiana and owned over 100 slaves on over 12,000 acres of land.[51] He is said to have instructed his slaves in the Bible, but the sinfulness of making other human beings into property never seems to have crossed Hennen's mind.

Of course it is not surprising that elite, and even non-elite, lawyers in New Orleans in the early nineteenth century would be slaveholders. Slave ownership was both a means to and symbol of success in the emerging slave society. Yet the fact that not one

---

50. *Interview with Etienne Mazureau, In Search of Tocqueville*, C-SPAN (Jan. 19, 1998), https://www.c-span.org/series/?tocqueville.

51. Hennen-Jennings Papers (1803-(1850-1870)-1918) (on file with Special Collections, Louisiana State University Libraries).

of these sixty-four men, former priests, reformers, and philanthropists among them, displayed any anti-slavery sentiment reveals the depth of the hold that the institution had on the region. Many lawyers had built considerable wealth and influence by practicing law in early New Orleans, and never once did any member of the legal profession spend this wealth or influence, or use his oratory skills, to challenge slavery.

After the Louisiana Purchase, aspiring lawyers poured into New Orleans from the United States, Europe, and the Caribbean to take advantage of the city's expanding economy and newly emerging legal system. They disagreed on many issues and fought among themselves, sometimes aggressively, both within and without the courtroom. Despite their differences, however, they were united on the issue of slavery. Immigrant lawyers from both the civil law and common law traditions were willing to compromise in their creation of New Orleans legal system so that they could combine forces in an effort to maintain local control in the face of national government attempts to place restrictions on slavery in the newly acquired territories. Such was the institution's importance in building and shaping the profession.

Name of Lawyer	Where From	When Arrived in New Orleans	When Born	When Died
Alexander, James	Boston, MA	1804	c. 1775: I don't have an exact birthdate, but the sources indicate that he was young when he arrived in New Orleans. He came with A. Ellery, who was born in 1773.	1811 (of suicide)
Arsmery [uncertain of the spelling of this name]	No information [hereinafter N/I]	N/I	N/I	N/I
Bradish, Ebenezer	Cambridge, MA	1804	1773	N/I
Brown, Henry	N/I	1804	N/I	N/I
Brown, James	Staunton, VA	1804	1766	1835

Where Died	Relationship to Law	Relationship to Slavery	Sources Used
New Orleans	He held a few civil service jobs when he first got to New Orleans but then looked to be on the path to being a career lawyer.	No evidence that he owned slaves; no evidence he was antislavery; tied to Burr and Livingston wing of the D-Rs	1811 City Directory; Records of the New Orleans City Court; *Claiborne Letters*; *Debate on a Memorial to Congress;* McCaleb, *The Aaron Burr Conspiracy; The Louisiana Gazette; The Columbian Centinel; The Panoplist*
N/I	N/I	N/I	City Court Records
N/I	Career lawyer	He owned some slaves while in New Orleans.	City Court Records; District Court Records; Court of Pleas Records; Louisiana Slave Records; *Claiborne Letters*; Massachusetts Town and Vital Records; Haynes, *The Mississippi Territory and South West Frontier; Territorial Records*
N/I	In addition to practicing law he was also a notary.	N/I	Court of Pleas Records; Thomas Jefferson Papers (Elizabeth Trist to Thomas Jefferson, Nov 26, 1804)
Philadelphia, PA	Lawyer, politician, and scholar	He was a planter.	James Brown Papers, LSU Libraries

Name of Lawyer	Where From	When Arrived in New Orleans	When Born	When Died
Bushnell, Charles	Salisbury, CT	1804	1782	1835
Caune, Charles Robert	N/I	1804	N/I	N/I
Cabell, Charles Joseph (changed his name from Joseph Meggison Cabell)	Abermarle County, VA	c. 1805	1788	c. 1811
Caune, Charles Robert	N/I	1804	N/I	N/I
Carleton, Henry Coxe	VA	1814	1785	1863

Where Died	Relationship to Law	Relationship to Slavery	Sources Used
Baton Rouge, LA	Lawyer and politician; he was a judge and a state representative.	Slave owner, but doesn't appear to have been a planter.	1811 City Directory; Michael Beauchampt, diss. "Instruments of Empire"; Baton Rouge Parish Probate Records; Connecticut Deaths and Burials Records
N/I	Career lawyer; his practice appeared to be both lucrative for him and related to slavery.	I found no evidence that he owned a plantation but he bought and sold dozens of slaves.	City Court Records; Court of Pleas Records; Michoud et. al. v. Girod et. al. 45 U.S. 503; Race and Slavery Petitions Project; Louisiana Slave Records
New Orleans	Career lawyer and part time soldier	N/I, but he is from VA and appears to have come from a planter family	1811 City Directory; *Encyclopedia of Virginia Biography*
N/I	Career lawyer and part time soldier	I found no evidence that he owned a plantation but he bought and sold dozens of slaves.	1811 City Directory; *Encyclopedia of Virginia Biography*
Philadelphia, PA	Lawyer politician; he later became a district attorney and a judge. He married Edward Livingston's wife's sister and read law in Livingston's office.	He was a wealthy man and a slaveholder while in New Orleans, but he was opposed to secession.	Papers of Henry Clay; Biographical Sketches of Graduates of Yale College

Name of Lawyer	Where From	When Arrived in New Orleans	When Born	When Died
Cauchoix, Eduard	France then St. Domingue	He likely arrived after Louisiana Purchase in one of the waves of refugees from St. Domingue.	1763 (I think) there is a typo in one of the records—17k3.	1824
Cuvillier, Pierre Ambroise	St. Domingue	by 1808	N/I	1835
D'argy, Francois Bouhourd	France	c. 1804—He was in Tours as late as 1789 as a witness in a wedding. He may have fled during the French Rev-olution, in which case he likely did not come directly to NO. He prob-ably came after the Purchase.	N/I	1813
De Armas, Michel	New Orleans	1783 (born there)	1783	1823

Where Died	Relationship to Law	Relationship to Slavery	Sources Used
New Orleans	Career lawyer; he appeared to have a successful practice.	He was a slave owner: there is evidence that he had a child with a slave in 1792 in SD. The slave was named Edouard and he was freed in 1822. Cauchoix also represented free people of color more than most lawyers.	City Court Records; Louisiana Supreme Court Records; St. Louis Cathedral Records; Race and Slavery Petitions Project; Louisiana Slave Records
Iberville Parish, LA	He did not practice law often. He was also part of a group that petitioned to form a Mason's lodge in New Orleans in 1808. By 1825 he was a planter. He served as clerk for the Louisiana Senate at one point early on. He was a party to a lot of lawsuits.	He became a planter.	City Court Records; 1811 City Directory; Martin's Reports; Louisiana Slave Records; Louisiana Wills and Probate Records; LSU Digital Collections
New Orleans	Career lawyer and little information on anything else he did.	He was a slave owner.	City Court Records; Court of Pleas Records; Orleans Parish Probate Records; Louisiana Slave Records; Civil Records of the canton of Tours-Nord; French National Archives—online edition
New Orleans	Notary-lawyer	He was a slave owner.	Biographical and Historical Memoirs of Louisiana; "The Winged Hourglasses of de Armas and Dupaquier"

Name of Lawyer	Where From	When Arrived in New Orleans	When Born	When Died
Davezac, Auguste	Les Cayes, St. Domingue	c. 1805—he came to study law in Livingston's office. He had been studying in France when the French Revolution broke out.	1780	1851
DeMahy (Desmontils), Joseph Henry	France	He was in New Orleans as early as 1791.	c. 1760s	N/I
Denis, Henry	France	by 1808	1787	1873
DePeyster, William	NJ	by 1807	1783	1817

Where Died	Relationship to Law	Relationship to Slavery	Sources Used
New York	Lawyer politician; he served under both Jackson and Van Buren.	He was a slave owner.	*American Biographical Dictionary*; John William Ward, Andrew Jackson; Charles Lanman, *Biographical Annals of the Civil Government of the United States*
N/I	Career lawyer; he was involved in several lawsuits for unpaid fees. He also appears to have come from at least minor nobility in France. His father got into some trouble in 1790 in France.	I do not have direct evidence that he owned slaves, but he was in communication with Nantes about the rice and indigo trade.	City Court Records; Court of Pleas Records; Michoud et. al. v. Girod et. al. 45 U.S. 503; Race and Slavery Petitions Project; Louisiana Slave Records
New Orleans	Career lawyer	He owned five slaves in the 1830 census.	City Court Records; 1811 City Directory; U.S. Census Records; Louisiana Death Records
New Orleans	Career lawyer	He owned at least two slaves at his death that he left to his infant son in his will.	City Court Records; Louisiana Statewide Death Index; Louisiana Probate Records; Louisiana Supreme Court Records

Name of Lawyer	Where From	When Arrived in New Orleans	When Born	When Died
De Quinones, Etienne	Spain	He arrived in New Orleans "many years" before the Louisiana Purchase.	1770	Territorial period or early statehood
Derbigny, Pierre	France	1797	1769	1829
Desdunes, Jean Baptiste	St. Domingue	c. 1802	1788	1842
Destroil [not sure of the spelling of the name]	N/I	N/I	N/I	N/I
Dewees, George William	Philadelphia, PA	c. 1804	1777	1834

Where Died	Relationship to Law	Relationship to Slavery	Sources Used
New Orleans	Lawyer notary but not much of a lawyer	He was involved in many slave transactions in the territorial period. Slave trading may have been a source of income.	Court of Pleas Records; St. Louis Cathedral Records; Claiborne Letters; Louisiana Slave Records
Gretna, LA	Lawyer politician	He was a pro slavery politician and had ten slaves in his household in the 1810 census.	*Encyclopedia of Louisiana*; Peter Kastor, *The Nation's Crucible*
New Orleans	He was more of a businessman than a lawyer. He was the son-in-law of Moreau Lislet for a while.	He became a big time planter in Louisiana. His father was known as "one of the cruelest planters of Artobonite plain" in colonial St. Domingue.	City Court Records; Louisiana Slave Records; Louisiana Wills; Carl Brasseaux, *The Road to Louisiana*; Baron De Vatsy, *The Colonial System Unveiled*
N/I	N/I	N/I	City Court Records
Vigo County, IND	He was a dabbler in the law. He moved around a lot, going from frontier to frontier. He appears to have left Louisiana after his wife died. He sold property in Louisiana in 1815.	He owned a lot of slaves while in Louisiana and may have been a planter—or at least an aspiring planter.	City Court Records; Court of Pleas Records; Louisiana Slave Records; Land Records of the United States Congress

Name of Lawyer	Where From	When Arrived in New Orleans	When Born	When Died
Duncan, Abner	Adams County, PA. He moved to Kentucky, then Natchez, then, in 1805, to New Orleans.	1805	1774	1823
Dupuy, L. Alexander	LA	1772—born in LA	1772	after 1850
Ellery, Abraham A.	Newport, RI	1803, as a surveyor at the behest of A. Hamilton	1773	1820
Fromentin, Eligius	France	1803. He lived in a lot of places. He left France during the French Revolution and went to PA, then MD, then LA. He also spent time as a judge in FL near the end of his life.	1767	1822

Where Died	Relationship to Law	Relationship to Slavery	Sources Used
New Orleans	He was a career lawyer, although he was involved in other business ventures. He received a monopoly in 1820 to run a steamboat ferry across the Mississippi River for five years. By all accounts he was a successful lawyer.	He was a slave owner.	City Court Records; Court of Pleas Records; Claiborne Letters; William Davis, *The Pirates Lafitte*
Iberville Parish, LA	I do not have much information about what he did outside of the law.	He was a slave owner.	City Court Records; Court of Pleas Records; U.S. Census
Bay St. Louis, MS	Career lawyer; he was one of the first seven before LA state bar in 1813.	He inherited from his father a plantation in Antigua with over 200 slaves.	City Court Records; Court of Pleas Records; Louisiana Supreme Court Records; Claiborne Letters; Bradley, Interim Appointment; Redwood Family Papers
New Orleans	Lawyer politician; Fromentin did lots of things. He was a priest first. He left the priesthood in MD to come to New Orleans and become a lawyer. He later served in the territorial legislature, was a judge and a U.S. senator from LA.	He was a slave owner.	City Court Records; American Antiquarian Society member biography; U.S. Census; Congressional Records

Name of Lawyer	Where From	When Arrived in New Orleans	When Born	When Died
Godefroy, Pierre Francois Simon	France	c. 1804	c. 1785	N/I
Gordon, Martin	VA	N/I	1773	after 1850
Gourrand, Jean Baptiste	N/I	N/I	N/I	N/I
Grymes, John Randolph	VA	1808	1786	1854
Grymes, Philip	VA	c. 1808	1774	1811

Where Died	Relationship to Law	Relationship to Slavery	Sources Used
N/I	Notary lawyer; he may have been a slave trader as well.	It appears that he traded in slaves. He certainly was involved in a lot of slave transactions.	City Court Records; 1805 and 1811 City Directories; New Orleans Notarial Archives; Louisiana Supreme Court Records; Louisiana Slave Records
N/I	He was a dabbler in the law. He was a "cultured gentleman from Virginia," a clerk to the Senate, a court clerk, and he bought and sold dozens of slaves.	He was a planter and/or trader. He bought and sold dozens of slaves in the territorial period and early statehood.	City Court Records; Louisiana Slave Records; U.S. Census; Stanley Arthur, *Old New Orleans*
N/I	N/I	N/I	Court of Pleas Records
New Orleans	Lawyer politician	He owned many slaves.	City Court Records; Louisiana Supreme Court Records; *Dictionary of Louisiana Biography;* Davis, *The Pirates Lafitte*
New Orleans	Lawyer politician	He was a slave owner.	Davis, *The Pirates Lafitte*; Thomas Jefferson Papers; *The Virginia Magazine of History and Biography*

Name of Lawyer	Where From	When Arrived in New Orleans	When Born	When Died
Guinault, Jacques Philipe	New Orleans	1758—born in New Orleans	1758	1838
Gurley, John	CT	1804	1778	1808 (in a duel with Philip Jones, esq.)
Hennen, Alfred	MD	1808	1786	1870
Keene, Richard Raynal	MD	1804	1779	1839
Kennedy, Thomas	MD	1804	1776	1831

Where Died	Relationship to Law	Relationship to Slavery	Sources Used
New Orleans	Notary lawyer; maybe a slave speculator as well	He bought and sold many slaves.	Court of Pleas Records; Louisiana Slave Records; Cabildo Records; New Orleans City Directories
New Orleans	Aspiring lawyer politician; he was attorney general in 1807; died in a duel in 1808.	He owned a lot of slaves and invested in plantations.	Court of Pleas Records; *Louisiana Gazette;* John Gurley Papers, LSU Libraries
New Orleans	Career lawyer and law professor	Planter; by 1830 he was the 3rd largest rice planter in La. with over 1 00 slaves.	City Court Records; Biographies of Early American Presbyterians; *New Orleans Times Picayune*
St. Louis, MO— while on a trip	Aspiring lawyer politician; his career was hurt when he was implicated in the Burr Conspiracy.	Slave owner or plant-er; he bought several slaves during the territorial period. He defended slavery as an aspiring politician.	City Court Records; Court of Pleas Records; Keene, "A Letter of Vindication to Colonel Munroe"; Luther Martin, *Modern Gratitude;* Louisiana Slave Records; Obituary
St. Louis, MO— while on a trip	He was dabbler in the law. He was one of Claiborne's early secretaries, along with Workman. He was also a court clerk of several different courts, including the City Court.	He was a slave owner.	City Court Records; New Orleans Passenger List; New Orleans Slave Manifests; Find a Grave Memorial; Bradley, *Interim Appointment*

Name of Lawyer	Where From	When Arrived in New Orleans	When Born	When Died
Kerr, Lewis	Dublin, Ireland	1803. He came with Claiborne from Natchez. He made many stops between Ireland and New Orleans, including India, PA, Ohio, and others.	1772	1834
Kidder, John	MA	1804	N/I	N/I
Lozano, Joachim	New Spain	N/I	N/I	N/I
Livingston, Edward	Columbia County, NY	1804	1764	1836
Mace, Abram	NY	N/I	N/I	N/I

Where Died	Relationship to Law	Relationship to Slavery	Sources Used
Philadelphia, PA	Lawyer scholar. He was implicated in the Burr conspiracy.	He was a slave owner.	Claiborne Letters; Bradley, *Interim Appointment*
N/I	He was a dabbler.	He was a slave owner.	Court of Pleas Records; 1805 City Directory; Louisiana Slave Records; Claiborne Letters; Bradley, *Interim Appointment*
N/I	N/I	He had a child with a free woman of color named Marie Chalon in 1813. It is unclear if he owned slaves.	City Court Records; Citizenship Affidavits; Louisiana Slave Records; St. Louis Cathedral Records
N/I	Career lawyer; his practice appeared to be both lucrative for him and related to slavery.	He was a slave owner.	City Court Records; Court of Pleas Records; Claiborne Letters; William Hatcher, *Edward Livingston: Jeffersonian Republican and Jacksonian Democrat*
Dutchess County, NY	Lawyer, politician, and scholar	He was a slave owner.	City Court Records; Orleans Parish District Court Records; Louisiana Slave Records

Name of Lawyer	Where From	When Arrived in New Orleans	When Born	When Died
Martin, Francois-Xavier	France	1809—via Martinique and NC	1762	1846
Mazureau, Etienne	France	c. 1804	1777	1849
McShane, Robert	Philadelphia, PA	c. 1804	1780	1811
McCurley [uncertain on spelling]	N/I	N/I	N/I	N/I
Meyere, Jean Lamon	N/I	N/I	N/I	N/I

Where Died	Relationship to Law	Relationship to Slavery	Sources Used
New Orleans	Lawyer politician	He was a planter.	City Court Records; Louisiana Slave Records; Louisiana Wills; Alexis de Tocqueville, *Democracy in America*; Thomas Ingersoll, *Mammon and Manon*
New Orleans	He appeared as counsel in the City Court a few times, but was not really a lawyer. He was a very successful businessman.	He was a planter. He developed a system for slaves to buy their freedom in fifteen years.	City Court Records; William Allen, *Life and Work of John McDonough*; Louisiana GenWeb Archives, *Biography of John McDonough*
Pointe Coupée Parish, LA	Lawyer politician; he became a judge in Pointe Coupee.	N/I	City Court Records; Court of Pleas Records; George Brubaker, *Families of the Wyoming Valley*
N/I	N/I	N/I	City Court Records
N/I	N/I	N/I	Court of Pleas Records

Name of Lawyer	Where From	When Arrived in New Orleans	When Born	When Died
Montesolo, Francisco	N/!	N/I	N/I	N/I
Moreau-Lislet, Louis	St. Domingue	1804	1766	1832
Morel, Pierre Louis	Vilaine, France	c. 1804	1776	1826
Nicholson, John	Philadelphia, PA	c. 1808	1783	1848
Nicholls, Edward	Cornwall, England	1804—via France, back to England, then MD	1746	1812

Where Died	Relationship to Law	Relationship to Slavery	Sources Used
New Orleans	Career lawyer	N/I	City Court Records
New Orleans	Lawyer, politician, and scholar	He was a slave owner.	City Court Records; Levasseur, *Moreau-Lislet: The Man Behind the Digest of 1808*
New Orleans	Made the occasional foray into the law but not really a career lawyer. He did serve in the House of Representatives.	He owned a lot of slaves.	City Court Records; St. Louis Cathedral Records; Obituary; the Morel Family Papers—Tulane's Howard Tilton Library
New Orleans	Career lawyer	He was a slave owner. He was involved in "shipping" some slaves but they all seem to involve the same slave named Hannah.	City Court Records; 1811 City Directory; Find a Grave Memorial; U.S. Census; Toledano, *New Orleans Architecture*; Louisiana Slave Manifests
Donaldsonville, LA	Lawyer politician; he was a lawyer in Prince George's County, MD, and DC before coming to New Orleans.	He was a slave owner.	City Court Records; Court of Pleas Records; LHA *Dictionary of Louisiana Biography*

Name of Lawyer	Where From	When Arrived in New Orleans	When Born	When Died
Paillette, Jacques Cesar	France, then St. Domingue, then Jamaica	c. 1804—via St. Domingue and Jamaica	1764	1847
Pedesclaux, Pedro	Basque Country, Spain	1770s or 1780s	1760	1816
Pignon, Claude Benoit	France	c. 1804	1762	1833
Pollock, George	Dublin, Ireland	c. 1804—via New York and Philadelphia	1755	1820

Where Died	Relationship to Law	Relationship to Slavery	Sources Used
New Orleans	Lawyer businessman; he came from wealth in France, bought a plantation in SD, lost it in the Haitian Revolution, and used the law to rebuild and become a planter in Louisiana—not verified, but very well could have happened this way.	He was a planter.	City Court Records; Court of Pleas Records; Louisiana Slave Records; Guide to the Historic French Quarter
New Orleans	Lawyer notary; he was one of those men who never broke into the New Orleans legal profession.	He was a slave owner.	Court of Pleas Records; New Orleans Notarial Archives; Louisiana Slave Records; Claiborne Letters
New Orleans	Lawyer businessman	He owned a lot of slaves.	City Court Records; Court of Pleas Records; Louisiana Wills; Louisiana Slave Records; Henry Clay Papers
Madisonville, LA	He was a lawyer, but he did dabble in many other jobs as well. He was a port warden, representative on city council and legislative council, and justice of the peace.	He was a slave owner.	City Court Records; Claiborne Letters; Bradley, *Interim Appointment*

Name of Lawyer	Where From	When Arrived in New Orleans	When Born	When Died
Porter, Andrew	Philadelphia, PA	c. 1804	1770s	N/I
Prevost, John Bartow	Paramus, NJ	1804	1766	1825
Roche, Charles (brother of merchant Pierre Roche)	Louisiana born	c. 1780s	c. 1780s	N/I
Rodriguez, Jean	Canary Islands	1778	1770s	N/I

Where Died	Relationship to Law	Relationship to Slavery	Sources Used
N/I	Lawyer merchant; he was mostly a merchant who dabbled in the law and had a lot of lawyer relatives. He was a port inspector but also operated Porter and Brown proc—and they show up in City Court cases.	N/I	City Court Records; 1811 City Directory; Bradley, *Interim Appointment*; *Journal of American Irish Historical Society*
Peru	Lawyer politician; his mother married Aaron Burr after his father died.	He was a planter.	Find a Grave Memorial; Lolita Buckner Inniss, "A Fugitive Slave in Princeton"; Nancy Isenberg, *Fallen Founder*; H.W. Brands, *The Heartbreak of Aaron Burr*
N/I	He was a career lawyer and his brother, Pierre, was a merchant.	He was involved in a lot of slave transactions.	City Court Records; Louisiana Slave Records; 1811 City Directory; Jill-Karen Yakubik, "Historical Investigations of the Civilian Occupation of the Chalmette Battlefield"
N/I	Lawyer planter	He was a planter.	City Court Records; Louisiana Death Index; Yakubik, "Historical Investigations of the Civilian Occupation of the Chalmette Battlefield"

Name of Lawyer	Where From	When Arrived in New Orleans	When Born	When Died
Seghers, Domingue	Brussels, Belgium	c. 1804—not clear exactly when he came. He fled Napoleonic rule, spent some time in Antwerp before coming to New Orleans.	1767	1848
Smith, W.T.	N/I	c. 1804	N/I	N/I
Trask, Israel	MA	1804—via MS	1773	1835
Workman, James	Ireland	1804—via stops in England, Norfolk, New York, Philadelphia, Alexandria, and Charleston	1770s	1832

Where Died	Relationship to Law	Relationship to Slavery	Sources Used
New Orleans	He was a career lawyer and owned a great deal of property.	He owned a lot of slaves although it is not clear whether or not he was a planter.	City Court Records; New Orleans Death Records; Louisiana Slave Records; Louisiana State Museum Online Exhibits Madame John's Legacy; Simon Delery, *Napoleon's Soldiers in America*
N/I	He was a career lawyer.	N/I	City Court Records; 1811 City Directory
MA	Lawyer civil servant	He was a slave owner.	Court of Pleas Records; Adam Rothman, *Slave Country*
Bay St. Louis, MS	Lawyer, politician, and scholar; he was an early judge of the County Court; part of the "Mexican Association"; one of the lawyers who represented Livingston in Batture Case.	Slave owner and ACS guy	City Court Records; Claiborne Letters; Bradley, *Interim Appointment*

Portrait of Almirante Antonio de Ulloa
Andrés Cortés y Aguilar, 1856

CHAPTER 5

SOUNDING THE RETREAT

The Exit of Spanish Law in Early Louisiana 1805-1808

Vernon Valentine Palmer

> "[Always] to be kept in mind is an interesting matter of prejudice: what is good in Louisiana law is attributed to France, what is medieval to Spain, and what is bad to the common law."
>
> Ferdinand Fairfax Stone[1]

> "From their English forbears and other non-Spanish Europeans, Anglo Americans had inherited the view that Spaniards were unusually cruel, avaricious, treacherous, fanatical, superstitious, cowardly, corrupt, decadent, indolent, and authoritarian—a unique complex of pejoratives that historians from Spain came to call the Black Legend, *la leyenda negra.*"
>
> David J. Weber[2]

INTRODUCTION

This essay focuses on a short period in Louisiana history, the first codification period 1805-1808. These four critical years encompassed key decisions about the future shape

1. Ferdinand Stone, 'The Law with a Difference and How It Came About', *in The Past as Prelude, New Orleans*, 1718-1968, at 42 (Hodding Carter ed., 1968).
2. David J. Weber, 'The Spanish Legacy in North America and the Historical Imagination', 23 *W. Hist. Q.* 7 (1992). Further on the Black Legend, see Thomas Ingersoll, *Mammon and Manon in Early New Orleans: The First Slave Society in the Deep South 1718-1819*, at 153-54 (1999).

and content of the legal system. A central question that could not be avoided was what would be the role, the scope, and the place of Spanish law in the future legal order. Spanish codes, *cédulas*, and decrees, both public and private, substantive and procedural, were the law of the land at the time of the colony's cession to the United States in 1803, and this law remained in force down to the beginning of the period under study. Spanish Governor Alejandro O'Reilly had the authority to introduce this system, and he in fact did so by an Ordinance of Nov. 25, 1769, which subsequently received approval by royal *cédula*.[3] The conjectures by President Jefferson, Gustavus Schmidt and John Tucker that Louisiana at the time of the Purchase was still governed by French law proved unhistorical and have ceased to be credited.[4]

A conventional view is that this period in Louisiana history was a contest between protagonists of the common law and those of the civil law, a characterization largely justified. But the common law/civil law question principally concerned the future orientation of the private or personal law of Louisiana, to the neglect of other Spanish laws which were also in force and could have a bearing on my subject. In the 1970s attention focused upon an interesting subtopic of the common law/civil law theme: to what degree was Spanish law or French law the inspiration behind the Digest of 1808? That question concerned the "inner identity" of Louisiana's private law and is often referred to as the "Pascal/Batiza debate."[5] John Cairns' important essay in this

---

3. *See* A.N. Yiannopoulos, 'The Early Sources of Louisiana Law: Critical Appraisal of a Controversy', in *Louisiana's Legal Heritage* 87-106 (Edward Haas, Jr. ed., 1983); Hans Baade, 'Marriage Contracts in French and Spanish Louisiana: A Study in 'Notarial Jurisprudence', 53 Tul. L. Rev. 1 (1978). O'Reilly's actions changed the official law but may not have changed all the "law in action" (French folkways, for instance, were still followed), for the province was culturally and linguistically French and still attached to a French way of life.

4.Gustavus Schmidt, 'Introductory Note, Were the Laws of France Which Governed Louisiana Prior to the Cession of the Colony to Spain Abolished by the Ordinances of O'Reilly?', 1 La. L.J. 23 (1842).

5. *See* R. Batiza, 'The Louisiana Civil Code of 1808: Its Actual Sources and Present Relevance', 46 Tul. L. Rev. 4 (1971); Robert Pascal, 'Sources of the Digest of 1808: A Reply to Professor Batiza', 46 Tul. L. Rev. 603 (1972); Yiannopoulos, *supra* note 3, at 98, 101-02.

collection of essays is the latest iteration of this continuing debate.[6] This essay may be of some relevance to this debate but it has a different starting point and treats a different subtopic: Conceding that a complete system of Spanish law was in force at the time of the Cession, then the broad and recurring question in the period 1805-1808 was what parts of that law to keep, what parts to discard, and what to replace it with? Some dismantling of the Spanish legal system was inevitable following the change of sovereignty and its American constitution, but after that point, where would it stop? What should remain? Legal and extralegal factors might affect legislative decisions on this issue, including cultural attachments, legal chauvinisms, economic and political considerations, the instructions to codifiers, and last but, I believe, equally important, the imbued preconceptions about Spanish law in the popular mind.

In deciding which laws to keep or discard, it seems reasonable to assume that each branch of Spanish law presented different considerations and conjured different perceptions. Spanish criminal law, for example, was burdened with a heavy stigma and was generally regarded as draconian, barbaric, and cruel. Torture as a means to extract evidence was approved by law and had been used in criminal trials in *Luisiana*,[7] and the horrific punishments outlined in O'Reilly's "Code" and in Las *Siete Partidas* were apparently still good law.[8] Spanish civil procedure, although

---

6. *See* John Cairns, 'Spanish Law, the *Teatro de la legislación universal de España e Indias*, and the Background to the Drafting of the Digest of Orleans of 1808', Chapter Six, this volume).

7. Torture as a means of acquiring evidence was not mentioned in O'Reilly's Ordinance and Instructions, but it was authorized by *Siete Partidas* and was used in criminal trials in Louisiana. *See* Laura Porteous, 'Torture in Spanish Criminal Procedure in Louisiana', 8 La. Hist. Q. 5 (1925); E.A. Davis, *Louisiana: A Narrative History* 139 (1961).

8. O'Reilly's Instructions called for brutal punishments. It was particularly severe on blasphemers against the Savior and his Mother (the reviler's tongue to be cut out and his property confiscated), and homosexuals who committed "the detestable crime against nature" (the body burned), and murderers (dragged to execution at the tail of some animal). Beccaria's famous work on criminal law *Dei delitte delle pene* (1764) was translated into Castilian in 1774, but by 1777 it was on the Inquisition's Index. *See* Alejando Agüero & Marta Lorente, 'Penal

similar to the Romano-canonical procedure prevalent in most of Europe, attracted a surprising degree of criticism. It was characterized in some quarters as being dilatory, prolix, secretive, and a source of corruption. In contrast, the substantive private law of Spain sometimes received lavish praise, at least from certain elite lawyers. Louis Moreau Lislet and Henry Carleton hailed *Las Siete Partidas* as "the most perfect of Spanish laws [which] could be advantageously compared with any code published in the most enlightened ages of the world." The *Partidas*, they wrote, were "the unceasing subject of the praise and admiration of every jurist acquainted with them."[9] James Workman, no hispanophile, acknowledged in a published letter, "The laws of Spain are generally excellent in themselves; for they are founded on the Roman Code, one of the most perfect and elegant systems of jurisprudence ever promulgated to the world."[10] While there was no question of the inner merit or the prestigious pedigree of Spanish private law, there were still problems in accessing and applying it. Lawyers regularly complained that the sources were labyrinthine, the confusion (as Livingston put it) "worse than that of babel,"[11] and needed books were scarce or unavailable.[12] Adding to the difficulty, many provisions found in texts such as

---

Enlightenment in Spain: From Beccaria's Reception to the First Criminal Code', FHI ¶¶ 13 et seq. (Nov. 15, 2012), http://fhi.rg.mpg.de/media/zeitschrift/1211aguero-lorente_1.pdf.

9. L. Moreau Lislet & Henry Carleton, 1 *The Laws of Las Siete Partidas Which Are Still in Force in the State of Louisiana* vii (New Orleans, n. pub. 1820). At another place in the Preface, the translators said "if it [the code of the Partidas] is not the best it is certainly equal to any the world has ever seen." *Id.* at xxv.

10. Letter of LAELIUS, Miss. Messenger, Nov. 30, 1804.

11. *Quoted in* Cairns, *supra* note 6, at 94 n.69.

12. As Professor Yiannopoulos summarized the chaos: "[T]here were at least six different compilations of Spanish laws and more than 20,000 individual laws, some of which were never intended to apply in the colonies. Conflicts among legislative provisions were not uncommon, and Spanish writers often disagreed as to which laws should take precedence." 'The Civil Codes of Louisiana', *in* 1 *Louisiana Civil Code XLVIII* (A.N. Yiannopoulos ed., 2016). It may be added that although needed books were often scarce or unavailable, certain elite lawyers such as Michel de Armas, Edward Livingston, Moreau Lislet, and Pierre Derbigny assembled remarkable libraries. For a detailed study of these libraries, see Florence M. Jumonville, '"Formerly the Property of a Lawyer"—Books That Shaped Louisiana Law', 24 Tul. Eur. & Civ. L.F. 161 (2009).

Siete Partidas (published 1263, promulgated 1348) were obsolete, archaic, and of uncertain application in modern society.[13]

The Louisiana legal system under construction during this period was built with the assistance of a talented corps of codifiers.[14] It might be asked, however, how much they knew about Spanish law. What were the sources of their knowledge? How objective was their judgment? None was native born. All were immigrants. None had trained in Spanish law, and none had lived under Spanish rule. It might be fair to say that these men carried their own impressions and information about that system

---

13. Moreau Lislet and Carleton faced this problem when they attempted to translate this "most perfect of Spanish laws." Large parts of this thirteenth-century code were either incompatible with the American Constitution or had to be disregarded as obsolete, irrational, or inhumane. Whenever Moreau Lislet and Carleton came across such problematic or incompatible provisions, they simply wrote "Not in Force" and made no translation of the material. In this way they passed over hundreds of pages, sometimes even entire Partidas. One estimates this shortened the translation by as much as 650 pages. *Partida* I, for example, which dealt with "all the things that relate to the Catholic Faith," enacted the mysteries of the Holy Trinity and the Seven Sacraments into positive law. It also codified the position of the Pope as the head of the church. None of this received translation into English. It must have seemed incompatible with the spirit of an American constitution that demanded separation of church and state. For similar reasons, the translators skipped nearly everything in *Partida* II since this dealt with the monarch as Emperor and King, his powers and qualifications, his duties toward his relatives, nobles, court, and his people, even his role as husband and father. These provisions must have seemed incompatible with a republican and democratic system of government. *Partida* VII, dealing with accusations, crimes, and punishments, was left untranslated in twenty-eight of its thirty-four titles. To mention some of the deleted titles, the translators skipped the provisions on trial by battle, *capitis diminutio*, homicide, adultery, stuprum, sorcery, heretics, sodomy, blasphemy, torture, and punishments. The dispositions on torture and trial by battle, for example, were obviously inhumane or irrational relics of a bygone era. The benign and approving manner in which the *Partida* accepted the use of torture in criminal proceedings, both arguing for its necessity and condoning its horrific methods, was no longer acceptable and needed no translation into modern law.

14. The principals alluded to in the text are Edward Livingston of New York, Louis Moreau Lislet of St. Domingue, James Brown of Kentucky, Pierre Derbigny of Laon, France, and James Workman of Ireland. As to the traits and backgrounds of the lawyers of the Territorial period, see Kenneth Aslakson, 'Immigrant Lawyers and Slavery in Territorial New Orleans' in this volume.

which affected its reputation, status and future acceptability in the new legal order.[15]

This essay is an enquiry into the factors, attitudes, and legislative choices that shaped the fate of Spanish law in early Louisiana. It will preliminarily consider a few of the legends, myths, and prejudices that affected the general reputation of Spanish law and Spanish rule in Louisiana, such as its reputation for corrupt judges, venal institutions, cruel and barbaric punishments, and the terrors of the Spanish Inquisition. Furthermore, by 1800 Spain was visibly in decline as a world power, and the prestige of its laws, inevitably, had declined as well.[16] It cannot be said with certainty that these impressions had direct effect upon legislative decisions and policy choices, but it can be said that such ideas were widespread and were not unknown to lawyers, codifiers, officials, and legislators. Secondly the essay will consider the major enactments of the period that impacted Spanish law prior to the Digest of 1808. These enactments show the areas and the extent to which the Spanish system in place at the Cession was surgically dismembered, sector by sector. It will show that by 1807 Spanish law was substantially expelled from the Territory in all legal areas except the field of private law. The pre-1808 measures show a consistent pattern of rejection—a consistent pattern of replacing Spanish law with American, English, and French laws. The last section of this essay briefly considers the Digest of 1808 and asks how it fits within this overall pattern. It is submitted that the preponderance of French sources found in the Digest may be appreciated as the continuation of a clear legislative trend. The turn to French legal sources was another manifestation of the general retreat of Spanish law in Louisiana.

---

15. Interestingly, the ancient Louisianians played a subdued role, or at least a less visible role, in the codification projects. This seems ironic in that they had more reason to understand the law of Spain. They lived under Spanish rule from 1769-1803.

16. *See* William H. Prescott, *Prescott's Histories: Rise and Decline of the Spanish Empire (*1990). Symbolic of Spain's decline was that upon gaining their independence, her former colonies made French law, not Spanish law, their "Northern Star." M. C. Mirow, *Latin American Law* 138 (2004).

OF LEGENDS, MYTHS AND PREJUDICE

Justice at the Cabildo

Though it may have generally operated as Alejandro O'Reilly decreed in his Ordinances and Instructions of 25 November 1769,[17] the justice administered at the Cabildo has often been portrayed as venal and corrupt. Only a few days after receiving possession of the Territory Governor Claiborne branded the erstwhile Spanish government and its Cabildo as corrupt and consumed in intrigue. In a letter to James Madison he informed the Secretary of State that "Government [under the Spaniards] had scarcely a nerve not wounded by corruption; the Business in every department was wrapped up in Mystery and intrigue and has been left in confusion perhaps inexplicable."[18] Referring to the last Spanish governor before the retrocession to France, Claiborne lamented "it is a shameful fact that under his [Salcedo's] administration not only many posts of Honour and profit in his gifts were sold, but that even when exercising the sacred Character of a Judge, he often vended his decisions to the highest bidder."[19] He expanded the charge: "the same depravities pervade the System in every direction." He reported that the arrears in the courts are very great: "Some of the causes have been pending for upwards of twenty years; corruption has put her Seal upon them ...."[20] Given that Governor Claiborne could not speak or read French or Spanish and that he had arrived in Louisiana only weeks earlier, one cannot be sure how he acquired this knowledge or how reliable his information was. For purposes of understanding attitudes about Spanish law in early Louisiana, however, there is little doubt that he himself clearly believed it.

As noted, the Cabildo operated during the Spanish domination as Alejandro O'Reilly had decreed in his Ordinances and

---

17. For the full text translated into English, see 'Ancient Jurisprudence of Louisiana', 1 La. L.J. 1 (Gustavus Schmidt ed. & trans., Aug. 1841).
18. Letter from Claiborne to Madison (Jan. 2, 1804), *in* 1 *Official Letter Books of W.C.C. Claiborne, 1801-1816*, at 323 (Dunbar Rowland ed., 1917) [hereinafter 1 *Official Letter Books*].
19. *Id.*
20. *Id.*

Instructions of 25 November 1769. Judgeships and other offices at the Cabildo were sold to the highest bidder,[21] and in contrast to the French policy that afforded free legal services to colonial subjects, justice in the Spanish era was expensive for litigants. Legal historian Henry Plauché Dart pointed out that "the system of charges was the real burden which affected the people in Spanish days."[22] Virtually every act, motion, or necessary signature by the judges required the litigant to pay a precise fee, as set forth in an elaborate fee schedule. A document signed by the judge with his baptismal and family name cost four reales in silver dollars. For sessions of the court lasting two hours and a half the charge was two ducats. The opening of a will and the examination of the witnesses to the will required payment of forty-eight reales.[23] Everywhere there seemed to be an outstretched palm, easily giving the impression the system was rigged and corrupt. Yet Dart was clear that this impression was unfounded. His careful review of the archival documents found that the system was not corrupt, indeed the contrary was true. Spanish justice on the whole was handled with "care and skill," and he found nothing to substantiate the stereotype of the "gold loving" Spanish judges, even though he was aware of contrary accounts.[24] A similar study of the New Mexico archives, 1621-1821, also concluded that the Spanish colonial judicial system, rather than being corrupt, was "painfully careful in its deliberations, and above all, remarkably humane in its judgements."[25] But these studies could hardly counter or correct impressions of

---

21. *See* Gilbert Din, *New Orleans Cabildo: Colonial Louisiana's First City Government 1769-1803* (1996); Derek Noel Kerr, *Petty Felony, Slave Defiance and Frontier Villainy: Criminal Justice in Spanish Louisiana 1770-1803*, at 21 et seq. (1983) (unpublished Ph.D. Dissertation, Tulane University) (on file with La. Research Collection, Tulane University; Henry Plauché Dart, *Courts and Law in Colonial Louisiana* 35 (1923).
22. *Id.*
23. *See* 'Table of Fees, Demandable by Judges, Lawyers, Escribanos, Attorneys, and the Other Officers of Justice, O'Reilly's Ordinances and Instructions (Nov. 25, 1769)', *in* 1 La. L.J. 55-60 (1841).
24. *Id.* at 46-47.
25. Robert J. Tórrez, 'Crime and Punishment in Colonial New Mexico', N.M. B.J. 23 (2000).

venality and corruption which existed in the popular mind and in the Governor's discourse.[26]

Laughing at Spanish Judges: "Liberty in Louisiana"

James Workman—codifier, critic of Spanish law, playwright, jurist, and would-be filibusterer—arrived in New Orleans in late 1804 and was appointed a judge of the County of Orleans. He was chosen to draft and reform the Territory's criminal law, a project he completed in 1805. He practiced law and represented Edward Livingston in his famous litigation over the New Orleans batture, and it was under Spanish law that Workman pressed the New Yorker's claims to the alluvial property.[27] Workman professed to have a certain admiration for the substantive Spanish law, stressing its prestigious Roman-law connection,[28] but he was sharply critical of its procedural law which, he said, tended to produce corrupt and venal judges. He boldly asserted that:

> [N]o rules of practice more efficacious for that purpose [inducing corruption] could have been framed than those which permit the judge to hear, to examine and decide in private: such a system offers strong temptation to the unprincipled, and

---

26. Thomas Ingersoll maintains that the final days of Spanish rule in Louisiana were characterized by levels of corruption that had not existed previously, and this development was responsible for the pejorative views formed by the incoming American officials: "In summary, the groaning descriptions of Spanish law by American officials who arrived in 1803 were based mostly on conditions that developed in New Orleans at the very end of the period when government did indeed become rotten with the love of gold." Ingersoll, *supra* note 2, at 154.
27. In this public debate over property rights, Spanish civil laws were generally perceived by the public in a positive light. Spanish legal authorities were conceded to be controlling, though Livingston's opponents alleged the American judges had misunderstood the meaning of them.
28. "The laws of Spain," he wrote in a public letter, "are generally excellent in themselves; for they are founded on the Roman Code, one of the most perfect and elegant systems of jurisprudence ever promulgated to the world." *Letter of LAELIUS, supra* note 10. Workman once proposed a book subscription to the public in which he would translate the entire Laws of Castile and the Spanish Indies into English.

> has been generally found to have produced a corrupt judiciary wherever it has been long established. On the other hand, where the Judge is obliged to act in public he is himself before the severe and vigilant tribunal of public opinion.[29]

In spreading prejudicial views of this kind, one may wonder whether the highly intelligent Workman was not an unwitting purveyor of the Black Legend in Louisiana.

His early writings contain signs of hispanophobia. In his *Political Essays* (a collection of his earlier writings), Workman deplored the "notorious" oppression of Spanish colonial rule and called for the emancipation of its "enslaved inhabitants." He proposed an invasion of Spanish America and later became an active organizer of a secret society in New Orleans, the Mexican Association.[30] General James Wilkinson arrested him as a Burrite or Burr conspirator during the so-called "Reign of Terror," which led to his being tried on charges of planning an invasion of Mexico. He was easily acquitted, however, because there was no evidence that he had taken active steps to that end.[31]

Prior to his arrival in New Orleans Workman wrote an amusing play called *Liberty in Louisiana* which was published and performed in Charleston in 1804 and subsequently performed in New York, Philadelphia, and Savannah. Apparently the play had a substantial run and was quite successful,[32] though curiously it was never performed in New Orleans where the scenes were located. Could it be that its hispanophobic humor played better with Anglo-American audiences than with Creoles who had experienced the reality of Spanish rule? The play brims with

---

29. *Quoted in* George Dargo, *Jefferson's Louisiana: Politics and the Clash of Legal Traditions* 218 n.76 (revised ed., Lawbook Exchange 2009) (1975).
30. *See* Dan Degges, 'The Mexican Association: The Secret Society Behind the Aaron Burr Conspiracy' (unpublished research paper), Academia, www.academia.edu/4358596/TheMexican_Association_the_Secret_Society_behind_the_Burr_Conspiracy (last visited July 17, 2017).
31. Charles S. Watson, 'A Denunciation on the Stage of Spanish Rule: James Workman's Liberty in Louisiana (1804)', 11 La. Hist. 245, 248 (1970).
32. The performance in Charleston was reportedly received "with the most unbounded applause." *Phila. Gazette*, July 3, 1804. The play ran through three printed editions. *Miss. Herald & Natchez Gazette*, Mar. 11, 1807.

contempt for Spanish colonial justice.[33] A comedy with a political aim, *Liberty in Louisiana* efficiently demonized and defamed the Spanish judges and officials who ruled *Luisiana*. It has been called a denunciation (from the stage) of Spanish rule and Spanish law.[34]

The opening scene takes place in the Hall of Audience of a corrupt Spanish judge, Don Bertoldo de la Plata, pictured on his last day in office in Louisiana, the day before the transfer of power to the American government.[35]

> <u>Don Bertoldo de La Plata</u>: "This, Senor Scrivano, is the last audience I shall hold in Louisiana. I hope it will not be an unprofitable one." [pulls out an empty bag and shakes it]

He calls for the most lucrative case on the docket, and Scrivano summarizes the case of *Don Antonio Gaspar v. Don Felix Pereira*:

> <u>Scrivano</u>: "[Don Antonio demands] to be put in possession of the plantation, consisting of one thousand acres, left him by his father, which Don Felix has, without any pretence or title, seized and occupied for five years past. It appears from the defendant's own declaration, that he has no right whatever to the property in dispute."
> <u>Don Bertoldo</u>: "Tell me not of right but tell me how much the parties have already given."
> Scrivano reports that Don Felix has given one thousand dollars to prolong the suit and has enjoyed five crops from the land, and Don Antonio has given exactly the same sum.
> <u>Don Bertoldo</u>: "Let me see—the parties have given equally, then I decree that the plantation be equally divided between them."
> <u>Scrivano</u>: "Nothing can be fairer."

---

33. Sayali Indulkar, 'Charleston Theatre 1790-1860' (2014) (unpublished M.A. research paper, University of Central Missouri), https://centralspace.ucmo.edu/xmlui/bitstream/handle/123456789/374/Indulkar_THEATRE2.pdf?sequence=1&isAllowed=y.

34. *See* Watson, *supra* note 31, at 248.

35. Here Workman seems to have assumed that Spain ceded Louisiana directly to the United States, without the interim retrocession to France.

No doubt the elegant simplicity of Don Bertoldo's depraved ruling must have produced audience laughter. The purpose was to hold up Spanish despotism to derision and abhorrence. As George Dargo pointed out, the work depicted "the arbitrary, corrupt and heavy-handed Spanish criminal justice system which existed prior to the retrocession to France and the subsequent American takeover."[36] But it may be worth noting that this depiction, written before the author came to Louisiana, caricatured a system that James Workman of Middle Temple had never observed in operation and seemed to know little about.[37] After he had worked firsthand with Spanish law as a lawyer and judge, his views became better informed. Eventually he appraised the merits and demerits of Spanish law with greater discrimination.

The Towering Shadow of the Inquisition

The Spanish Inquisition was an established institution in Spanish colonies, but it was never officially introduced in *Luisiana,* at least not in the form of an *ecclesiatical jurisdiction*.[38] Nevertheless, even at a distance, its presence was felt and feared. The Inquisition's jurisdiction over the importation of prohibited books and materials gave it a particular reason to police behavior in port cities such as New Orleans.[39] Thus in 1786 the Cartagena Inquisition appointed a Capuchin friar in New Orleans to be its investigating Commissary. Father Antonio de Sedella conducted investigations into cases of heresy, blasphemy, bigamy, the reading of books on the Index (which burgeoned with works of

---

36. Dargo, *supra* note 29, at 211-12.
37. Although Workman claimed that he had researched all books about the Spanish colonies in the languages known to him, which included Spanish and French. Watson, *supra* note 31, at 250.
38. O'Reilly introduced, at least nominally, the tribunal of the Saint Hermandad, whose principal object was "to repress disorders and to prevent the robberies and assassinations committed in unfrequented places by vagabonds and delinquents ...." In practice the brotherhood's members worked and were allied with the Inquisition tribunals.
39. Mirow, *supra* note 16, at 28.

the Enlightenment), and lack of orthodoxy among the Indians.[40] He collected dossiers on Louisianians, which in some cases led to their arrest and prosecution when they ventured abroad.[41] After his appointment was renewed and reaffirmed in 1789 by the Inquisitor General of Spain, Père Antoine (as locals frenchified his name) began to assert his authority more forcefully, putting pressure on Governor Esteban Miró to supply him with the necessary troops "to carry on my operations."[42] These demands alarmed the Governor, who had the friar arrested and deported back to Spain. In defense of his action the Governor stated that the spectre of the Inquisition operating in *Luisiana* would be a hindrance to trade, commerce, and the ability to attract foreign immigrants.[43] As he explained to his superior in Madrid, "these foreigners are imbued with, and very frightened of the power of the Holy Office which they consider absolutely despotic and discriminatory, notwithstanding the uprightness, stature, and circumspection of its most just proceedings."[44] It was a tactful warning that the Inquisition's reputation for fanaticism, cruelty, and torture was a serious liability for a Spanish administrator attempting to govern non-Catholics and non-Spaniards. In short, the Inquisition was perhaps the most powerful negative image associated with Spanish law in the popular mind.

---

40. Richard E. Greenleaf, 'The Inquisition in Spanish Louisiana 1762-1800', 50 N.M. Hist. Rev. 45, 51 (1975).
41. The arrest of Don Juan Longouran, a prominent New Orleanian while traveling abroad, led to his trial by the Holy Office in Mexico City. He was subjected to a lengthy incarceration and confiscation of his property. *Id.* at 58-60.
42. "[I]t is necessary that I have recourse at any hour of the night to the Corps de Garde from which I may draw the necessary troops to assist me if they are necessary to carry on my operations." *Id.* at 53-54.
43. The traveler Berquin Duvallon gave this fanciful account of de Sedella's deportation: "Once it was contemplated to establish the tribunal of the inquisition in New-Orleans; but the Monk charged with the mission of the holy office, found himself so obnoxious to the people, that, to avoid being stabbed, or thrown over the pier, he decamped back in haste to Spain." Pierre-Louis Berquin-Duvallon, *Travels in Louisiana and the Floridas, in the Year, 1802* (John Davis transl., New York, I. Riley & Co. 1806).
44. *Id.* at 55.

Creole Mythology

Gilbert Din and John Harkins speak of a Creole mythology of the late 19th century, of which Alcée Fortier and Grace King were leading exponents, that portrayed Spanish government as intolerant, cruel, and corrupt.[45] The mythology characterized Spain's thirty-four year "domination" of Louisiana as a kind of superficial occupation with no lasting effect, except for a few place names to commemorate their stay.[46] French Creoles survived the domination by not learning or speaking Spanish, and French life and culture was uninterrupted in any appreciable way.[47]

The narrative resembles a Creole version of the Black Legend. Certainly it denigrates and minimizes the Spanish contribution to Louisiana.[48] It overlooks, for example, that in material terms Louisiana flourished under Spain as it had never done under France. The population rose from 12,000 under France to 50,000 under Spain; shipping increased many times over; the value of exports rose five fold.[49] After the great fires of 1788 and 1794 reduced New Orleans to ashes, Spain rebuilt the city largely at the Crown's expense, in the process altering its architectural styles.[50] According to Din and Harkins, the long-held idea that French

---

45. Gilbert Din & John Harkins, *The New Orleans Cabildo: Colonial Louisiana's First City Government 1769-1803*, at xvi-xvii (1996).
46. *Id.*
47. Christina Vella, *Intimate Enemies: The Two Worlds of Baroness de Pontalba* 13 (2004):

> French remained the language of the colony throughout the Spanish period—even the deliberations of the Cabildo might lapse into French—and when Spanish was required for a formal proceeding, a translator was generally present. The Spaniards in Louisiana, right up to Governors Gálvez and Miró, married the daughters of Creole planters, served Bordeaux at their official dinners, danced the galopade, sedulously gambled their money at bourré, and reared children who could not speak a word of Spanish.

48. For a full restrospective on the Spanish contribution (demographically, architecturally, linguistically, in the arts, in medicine, etc.), see Jose Montero de Pedro, *Españoles en Nueva Orleans y Luisiana* (1979).
49. Arthur P. Whitaker, 'The Commerce of Louisiana and the Floridas at the End of the Eighteenth Century', 8 Hisp. Am. Hist. Rev. 190 (1928).
50. Richard Campanella, *Bienville's Dilemma: A Historical Geography of New Orleans* 304-08 (2008).

Creoles did not learn Spanish is blatantly untrue. Two of the first newspapers established in New Orleans were in Spanish: *El Misisipi* appearing in 1808 and *El Mensajero* in 1810, indicating that there was a substantial Spanish-literate population. According to one estimate, 50% of New Orleans' white population in 1803 was Spanish, that is, about twelve hundred persons, not including Spanish soldiers and sailors who numbered another thousand.[51]

Perhaps for legal historians the most glaring omission in the Creole narrative is the neglect of Spain's contributions to Louisiana civil law. A demographic effect still reverberating in modern times was the exceptional number of free people of color who gained their freedom as a result of Spanish emancipation laws.[52] Spanish private law governed the lives of Louisiana citizens for decades after the Spanish departed. Under the Digest methodology, Louisiana judges went well outside the rules found in the Digest of 1808 and enforced some of the most obscure provisions of Spanish law.[53] Having mastered the Spanish system, the judges clung to it with unequalled tenacity, refusing to recognize several repeals passed by the Legislature. The situation eventually drove the Legislature to commission the translation of the *Siete Partidas* into English.

The point here is not to refute or correct legends or myths of this sort but rather to suggest they would have had an attitudinal impact on legal decisions in the first codification era. They form one of the extralegal factors that seem to have expedited the expulsion of Spanish law in early Louisiana. They may help us understand why the legislative pattern to be discussed below is clear and consistent.

---

51. Din & Harkins, *supra* note 45, at 10. All of the codifiers mentioned above (*see supra* text accompanying note 14) were literate in Spanish or spoke it fluently.

52. By the time of the Cession, the number of *gens de couleur libre* reached 1819. Din & Harkins, *supra* note 45, at 12.

53. *See* Vernon Valentine Palmer, *Through the Codes Darkly* 141 (2012); *see also* Vernon Valentine Palmer, 'The Quest To Implant the Civilian Method in Louisiana: Tracing the Origins of Judicial Methodology', 73 La. L. Rev. 793 (2013). For enforcement of obscure Spanish laws, see *Cottin v. Cottin*, 5 Mart. (OS) 93 (La. 1817).

THE DISMEMBERMENT OF THE SPANISH SYSTEM

The Dismantlement of the Cabildo

The rejection of Spanish law in the Territory of Orleans started even before the Cession to the United States had taken place. French Prefect Pierre Clément de Laussat, whose Memoirs betray his visceral antipathy toward Spain,[54] by an *arrêté* of 10 November 1803 dismantled the Cabildo, the complex Spanish institution that had exercised unseparated executive, legislative, and judicial powers in *Luisiana*.[55] The abolition of the Cabildo effectively deprived Louisiana of a court system, and his further decree creating a Municipal Council in New Orleans, to consist of a Mayor and twelve Council Members, did nothing to fill the judicial vacuum he had created.[56] The demise of this organ of government would soon create an institutional opening for Governor Claiborne to Americanize the judiciary and court

---

54. See, for example, his description of the Spanish Judge-Advocate, Nicolas Maria Vidal, ("There was not a more diseased heart, a more twisted mind, a more mealymouthed disposition hidden behind a yellow countenance shaded by black ....") but then his effort to generalize Vidal's character traits as being typically Spanish, i.e. "the personification of the Spanish spirit in this country." This appears to be the rhetoric of the Black Legend. Pierre Clément de Laussat, *Memoirs of My Life* (Robert D. Bush ed., Sister Agnes Josephine-Pastwa trans., 1978).

55. On Laussat's twenty days in power and governmental changes he made, see Eberhard L. Faber, *Building the Land of Dreams: New Orleans and the Transformation of Early America* 103-06 (2016).

56. *See* Arrêté 30 November 1803, *reprinted in* Laussat, *supra* note 54, at 30. Laussat acknowledged "le pays se trouve en ce moment sans Tribunaux" but he anticipated that the American government would soon create a court system. At the persistent request of creole planters, Laussat also ordered the repeal of Spanish slave law on December 17, 1803, but this last-minute decree was apparently ignored. ("The members of the local government tormented me to sanction yet one more decree relative to the regulation of the Negroes. They pointed out that they daily felt an extreme need for it. They came back to the charge several times. I kept refusing on the grounds that this was on the eve of my laying down my ephemeral power. Finally, I gave in.") Laussat, *supra* note 54, at 87.

system. In a letter to Madison in late December 1803, Claiborne embraced Laussat's decision completely: "*He [the French Prefect] abolished the Cabildo, or City Council: This body was created on principles altogether incongruous with those of our Government;*—It was in part an Hereditary Council. In action feeble and arbitrary and supposed to be devoted to the views of the Spanish Government."[57] Claiborne soon introduced American-style courts onto the scene, a move which soon made it pointless to continue to use Spanish procedural law and rules of evidence. Those laws were basically incompatible with the way common-law courts operated. Governor Claiborne began to fill the judicial void by establishing a Court of Common Pleas, modeled after the common law tribunal of the same name, which he staffed with American appointees.[58] Thereafter Congress created the Superior Court, a three-judge court on the American pattern, with general jurisdiction in criminal and civil matters.

Replacing Spanish Civil Procedure

Edward Livingston's Practice Act of 1805 became the first legislation to repeal an entire sector of Spanish law.[59] It recognized the Superior Court of the Territory, provided simplified rules for civil causes, established trial by jury, required testimonial evidence to be given in open court, and made the acceptance

57. Letter from Claiborne to Madison (Dec. 27, 1803), *in* 1 *Official Letter Books*, *supra* note 18, at 312-14 (emphasis in original).

58. This court dealt only with civil matters under $3000. It met for the first time on January 10, 1804. The more important cases would go to the Governor's Court. H. Ward Fontenot, 'The Louisiana Judicial System and the Fusion of Cultures 1803-2003', 63 *La. L. Rev*. 1149, 1158 (2003). Claiborne noted in his *Letter Book*, "On my arrival in Louisiana I found a disorganized Government and a dissatisfied People. The colonial prefect had abolished all the former Spanish Tribunals. In lieu of the Cabildo, I found a Municipality, organized upon French principles and no regular Judiciary in existence." 2 *Official Letter Books of W.C.C. Claiborne 1801-1816*, at 354-55 (Dunbar Rowland ed., 1917) [hereinafter 2 *Official Letter Books*].

59. An Act regulating the practice of the Superior Court in civil causes, ch. XXVI, 1805 Stat. 210-60.

of the common law rules of evidence inevitable.[60] Historians have sometimes debated whether Livingston's code of practice was principally inspired by Chancery practice or whether it in fact owed a debt to Spanish procedural ideas,[61] but in truth Livingston's code represented a more revolutionary step than the debate acknowledges. It was designed to regulate an adversarial "trial" in the American sense, that is, a type of trial unknown to Spanish law. The Practice Act presupposed an open, public, adversarial proceeding in the common law manner, in which the judge presided and played no role as a fact gatherer. It represented a sea change from the *in camera*, inquisitorial judicial proceedings formerly conducted by Spanish colonial tribunals. The Practice Act was fundamentally incompatible with the Spanish civil procedure set forth in Governor O'Reilly's Instructions of 1769.

The changeover to the American mode of trial may well have been animated by a confident belief in the superiority of American courts, but it also reflected the low value placed upon Spanish procedural law. Many American lawyers and officials apparently arrived in Louisiana already imbued with negative impressions, and Spanish procedure was a convenient target. American litigants entangled in Spanish courts complained that the proceedings were slow, oppressive, overly written, and lacking in finality. Writing of an experience in the courts of Puerto Rico, one merchant complained that:

---

60. *See* Henry George McMahon, 'The Exception of No Cause of Action in Louisiana', 9 Tul. L. Rev. 17, 19 (1934): "The Practice Act of 1805 ... was nothing less than a grossly inadequate and extremely refined common law system." Professor McMahon later modified his original view, however, finding there was more Spanish influence than he previously thought. Henry G. McMahon, 'The Louisiana Code of Civil Procedure', 21 La. L. Rev. 1, 7 (1960). Professor Robert W. Millar believed that the Practice Act was primarily a refinement and simplification of contemporary American chancery practice. Robert Wyness Millar, 'The Fortunes of the Demurrer', 21 *Ill. L. Rev.* 596, 604 (1937); *see also* Kent A. Lambert, 'An Abridged History of the Absorption of American Civil Procedure and Evidence in Louisiana', *in* Vernon Valentine Palmer, *Louisiana—Microcosm of a Mixed Jurisdiction* 110 (1999).
61. The various points of view are discussed in McMahon, 'The Exception of No Cause of Action,' *supra* note 60, at 8 et seq.

> It is not merely against the results of the adjudications in Spanish tribunals that we have to complain, but against the slow and deleterious nature of their proceedings. With them every thing must be done in writing, and must originate with the governors. No oral testimony is received and no oral pleadings permitted. The accused is [not] confronted with the accuser; the defendant never heard at the same time with the plaintiff. The first step is always a petition to the governor intendant in which the case is stated and justice demanded. He seldom decides himself but refers to the auditor of war, or of marine as the case may be. Perhaps after a detention of a fortnight or three weeks, the judge may decide upon it; perhaps he may refer it to the other party, who applies by another petition which is proceeded upon in a similar manner. Each however or each decree produces a new remonstrance: and thus memorial follows memorial, answer follows answer, and decree follows decree, until circumstances are multiplied to a countless number and the proceeding in a trifling cause swells to immeasurable volume. The process ... would make a volume larger than Coke upon Littleton.[62]

Digression on Spanish Procedure and the Treason Trials

General O'Reilly introduced Spanish procedure in 1769 when he established a Cabildo in New Orleans composed of six regidors and two elected 'ordinary judges' (*alcaldes ordinarios*) in accordance with the *Recopilación de las Indias*. At that time

---

62. Telegraphe & Daily Advertiser (Baltimore, Maryland), Mar. 5, 1806. For a more favorable view of Spanish procedure, see Amos Stoddard, *Sketches of Louisiana: Historical and Descriptive* 281 (Applewood books reprint 2016) (1812) ("The change produced by the operation of the laws of the United States, the dilatory proceedings of our courts, the introduction of the trial by jury, and the expenses of legal contests, gave a temporary check to trade, and to the credit of merchants, particularly in Upper Louisiana. Experience led them [the merchants] to believe, that the Spanish mode of decision, grounded on equitable laws, was much the most wise and salutary; and they murmured at a system calculated to produce delays, and in many instances to create expenses equal in amount to the sums demanded. They preferred the judgment of one man to that of twelve; and it is but justice to observe that their judicial officers were in most instances upright and impartial in their decisions.").

he promulgated, in French, a small Code summarizing the procedures which the alcaldes should follow in deciding civil and criminal cases. It was basically a procedural and administrative guidebook for Cabildo officials and alcaldes, with almost no substantive law content.[63] The Governor explained his purpose as follows:

> And as the want of advocates in this country, and the little knowledge which his new subjects possess of the of the Spanish laws might render a strict observance of them difficult, and as every abuse is contrary to the intentions of His Majesty, we have thought it useful, and even necessary to form an abstract or regulation drawn from the said laws, which may serve for instructions and elementary formulary in the administration of justice and in the economical government of this city, until a more general knowledge of the Spanish language may enable every one, by the perusal of the aforesaid laws, to extend his information to every point thereof.[64]

Thus the O'Reilly Code was not an attempt to summarize or translate the private law of Spain, and it did not make Spain's substantive law accessible to its new Francophone subjects.

The drafters of the code were Dr. Don Manuel Joseph de Urrustia and Don Felix Rey, and their main sources, as identified in their footnotes, were the *Nueva Recopilación de Castilla* and the *Recopilación de las Indias*.[65] Under the regulations, the regidors would elect on the first day of every year two judges (the alcaldes ordinarios). The office of alcalde was to be given to "capable persons" at least twenty-six years of age, though "new converts" to the faith were ineligible. Alcaldes should make their appearance in public "with decency and modesty, bearing the wand of royal justice" and were to "hear mildly" the cases of those who sought justice. An alcalde must be impartial and must

---

63. The one exception is that the code set forth the law governing wills and testaments, apparently due to the practical significance of the subject.
64. *Ancient Jurisprudence of Louisiana*, *supra* note 17, at 2-3.
65. Section II, Article 12, Ordinances and Instructions, *translated in* 1 *La. L.J.* 1 (1841-1842) (Gustavus Schmidt trans.).

recuse himself in certain cases of blood relationship or friendship with an adverse party.

Civil litigation was essentially conducted in writing, beginning with the plaintiff's opening petition and followed by a series of replies, declarations, and exceptions taken by the parties.[66] Criminal proceedings would commence with the judge drawing up a *procès-verbal*, then the conducting an inquiry that led to the *escribano's* draft of a statement of facts. In both civil and criminal proceedings the testimony of witnesses was taken in secret and not made "public" until shared with the parties at a given point later on. The Instructions required that "The testimony of the witnesses shall be so secretly given that neither of the parties shall have knowledge of the depositions of his own witnesses, nor of those of the adverse party." A judge's reasons for judgment were secret too and were not to be revealed. Castilian law, and by extension colonial legal systems, forbade magistrates from issuing a written explanation (*sentencia fundada*) of their decision.[67]

Governor O'Reilly followed these procedures in the treason trials he conducted after his arrival, in which six colonists (headed by Lafrenière) who had revolted against the Spanish Crown were executed.[68] To those accustomed to English or American notions of due process, those proceedings have been remembered, understandably, as appallingly unfair. Historian Henry Plauché Dart relates that the rebels were separated and detained in dungeons, where lawyers brought from Havana conducted a secret investigation.

> It was a secret inquiry, the witnesses ... were examined secretly and under instruction not to disclose either the fact that they had testified nor the substance of their testimony .... It is probable O'Reilly was the sole judge and at best he may have been attended only by his military attachés .... Gayarré's report indicates the accused were not present at this "trial."

---

66. From plaintiff's opening petition down to the taking of an appeal, the procedure called for no less than thirteen written interactions between the parties.
67. Mirow, *supra* note 16, at 52-53; Charles R. Cutter, *The Legal Culture of Northern New Spain 1700-1810*, at 36 (1995).
68. Dart, *supra* note 21, at 27.

> They were convicted, so far as we know, by a decree rendered out of their presence.

The treason trials undoubtedly exacerbated negative perceptions of Spanish justice, but the charge that O'Reilly conducted a *secret* trial may actually amount to the charge that he followed the romano-canonical procedure of Spanish law.

The Swift Overthrow of Spanish Criminal Law

The next blow to the Spanish law in place was struck by the Crimes Act of 1805 drafted by James Workman. In a single stroke, it repealed and replaced the Spanish criminal law with the English law of crimes.

The Crimes Act succinctly listed the English crimes that it recognized, without providing definitions or any elaboration. It then stated that the forms of indictment, method of trial, and rules of evidence would conform to the common law of England.[69] Something of an expository work was thought to be desirable in order to explain the Crimes Act in more detail, so Lewis Kerr in his *Exposition of the Laws of the Territory* set forth the elements of the individual crimes, often relying upon definitions and distinctions drawn from the *Commentaries* of Sir William Blackstone.[70]

---

69. Section 33 of the Act provided:

> That all the crimes, offences and misdemeanors herein before named, shall be taken, intended and construed , according to and in conformity with the common law of England; and that the forms of indictment, (divested however of unnecessary prolixity) the method of trial; the rules of evidence, and all other proceedings whatsoever in the prosecution of the said crimes, offences and misdemeanors, changing what ought to be changed, shall be except as is by this act otherwise provided for, according to the said common law.

An Act for the punishment of crimes and misdemeanors, ch. 50, 1805 Stat. 416-52.

70. Lewis Kerr, *An Exposition of the Criminal Laws of the Territory of Orleans* (New Orleans, Bradford & Anderson 1806). Kerr's English draft was translated into French by Moreau Lislet.

Research has not uncovered any public protest or outcry about this abrupt shift to the English law of crimes, even by the French population. On the one hand the American constitution now imposed the right to trial by jury, the protection of habeas corpus, relief from cruel and unusual punishments, and other guarantees that were either in conflict with Spanish law or in some cases were unknown to that system. Those requirements were not debatable. Spanish criminal law was swiftly overthrown probably because of its unflattering reputation for harsh punishments, use of torture, and secret proceedings closed to the public. Those perceptions helped hasten its exit.

Claiborne's inspection of the prisons in New Orleans may have been the initial catalyst for his later actions. The small cells of the Calabozo, some of which were underground, afforded little light or air. According to Amos Stoddard's description "[the Calabozo] was a wretched receptacle of vice and misery; like the grave it received many tenants, who were soon forgotten by the world: Some of them perished with age and disease, and others by the hands of assassins."[71] Apparently Claiborne became further appalled after his interviews with prisoners. A few weeks after assuming the duties of governor, he gave an account of his impressions to Secretary of State James Madison in a letter dated January 2, 1804. He informed Madison of his intent to make a general jail delivery, which meant freeing all prisoners held in the jails. It appeared he had no trust or faith in the judicial system which had led to their incarceration.

> In the different prisons of this City I have found upwards of one hundred prisoners, some of whom had been there from ten to thirteen years, on Suspicions of Crimes of which it does not appear they were ever convicted; and Some for offences of a very trivial nature .... I have already released five and shall proceed to set I believe the whole at large. Their detention would be attended with a heavy public expense, and would answer no good purpose, as it appears to me very questionable, whether any principle of law would justify our noticing offences of which we had no cognizance at the time of their

71. Stoddard, *supra* note 62, at 154.

> commission. It is also to be presumed that many of them are innocent, and if others less deserving should be included in the general Amnesty, it is more pleasing that our error should be on the Side of Mercy.[72]

Approximately eleven months later Claiborne addressed the Legislative Council and recommended a whole new system. "You will find the existing code of criminal law imperfect and not adapted to the present constitution of the territory."[73] He spoke of the need for an "energetic" system of criminal jurisprudence but not a "sanguinary or cruel" one, and these adjectives may have been an allusion to traits attributed to Spanish law. In replying to a pamphlet highly critical of his administration, he simply remarked, "The criminal System of Jurisprudence could not be preserved for the Liberty of the Citizen was not secured thereby."[74]

The Repeal of Spanish Slave Law

The new Black Code passed in 1806-1807 suppressed Spanish slave law and replaced it with a repressive, security-conscious law of the Creoles' own devising that was drawn from American sources.[75]

The old Spanish *Código Negro*, with its liberal (and thus objectionable) concepts of slave self-purchase (*coartacíon*), recognition of the slave's *peculium* (slave property), religious entitlements, and more egalitarian stance toward free persons of

---

72. 1 *Official Letter Books*, *supra* note 18, at 325-26.
73. *Address to the Legislative Council*, Wilmington Gazette, Feb. 26, 1805.
74. The pamphlet was entitled *Esquisse de la situation.* It appeared anonymously but was widely attributed to Pierre Derbigny. *See* 2 *Official Letter Books*, *supra* note 58, at 356.
75. For details, see Palmer, *supra* note 53, at 115-23. I am treating two different statutes as comprising one Black Code. The first, consisting of forty provisions, was dated June 7, 1806, and was actually entitled "Black Code." The second, entitled "An Act to regulate the conditions and forms of the emancipation of slaves" was dated March 9, 1807, and covered a subject normally dealt with in such a code.

color, had for many years been an irritant to the planters and other slave owners. On more than one occasion during the Spanish domination the wealthy *regidors* who controlled the Cabildo had signaled their displeasure with it, taking steps, ultimately to no avail, to bring about a return of the old French *Code Noir*.[76] From their point of view Spanish law was excessively liberal regarding the emancipation of slaves, and it produced a dangerously large class of free people of color that was a threat to public security. Probably, if the slaves and free people of color could have expressed themselves, they might have said Spanish law was actually preferable to French or American laws since they obtained greater rights under the former. As mentioned earlier, the number of *gens de couleur libre* in the population greatly increased during the Spanish domination as a direct result of it.[77]

The Black Code passed by the Territorial legislature in 1806 was not a civilian document in any sense; it was a crude statute probably drafted by the same committee of the Legislature that authored the 1807 law on slave emancipations.[78] It marked the first occasion when the Creoles felt free to fashion a law of their own choosing, without interference from the French or Spanish Crowns. They now borrowed legal ideas from a reactionary source, the South Carolina Act of 1740.[79] A significant transplant from South Carolina was the establishment of lay tribunals (consisting of "freeholders" sitting with a judge or justice of the peace) to deal with slave crimes. Slave self-purchase was suppressed, and the formerly recognized spiritual entitlements of

---

76. There were two attempts to resuscitate the old *Code Noir* of 1724, once by the Cabildo around 1777 when it produced a draft *Code Noir* or *Loi Municipale*, and again in 1803 when Creole leaders prevailed upon Prefect Laussat to resurrect it. *Id.* at 113.

77. See *supra* note 52.

78. The Legislature resolved in January 1807 "That Messrs. Boré, Parrot and Hazure de L'Orme be a committee to revise the *Black Code.*" —*Orleans Gazette & Com. Advertiser*, Feb. 5, 1807, at 2. One section of the Crimes Act of 1805 directed that slaves would continue to be punished for crimes in accordance with Spanish criminal law, but this vestige of Spanish criminal law was repealed shortly thereafter.

79. For details on this source of slave law, see Palmer, *supra* note 53, at 116-18.

slaves, such as baptism, marriage, Sunday rest, and burial within the church, simply disappeared from the law. In many provisions the Code embodied the *angst* and fear of a society on high alert against slave uprisings.[80] It strictly controlled slave assemblies, free movement, and the amassing of weapons. It provided that any slave away from his usual place without a white accompanying him could be questioned, seized, and subdued by any "freeholder." Many provisions dealt with the capture and return of runaway slaves. The tremors of the slave rebellion in Haiti increased fears of similar uprisings in Louisiana, fears which soon proved warranted. In 1811, a few miles from New Orleans, Louisiana witnessed the largest slave rebellion in the history of the United States.[81]

The Gradual Ouster of Spanish Commercial Law

Gradually but steadily, the American law merchant ousted the Spanish commercial law. At first it was by judicial decisions, rather than legislation, that this began to occur. The main source of commercial law at the time of the Cession was a Spanish Ordinance, the Ordenanza de Bilbao of 1737, and ambiguously enough, this law was never explicitly repealed. What occurred instead was a studied movement, led from the bench, to supple-

---

80. As Christina Vella expressed the level of fear:

> Rumors of rebellion were constantly in the air, and the events at Pointe Coupee and Santo Domingo haunted the whites. "I can recall when our position in this colony was ever so critical," Pontalba wrote to his wife a year after Pointe Coupée, "when we used to go to bed only if armed to the teeth. Often then, I would go to sleep with the most sinister thoughts creeping into mind, taking heed of the dreadful calamities of Saint Domingue, and of the germs of insurrection only too widespread among our own slaves. I often thought, when going to bed, of the means I would use to save you and my son, and of the tactics I would pursue if we were attacked." Pontalba's wife must have had her own sinister fears; when she was a young girl, her father had been murdered by one of his slaves.

Vella, *supra* note 47, at 20.

81. Recounted in Daniel Rasmussen, *American Uprising: The Untold Story of America's Largest Slave Revolt* (2011).

ment, replace, or disregard the Ordenanza. Its "gradual death" commenced as early as the period under study (1805-1808), as the Louisiana judges began to accept American law as authority in such fields as bills of exchange, promissory notes, and insurance.[82]

A Turn 'In Advance' to French Private Law: The Marriage Act of 1807

Adding to this pattern is a statute that was passed immediately before the 1808 Digest. This was the Marriage Act of 1807 in which, without explanation or prior warning, many provisions were taken verbatim or almost verbatim from the *Projet* of 1800 and the *Code civil* of 1804. It was the first clear turning away from Spanish law in a sensitive area of personal law. It mimicked, in technique and sources, the large-scale shift to French law that took place in the drafting of the Digest of 1808, but now with an interesting difference: in 1807 there were no accompanying instructions to the drafter(s) of the statute about permitted sources, and hence there was no question of whether they did or did not follow their instructions.[83] Up to twenty-three provisions of the Marriage Act were drawn verbatim or almost verbatim from these sources. It became a two-step reception of French law. Firstly the redactors of 1807 borrowed directly from the *Projet* or the *Code civil*; then the jurisconsults in 1808 inserted those provisions into the Digest with no alterations whatsoever.[84]

---

82. In the second half of the century, the Legislature took the lead in enacting a host of uniform commercial laws, and before the century was out, Louisiana's law merchant was decidedly American. For details, Vernon Valentine Palmer, *A Descriptive and Comparative Overview, in Mixed Jurisdictions Worldwide: The Third Legal Family* 80 (V. V. Palmer ed., Cambridge Univ. Press, 2012).
83. Because of its style, sources, and subject matter, one suspects the drafters of the Act were probably Moreau Lislet and Brown, but this is conjecture.
84. In some provisions, there is such complete identity between all three sources that it is impossible to be sure about the sequence of borrowing. The English translation in the Marriage Act was also inserted verbatim into the Digest.

(A) The following is an example in which the *Code civil* (1804) provided the source of the Marriage Act (1807) provision, which in turn, both in French and in English translation, became a provision of the Digest (1808):

Code civil, article 212:

Les époux se doivent mutuellement fidélité, secours, assistance.

Marriage Act (1807), section LX, page 127:

Le mari et la femme se doivent mutuellement fidélité, secours et assistance.

Digest (1808), article XIX, page 26:

Le mari et la femme se doivent mutuellement fidélité, secours et assistance.

(B) The following is an example in which the French *Projet* (1800) was the source of the Marriage Act (1807) provision, which in turn, in French and in English translation, became a provision of the Digest (1808):

Projet (1800), article II, page 31:

Elle [la Loi] ne reconnaît que le mariage contracté conformément à ce qu'elle a prescrit.

Marriage Act (1807), section III, page 105:

La Loi ne reconnait que les mariages qui sont contractés et solemnisés conformément aux règles qu'elle prescrit.

Digest (1808), article II, page 25:

La loi ne reconnaît que les mariages qui sont contractés et solemnisés conformément aux règles qu'elle prescrit.

Obviously those who drafted the Marriage Act had copies of the *Projet* and *Code civil* in their possession (it was once incorrectly claimed that only the *Projet* was available).[85] They allowed themselves a certain freedom to depart from Spanish law in this area of personal law. For example the Marriage Act now revived a distinct French institution that did not exist in Spanish law, spontaneously resurrecting an old institution known as the "family council" (*assembleé de la famille*). Spanish law did not recognize this institution (its roots were in the *Coutume de Paris*). It had been expressly abolished by Governor Unzaga's

85. *See* François-Xavier Martin, *The History of Louisiana From The Earliest Period* 344 (New Orleans, Pelican Press reprint 1963).

decree thirty-six years earlier, yet it sprang to life due to the turn toward the *Code civil*.[86]

As mentioned earlier, there were no specific instructions to explain this free dependency on French texts. We also cannot be sure who the redactors were. So far as I have been able to discover, it produced no public expression of surprise or displeasure, either from the Legislature or in the press. It is therefore tempting to believe that this recourse to French sources was expected all along by the Legislature and was, in their minds, consistent with the instructions applicable to the Digest ("to make the civil law the groundwork"), which had been issued in 1806.

THE DIGEST OF 1808 AND THE RETREAT OF SPANISH PRIVATE LAW

Thus far we have seen six instances in which a consistent pattern of rejecting Spanish law took place. This background is often neglected or forgotten in the debate over the sources of the Digest of Orleans. As a backdrop it allows us to ask whether the Digest should be considered a deviation from the pattern or merely a continuation of it.

Commissioned in 1806 and completed in 1808, the Digest was, on the face of the legislative instructions, to have been a continuation of the laws then in force in Louisiana. The Legislative Council and House of Representatives resolved "That the two jurisconsults shall make the civil law by which this territory is now governed, the ground work of said code."[87]

---

86. This was not the only instance of spontaneous reversion to French law in this early period. Professor Baade's research shows that during the Spanish period, formal Castilian law did not govern the notarized marriage contracts except in New Orleans. Paris notarial prototypes were used in the rest of the province. Soon after the Purchase, however, registered marriage contracts in New Orleans stopped following Castilian law and reverted to the Paris notarial forms. *See* Vernon Valentine Palmer, *The Louisiana Civilian Experience: Critiques of Codification in a Mixed Jurisdiction* 78-79 (2005).

87. Resolutions of June 7, 1806, *in Acts Passed at the First Session of the First Legislature of the Territory of Orleans* 214-19 (New Orleans, Bradford & Anderson Printers 1807).

The meaning of these instructions has received different interpretations. For some scholars it is plain that by the words "the civil law by which this territory is now governed," the Legislature instructed the redactors to follow the subsisting Spanish civil law that had been in force since Governor O'Reilly took possession of the province.[88] When the Digest was finally produced, however, it appears the drafters interpreted their remit more widely. The instruction to make *the civil law* "the groundwork" was taken to mean that the civil laws of Rome would form the ground work, not the civil law of a particular national system. The words "ground work" were quantitatively indefinite and fell short of requiring more than a foundation of Roman civil law. This wider reading of the instructions was supported by two other documents in the legislative history of the code—the Declaratory Act of 1806 and the Manifesto of 1806—both of which ranked the sources of the "existing laws" in the following order: first, the Roman civil law; second, the Spanish civil law.[89] The primary emphasis given to Roman civil law would permit

---

88. See Pascal, *supra* note 5.

89. The Declaratory Act of 1806 ranked Roman civil law in first place and treated Spanish law as a secondary source. The Legislature was attempting to answer the question—"What laws are presently in force in the Territory?"—by declaring in part:

> 1. The Roman civil code, as being the foundation of the Spanish law, by which this country was governed before its cession by France and to the United States .... 2. The Spanish law, consisting of the books of the recopilation de Castillo and autos acordados being nine books in the whole; the seven parts or partidas of the king Don Alphonse the learned, and the eight books of the royal statute (fueroreal) of Castilla; the recopilation de indias ....

The Act's full title was "An Act declaring the laws which continue to be in force in the Territory of Orleans, and authors which may be recurred to as authorities within the same." The Act is set forth in full in Elizabeth Gaspar Brown, 'Legal Systems in Conflict: Orleans Territory 1804-1812', 1 Am. J. Legal Hist. 35 (1957).

In *The Manifesto of 1806*, the Creoles spoke of the "old laws," which they desired to keep as being "nothing but the civil or Roman law modified by the laws of the government under which this region existed ...." The document connected these "old laws" of Louisiana to the *ius commune* of Europe by saying: "the Roman law which formed the basis of the civil and political laws of all the civilized nations of Europe presents an ensemble of greatness and prudence which is above all criticism."

either French or Spanish sources of that law (even the works of leading French, Spanish, and English authors expressing the civil law) to make up the foundation of the code. Under this reading, heavy borrowing from codified French law was not necessarily a violation of their instructions. Professor Batiza's research revealed that nearly 85% of the provisions of the Digest had sources in French law, with more than 1500 provisions taken directly from the *Code civil* of 1804 and the *Projet du Gouvernement* of 1800.[90] His research confirmed that Spanish law was the source of a considerable number of provisions, yet in relatively small proportion compared to the far greater number of provisions taken from the French legislation.[91] Batiza's research showed too that the drafters drew upon English, French, and Spanish writers such as Blackstone, Domat, Febrero, and Pothier. Clearly this was a cosmopolitan selection from across national systems. Their decision to choose in this way may have owed much to the liberating influence of natural law thinking on their method. Their decision to take so much material from non-Spanish sources furthered the process of expelling Spanish law from Louisiana.

Concluding Observations

Mitchell Franklin once observed that the Louisiana legal system proposed by the Territorial Legislature in 1806 would have consecrated a complete system of medieval Spanish law in

---

90. *See* Batiza, *supra* note 5, at 11. Professor Pascal dismisses this research as purely "philological" since in his view it does not trace the *substantive* sources of the Digest, but merely dwells upon word and phrase analysis. Pascal, *supra* note 5. Professor Yiannopoulos subsequently analyzed the meaning of the word "sources" and opined that Batiza's use of the word—which identified a verbatim or almost verbatim borrowing as a source—was a "legitimate" one and one which is commonly used by legal historians. Yiannopoulos, *supra* note 3, at 98, 101-02.

91. For example, Batiza's research found that *Siete Partidas* was the source of sixty-seven provisions and *Febrero Adicionado* of fifty-two provisions. Batiza, *supra* note 5, at 12.

Louisiana.[92] The Declaratory Act of that year used compendious terms to designate the law then in force in the Territory of Orleans. Franklin apparently read the Act's broad language as a proposal to receive the ultramarine Spanish system *in globo*. It would have continued the laws instituted by Governor O'Reilly in 1769, though now stating them in a more expansive way that would have produced the same system as then obtaining in Mexico as well as in the whole Spanish colonial world.[93]

In my view, however, the sweeping reception of Spanish law described by Professor Franklin simply could not have been the intent of the Legislature in 1806. By that date, as we have seen, Spanish law had already been substantially expelled from the Territory. The Cabildo had been abolished, and an American court system was in place. Rules of Spanish civil procedure, criminal procedure, and evidence were no longer in force. The English criminal law replaced Spanish penal law. The commercial law was moving toward an American footing. The old Código Negro was about to be repealed.[94] Thus far from resembling the legal system of Mexico or other Spanish colonies, the Territory's legal system resembled in many respects Louisiana's

---

92. Mitchell Franklin, 'The Eighteenth Brumaire in Louisiana: Talleyrand and the Spanish Medieval Legal System of 1806', 16 *Tul. L. Rev.* 514 (1942) [hereinafter Franklin, *Eighteenth Brumaire*]; *see also* Mitchell Franklin, 'The Place of Thomas Jefferson in the Expulsion of Spanish Medieval Law from Louisiana', 16 Tul. L. Rev. 319 (1942) [hereinafter Franklin, *Place of Thomas Jefferson*].

93. Franklin, *Eighteenth Brumaire*, *supra* note 92, at 547. Professor Batiza noted that the Spanish regime in Louisiana replaced the French legal system with a simplified version of the system in force throughout the Spanish Empire. Based primarily on the Compilation of the Laws of Castile and the Compilation of the Laws of Indies, Spanish law in Louisiana was supplemented by other enactments, principally *las Siete Partidas*. R. Batiza, 'The Actual Sources of the Louisiana Projet of 1823: A General Analytical Survey', 47 Tul. L. Rev. 1, 5-6 (1972).

On the other hand, Professor Baade held that O'Reilly's laws transformed Louisiana into a Spanish ultramarine province, governed by the same laws as the other Spanish possessions in America and subject to the same system of judicial administration. Constitutionally, these possessions were part of the Crown of Castile, and their legal orders were derived from Castilian law to the exclusion of other peninsular *fueros*. Baade, *supra* note 3, at 40.

94. The Black code was apparently pending in the Legislature on the date of the Declaratory Act and became law a few days later.

present-day mixed system. It is difficult to see the Declaratory Act as an attempt to undo the sector-by-sector dismemberment of Spanish law that had already taken place. Actually the Declaratory Act avoided that possibility by saving clauses that expressly maintained "the changes and modifications which may have already been made by the Legislatures of the said Territory" and also excluded "whatever might be contrary to the constitution of the United States."[95] In my view the most that could have been expected or intended by the 1806 proposal was a general reception (by reference) of the *substantive* private law of Spain. Even within the private law sector, however, the 1806 proposal was qualified and would have permitted a discerning selection. It emphasized Roman civil law ("which is composed of the institutes, digest and code of the emperor Justinian, aided by the authority of the commentators of the civil law")[96] as the principal legal element to be extracted from Spanish law, as opposed to the idiosyncratic features of Spain's *ius proprium*, such as Castilian fueros, special jurisdictions, and obsolete legal rules. An important indication of Creole sentiment on the eve of codification, the 1806 proposal was intended as a placeholder to last "untill (sic) the Legislature may form a civil code for the Territory."[97] It demonstrated a willingness to preserve Roman-Spanish law, but no more than temporarily; it was meant to give interim protection against the efforts of Governor Claiborne and President Jefferson to implant the common law.

---

95. The full text of the Act is found in Franklin, *Place of Thomas Jefferson*, *supra* note 92, at 323-24.
96. *Id.*
97. *Id.*

A DIGEST

OF THE

CIVIL LAWS

NOW IN FORCE

IN THE

TERRITORY OF ORLEANS,

WITH

ALTERATIONS AND AMENDMENTS

ADAPTED TO ITS

PRESENT SYSTEM OF GOVERNMENT

By Authority.

NEW-ORLEANS:

PRINTED BY BRADFORD & ANDERSON, PRINTERS TO THE TERRITORY.

1808.

Title page
1808 *Digest*

CHAPTER 6

SPANISH LAW, THE *TEATRO DE LA LEGISLACIÓN UNIVERSAL DE ESPAÑA E INDIAS*, AND THE BACKGROUND TO THE DRAFTING OF THE DIGEST OF ORLEANS OF 1808

John W. Cairns

INTRODUCTION

It is tempting to see the work of redaction of the Digest of the Civil Laws Now in Force in the Territory of Orleans of 1808 as an event within the history of the Territory in the United States, and largely contingent on local and U.S. concerns. And, of course, so it was; but this was far from the entire story. Global politics in an era of warring empires had a major impact on the development of thinking about the law in the Territory and on the attitudes of all the inhabitants to the law. Three sets of interlocking events in particular had an understandable and significant impact on the development of the law.

First, the newly acquired U.S. Territory had boundaries, sometimes ill defined, with Spanish colonies. France had sold Louisiana to the United States of America; but for the Spanish the validity of the Louisiana Purchase was questionable. It is easy to understand why. Not only in negotiations to return Louisiana to France had France undertaken not to cede Louisiana to a third party, but the U.S. occupation of Louisiana also threatened the

Spanish territories of East and West Florida—not long regained from the British—and its province of Texas. The U.S. Governor of the Territory of Orleans, William C. C. Claiborne, thus spent much of the territorial period understandably anxious about the intentions of Spain and frustrated and alarmed by the behavior of the local representatives of the Spanish crown, whose activities he saw as likely to encourage the creole population, whom he tended to distrust, in a belief that Spain might recover the Territory.[1] This led him to worry about Spanish troop movements.[2] And indeed his correspondence with the President, Thomas Jefferson, the Secretary of State, James Madison, and the Secretary of War, Henry Dearborn, is full of concerns about the military activities of Spain.[3] Claiborne did not immediately feel secure in the newly acquired territory. The authority of the U.S. government may have seemed potentially fragile.

Secondly, the slave revolt on St. Domingue led by Toussaint L'Ouverture and Jean-Jacques Dessalines not only eventually encouraged Napoléon to sell Louisiana, but it also had a direct impact on the development of the Territory.[4] French colonists and free people of color fled St. Domingue; many of these came to the Territory of Orleans, sometimes with their slaves. This was another group distrusted by Claiborne; but it was one—large, powerful, and often well educated—that had a major impact on

---

1. J.C.A. Stagg, *Borderlines in Borderlands: James Madison and the Spanish-American frontier, 1776-1821*, at 54-56 (2009); Jared W. Bradley, 'W.C.C. Claiborne and Spain: Foreign Affairs Under Jefferson and Madison, 1801-1811', 12 La. Hist. 297, 300-02 (1971).
2. Bradley, *supra* note 1, at 312-14.
3. *See, e.g.*, Letter from William C.C. Claiborne to James Madison (Feb. 26, 1804), *in* 1 William C.C. Claiborne, *Official Letter Books of W.C.C. Claiborne, 1801-1816*, at 387-88 (Dunbar Rowland ed., 1917) [hereinafter Claiborne, *Letter Books*]; Letter from William C.C. Claiborne to Henry Dearborn (Apr. 20, 1804), *in* 2 Claiborne, *Letter Books* 108; Letter from William C.C. Claiborne to James Madison (Oct. 24, 1805), *in* 3 Claiborne, *Letter Books* 211-13; Letter from William C.C. Claiborne to Henry Dearborn (Oct. 30, 1805), *in* 3 Claiborne, *Letter Books* 216-17.
4. *See* Laurent Dubois, 'The Haitian Revolution and the Sale of Louisiana; or, Thomas Jefferson's (Unpaid) Debt to Jean-Jacques Dessalines', *in Empires of the Imagination: Transatlantic Histories of the Louisiana Purchase* 93 (Peter J. Kastor & François Weil eds., 2009).

the culture of New Orleans and the Territory.[5] The refugees from St. Domingue came to New Orleans in waves, first in 1803, and then 1803-1804 after they were expelled from Jamaica, and then in 1809 after they were expelled from Havana.[6] This reflected developments in the war in Europe as well as events on the island. Again, the arrival of these groups worried Claiborne.[7]

Thirdly, as Eberhard Faber has convincingly argued, the brief French regime under Napoléon's *Prefet*, Pierre Clément de Laussat, had longer-term ramifications than has hitherto been thought, contributing to the initial instability of the American regime under Governor Claiborne. Laussat's activities solidified a certain type of francophone nationalism among the creoles that gave them a means of resistance to Jeffersonian republican assimilation, while also presenting images of a possible French future that was never to be, but which would have an impact on the creoles' attitudes to their new government.[8]

These tensions and conflicts played a significant part in the production of the Digest of 1808. The debate initiated by professors Pascal and Batiza over the sources used in compiling the Digest of the Civil Laws Now in Force in the Territory of Orleans of 1808 lacked a significant depth of richness through not paying sufficient attention to them. This debate has probably now run its course.[9] But it is important to say a little about it so that what

---

5. Nathalie Dessens, *From Saint-Domingue to New Orleans: Migration and Influences* 24-28 (2007) (providing the vital demographic study).
6. Nathalie Dessens, 'The Saint-Domingue Refugees and the Preservation of Gallic Culture in Early American New Orleans', 8 French Colonial Hist. 53, 56 (2007); Paul F. Lachance, 'The 1809 Immigration of Saint-Domingue Refugees to New Orleans: Reception, Integration and Impact', 29 La. Hist. 109 (1988).
7. Letters from W.C.C. Claiborne to James Madison (Feb. 6 & Feb. 26, 1804), *in* 1 Claiborne, *Letter Books*, *supra* note 3, at 363-65, 387-88; Letters from W.C.C. Claiborne to James Madison (Apr. 9 & May 8, 1804), *in* 2 Claiborne, *Letter Books*, *supra* note 3, at 88-89, 134; Letter from W.C.C. Claiborne to Robert Smith (Nov. 12, 1809), *in* 5 Claiborne, *Letter Books*, *supra* note 3, at 1-3.
8. Eberhard L. Faber, 'The Passion of the Prefect: Pierre Clément de Laussat, 1803 New Orleans, and the Bonapartist Louisiana that Never Was', 54 La. Hist. 261 (2013) [hereinafter Faber, 'Passion of the Prefect']; Eberhard L. Faber, *Building the Land of Dreams: New Orleans and the Transformation of Early America* 83-117 (2016) [hereinafter Faber, *Land of Dreams*].
9. Rodolfo Batiza, 'The Louisiana Civil Code of 1808: Its Actual Sources and Present Relevance', 46 Tul. L. Rev. 4 (1971) [hereinafter Batiza, 'Actual Sources

follows can be grounded in the existing literature. The ingenious idea that the Digest was French in language but Spanish in essence will probably linger on for a while, as it is now woven into some of the more general discussions of the legal history of Louisiana. It has no doubt joined those other disproven and untenable views that continue to exercise influence—if decreasing—from their graves. But the accumulated weight of evidence is, however, firmly against it.[10] That the Digest is not Spanish law in French dress does not mean, however, that it is entirely French. The issue is much more complicated. The Digest is a unique and fascinating civil code.

All debates are creative in the long run; they stimulate and inspire others to carry out work to prove or disprove differing points of view. But they can sometimes suppress endeavor and new research; and, indeed, the debate over the sources of the Digest was one that has in many ways served to obscure or to distract from interesting questions. For example, some important issues—such as the creativity of the codifiers, James Brown and Louis Moreau Lislet, and the manner in which they collaborated—have become obscured in the heated discussions of whether the code they produced was "French" or "Spanish."

It is tempting to write that the Digest is a code in the tradition of the French *Code civil*; this is correct only in so far as in 1808 it was helping constitute such a tradition, and both it and in particular its successor Civil Code of the State of Louisiana of 1825 were to

---

1808']; Robert A. Pascal, 'Sources of the Digest of 1808: A Reply to Professor Batiza', 46 Tul. L. Rev. 603 (1972); Rodolfo Batiza, 'Sources of the Civil Code of 1808, Facts and Speculation: A Rejoinder', 46 *Tul. L. Rev.* 628 (1972); Joseph Modeste Sweeney, 'Tournament of Scholars over the Sources of the Civil Code of 1808', 46 Tul. L. Rev. 585 (1972). For an overview of the debate, see John W. Cairns, 'The de la Vergne Volume and the Digest of 1808', 24 Tul. Eur. & Civ. L.F. 31, 35-38 (2009) [hereinafter Cairns, 'De la Vergne Volume']; John W. Cairns, *Codification, Transplants and History: Law Reform in Louisiana (1808) and Quebec (1866)* 433-40 (2015) [hereinafter Cairns, *Codification, Transplants and History*]; Asya Ostroukh, Reception of the French Civil Code in Quebec, Louisiana and Francophone Switzerland: A Socio-Legal Study 13-23 (unpublished Ph.D. thesis, University of Edinburgh, 2016).

10. Olivier Moréteau, Book Review, 4 *Comp. Leg. Hist.* 94, 97-98 (2016) (reviewing Cairns, *Codification, Transplants and History*, *supra* note 9); Olivier Moréteau, 'The Louisiana Civil Code in French: Translation and Re-Translation', 9 J. Civ. L. Stud. 223, 229-31 (2016).

exercise significant influence within that tradition.[11] But that civil codes may constitute a tradition does not mean that they are identical. Though very strongly influenced by the *Code civil*, the Digest is also unique and different in all kinds of ways. For example, while the first book of the French code has a significant focus on the idea of citizenship, that of the Digest is organized around the more traditional civilian category of "persons," probably as conceptually better for the inclusion of slavery.[12]

One of the important issues not as thoroughly explored as it might have been is the use of Spanish sources in the early Territorial period, with their impact on the eventual drafting of the Digest. It has long been recognized that contemporaries considered there to have been a problem of access to relevant legal materials in the immediate aftermath of the Louisiana Purchase. This chapter will assess afresh much of the primary evidence of this, often in greater detail than has been done before, to present a new argument about the sources used and the actual work of the codifiers, with a concern for some of the language used.

Here we will first examine the redactors and their work, reflecting on the evidence we have of the task before them and how they carried it out. We will then explore the problem of the sources of the law in the early territorial period, before moving to a consideration of the changing nature of government in the Territory and the impact this had on the issue of codification and sources of law, leading to an act, vetoed by the governor, that set out the sources of law for the Territory. We will next reflect on

---

11. *See, e.g.*, Rolf Knütel, 'Influences of the Louisiana Civil Code in Latin America', 70 Tul. L. Rev. 1445 (1996); Jean-Louis Halpérin, *Le code civil* 135-36 (2nd ed. 2003); Agustín Parise, 'The Place of the Louisiana Civil Code in the Hispanic Civil Law Codifications: Inclusion in the Comments to the Spanish Civil Code Project of 1851', 68 La. L. Rev. 823 (2008); Olivier Moréteau & Agustín Parise, 'Recodification in Louisiana and Latin America,' 83 Tul. L. Rev. 1103 (2009); Agustín Parise, *Ownership Paradigms in American Civil Law Jurisdictions: Manifestations of the Shifts in the Legislation of Louisiana, Chile, and Argentina (16th-20th Centuries)* 139-43 (2016).

12. John W. Cairns, 'Blackstone in the Bayous: Inscribing Slavery in the Louisiana Digest of 1808', *in Re-interpreting Blackstone's Commentaries: A Seminal Text in National and International Contexts* 73, 88-90, 93-94 (W. Prest ed., 2014) [hereinafter Cairns, 'Blackstone in the Bayous'].

the vetoed act and the Spanish law, followed by an assessment of the reaction to the veto and a call for codification. The conclusion will explain why the redactors acted as they did.

CODIFICATION AND CODIFIERS, 1806-1808

In 1806, the Legislative Council and House of Representatives of the Territory of Orleans issued Resolutions appointing "James Brown and Moreau Lislet ... to compile and prepare, jointly, a Civil Code for the use of this territory;" it also instructed them to "make the civil law by which this territory is now governed, the ground work of said code." Brown and Moreau Lislet were to work in consultation with a committee of both houses of the legislature, four from the House of Representatives and two from the Legislative Council, which would monitor their work.[13] The code finally enacted and promulgated in 1808 was entitled A Digest of the Civil Laws Now in Force in the Territory of Orleans, With Alterations and Amendments Adapted to its Present Form of Government.[14]

Both James Brown (1766-1835) and Louis Moreau Lislet (1766?-1832) were recent incomers: Brown from the United States and Moreau Lislet from St. Domingue. Brown was one of the many individuals who came to Louisiana from anglophone North America immediately after the Purchase. Moreau Lislet's situation was more complicated. He came at the time of the first great influx into Louisiana of refugees from St. Domingue.[15] A sense of the lives of these two men is important in explaining their work on the Digest.

---

13. Resolutions of June 7, 1806, *in Acts Passed at the First Session of the First Legislature of the Territory of Orleans* 214-19 (New Orleans, Bradford & Anderson Printers 1807) [hereinafter Resolutions of June 7, *1806*].
14. Act Providing for the Promulgation of the Digest of the Civil Laws Now in Force in the Territory of Orleans, 1808, ch. 29, *in Acts Passed at the First Session of the Second Legislature of the Territory of Orleans* 120-29 (New-Orleans, Bradford & Anderson Printers 1808) [hereinafter Acts First Session of Second Legislature].
15. Dessens, *supra* note 5, at 24-28.

The Virginian-born Brown had studied at Liberty Hall (later Washington and Lee University) and the College of William and Mary before training as a lawyer in Kentucky, where his elder brother (who had trained as a lawyer with Thomas Jefferson) was U.S. Senator after having pursued a public career in Virginia. Through his wife Anna or "Nancy" Hart James Brown was the brother-in-law of Henry Clay. Brown had served as Secretary of State in Kentucky. He was one of the many Americans who came to New Orleans after the Louisiana Purchase in search of lucrative government office to be secured through patronage (which his networks would aid him in acquiring) and opportunities to acquire land and make money. In all of these Brown succeeded, acquiring a substantial plantation on the German Coast upriver from New Orleans, becoming Secretary to the Territory (1804-5), then District Attorney for Orleans (1805), and U.S. Agent to investigate land claims in the eastern district of the Territory (1805). He held these offices during the work on preparation of the Digest, as well as becoming a lieutenant of the militia (1805) and a Justice of the Peace (1806). He later served twice as U.S. Senator for Louisiana after statehood in 1812, before becoming U.S. minister to France in the 1820s.[16] Brown knew both French and Spanish.[17]

Moreau Lislet was born in St. Domingue, the son of Jacob Vincent Moreau and Elizabeth Torel, part of the island's white, French elite.[18] He was evidently marked by his origins in the Caribbean island, as when one critic, Jeremiah Brown, attacked his work on the Digest, he described him as the "St. Domingo

---

16. Jared William Bradley, 'James Brown,' *in Interim Appointment: W.C.C. Claiborne Letter Book, 1804-1805, with Biographical Sketches* 258 (J. W. Bradley ed., 2002).

17. *See* Letter from James Brown to the President [Thomas Jefferson] (Jan. 8, 1805), *in Territorial Papers of the United States. Volume IX. The Territory of Orleans 1803-1812*, at 365-66 (Clarence Edwin Carter ed., 1940) [hereinafter *Orleans Territorial Papers*]. Bradley, *supra* note 16, at 261 points to problems in the translations of the Digest and suggests they indicate that Brown may not have been so skilled in languages as usually suggested. Bradley, however, is unaware of the role of the translators.

18. Alain Levasseur, *Moreau Lislet: The Man Behind the Digest of 1808*, at 71-78 (rev. ed. 2008) [hereinafter Levasseur, *Moreau Lislet*].

Lycurgus."[19] Brown, however, attacked the lawyers from St. Domingue more generally.[20] Moreau Lislet studied law in Paris in the 1780s, and was admitted as an *avocat au Parlement*.[21] There he married Anne Elisabeth Philippine de Peters (his brother-in-law Augustin was also a law student and a future *avocat*). Moreau Lislet's father-in-law Johann Anton (Jean Antoine) was the official painter of the King of Denmark.[22] It is worth noting that Moreau Lislet's sister married another lawyer from St Domingue.[23] Moreau Lislet's guardian in his marriage contract was his distinguished fellow lawyer from St. Domingue and *Conseiller du Roy* in the Council of St. Domingue, Médéric Louis Moreau de St Méry, at the same time both philosophe and defender of colonial slavery.[24] Moreau Lislet was clearly well connected in the legal profession and in the society of St. Domingue. He returned to the island with his wife to hold the office of *Premier substitut du procureur général au Conseil supérieur de Saint Domingue*, based at Cap Français. Apart from a brief spell in Philadelphia during the height of the revolt, Moreau Lislet spent the troubled years of the 1790s in St. Domingue once Toussaint L'Ouverture and Jean-Jacques Dessalines, as the leaders of the revolt, had accepted the validity of French authority in the colony consequent on the French abolition of slavery. Moreau Lislet held various government and legal offices and acted as an attorney for emigrés trying to protect their property, while also trying to keep secure that of his own family. In August 1803, according to a colonial document, Moreau Lislet was sailing from Port Républicain (Port-au-Prince) to Cap Français on government business, when, to avoid enemy ships

---

19. Jeremiah Brown, *A Short Letter to a Member of Congress Concerning the Territory of Orleans* 21 (Washington City, n. pub. 1806) [hereinafter Brown, *Short Letter*].
20. *Id.* at 8-10, 20-22. On the lawyers from St. Domingue, see Dessens, *supra* note 5, at 71.
21. Levasseur, *Moreau Lislet*, *supra* note 18, at 95.
22. *Id.* at 76-77, 95-97.
23. *Id.* at 77-78.
24. *Id.* at 96; Joseph G. Rosengarten, 'Moreau de Saint Mery and His French Friends in the American Philosophical Society', 50 Proc. Am. Phil. Soc'y 168 (1911).

(there was a British blockade), the vessel he was on took refuge in Santiago in Cuba. The British Blockade prevented his return to St. Domingue should he have wished it, but there was already bitter warfare in St. Domingue as the Napoleonic regime tried but failed to establish control over the colony. Moreau Lislet seems to have stayed in Cuba for about a year, before making his way to New Orleans.[25]

Moreau Lislet held a number of patronage posts in the city. For some years he was an official translator. He practiced law, served as judge of the City and Parish of New Orleans (this office allowed him still to practice law and included significant administrative responsibilities), and was appointed to the post of judge of the Superior Court of the Territory (an office in the gift of the President that he declined), as well as being involved in a variety of civic projects. He also served as attorney for the city of New Orleans. After the Territory of Orleans had become the State of Louisiana, he was briefly a State Senator, then Attorney General of the State, while also continuing in private practice and as attorney for the city. He became a member of the Louisiana House of Representatives for a number of years, before being appointed to the Commission to draft the Civil Code. He was now elected a State Senator and participated in a variety of other activities, including practice as an attorney. Despite all these endeavors, he died a poor man.[26]

Thus, in 1806 to 1808, both men, in vigorous middle age, were making their way as highly educated and engaged members of the rising white elite of New Orleans, an elite of merchants, planters, and professionals that transcended the real divisions of language and origins.[27] Both had extensive legal and administrative experience. Brown had better links with the networks of power around Jefferson and the Federal Government, but Moreau Lislet was also forging connections more locally. We know that Brown had earlier been in favor of a code to sort out difficulties

---

25. Levasseur, *Moreau Lislet*, *supra* note 18, at 95-113.

26. *Id.* at 114-66.

27. Faber, *Land of Dreams*, *supra* note 8, at 215-45. The significance of this elite is a strong theme in this important work, which stresses class over ethnic tensions, while not denying the latter.

with the law in the territory, and that he had drafted legislation relating to the administration of justice for the Legislative Council "to assimilate it to the American Jurisprudence."[28] Moreau Lislet's work as a translator of the legislation of the Legislative Council under the first government, and then as translator of the legislation passed by the First Legislature of the Territory under the new constitution, gave him both familiarity with legislative practice and access to the influential men of the Territory, such as Brown. Indeed, Moreau Lislet had translated Livingston's important Act organizing the procedure of the Superior Court, and Richard Kilbourne has persuasively argued that Brown may have co-authored this.[29]

Brown and Moreau Lislet must have been picked, not only because of their legal knowledge, but also because of their knowledge of the French, Spanish, and English languages. Moreau Lislet's year in Cuba will have allowed him to learn Spanish, if he did not know it before, while, virtually from his arrival in New Orleans, he was working in English and French. Jefferson had appointed Brown Secretary of State of the Territory because of "his possession of the languages," and later appointed him to the Superior Court because of his knowledge of French.[30] Brown later told the President that his "knowledge of the French

---

28. Letters from James Brown to John Breckinridge (Jan. 22 & Sept. 17, 1805), *in Orleans Territorial Papers*, *supra* note 17, at 378-80, 506-513, at 507; James Workman, 'A Letter to the Respectable Citizens, Inhabitants of the County of Orleans, Together with Several Letters to Governor Claiborne, and Other Documents Relative to the Extraordinary Measures Lately Pursued in This Territory', *in* James Workman, *Essays and Letters on Various Political Subjects* [107], 113-15 (2nd ed., New York, I. Riley 1809). This might include the Act Regulating Practice of the Superior Court in Civil Causes, 1805, ch. 26, *in Acts Passed at the first Session of the Legislative Council of the Territory of Orleans* 210 (New-Orleans, James M. Bradford 1805) [hereinafter *Acts Passed at the first Session of the Legislative Council*].

29. Levasseur, *Moreau Lislet*, *supra* note 18, at 115-16; *see* Act Regulating Practice of the Superior Court in Civil Causes, 1805, *supra* note 28, at 261; Richard Holcolme Kilbourne, Jr, *A History of the Louisiana Civil Code: The Formative Years, 1803-1839*, at 25-26, 26 n.75 (1987).

30. *See* Letter from the President [Thomas Jefferson] to Governor [William C.C.] Claiborne (Aug. 30, 1804), *in Orleans Territorial Papers*, *supra* note 17, at 281-84; Letter from the President [Thomas Jefferson] to Secretary [James] Brown (Dec. 1, 1804), *in Orleans Territorial Papers*, *supra* note 17, at 341-42.

and Spanish languages and ... reputation ... as a Lawyer ... insured [him] success."[31]

The work on codifying the law that resulted in promulgation of the Digest has generated no surviving records or other archival material. The Resolutions of June 7, 1806, stated that the committee of four members of the House of Representatives and two members of the Legislative Council was to meet "whenever requested to do so by the jurisconsults, in order to examine and to discuss such parts of the new code as may be completed." The committee was to fix the place of meeting and then intimate it to the "jurisconsults," who had to be present at the meeting and were to "have the right to debate." Further, the Resolutions stated that "whenever the opinion of the committee, after the discussion of any article of the new code shall be in opposition with the opinion of the two jurisconsults, this opinion of the committee shall be put down in writing and submitted to the legislature, when the legislature shall take up the discussion of the said code."[32] This committee was known as "the committee for the revision of the civil code," and it had a president.[33] Unfortunately, we do not know who served in this office, nor, indeed, the names of any members of the committee. Thus, Moreau Lislet and Brown drafted and the committee revised. There is no evidence as to how this worked, nor of how Brown and Moreau Lislet worked together, nor of how they cooperated with the committee nor with the translators and other individuals involved in the project, such as clerks.[34]

There is some slight and unclear evidence on the relationship between James Brown and Moreau Lislet. Jeremiah Brown, who opposed the preservation of the Civil Law in Louisiana, stated in

---

31. Letter from James Brown to the President [Thomas Jefferson] (Jan. 8, 1805), *in Orleans Territorial Papers*, *supra* note 17, at 365-66.
32. Resolutions of June 7, 1806, *supra* note 13, at 214-17.
33. An Act Providing for the Payment of Sundry Expences Incurred in Revising and Copying the Civil Code, 1808, ch. 23, *in Acts First Session of Second Legislature*, *supra* note 14, at 92-93.
34. *Id.* (citing the names of the men paid); *see also* Vernon Valentine Palmer, 'The Secret Translators of the Louisiana Civil Codes', Unpublished Paper Delivered to the World Society of Mixed Jurisdiction Jurists, Montréal (June 24, 2015).

November 1806 that, as a common lawyer, James Brown's role was "to serve as a mask" for the designs of those who wished to preserve the Civil Law, as James Brown could "know but little of the civil law and still less of the Bonapartian code."[35] He referred to the fact that the drafting of the code, and hence the choice of the law, was "now left to the two *jurisconsults*," one of whom was "a native frenchman" from St. Domingue. He had already fulminated against what he saw as the malign influence of lawyers from St. Domingue as likely to inhibit the reception of the common law in Louisiana. He now commented of Moreau Lislet that "our St. Domingo Lycurgus is avowedly copying his new code from that of Bonaparte, to the infinite delight of the whole party by whom he is employed."[36] This suggests that Moreau Lislet was dominant in drafting the proposed code. It should be remembered, however, that Jeremiah Brown's aim was to attack the code through its association with the lawyers from St. Domingue;[37] this meant that he necessarily downplayed the role of James Brown. That Jeremiah Brown was so *parti pris* suggests we should take *cum grano salis* his claims that the energetic and well-educated James Brown knew nothing about the French *Code civil* and the civil law generally, and that he was willing to act—or unable to realize he was acting—as some kind of cover for Moreau Lislet's malevolent Gallic scheming. It is difficult to think of Brown as anyone's dupe.

Rodolfo Batiza and Thomas Tucker have suggested that James Brown took no part in the drafting of the Digest.[38] They founded this claim on a statement in the Preliminary Report published in 1823 by the Committee Appointed in 1822 for the

---

35. Brown, *Short Letter*, *supra* note 19, at 36 n.*. The *Short Letter* is dated November 1, 1806: *id.* at [3].
36. *Id.* at 8-11, 21-22.
37. *Id.* at 8-11.
38. Batiza, 'Actual Sources 1808', *supra* note 9, at 28 n.164; Thomas W. Tucker, 'Interpretations of the Louisiana Civil Codes, 1808-1840: The Failure of the Preliminary Title', 19 Tul. Eur. & Civ. L.F. 57, 131-32, 32 n.211 (2004); *see also* Vernon Valentine Palmer, *The Louisiana Civilian Experience: Critiques of Codification in a Mixed Jurisdiction* 21 n.3 (2005) [hereinafter Palmer, *Louisiana Civilian Experience*]. Palmer cautiously describes Moreau Lislet as the "mastermind."

Revision of the Civil Code.[39] After an account of proposals to perfect the proposed new Code, and reflections on the respective roles of the judiciary and the legislature in doing so, the Committee made an interesting set of remarks on the Digest. It is necessary to quote them at length so the context can be understood:

> Its rules being concise, and in general easily understood, have been read by the people and have enabled them to avoid disputes, on the subjects embraced by its provisions, that without them, would have led to endless litigation; and if some parts have given rise to questions of construction, they have arisen chiefly either from a faulty translation, or from errors inevitably attending a work so hastily compiled. Sufficient time was not given for an accurate examination of the existing Law in its various sources. No decisions had then been reported to throw light on their operation, and the unaided exertions of one person were not sufficient for the completion of the task.[40]

This quotation has a variety of interesting implications. First, it suggests that the Digest had largely been a success in resolving the immediate legal problems faced in the Territory. Secondly, it emphasizes the speed of compilation of the Digest as a factor in any defects that it might have. Thirdly, it states that because of the lack of time devoted to preparing the Digest, the "existing Law" had not been thoroughly examined "in its various sources." Moreover, there were as yet no "decisions ... reported" to throw light on "their operation." Grammar would suggest that this refers to the "sources"; but this must mean something like operation of the "existing Law." The following comment is the crucial one for Batiza's and Tucker's claims: "and the unaided exertions of one person were not sufficient for the completion of the task." They took this as meaning that Moreau Lislet *alone* compiled the Digest; but this is not in fact what the passage

---

39. Tucker also alludes to a tradition that Brown left the Territory: Tucker, *supra* note 38, at 131-32, 32 n.211. This is inaccurate.

40. Edward Livingston, Louis Moreau Lislet & Pierre Derbigny, 'Preliminary Report of the Code Commissioners (Feb. 13, 1823)', *in Louisiana Legal Archives. Volume 1. A Republication of the Project of the Civil Code of Louisiana of 1825*, at LXXXV, XCIII (1937) [hereinafter Livingston, Moreau Lislet & Derbigny, 'Preliminary Report'].

states. The "task" referred to must be the collecting of the decisions or, most likely, the investigation of the existing law, not the drafting of the Digest, which was, after all, a task that was completed. The previous two paragraphs in the Preliminary Report had been devoted to the relationship between the Code enacted by the legislature and the role of the judges in interpretation. Thus, this provides no real or, at best, very ambiguous evidence that Moreau Lislet was the sole author of the Digest.

There are two further, more reliable, pieces of evidence. The first is the address Governor Claiborne made to the Legislature in 1808, in which he stated that the work of compiling the Digest "principally devolved" on one Gentleman, who "evidenced a great share of zeal."[41] If this is a reference to Moreau Lislet, as surely it must be, then it does not mean he drew it up on his own, but only that he took on the greater proportion of the work, a conclusion in line with Jeremiah Brown's critical remarks. The second piece of evidence comes from legislation. By January 1807, work on the Digest was proceeding apace.[42] On April 14, 1807, Governor Claiborne signed an Act of the Territorial Legislature providing for the payment to Brown and Moreau Lislet of $2000 each, three-fifths to be paid immediately, with the remainder to be paid on completion of the Digest. Brown may have been well connected in Washington; but, if he had made no contribution or very little contribution, such a payment would seem unlikely and would surely have caused comment, if not scandal, in the febrile political atmosphere of 1807.[43] Underscoring this is the fact that, by now, the governor considered Brown

---

41. Letter from Governor Claiborne to the Legislature (Mar. 31, 1808), *in Orleans Territorial Papers*, *supra* note 17, at 780.

42. The Code was "far advanced" according to Julien Poydras President of the Council, in Reply to Governor W.C.C. Claiborne's Address to the Legislature (Jan. 22, 1807), *in* 4 Claiborne, *Letter Books*, *supra* note 3, at 110-12, at 111.

43. An Act To Fix the Compensation To Be Allowed to the Two Jurisconsults, Appointed to Prepare a Civil Code for the Use of the Territory of Orleans, by the Resolution of Both Branches of the Legislature of this Territory, Under the Date of June the 7th, 1806, and to the Translators of the Said Code, 1807, ch. 31, *in Acts Passed at the Second Session of the First Legislature of the Territory of Orleans 190-93* (New-Orleans, Bradford & Anderson Printers 1807) [hereinafter *Acts Passed at the Second Session of the First Legislature*]; *see also* Cairns, *Codification, Transplants and History*, *supra* note 9, at 77-78.

to be a political enemy, largely because of his association with Edward Livingston.[44]

Thus, we can see Moreau Lislet as leading the project under the direction of the Legislature's committee, working with Brown, the two translators, and other assistants.[45] It was the committee that had the authority to appropriate funds for the expenses of copying, translating, and the like.[46] Governor Claiborne stated that the Digest was drafted in French and translated into English. He also stated that the English translation was very poor indeed.[47] Moreau Lislet made a similar remark in court in 1822.[48] As Batiza has pointed out, the matter is obviously rather more complicated than that, since there are a number of articles drawn from the text of Blackstone's *Commentaries on the Laws of England* in which the language of drafting was presumably English, with the text translated into French.[49] Indeed, Guzmán has recently shown that the redactors also drew on Edward Christian's notes to Blackstone;[50] again, these articles must have been drafted in English with a subsequent translation into French.

It is easy to imagine Moreau Lislet and Brown working together, dividing tasks, drawing up an outline of the Digest, filling it in with articles, moving between French and English, working with the translators and others associated with the work (seven

---

44. Bradley, *supra* note 16, at 262-63.

45. In 1807, the Legislature awarded each of the two translators $750, with three-fifths to be paid immediately and the remainder on completion: *An Act to Fix the Compensation To Be Allowed*, *supra* note 43, at 192-93.

46. Resolutions of June 7, 1806, *supra* note 13, at 218-19.

47. Letter from Governor [W.C.C.] Claiborne to the Legislature (Mar. 31, 1808), *in Orleans Territorial Papers*, *supra* note 17, at 780; Letter from Governor [W.C.C.] Claiborne to the Secretary of State [James Madison] (Oct. 7, 1808), *in Orleans Territorial Papers*, *supra* note 17, at 802-03.

48. "We have nothing to do with the imperfections of the translation of the *Code*—the French text in which it is known that work was drawn up, leaves no doubt." Dufour v. Camfranc, 11 Mart. (O.S.) 675, 701 (La. 1822), *quoted in* John H. Tucker, 'Source Books of Louisiana Law', 6 Tul. L. Rev. 280, 285 (1932).

49. Batiza, 'Actual Sources 1808', *supra* note 9, at 13-14, 25-28; *see also* Cairns, 'Blackstone in the Bayous', *supra* note 12, at 81-84.

50. Alejandro Guzmán Brito, 'Las fuentes de las normas sobre interpretación de las leyes del "Digest des lois civiles" ("code civil") de la Luisiana (1808/1825)', 31 Revista de estudios histórico-jurídicos 171, 185 (2009).

men in total),[51] and reporting to the Legislature's Committee for the Revision of the Civil Code, with Moreau Lislet taking the lead and perhaps undertaking the bulk of the work.

SOURCES OF LAW, 1804-1806

The precise original intention (supposing there was one) lying behind the drafting of the legislative phrase "the civil law by which this territory is now governed" (les lois civiles qui régissent actuellement ce Territoire) as forming "the ground work" (base) of the Code can only be the subject of speculation.[52] It was later to be loosely echoed in the extended title given to the Digest in 1808.[53] This issue will be returned to below.

From a modern perspective it is obvious that the law theoretically in force at the time of the Purchase was Spanish colonial law—the Laws of the Indies—which provided, in default of provision in the colonial laws, for Castilian law to be applied.[54] During the brief French period in 1803, Napoléon's *Préfet*, Pierre Clément de Laussat, had made significant structural reforms, notably replacing the Spanish Cabildo with a Municipal Council;[55] but he had not changed the substantive law in force, except as regards slavery, though this reform does not seem to have had any significant impact on practice.[56] Indeed the Act for the Punishment of Crimes and Misdemeanors of 1805 specifically

---

51. Act Providing for the Payment of Sundry Expences, *supra* note 33, at 92-93.
52. Resolutions of June 7, 1806, *supra* note 13, at 214-15.
53. See the important discussion in Asya Ostroukh, 'The Mystery of the Mixité Around the Title of the Louisiana Digest of Civil Laws of 1809', 62 Loy. L. Rev. 725 (2017).
54. Cairns, *Codification, Transplants and History*, *supra* note 9, at 44-48, 53-54.
55. *See, e.g.*, Faber, 'Passion of the Prefect', *supra* note 8; Julien Vernet, 'More than Symbolic: Pierre Clément de Laussat's Municipal Council and French Louisianan Protest Against American Territorial Government', 4 French Colonial Hist. 133 (2003); André Lafargue, 'Pierre Clement de Laussat, Colonial Prefect and High Commissioner of France in Louisiana: His Memoirs, Proclamations and Orders', 20 *La. Hist. Q.* 159 (1937).
56. Pierre Clément de Laussat, *Memoirs of My Life* 87 (Agnes-Josephine Pastwa trans., 1978); Hans W. Baade, 'The Law of Slavery in Spanish Luisiana, 1769-1803', *in Louisiana's Legal Heritage* 43, 70-74 (Edward F. Haas ed., 1983).

stated it was not to apply to any slave and that "every slave accused of any crime shall be punished according to the laws of Spain for regulating her colonies."[57] In the Territorial period to 1808, a common-law-style court system was introduced, as well as English-style criminal law, while there had been major reform of the law on slavery in 1806 and of that on marriage in 1807.[58] Study of surviving records shows this legal regime in practice.[59]

But it is wrong to assume that the redactors would necessarily have based their new code on Castilian law, understanding it as the "civil law by which this territory is now governed."[60] They neither had the clarity of hindsight nor—one suspects—a strict and narrow sense of legislative positivism. All that one can know for certain is what the redactors in fact did; study of the provisions of the Digest can reveal with some degree of certainty what they considered, rejected, and adapted to create the new code. Much, of course, was taken from the *Code civil des Français* of 1804, its *projet* of 1800, and territorial legislation; but the redactors also drew on provisions and texts of Castilian law, Roman law, Blackstone's *Commentaries*, Christian's notes to Blackstone, and even the translation of Blackstone into French.[61] They may even have drawn on other sources as yet unrecognized. In fact, the men who compiled the Digest of the Civil Laws were

---

57. An Act for the Punishment of Crimes and Misdemeanors, 1805, ch. 50, § 47, *in Acts Passed at the first Session of the Legislative Council*, *supra* note 28, at 416, 450.
58. Mark F. Fernandez, *From Chaos to Continuity: The Evolution of Louisiana's Judicial System, 1712-1862*, at 16-39 (2001); Warren M. Billings, 'A Neglected Treatise: Lewis Kerr's Exposition and the Making of Criminal Law in Louisiana', 36 *La. Hist.* 261 (1997) [hereinafter Billings, 'Neglected Treatise']; Warren M. Billings, 'Origins of Criminal Law in Louisiana', 31 La. Hist. 63 (1991); Kilbourne, *supra* note 29, at 17-30; Vernon Valentine Palmer, 'The Strange Science of Codifying Slavery', 24 *Tul. Eur. & Civ. L.F.* 83, 94-101 (2009); An Act Concerning the Celebration of Marriages, 1807, ch. 17, *in Acts Passed at the Second Session of the First Legislature*, *supra* note 43, at 102-31.
59. Kilbourne, *supra* note 29, at 44-60.
60. Such a false assumption in part underlies the views of Robert Pascal in the Pascal-Batiza debate: *see* Pascal, *supra* note 9 (responding to Batiza, 'Actual Sources 1808', *supra* note 9).
61. Batiza, 'Actual Sources 1808', *supra* note 9, at 36-44; Palmer, *Louisiana Civilian Experience*, *supra* note 38, at 19-49; Guzmán Brito, *supra* note 50, at 185; Cairns, 'Blackstone in the Bayous', *supra* note 12, *at 81-84*.

creative and eclectic in the choices they made in drafting their code, even if they relied most on that of France and its *projet*. A hundred years later, F. P. Walton was jocularly to remark that "[c]odifiers are arrant thieves;"[62] this comment was already applicable to Moreau Lislet and Brown.

Moreover, for a period around the U.S. takeover of the colony, there had been considerable uncertainty over knowledge of the laws in force and problems with their accessibility. This created a potential for confusion. Thomas Jefferson had sought information about the province, including its laws, from a number of interlocutors.[63] One of them, possibly William Dunbar, told him, perfectly correctly, that "the province is governed entirely by the laws of Spain, and ordinances formed expressly for the colony."[64] But there was an initial measure of confusion, perhaps arising from the perception of the colony as "French." Thus, in August 1803, Governor Claiborne wrote to President Jefferson:

> Louisiana, like most other Countries which have undergone a change of Masters, derives many of its Municipal Customs & regulations from different sources; By what kind of Laws, the French formerly governed the Province is unknown to me.— After its session [*sic*] by them to Spain, General O'Reily [*sic*] the Governor of the Province, published a Collection of Laws (as I am informed) of a general nature, but few in number. But whether that small code was a selection from the previous Laws of the Country, to which he intended to give new force, or were certain Ordinances, then for the first time promulgated

---

62. F.P. Walton, 'Civil Codes and Their Revision: Some Suggestions for the Revision of the Title "Of Ownership"', 1 *S.L.Q.*, 95, 116 (1916).
63. George Dargo, *Jefferson's Louisiana: Politics and the Clash of Legal Traditions* 190-93 (rev. ed. 2009) [hereinafter Dargo, *Jefferson's Louisiana*].
64. 'Condition of Louisiana in 1803, When the American Government Took Possession', *in* 2 Joseph M. White, *A New Collection of Laws, Charters and Local Ordinances of the Governments of Great Britain, France and Spain, Relating to the concessions of Land in Their Respective Colonies; Together with the Laws of Mexico and Texas on the Same Subject* 690-698, at 692-693 (Philadelphia, T. & J. W. Johnson 1839). The late Professor J.W. McKnight brought this to my attention. He speculated that these may be the lost answers of William Dunbar of Natchez, especially since some of the answers suggest the author was not in New Orleans.

> by authority of the new Government, I have not ascertained. O'Reily's Code is said still to be in print, but I have not been enabled to procure a Copy. Under the Spanish government at present, the Laws are enacted in the Council of State by order of the King. But in cases of small local Concern; I understand that the Governor General, with the advice of certain other officers of State at New-Orleans, has occasionally published some Regulations providing for the redress of Grievances in a summary way.[65]

Daniel Clark had less excuse for uncertainty, having lived in New Orleans since the 1780s;[66] but he nonetheless informed Jefferson: "The Code of Laws is derived from the Recopilacion de Indias, & Leyes de Castilla & les uses & *Coutumes de Paris* for what respects usages & Customs."[67] He may simply have been mistaken, or perhaps he was referring to the continuance outside New Orleans of French "folkways" of the type noted by the late Professor Hans Baade.[68] Edward Livingston wrote to his brother:

> The Spaniards when they took possession of the Province abrogated the French and introduced the Spanish laws. Laussat during his ephemeral reign restored a very important part of the French municipal law, and when he gave over the country to us we promised to preserve its laws until they should be altered by the constituted authorities. The Governor having the powers conferred on him by the president of both Governor General and Intendant conceives himself authorized to legislate and his ordinances in English mixed with those of his predecessors in Spanish and French, the laws of Castille, the Cus-

---

65. Letter from Governor [William C.C.] Claiborne to the President [Thomas Jefferson] (Aug. 24, 1803), *in Orleans Territorial Papers*, *supra* note 17, at 16-25, at 19.
66.On the Irish Old Etonian, Clark, *see, e.g.*, Julien Vernet, *Strangers on their Native Soil: Opposition to United States' Governance in Louisiana's Orleans Territory, 1803-1809*, at 13-14 (2013). Clark features extensively in Vernet's book.
67. Letter from Daniel Clark to the Secretary of State [James Madison] (Sept. 8, 1803), *in Orleans Territorial Papers*, *supra* note 17, at 28-47, at 35.
68. Hans W. Baade, 'Marriage Contracts in French and Spanish Louisiana: A Study in Notarial Jurisprudence', 53 Tul. L. Rev. 1, 57-75, 79-80 (1978); Hans W. Baade, 'The Bifurcated Romanist Tradition of Slavery in Louisiana', 70 Tul. L. Rev. 1481, 1482 (1996).

> toms of Paris, the Leyes de Partidas, les Edits du Roi, the Statutes of the United States, and the omnipresent Common Law of England make a confusion worse than that of babel ... .[69]

Of course, Livingston was writing in a rhetorical style both to amuse his brother and to convey an understanding of the complexity of the situation; but his acceptance that there might plausibly still be some French law in force or with some type of authority is notable. At much the same time, the authors of the Louisiana Remonstrance, another work written in a highly-colored rhetorical style, in discussing the first Territorial period, painted a similar picture. Its authors complained to Congress of

> the involuntary errors, of necessity committed by judges uncertain by what code they are to decide, wavering between the civil and the common law, between the forms of the French, Spanish, and American jurisprudence, and with the best intentions unable to expound laws of which they are ignorant, or to acquire them in a language they do not understand.[70]

It certainly did not take long for the new Governor to have a more precise grasp of the actual situation in law. In October 1804, the arrival of J. B. Prevost to serve as judge of the new court prompted him to write to the Secretary of State that the introduction of common-law forms would mean the court would "be accused by the designing few, of making injurious innovations on the Spanish law," as indeed he himself already had been.[71] But knowing that the law was Spanish merely revealed other problems. In 1803, Jefferson had also asked his corre-

---

69. Letter from Edward Livingston to Robert Livingston (May 6, 1804), *quoted in* Dargo, *Jefferson's Louisiana*, *supra* note 63, at 196-97.
70. 'Remonstrance of the People of Louisiana, Against the Political System Adopted by Congress for Them', *in* 1 *American State Papers [Miscellaneous], Documents, Legislative and Executive, of the Congress of the United States, From the First Session of the First to the Second Session of the Tenth Congress, Inclusive* 396, 396 (Walter Lowrie & Walter S. Franklin eds., Washington, Gales & Seaton 1834).
71. Letter from Governor [William C.C.] Claiborne to the Secretary of State [James Madison] (Oct. 29, 1804), *in Orleans Territorial Papers*, *supra* note 17, at 317.

spondents about the sources of the law. Claiborne, as already quoted, simply stated that he had not been able to obtain a copy of O'Reilly's code; Clark, however, rather dishearteningly replied that "The Marquis de Yrujo & John Vaughan of Philadelphia had copies of the Spanish laws,—the French uses & Coutumes may I presume be easily found among the booksellers of the United States, they are not to be had here."[72] Yrujo was the Marques de Casa Irujo, Spanish minister to the United States from 1796-1808;[73] John Vaughan was the Philadelphia wine merchant, who, from 1803, was Librarian of the American Philosophical Society.[74] The correspondent who may be Dunbar simply stated: "it is believed that no correct code can possibly be procured; excepting only a few ordinances promulgated and printed by order of General O'Reilly, respecting principally the laws of inheritance and rights of dower."[75]

It is thus clear that access to the laws was a major problem, once it had been recognized that the law applicable in the Territory of Orleans was the Spanish colonial law as found in the Laws of the Indies, with a default reference to the Laws of Castile. Also, once the U.S. Government started to organize its newly acquired colony—first through the Governor, then the Governor with the appointed Legislative Council, and finally the Governor and Territorial Legislature—new sources of law and new legislation developed that had to be accommodated to the existing law of Spanish origin, which in itself had to be accommodated to the principles of the U.S. constitution.

A decade later, in the course of the long-running dispute over the New Orleans Batture, Edward Livingston explained reasonably clearly what these laws were and the main sources:

---

72. Letter from Daniel Clark to the Secretary of State [James Madison] (Sept. 8, 1803), *in Orleans Territorial Papers*, *supra* note 17, at 28-47, at 35.

73. Eric Beerman, 'Spanish Envoy to the United States (1796-1809): Marques de Casa Irujo and His Philadelphia Wife Sally McKean', 37 Americas 445 (1981).

74. Roy Goodman & Pierre Swiggers, 'John Vaughan (1756-1841) and the Linguistic Collection in the Library of the American Philosophical Society', 138 Proc. Am. Phil. Soc'y 251 (1996).

75. 'Condition of Louisiana in 1803, When the American Government Took Possession', supra note 64, at 693.

> A code had long been prepared for the government of the Spanish colonies in the *Indies*, by which name they designated all their American possessions. It is called the "*Recopilacion de las Leyes de las Indias*." It introduced the law of Castile, those of the Partidas, and of Toro; that is to say, the whole body of the laws of Spain, in all cases not provided for by the laws of the Indies, and declares that the laws of that collection shall prevail in all the Spanish colonies, as well those then established, as those which might in future be discovered or established.[76]

Thus, to know what the law in Louisiana might be, it was necessary to examine a variety of collections. The matter was rather more complex than the quotation from Livingston might suggest. First to be considered was the *Recopilación de leyes de los reinos de las Indias* of 1680, which collected together Spanish colonial legislation, and any other general legislation for the Indies or legislation specifically for Louisiana. One law in this *Recopilación* stated that if there were no such laws, then recourse was to be had to the laws of the kingdom of Castile in conformity with those of Toro.[77] The *Leyes de Toro* dated from 1505 and, in their first provision, set out a hierarchy for Castilian law: first the *Leyes de Toro* themselves; second, the *Ordenamiento de Alcalá* and other *ordenamientos* and *pragmaticas*; third, *fueros municipales y reales*, especially the *Fuero real*, and last the *Siete Partidas*. Although the *Siete Partidas* were last in precedence, they were in effect the most important source. Of great practical significance was the *Nueva Recopilación de las leyes de estos reynos*, first issued in 1567, that gathered together much Castilian legislation to that date, including, for example, many of the laws of Toro. In 1745, a collection of *Autos Acordados*, that is of further Castilian laws, was published arranged in the order of the *Recopilación*. As well as these sources, there were important commentaries and glosses, notably those of Gregorio López on the *Siete Partidas*, Antonio Gómez on the *Leyes de Toro*, and Alfonso Díaz de Montalvo on the *Fuero real*, as well as more

---

76. Edward Livingston, *An Answer to Mr. Jefferson's Justification of his Conduct in the Case of the New Orleans Batture* 31 (Philadelphia, William Fry 1813).
77. *Recopilación de leyes de los reinos de las Indias* II.i.2 (4th imp., Madrid, viuda de D. Joaquin Ibarra 1791).

general juristic literature. Further, the *Siete Partidas* were Romanizing in effect, and Roman law had a significant impact on the interpretation and development of the law of Castile. It is finally worth noting that on any topic it might be necessary to consult a number or even all of the collections to develop a picture of the law.[78] One modern author, reflecting on the Spanish legal system at the end of the eighteenth century, described the range and multitude of texts, both of royal and canon law, along with the practice of using Roman law in support, together with the huge number of authors who had commented on the texts, as constituting a labyrinth for the lawyer trying to find relevant doctrine and current legislation.[79]

Anxiety about the law in the early territorial period might indeed seem a sensible response to the circumstances. The makeshift judicial system put together by Claiborne pending Congress's establishment of a more regular government for its new colony must have been the initial cause of disquiet. As the population increased and more lawyers entered the Territory, the fact that most of the laws in force were written in Spanish was hardly desirable for a population that tended to be either anglophone or francophone; that copies of these laws were also not readily obtainable was a further problem. Jeremiah Brown commented that, "at the time of the transfer to the United States ... there was scarcely a law book in the country except those of the intendant and the auditor."[80] Brown is an overtly hostile source; but Allan B. Magruder still stated in 1807 that in "civil concerns, rules of right are sought from a thousand sources, often enveloped in the mysteries of unknown languages, and the unwritten customs and usages of the descendants of European

---

78. *See, e.g.*, Kate Wallach, *Biographical History of Louisiana Civil Law Sources: Roman, French and Spanish* 61-79 (1955); Cairns, *Codification, Transplants and History*, *supra* note 9, at 44-52. On the Autos Acordados, see now José Luis Bermejo Cabrero, 'Nueva Recopilación y Autos Acordados (1618-1745)', 70 Anuario de Historia del Derecho Español 37 (2000).

79. José M. Mariluz Urquijo, 'El "Teatro de la legislación universal de España e Indias" y otros recopilaciones indianas de carácter privado', 8 Revista del Instituto de Historia del Derecho 267, 267 (1957).

80. Brown, *Short Letter*, *supra* note 19, at 14.

nations ... ."[81] As late as 1811, François Xavier Martin, then one of the judges of the Superior Court of the Territory, remarked that the "arduous task" imposed on the judges of the Territory of examining and comparing "a number of foreign laws" was made "extremely so here, from the scarcity of the works of foreign jurists."[82] It is easy to imagine that the situation had been even more extreme in the earlier territorial period. Such information as there is about the book trade in territorial Louisiana tends to confirm that law books would not be readily accessible, even if we find mention of some in newspaper advertisements.[83]

LEGISLATURES AND CODES

Congress had established a first level of territorial government by an act passed on March 26, 1804 that came into force on October 1. This formally divided the Territory of Orleans from the rest of the former huge province of Louisiana.[84] It continued "the laws in force" as in effect.[85] It created a Legislative Council, the members of which were to be appointed by the President;[86] it also erected a superior court, empowering the legislature to create inferior courts.[87] The Legislative Council first met on December

---

81. *Quoted in* Dargo, *Jefferson's Louisiana*, *supra* note 63, at 199.
82. François-Xavier Martin, 'Preface', *in* 1 François-Xavier Martin, *Orleans Term Reports, Or Cases Argued and Determined in the Superior Court of the Territory of Orleans* [iii], v (New-Orleans, John Dacqueny 1811). On Martin, see Michael Chiorazzi, 'François-Xavier Martin: Printer, Lawyer, Jurist', 80 Law Libr. J. 63 (1988).
83. John M. Goudeau, 'Booksellers and Printers in New Orleans, 1764-1885', 5 J. Libr. Hist. 5, 7-11 (1970); Roger Philip McCutcheon, *Books and Booksellers in New Orleans, 1730-1830*, 20 La. Hist. Q. 606, 610-11 (1937).
84. 'An Act Erecting Louisiana into Two Territories, and Providing for Temporary Government Thereof, 1804, ch. 38, § 1', *reprinted in* 2 U.S. Congress, *Public Statutes at Large of the United States of America* 283-89, 283 (Richard Peters ed., Boston, Charles C. Little & James Brown 1845).
85. *Id.* § 11, at 286.
86. *Id.* § 4, at 284.
87. *Id.* § 5, at 284.

4, 1804.[88] The recently arrived Judge Prevost convened the Superior Court for the first time on November 5, 1804.[89] By December 19, he was pointing out to Madison the difficulties with the legal system, and the problems with reconciling "the antient laws of the country with the provisions of the act organizing this government and with the principles of our Constitution." He had concluded that a code was what was necessary to resolve the difficulties. He accordingly informed Madison that he had

> interested [himself] much with the Council to induce them to employ some of the bar in forming a code of laws, they have at length consented to unite Mr Brown and Mr Livingston for the purpose, the governor however opposes this arrangement either from an enmity to the[se g]entlemen or from a persuasion that the laws of Tennessee se[ver]al of which he has actually presented, are fit for every state of Society in whatever clime ... .

Prevost sought Madison's assistance in this project, which he saw as a means of promoting a reception of the common law.[90] A month later James Brown himself discussed this project in his correspondence:

> Should the present system [of Territorial Government] be continued until October I have conceived that much good might be done by availing ourselves of the assistance of the Council to adopt a good code of Laws for the Government of the Territory. We possess all the materials for the able execution of such a work[.] The Civil law—the Spanish ordinances—the British Statute and Common Laws, and the codes of all the States are spread before us, and the people are prepared for the reception of a code ably compiled from these several systems—The Council is composed of characters ready to adopt a code which would meet the approbation of our Judges and American Lawyers... . If such a code is not in operation on the commencement of the second grade of Government, it is but too probable we

---

88. Letter from Governor [William C.C.] Claiborne to the President [Thomas Jefferson] (Dec. 8, 1804), *in Orleans Territorial Papers*, *supra* note 17, at 348.
89. Dargo, *Jefferson's Louisiana*, *supra* note 63, at 200.
90. Letter from Judge [John B.] Prevost to the Secretary of State [James Madison] (Dec. 19, 1804), *in Orleans Territorial Papers*, *supra* note 17, at 356-57.

> shall remain sometime without Laws or with a system too motley and complicated to be understood by our ablest jurisprudents... . Impressed with these ideas the council appear disposed to engage Mr Livingston and myself to digest a Code; but such is the unfortunate dislike of the governor towards the only man in whom the Council seems disposed to confide as my assistant, that it is beleived [*sic*] the measure will fall.[91]

Like Prevost, Brown was anxious that, if there were not a code by the time representative government was introduced, the new legislature would "generally be attached to the French Laws and will pass only acts resembling the Civil Law and the Spanish ordinances formerly in force here[.]"[92] (The phrase "formerly in force" is intriguing.) The Legislative Council had in fact quickly established a committee to draft a civil and a criminal code;[93] on February 5, it resolved jointly with the Governor: "That the committee appointed by the said legislative council, to draught and report a civil and criminal code for the said territory, are hereby authorised to employ two counsellors at law, to assist them in the draughting of the said codes." Five thousand dollars was to be appropriated to compensate these lawyers.[94] If this stalled as an attempt to have a civil code drafted, in a few months the Legislative Council had nonetheless enacted a statute on criminal law and procedure. This specified individual crimes, and provided that they should "be taken, intended and construed, according to, and in conformity with, the common law of England," and authorized the Governor to provide an exposition providing the details of individual crimes.[95] On August 12, 1805, Claiborne appointed Lewis Kerr to undertake this task.[96] This

---

91. Letter from James Brown to John Breckinridge (Jan. 22, 1805), *in Orleans Territorial Papers*, *supra* note 17, at 378, 379.
92. *Id.*
93. La. Gazette, Dec. 21, 1804, *cited in* Dargo, *Jefferson's Louisiana*, *supra* note 63, at 226.
94. Joint Resolution of Both Branches of the Legislature, Feb. 4, 1805, *in Acts Passed at the First Session of the Legislative Council*, *supra* note 28, at 458-61.
95. An Act for the Punishment of Crimes and Misdemeanors, 1805, ch. 50, §§ 33, 48, *supra* note 57, at 416-53.
96. *See* Letter from W.C.C. Claiborne to Lewis Kerr (Aug. 12, 1805), *in An Exposition of the Criminal Laws of the Territory of Orleans: The Practice of the*

mode of proceeding apparently had a precedent in Kentucky.[97] Kerr was able to transmit a manuscript to the Governor on January 1, 1806.[98]

On March 2, 1805, Congress enacted a new statute reorganizing the government of the Territory of Orleans, to come into force on July 4. The new structure of government was stated to be "in all respects similar" to that in the Mississippi Territory. There were to be two houses in the Legislature, a Legislative Council of five appointed by the President from ten nominations made by the elected General Assembly or House of Representatives, which was to be convened in November 1805.[99] These institutions for territorial government were first laid down in the Northwest Ordinance of 1787, which had provided a template for a number of other territories as well as that of Mississippi.[100] The new organic act for the Territory of Orleans stated that the President was to appoint the necessary officers "in conformity with the ordinance" of 1787, while the inhabitants of Orleans were to "be entitled to and enjoy all the rights, privileges, and advantages secured by the said ordinance." A provision preserved "the laws in force"; another excluded from extension to the Territory of Orleans the Ordinance's provisions on "the descent and distribution of estates" as well as an article in the ordinance prohibiting slavery.[101]

Courts of Criminal Jurisdiction, the Duties of Their Officers, with a Collection of Forms for the Use of Magistrates and Others [iv-vii] (Wm. W. Gaunt 1986) (1806) [hereinafter *Exposition of the Criminal Laws*]; Billings, 'Neglected Treatise', *supra* note 58.

97. Kilbourne, *supra* note 29, at 29, 29 n.90.

98. Letter from Lewis Kerr to W.C.C. Claiborne (Jan. 1, 1806), *in Exposition of the Criminal Laws*, *supra* note 96, at [viii]-xiii.

99. An Act Further Providing for the Government of the Territory of Orleans, 1805, ch. 23, §§ 1-22, *reprinted in* 2 U.S. Congress, *Public Statutes at Large of the United States of America* 322-23 (Richard Peters ed., Boston, Charles C. Little & James Brown 1845) [hereinafter Act Further Providing for the Government of the Territory of Orleans].

100. An Ordinance for the Government of the Territory of the United States North West of the River Ohio, July 13, 1787, *reprinted in* 32 Library of Cong., *Journal of the Continental Congress 1774-1789*, at 334-43 (1936) [hereinafter Northwest Ordinance]; Denis P. Duffy, 'The Northwest Ordinance as a Constitutional Document', 95 Col. L. Rev. 929, 930 (1995).

101. An Act Further Providing for the Government of the Territory of Orleans, *supra* note 99, §§ 1, 4, 5.

The Act erecting the Territory of Mississippi, on the government of which that of Orleans was to be based, had few specific provisions, instead relying by reference on the terms of the Northwest Ordinance.[102] This stated: "There shall also be appointed a court to consist of three judges any two of whom to form a court, who shall have a common law jurisdiction ... ."[103] This inevitably raised a question of interpretation. The Congressional Act of 1805 did not reconstitute the Territorial Court established in 1804; but, nonetheless, its references to the Government of the Territory of Mississippi and to the Northwest Ordinance raised two obvious questions: did this provision apply to the Territorial Court? If it did, how was the term "common law" to be understood? In the early 1800s, the primary understanding of the term "common law" in the Ordinance would have been in terms of a comparative-law analysis, so it would have generally been seen as meaning "common law" in an opposition to "civil law." The fact that the 1805 Act specifically stated that the provisions of the 1787 ordinance on descent and distribution of estates were not to be applied might be taken to imply that this provision was indeed applicable, whatever it meant.

Towards the end of June 1805, the Legislative Council created under the Congressional Act of 1804 convened for the second and last time for a very short legislative session.[104] Claiborne sent a message to the Council, urging subjects for its consideration, in which he alluded to the recent Act of Congress and the Northwest Ordinance, noting that the latter "declared that the Court to be established in virtue of it, Shall have a 'common law Jurisdiction,' and that the Citizens shall be entitled to the benefit of Judicial proceedings according to the course of the common Law." He recommended that the Council "consider how far this constitutional provision will necessarily innovate upon your

102. An Act for an Amicable Settlement of Limits with the State of Georgia, and Authorizing the Establishment of a Government in the Mississippi Territory, 1798, ch. 28, *reprinted in* 1 U.S. Congress, *Public Statutes at Large of the United States of America* 549-50 (Richard Peters ed., Boston, Charles C. Little & James Brown 1845).

103. Northwest Ordinance, *supra* note 100, at 336.

104. *Acts Passed at the Second Session of the Legislative Council of the Territory of Orleans* (New-Orleans, James M. Bradford 1805).

present System, and what measures may be expedient to prevent the inconveniences that might attend an unprepared transition from one mode of practice to another."[105] It is not entirely clear what Claiborne had in mind. Perhaps he was considering the work of the Council's committee on codification, established in December 1804.[106] But this obviously raised in the minds of some the possibility that Claiborne was encouraging a reception of the common law.

As it turned out, in this very short, second, legislative session, prorogued *sine die* on July 3 after first meeting on June 22, the Legislative Council did enact a number of statutes concerning the legal system;[107] but there was nothing that could be identified as fulfilling Claiborne's suggestion. Indeed, on the day of the prorogation, Julien Poydras, hitherto one of Claiborne's most significant supporters among the francophone community, in a speech in response to that of the Governor, addressed directly the issue of the laws. After indicating that laws should be "simple, natural, clear, intelligible to those whose conduct is to be regulated thereby," they had also to be "adapted to the local circumstances, the necessities, the manners of the people which they are to rule." They ought not to have complicated forms, and have a style that is "pure, correct, and purged of those barbarous foreign expressions" that make the laws unintelligible and create the necessity of having interpreters. He also stated that one should avoid "servile attachment to ancient usages, whether good or bad; to ancient laws though most absurd, and formed in the midst of tyranny and barbarity." This may initially have suggested to Claiborne that he had convinced at least Poydras; but, if so, he was about to be disabused. Poydras next commented "on of the consequences of this fatal prejudice:"

---

105. Message from Governor Claiborne (June 22, 1805), *in* 3 Claiborne, *Letter Books*, *supra* note 3, at 103-04.

106. Dargo, *Jefferson's Louisiana*, *supra* note 63, at 226.

107. Letter from William C. C. Claiborne to James Madison (June 26, 1805), *in* 3 Claiborne, *Letter Books*, *supra* note 3, at 105; Speech—Delivered by Governor Claiborne, to the Legislative Council, on Proroguing Them (July 3, 1805), *in* 3 Claiborne, *Letter Books*, *supra* note 3, at 108-13.

> We are on the eve of seeing confusion established on the banks of the Mississippi, by the forced introduction of a voluminous body of common law to which we are total strangers; laws which are quite foreign to our constitution, our liberty, our circumstances and our manners, and are wholly unknown and inapplicable to us. And why is this to take place? Because our ancestors of glorious memory were children of the Thames, had they been natives of Japan or China, the Bambou would be justice of the peace amongst us, as it has been for numberless ages amongst the inhabitants of those empires.[108]

After this bombshell lobbed at the Governor, Poydras finished his speech with an uplifting peroration; but he had made his point. He had turned the typical critique of the civil law into one of the common law in a strong argument for codification.

The House of Representatives of the new legislature met on November 4, 1805.[109] The Governor reminded them that their first duty, after electing a Speaker, was to nominate by ballot ten men, each with a freehold of 500 acres, whose names were to be returned to the President, who would select five from these to serve in the new Legislative Council.[110] On November 11, Hazure de l'Orme moved before the House that its committee, already instructed to draft a memorial to Congress, should "pray for a repeal of that part of the act granting to the territory the second grade of government, as provides for the introduction of the common law, owing to the great confusion it will introduce in the courts of justice." The House accepted a proposal to postpone consideration of this until after "the opinion of the superior court should be known on the subject, understanding that the subject would be agitated tomorrow."[111]

---

108. Address, Delivered by Julien Poydras, to the Legislative Council, on Its Being Prorogued (July 3, 1805), *in* Nat'l Intelligencer & Washington Advertiser, Sept. 9, 1805.
109. Letter from W.C.C. Claiborne to James Madison (Nov. 5, 1805), *in* 3 Claiborne, *Letter Books*, *supra* note 3, at 225-27.
110. Address to the House of Representatives (Nov. 4, 1805), *in* 3 Claiborne, *Letter Books*, *supra* note 3, at 223-24.
111. Proceedings of the Territorial House of Representatives, *in Orleans Territorial Papers*, *supra* note 17, at 520-21.

This is a reference to an inadequately recorded event, when a debate about the laws in force and the impact of the Northwest Ordinance was held before Judge Prevost on November 12. From Étienne Mazureau, a French-born lawyer, we know that he, Moreau Lislet, James Brown, Pierre Derbigny, and Edward Livingston argued against the claim that the Act of Congress had introduced the common law. He did not name counsel who took the opposing view, but remembered that they—"Scotch, English, Irish, and others"—relied on "the organic law of the Court" as carrying with it "the jurisdiction of common law." Mazureau attributed the success of those arguing for the civil law to the outstanding argument of Edward Livingston. He also noted that the organic acts had also preserved the laws in force.[112] There are only very general accounts of Prevost's opinion. He apparently recognized Roman, Spanish, and French civil law as the law of the territory, on the basis that "common law" in the Ordinance meant the common law of the territory, that is, in the case of that of Orleans, the civil law in force.[113] Jeremiah Brown stated that the basis of Prevost's decision was the view that "Congress ... could never have intended ... to subvert the laws of a country."[114] Given the understandable concerns about the actions of the Spanish, all of this will have troubled the ever-anxious Claiborne even more, and led to further doubts about the loyalty of the creoles.[115]

The new legislature, dominated by the francophone elite of the Territory, had its first meeting on March 24, 1806.[116] In a

---

112. Henry Plauché Dart, 'Mazureau's Oration on Mathews', 4 La. Hist. Q. 149, 173-74 (1921). Brown, *Short Letter*, *supra* note 19, at 17 states that of all the lawyers who argued there only Livingston and Derbigny "favored the civil law." It may be that the others mentioned by Mazureau presented no direct oral argument. On Mazureau, *see* Tara Lombardi, 'The Great Advocate: Étienne Mazureau, Accomplished Attorney and Statesman (1777-1849)', 7 De Novo (Law Library of La., New Orleans, La.), Fall 2009, at 6.

113. Dargo, *Jefferson's Louisiana*, *supra* note 63, at 230; Faber, *Land of Dreams*, *supra* note 8, at 237.

114. Brown, *Short Letter*, *supra* note 19, at 17.

115. On the activities of the Spanish, see, e.g., Faber, *Land of Dreams*, *supra* note 8, at 219-25.

116. Letter from Governor [William C.C.] Claiborne to the Secretary of State [James Madison] (Mar. 27, 1806), *in Orleans Territorial Papers*, *supra* note 17, at 616; Letter from James Brown to John Breckinridge (Sept. 17, 1805), *in*

lengthy address to it, the Governor drew attention to the "revision of the Judiciary System" as "of primary importance." The final section on military matters indicates how anxious Claiborne remained about the possibility of a Spanish invasion.[117] The reply of the Legislative Council was in very general terms, but that of the House of Representatives alluded to the issue of the "Revision of the judiciary system."[118] By April 10, Claiborne was anxious about the activities of the Legislature. He predicted: "Many laws will be offered for my approbation & my duty will compel me to reject several." He also saw tensions between the "ancient Louisianians" and the "few Native Americans" in the House of Representatives.[119] On May 6, the governor vetoed a bill that set out conditions necessary to be fulfilled in order to be a member of the Legislature.[120] He complained to Madison, justifying himself, noting that the tensions between the "Ancient and modern Louisianians" meant that the Legislature had achieved little. The most "fruitful sources" of the discontent were "the introduction of the English language in our Courts of Justice; the Judicial System generally and particularly the Trial by Jury, and the admission of attorneys." He hoped, however, that once the difficulties with Spain were settled matters would settle down.[121]

Claiborne was correct to identify the members of the Legislature as dissatisfied with the legal system. They remained anxious about the administration's intentions as regards the law. Around or just after May 20, a bill was introduced into the Legislature that

---

Orleans Territorial Papers, *supra* note 17, at 506-13 (discussing the likely composition).

117. Address to the Legislature of the Territory of Orleans (Mar. 24, 1806), *in* 3 Claiborne, *Letter Books*, *supra* note 3, at 274-81.

118. Answer of the Legislative Council (Mar. 29, 1806); Answer of the House of Representatives (Apr. 2, 1806), *in Orleans Territorial Papers*, *supra* note 17, at 618-22.

119. Letter from William C. C. Claiborne to Thomas Jefferson (Apr. 10, 1806), *in* 3 Claiborne, *Letter Books*, *supra* note 3, at 288-89.

120. Letter from William C.C. Claiborne to the Legislative Council and House of Representatives of the Territory (May 6, 1806); Letter from William C.C. Claiborne to James Madison (May 8, 1806), *in* 3 Claiborne, *Letter Books*, *supra* note 3, at 296-98.

121. Letter from William C.C. Claiborne to James Madison (May 16, 1806), *in* 3 Claiborne, *Letter Books*, *supra* note 3, at 299-300.

was intended to clarify Prevost's decision of November 12 preceding; if the judge's words were as indeterminate as they seem to have been according to the accounts preserved, this may even have been necessary or wise. But the bill was intended to give legislative force to his ruling. Though the text of this bill is reasonably well known, it is necessary to repeat it here *in extenso*:

> An Act declaring the laws which continue to be inforce in the Territory of Orleans, and authors which may be recurred to as authorities within the same
>
> Whereas by the effect of the reiterated changes which the government of this Territory has undergone, the divers matters which now compose its judiciary system, are in some measure wrapped in obscurity, so that it has become necessary to present to the citizens the whole of these different parts, collected together by which they may be guided, whenever they will have to recur to the laws, untill the Legislature may form a civil code for the Territory; and whereas by the 11th section of the act of Congress intitled "an act dividing Louisiana into two Territories and providing for the temporary government thereof" passed the 22d march 1804, and by the 4th section of the act of the said Congress, intitled "an act further providing for the government of the Territory of Orleans" it is said, that the laws which shall be inforce in the said Territory, at the Commencement of the said acts, and which shall not be contrary to the dispositions thereof, shall continue to be in force untill altered, modified or repealed by the Legislature of the Territory.
>
> Sect. 1st. Be it therefore declared by the legislative Council and the House of Representatives of the Territory of Orleans in general assembly convened, that by virtue of the said dispositions, the laws which remain in force, and those which can be recurred to as authorities in the tribunals of this Territory, save the changes and modifications which may have already been made by the Legislatures of the said Territory, save also whatever might be contrary to the constitution of the United States, to the laws of the federal government which have been extended to the said Territory by Congress, and to the acts of the said Congress which direct the present governement of the said Territory, and save therefore the modifications, which necessarily result from the introduction which the act of the 22d march 1804, has made into the said Territory

of the two most important principles of the judiciary system of the common law, to wit, the writ of habeas corpus, and the trial by jury, are the laws and authorities following, to wit: 1. The roman Civil code, as being the foundation of the spanish Law, by which this country was governed before its cession to France and to the United States, which is composed of the institutes, digest and code of the Emperor Justinian, aided by the authority of the commentators of the civil law, and particularly of Domat in his treaty of the Civile Laws; the whole so far as it has not been derogated from by the Spanish law; 2. the Spanish law, consisting of the books of the *recopilation* de *Castilla* and *autos acordados* being nine books in the whole; the seven parts or *partidas* of the king Don Alphonse the learned, and the eight books of the royal statute (*fueroreal*) of Castilla; the *recopilation* de *indias*, save what is therein relative to the enfranchisement of Slaves; the laws de *Toro*, and finally the ordinances and royal orders and decrees, which have been formally applied to the Colony of Louisiana, but not otherwise; the whole aided by the authority of the reputable commentators admitted in the courts of Justice.

Sect. 2. And be it further declared, that in matters of commerce the ordinance of Bilbao is that which has full authority in this Territory, to decide all contestations relative thereto; and that wherever it is not sufficiently explicit, recourse may be had to the roman laws; to Beawes lex mercatoria, to Park on insurance, to the treatise of insurences by Emorigon, and finally to the commentaries of Valin, and to the respectable authors consulted in the United States.[122]

---

122. For the text, *see* Mitchell Franklin, 'The Place of Thomas Jefferson in the Expulsion of Spanish Medieval Law from Louisiana', 16 Tul. L. Rev. 319, 323-26 (1942); Levasseur, *Moreau Lislet*, *supra* note 18, at 55-57; Elizabeth G. Brown, 'Legal Systems in Conflict: Orleans Territory 1804-1812', 1 Am. J. Legal Hist. 35, 46-48 (1957). I have copied exactly the version given by Franklin, including obvious errors, though correcting "Civils Laws" to "Civile Laws" for Domat's work. These errors are intriguing: was this a document in English produced by a francophone? Without access to the original it is impossible to say, as there may be printing errors in Franklin's text.

By May 22, Claiborne had decided to veto this bill.[123] His intention must have already been clear, as, from May 21 onwards, members of the Legislative Council started to intimate to him their resignations.[124] He vetoed the Act on May 26.[125]

THE VETOED ACT AND THE SPANISH LAW

The proposed statute was rather strange, as contemporaries realized. Indeed, it is sufficiently unusual that it is tempting to suspect that it may have been passed with the aim that Claiborne should veto it, so that those in favor of the civil code mentioned in it should gain some political advantage by putting the governor on the defensive, through requiring him to justify his actions in vetoing the act.

The first thing to note is that the act refers to an unusual mix of primary and secondary sources, though this perhaps could be justified given the state of legal science in the Territory. After all, the previous year the statutory reform of criminal law and procedure had led to the authorized publication by Lewis Kerr of an *Exposition of the Criminal Laws of the Territory of Orleans*, as it was necessary to explain the new criminal laws of English origin.[126] The existing legal culture was not one into which the

---

123. Letter from W.C.C. Claiborne to James Madison (May 22, 1806), *in* 3 Claiborne, *Letter Books*, *supra* note 3, at 305-06.
124. Letter from Pierre Sauvé to Governor [William C.C.] Claiborne (May 21, 1806), *in Orleans Territorial Papers*, *supra* note 17, at 641; Letter from W.C.C. Claiborne to Pierre Sauvé (May 26, 1806), *in* 3 Claiborne, *Letter Books*, *supra* note 3, at 308-09; Letter from Jean Noël Destréhan to Governor [William C.C.] Claiborne (May 24, 1806), *in Orleans Territorial Papers*, *supra* note 17, at 641; Letter from W.C.C. Claiborne to John Noel Destrehan (May 26, 1806), *in* 3 Claiborne, *Letter Books*, *supra* note 3, at 308.
125. Letter from W.C.C. Claiborne to James Madison (May 26, 1806), *in* 3 Claiborne, *Letter Books*, *supra* note 3, at 309-11; Message to the Legislative Council, and to the House of Representatives (May 26, 1806), *in* 3 Claiborne, *Letter Books*, *supra* note 3, at 313.
126. See Billings, 'Neglected Treatise', *supra* note 58.

new criminal laws could readily be fitted. The *Exposition* was intended to assist understanding and application.

Another point to note is that the vetoed act contains one very obvious error, should the copy initially printed by Franklin in 1942 be accurate: the Fuero Real had only *four* rather than the *eight* books the statute apparently ascribes to it. This will be discussed further below, and an explanation suggested.

The statute also raised a number of practical problems, as one correspondent in a newspaper pointed out, in a series of rhetorical questions addressed to three members of the Legislature:

> [I]n which century was the code of the emperor Justinian written? of how many volumes was it composed? and whether the seven parts or partidas of the king don Alphonso the learned can be purchased in this City?
>
> If the Recopilacion de Castille, and Autos acordados, the laws of Toro, and the ordinance of Bilbao are in ether of your libraries?[127]

These were fair and entirely justified questions. Of course, the writer raised them as an attack on the civil law; but his motivation does not diminish their cogency.

Jeremiah Brown also emphasized the problems posed by the vetoed act, suggesting in his sarcastic invective that the works listed were "apparently copied with indecent accuracy from the shelves of one of those french lawyers," whom he has just criticized. He mockingly suggested that some important works had perhaps been omitted simply because the lawyer's shelves had been organized by the "rank and quality" of the binding not of the authors:

> So uncouth was the confusion in which books ancient and modern were ushered in, books of high authority and books of none, and so awkwardly were roman, french, spanish, english and american laws thrown as it were at random into the small space of this one short act, that before any legislature it might well have passed for a burlesque on the object of its compilers.

---

127. Letter from A. Merchant, La. Gazette, June 10, 1806, *quoted in* Levasseur, *Moreau Lislet*, *supra* note 18, at 57.

> It was carried through both houses by a large majority, but from the executive happily met with the fate it merited.[128]

Despite the witty hyperbole, Brown was indeed correct that it is an odd listing of primary and secondary works. But this turns out to be very revealing.

It is important to single out one citation in particular, that of *Les lois civiles dans leur ordre naturel* written by the notable French jurist, Jean Domat, and first published in 1689. This was one of the most important law books of the eighteenth century; but it is not immediately obvious why Domat was here selected out of all the possible commentators on the civil law that could have been named. In modern scholarship Domat is regarded as important for his rationalist account of natural law and as part of the story of the movement towards codification in France, and as having exercised an important influence on the *Code civil des Français* of 1804 and on the Civil Code of Lower Canada of 1866.[129] He is not generally discussed as a commentator on the Roman law, but seen as systematizing law in France; of course, by the very nature of his work, a natural-law exposition of the substance of Roman law, he is expounding and explaining Roman law in an accessible way. The very popularity of the book indicates his success in achieving this, setting out principles in an abstract way that often resembles the articles of a code, with quotations of relevant sections of the Roman texts. But it is not a conventional commentary on the Roman law; rather, it is more a type of rationalist and idealist account of law treated as a universal on a foundation of Roman law, with didactic and explanatory introductions to its various titles, developed in an essentially French context. In reality it is a

---

128. Brown, *Short Letter*, *supra* note 19, at 19-20.

129. Alejandro Guzmán Brito, 'La doctrina de Jean Domat sobre la interpretación de las leyes', 31 Revista Chilena de Derecho 39 (2004); Simone Goyard-Fabre, 'Montesquieu entre Domat et Portalis', 35 McGill L.J. 715 (1990); David Gilles, 'Les Lois civiles de Jean Domat, prémices à la Codification? Du Code Napoléon au Code civil du Bas Canada', 43 R.J.T.U.M. 1 (2009).

distinctively French work. It is easy to understand its influence on later francophone codifications.[130]

The question then remains: why was Domat's treatise privileged in the draft act of 1806 as a commentary on Roman law? The answer lies in the researches in the Spanish sources carried out by Louisiana lawyers. As indicated above, the Spanish sources were complex to use; but between 1791 and 1798 an important work, the *Teatro de la legislación universal de España e Indias, por orden cronológico de sus cuerpos, y decisiones no recopiladas y alfabético de sus títulos y principales materias*, was issued in Madrid in twenty-eight volumes. It was authored by Antonio Xavier Pérez y López. The work was, as the title indicates, organized alphabetically by legal topic. Entries on each topic would vary according to need. A full entry on a topic would start with a list of texts of Roman and Canon law, followed by a listing of the relevant Spanish legislation. There then could follow a brief introduction, before the quotation in full of any texts of canon law, and then in full of the relevant Spanish or Castilian law, including the laws of the Indies where relevant. Pérez had carried out the hard work of finding the relevant material in the Spanish sources for each topic, and had then quoted it; thus, if his texts were reliable, he had replaced the need to own an extensive library of individual collections of laws, while his selections and introductions had a didactic effect, allowing someone with a basic knowledge of the structures and vocabulary of the civilian legal tradition to negotiate the Spanish law by topic without having been educated in it. In other words, it was very useful in conditions such as those in the Territory. There is relatively little literature on this work; but it was of great importance in the Spanish Indies.[131]

The first volume of the *Teatro* has a lengthy introduction—the 'Discurso Preliminar'—to the history, sources, and collec-

---

130. David Gilles, 'La doctrine comme source des codifications: Jean Domat', Studia Universitatis Babes-Bolyai Jurisprudentia 61 (Apr. 2009).

131. Mariluz Urquijo, *supra* note 79; Frederico de Castro, 'Nueva Biografía del Doctor Don Antonio Xavier Pérez y Lopez, con un breve studio sobre su sistemo filosófico', 1 Revista de la Universidad de Madrid 83 (I), 351 (II), 687 (III) (1873). Pérez and his *Teatro* are also mentioned incidentally in studies of Spanish dictionaries of law.

tions of Spanish laws, including those of the Indies. In the historical account towards the beginning, Pérez mentioned the spread of study of the Civil Law through Europe. He then noted he would not touch on the issue of the order or disorder of the *Corpus iuris*, or on that of the justice or utility of its provisions, on which law professors debated. Instead, he wrote: "I see the famous Domat has only arranged them, organizing them according to method in his work known by the name of the Civil Law organized according to its natural order." He also noted that the celebrated Christian Wolff, and other authors on the law of nature and nations, who treated jurisprudence in a philosophical and geometrical method, differed very little from the Civil Law as regards contracts, last wills and other specific parts of the law, while the same could also be said of the famous Code of Frederick the Great.[132] As a scholar Pérez was very interested in natural law (he was a doctor of canon law);[133] this is the context of his comments about Domat.

It seems very likely that the drafters of the vetoed act of 1806 had read Pérez's 'Discurso Preliminar'. The twenty-eight volumes of his *Teatro* would be by far the most useful legal work for any lawyer practicing in the Territory of Orleans before the enactment of the Digest. It is clear that later the *Teatro* was very familiar to Moreau Lislet, since he used it both in compiling the de la Vergne volume and in his later translation of the Partidas, again alluding to Domat as a commentator on Roman law.[134] Indeed, one wonders if it was to the *Teatro* that Brown referred in 1805 when he talked of "the Spanish ordinances" as among the works "spread before us."[135] It is a plausible description.

Supporting this suggestion is the observation that the draft act also refers to the "the *recopilation* de *Castilla* and *autos acordados* being nine books in the whole;" this rather resembles

---

132. 1 Antonio Xavier Pérez y López, *Teatro de la legislación universal de España e Indias, por orden cronológico de sus cuerpos, y decisiones no recopiladas y alfabético de sus títulos y principales materias* VIII (Madrid, Imprenta de Manuel Gonzalez 1791) [hereinafter 1 Pérez, *Teatro*].

133. Castro, *supra* note 131, at 352 (II).

134. Cairns, 'De la Vergne Volume', *supra* note 9, at 52-60.

135. Letter from James Brown to John Breckinridge (Jan. 22, 1805), *in Orleans Territorial Papers*, *supra* note 17, at 378-80.

Pérez's remark that the Recopilación and the Autos Acordados are "two bodies that are divided into nine books," a comment which, as in the act, is then followed by an allusion—if here brief and incidental—to the Siete Partidas.[136] Likewise, the error attributing eight books to the Fuero Real may be the product of careless reading, note-taking and understanding of Pérez's 'Discurso Preliminar'. Pérez refers to publication of collections of disparate types of royal legislation before and after the Cortes of Castille held at Toro. He writes that the first of these was known as *Ordenamiento Real*, authorized and published in 1496 by the Reyes Católicos, Ferdinand and Isabella, adding that it was divided into eight books, and these into diverse titles. Pérez comments that because the major part of the laws of this *Ordenamiento* were inserted in the *Recopilación*, and because its titles corresponded with those of the latter, it was unnecessary to say more about it.[137] Given that this passage is found in Pérez' 'Discurso Preliminar', just prior to the remark about the nine books of the *Recopilación* and *Autos Acordados*, it is tempting to conclude that the drafter of the act had this passage in front of him and has mistakenly confused the *Ordenamiento Real* with the *Fuero Real*.

If this argument is correct, a number of conclusions may be drawn and conclusions reinforced that were based on other evidence. First of all, the very nature of the Spanish legal material was causing problems. If the Spanish sources constituted a "labyrinth" for the Spanish lawyer, they must have been very difficult to negotiate in the territory of Orleans with its lack of books. If the *Teatro* offered a solution, ignorance could still cause problems, as the 1806 draft act showed. Secondly, the *Teatro* presented texts of law in an accessible way, but they still needed to be understood. The Act suggests a rather crude level of comprehension. Training in a civil law system, and a knowledge of its vocabulary, was probably necessary to utilize the *Teatro* efficiently and well. Thirdly, the act focuses on the significance of the Roman or civil law as the foundation of Spanish law. Fourthly, it should always be recalled that those lawyers in the

---

136. 1 Pérez, *Teatro*, *supra* note 132, at XXVII.
137. *Id.* at XXVI.

Territory who were trained civilians had trained in the French tradition, not in the Spanish, and it would be interesting to know how widespread was knowledge of the Spanish language—one suspects not very. Finally, it is difficult to accept that the act was seriously intended, other than to goad the governor into exercising a veto. His veto then cleared the way for the preparation of a bilingual civil code drawing on the best modern sources.

THE MANIFESTO AND THE CODE

Since the Governor's veto was expected, the Legislative Council, with the support of ten members of the House of Representatives, was able on the same day to issue a "Manifesto" that embodied a resolution for the dissolution of the Legislature, as well as presenting a relatively detailed argument on the law. The main thrust of this clever document—entitled Address of the Legislative Council to the People—was to argue for a bilingual civil code and to identify the law of the Territory with the authority and prestige of the Civil or Roman law. It was also concerned to stress that opposition to Claiborne's policies on the law was not evidence of disloyalty to the American regime.[138] To demonstrate this it is worth examining parts of it in some detail.

The reason given for the dissolution was the Governor's vetoing of the laws passed, most notably, of course, the declaratory law quoted above. The Manifesto emphasized, however, that, as stated in the preamble to the draft Act, the aim was to clarify "our present judicial system and [do] away with its uncertainty until [the Legislature] should have time to draw up a civil code."[139] It

---

138. Le Telegraphe—Nouvelle Orleans—Mardi 3 Juin 1806—Extrait de la Seance du Conseil Legislatif, Du 26 Mai, 1806, *in Orleans Territorial Papers*, *supra* note 17, at 643-57. This contains both the French and English texts. I shall quote from the English text in this source. A very slightly different version of the English text is found on the front pages of the Nat'l Intelligencer & Washington Advertiser, Aug. 11 & 13, 1806, reflecting a different translation from the original French. I shall here quote from the *Orleans Territorial Papers*, *supra* note 17, though I have checked them against the version in the Washington newspaper.

139. Manifesto, *in Orleans Territorial Papers*, *supra* note 17, at 656.

also claimed that "[t]he most inestimable benefit for a people is the preservation of its laws, usages, and habits."[140] It stated that this had been the intention of the U.S. Congress in its Act of 1805 on the government of the Territory, noting that Congress had applied to the territory "all of the common law [*la Loi Commune*] which it considered indispensible to prescribe for us ... the right to be judged by one's peers and the *writ of habeas corpus*."[141] The Manifesto commented:

> [T]he Constitution of the United States and the other Federal laws being general for the whole Union, it would be absurd to claim that this Territory ought not to be subject to them: but as to laws regarding contracts, wills and successions, what difference does it make that here such acts should be governed by the civil law [*le droit civil*] while in the other States of the Union they are governed by the common law [*la loi commune*].[142]

Hinting at the current problems the administration had due to anxiety about the intentions of Spain, and playing on Claiborne's suspicions of the loyalty of the creoles, it added that "it would be exposing [a citizen's] affection to the danger of being alienated and exciting disorder and general discontent to disturb those customs to which each province is attached by bonds of experience and long habit."[143]

The Manifesto pointed out, perfectly reasonably, that in "the United States itself there is no general civil code." Each state has been allowed its own unique common law.[144] This was why the Congress granted to the Territory "the privilege of keeping its old laws or of changing or modifying them ... ."[145] But the Manifesto was keen to claim the reputation of the Roman laws for the law of Louisiana: "Now, every one knows that those old laws [*anciennes lois*] are nothing but the civil or Roman law [*la loi civile ou romaine*] modified by the laws of the government under

---

140. *Id.* at 650.
141. *Id.* at 651.
142. *Id.*
143. *Id.*
144. *Id.* at 651-52.
145. *Id.* at 652.

which this region existed before the latter's cession to the United States."[146] If the titles of the old laws might seem "barbarous or ridiculous," the fact that hitherto citizens had been happy under them showed "their mildness and their wisdom:"

> In any case it is no less true that the Roman law [*la loi romaine*] which formed the basis of the civil and political laws [*la base des lois civiles et politiques*] of all the civilized nations of Europe presents an ensemble of greatness and prudence which is above all criticism. What purity there is in these decisions based on natural equity; what clearness there is in the wording which is the work of the greatest jurists, encouraged by the wisest emperors; what simplicity there is in the form of those contracts and what sure and quick means there are for obtaining the remedies prescribed by the law, for the reparation of all kinds of civil wrongs.
>
> We certainly do not attempt to draw any parallel between the civil law and the common law [*la loi civile et la loi commune*]; but, in short, the wisdom of the civil law [*la loi civile*] is recognized by all Europe; and this law is the one which nineteen-twentieths of the population of Louisiana know and are accustomed to from childhood, of which law they would not see themselves deprived without falling into despair.[147]

The Manifesto emphasized that everyone knew the basics of the existing legal system—succession, parental authority, marriages and marriage contracts, buying and selling, and remedies—and had a "tincture of this general and familiar jurisprudence." Overthrowing this all at once would cause great dislocation.[148] The Manifesto explained:

> The first legislature of this Territory has to be particularly interested in establishing the fundamental bases; the secondary laws, accessory laws and details should only come later, otherwise one is exposed to making parts which will be found inconsistent with the whole. Now, what is the first law, the most important law in the present situation of this country; what is the fundamental basis of the great edifice of its future

---

146. *Id.*
147. *Id.*
148. *Id.* at 653.

> legislation? It cannot be denied that it is the matter of giving to it a civil code.[149]

This was particularly necessary when the judges in the courts and the lawyers pleading before them were "almost all strangers to the French language and still more so to the language in which the greater part of the laws of this country are written" and given "the very scarcity even of the elementary authors who deal with them."[150] But before undertaking this, it was necessary to determine "what would be its basis and what would be the canvas on which one would do the work." It was in the interest of the inhabitants to keep "of the old laws, everything which can be saved without disadvantage and without going contrary to the system of our Government, and of not having recourse to foreign codes except in so far as the old may be found defective or prejudicial."[151] Continuity was required:

> For all the contracts which have been made till now must necessarily be judged by the laws under which they were made; so how great would be the embarrassment of the courts if, while canceling everything which remains of the civil law [*la loi civile*], the courts should nevertheless be left under the necessity of judging, under that same law, of the effects of all contracts and documents made down to today?[152]

It was thus necessary that the Legislature make "a code which shall be as near to [our old laws] as possible." These principles had led the Legislature "to place, before its act on the formation of the code, a preliminary and declaratory law regarding the laws which were to serve as a basis for that work."[153] It was necessary, because both "[t]he debate in the Chamber of Representatives and even the refusal of the sanction of the Governor" might suggest "that there is a secret intention of throwing us, despite ourselves, into the frightful chaos of the common law." Against

---

149. *Id.*
150. *Id.* at 653-54.
151. *Id.* at 654.
152. *Id.*
153. *Id.*

those who had claimed that, "by keeping the civil law we are adopting everything that is most revolting and contrary to the Republican régime," it was argued that nothing would be retained that was contrary to the Constitution of the United States.[154] All of this justified the resolution to dissolve the Legislature.[155]

The Legislature did not act on the proposed Resolution to dissolve, which, according to Claiborne, was rejected by the House of Representatives on May 27, 1806.[156] But the text of the Manifesto was published in New Orleans in both *Le Télégraphe* and the Louisiana Gazette in early June.[157] It undoubtedly raised anxiety among those hoping for a reception of the common law.

On the other hand, the manifesto's argument for a bilingual civil code undoubtedly had the potential to draw the sting from the criticisms leveled at the civil law in force. Simple arguments about accessibility and comprehensibility would be of no force against a comprehensive bilingual civil code. The code would be in both the major languages in the Territory and accessible to all. It is therefore unsurprising that Governor Claiborne accepted the Resolutions of both Houses on June 7, 1806, appointing Moreau Lislet and James Brown to draft a civil code.[158] Given he had already agreed in 1805 to a similar Resolution, it would have been politically difficult for him to refuse to do this.[159]

CONCLUSION

Jared Bradley in his study of Governor Claiborne's relations with the Spanish remarks:

---

154. *Id.* at 654-55.

155. *Id.* at 656-57.

156. Letter from William C.C. Claiborne to James Madison (May 28, 1806), *in* 3 Claiborne, *Letter Books*, *supra* note 3, at 319.

157. *Orleans Territorial Papers*, *supra* note 17, at 643; Joseph T. Hatfield, *William Claiborne: Jeffersonian Centurion in the American Southwest* 148-49, 350 nn.23-25 (1976); *see also* Nat'l Intelligencer, Aug. 11 & 13, 1806.

158. Resolutions of June 7, 1806, *supra* note 13, at 214-19.

159. Joint Resolution of Both Branches of the Legislature, Feb. 4, 1805, *supra* note 94. Both branches in this case being the Governor and Legislative Council.

> By the summer of 1806 tensions on both sides of the border in the Southwest had been pushed to the breaking point. Late in July, it appeared that the long talked of war with Spain had begun: the Spanish troops stationed on the Trinity marched to the Sabine; on the twenty-ninth of the month they crossed the Sabine and moved to within ten miles of Natchitoches.
>
> The situation on the Louisiana-Texas border was potentially explosive.[160]

War did not come; but through the period of the vetoed act and the Manifesto culminating in the Resolutions of June 7 on the drafting of a civil code, Claiborne had been anxious about the military activities of Spain. Thus in March he was concerned about their "intriguing with the Indians," and their distributing "a quantity of powder."[161] In the next month he worried that the French citizens who had not taken an oath of loyalty to the U.S.A. could not be tried for treason "if they were to take arms against us in the event of a War between Spain and the United States."[162] He raised with the Secretary for War, Henry Dearborn, the issue of the French Artillery in New Orleans that the Spanish wanted transported to Mobile, as the Spanish Governor there was "under an impression that a war between the United States and Spain was likely to ensue."[163] In a letter to Jefferson about international politics and the possibility of war, he alluded to the "ancient Louisianians" being "greatly jealous of the few Native Americans" in the House of Representatives, and he saw there as being malcontents sowing "the Seeds of distrust & discontent." It was in this letter that he alerted Jefferson to that fact that he would probably need to veto legislation.[164] He also discussed the supposed royal authorization of a Spanish settlement on the

---

160. Bradley, *supra* note 1, at 313.
161. Letter from William C.C. Claiborne to James Madison (Mar. 25, 1806), *in* 3 Claiborne, *Letter Books*, *supra* note 3, at 281.
162. Letter from William C.C. Claiborne to James Madison (Apr. 2, 1806), *in* 3 Claiborne, *Letter Books*, *supra* note 3, at 283.
163. Letter from William C.C. Claiborne to Henry Dearborn Madison (Apr. 8, 1806), *in* 3 Claiborne, *Letter Books*, *supra* note 3, at 286.
164. Letter from William C.C. Claiborne to Thomas Jefferson (Apr. 10, 1806), *in* 3 Claiborne, *Letter Books, supra* note 3, at 288-89.

Trinity River.[165] He continued to see the Territorial Legislature as dominated by men "whose politics and views are ... in opposition to the interests of the United States."[166] He did think that time and the dominance of the English language would eventually reconcile them to the United States.[167] He shortly thereafter rejected the act setting out the sources of the law.[168] Anxiety about the relationship with Spain continued and Claiborne continued to organize against a Spanish invasion, although as the summer wore on, he expressed less alarm, until the Spanish again crossed the Sabine to garrison an area near Natchitoches, as Bradley mentions.[169]

Of course, though there was to be no war with Spain, only the year before it had been rumored that the Territory was to be returned to Spain, so that political and military affairs will have seemed rather more delicate and dangerous than they now do with the benefit of hindsight.[170] But this background helps explain both Claiborne's veto of the act and acceptance of the Resolution for the drafting of a Civil Code. At a time when the rumor that the Territory might be returned to Spain was strong, and when there were suspicious Spanish troop movements, allowing the enactment of a statute specifically enforcing and embedding Spanish law in the Territory was not a political possibility, given Claiborne had to deal with the potential threat from Spain, and suspected the loyalty of the incoming Europeans. It is this that suggests he may have been manipulated into using his veto. He was then most likely to try to assuage the resentment of the creole elites by acting in a pragmatic fashion,

---

165. Letter from William C.C. Claiborne to James Madison (Apr. 16, 1806), *in* 3 Claiborne, *Letter Books*, *supra* note 3, at 289-90.
166. Letter from William C.C. Claiborne to James Madison (May 14, 1806), *in* 3 Claiborne, *Letter Books*, *supra* note 3, at 298.
167. Letter from William C.C. Claiborne to James Madison (May 16, 1806), *in* 3 Claiborne, *Letter Books*, *supra* note 3, at 299-300.
168. Letters from William C.C. Claiborne to James Madison (May 22 & May 26, 1806), *in* Claiborne, *Letter Books*, *supra* note 3, at 305-06, 309-10.
169. Letter from William C.C. Claiborne to Richard Claiborne (Aug. 17, 1806), *in* 3 Claiborne, *Letter Books*, *supra* note 3, at 378-81.
170. Paul D. Gelpi, 'Mr Jefferson's Creoles: The Battalion d'Orléans and the Americanization of Creole Louisiana, 1803-1815', 48 La. Hist. 295, 310 (2007).

by capitulating or perhaps compromising over the law, thus allowing the drafting and then promulgation of a civil code. And this in any case is what he did.

Much attention has been devoted to the clash of legal traditions or the conflict between the civil law and the common law in the Territorial period.[171] There can be no doubt but that many incoming anglophone Americans, including Governor Claiborne, had hoped for a reception of Anglo-American common law that went beyond courts, crimes, and procedure to include private law.[172] But by 1806 it was also perfectly clear that this was not going to happen. The creole elite was simply too powerful, while also being reinforced through 1804 and onwards by the arrival of further francophone refugees and migrants from France and the Caribbean—as we have seen, a matter of considerable and continuing concern to the Governor.[173] But wider international politics also had an impact.

This then returns us to the Digest of 1808. How did Moreau, Brown, and the Committee for the Revision of the Civil Code interpret the legislature's instructions? Why did they not codify on the basis of the Law of Castile? With Pérez's *Teatro* they had easy access to the rules of the Castilian law. They could have used it to draw up a code founded in that law, though this might have been a rather difficult task. But in November 1806, a mere five months after the Resolution, Jeremiah Brown was able to write that "our St. Domingo Lycurgus is avowedly copying his new code from that of Bonaparte, to the infinite delight of the whole party by whom he is employed."[174] As noted above, this is broadly correct, though the Digest is rather more original than this might suggest.[175] The "party" to whom Brown refers must be

---

171. Brown, *supra* note 122; Dargo, *Jefferson's Louisiana*, *supra* note 63, at 185-266.

172. Dargo, *Jefferson's Louisiana*, *supra* note 63, at 188-200, 210-18.

173. Letters from W.C.C. Claiborne to James Madison (Feb. 6 & Feb. 26, 1804), *in* 1 Claiborne, *Letter Books*, *supra* note 3, at 363-65, 387-88; Letters from W.C.C. Claiborne to James Madison (Apr. 9 & May 8, 1804), *in* 2 Claiborne, *Letter Books*, *supra* note 3, at 88-89, 134.

174. Brown, *Short Letter*, *supra* note 19, at 21-22.

175. Cairns, *Codification, Transplants and History*, *supra* note 9, at 137-234, 357-96, 427-33 (demonstrating clearly and conclusively that in crucial areas of

the creoles, some of the Americans, and the immigrants from St. Domingue and elsewhere.

The evidence of Jeremiah Brown demonstrates that to contemporaries there could have been no surprise in observing that the Digest was modeled on the *Code civil des Français*. As Professor Palmer has shown, it was common knowledge that the Digest was based on the French *Code civil.*[176] It was not a code of the Castilian private law supposedly in force, though it undoubtedly has some provisions drawn from that law, probably relying on the *Teatro* for knowledge of the actual texts of Castilian law as well as on Febrero's work for notaries, also influential in the Spanish Indies, for a discussion and exposition of certain topics.[177]

The Resolutions of June 7, 1806 (in the French text with the heading "Résolution relative à la formation d'un code civil") provided that the code was to be based on "the civil law by which this territory is now governed" or, in French, "les lois civiles qui régissent actuellement ce Territoire."[178] To understand what was meant by the terms "civil law" and "lois civiles," it is important to examine the contemporary language used in Louisiana about law. The vetoed act of 1806 and the consequent Manifesto provide important examples of context. The first had emphasized that the "roman Civil code" was "the foundation of the spanish Law."[179] The Manifesto had argued that the "old laws," the

---

family law, persons, and contract the Digest is not Spanish law in French dress); Ostroukh, *supra* note 9, at 166-85 (showing how the account of property law in the Louisiana Code of 1825 is essentially French); Palmer, *Louisiana Civilian Experience*, *supra* note 38, at 19-49 (presenting a strong and convincing argument about a French origin for a great many articles).

176. Palmer, *Louisiana Civilian Experience*, *supra* note 38, at 25 n.24, 82.

177. Josef Febrero, *Librería de escribanos, é instrucción juridíca theórico práctica de principantes. Prima parte divida en tres tomos. Trata de testamentos y contratos* (Madrid, Impr. de P. Marín 1789); Josef Febrero, *Librería de escribanos, é instrucción juridíca theórico práctica de principantes. Secunda parte divida en tres tomos. Trata de los juicios de inventario, y partición de acreedores, bienes de difunto, ordinario, executive, y de concurso, y prelación* (Madrid, Impr. de P. Marín 1790); *see* Alberto David Leiva, 'Aportes para un studio de la Librería de escribanos de Joseph Febrero', 22 Revista del Istituto de Historia del Derecho 302 (1971).

178. Resolutions of June 7, 1806, *supra* note 13, at 214-15.

179. Franklin, *supra* note 122, at 324.

"anciennes lois," in the Territory were "nothing but the civil or Roman law," "la loi civile ou romaine," modified by the laws of the former government of the colony. The "Roman law," "la loi romaine," was the "basis of the civil and political laws," "la base des lois civiles et politiques," of the civilized nations of Europe, while "the wisdom of the civil law [la loi civile] is recognized by all Europe" and, moreover, it claimed that this law was "the one which nineteen-twentieths of the population of Louisiana know and are accustomed to from childhood, of which law they would not see themselves deprived without falling into despair."[180]

The Act and the Manifesto emphasized that the law in the Territory of Orleans was the civil law in the sense of laws based on the Roman law. The Spanish law was represented as just a modern variation. What was most significant was that the law should not be the common law. This is not to say that the instructions in the Resolutions were deliberately couched in a particular way or were designed to be interpreted in a particular way. But it is certainly the case that the phrasing—"the civil law by which this territory is now governed" or "les lois civiles qui régissent actuellement ce Territoire"—was open enough to justify the nature of the code that was drawn up. The Manifesto is minimizing the differences between French law and Castilian law by focusing on the concept of civil law. French law could be represented as just another variation of the civil law. It should also be recalled that this was a period in which there was a continuing intensification of French culture in the Territory.

This said, the codifiers were undoubtedly eclectic and imaginative in their "arrant thievery," to adapt Walton's phrase. In 1847, Henry Bullard rather cruelly described the Digest as "little more than a mutilated copy of the Code Napoléon."[181] This is rather unfair and also quite misleading; the *Code civil* and its *projet* provided a basic structure, but there were other influences

180. Manifesto, *in Orleans Territorial Papers*, *supra* note 17, at 651-52.
181. Henry Bullard, *A Discourse on the Life and Character of the Hon. François Xavier Martin; Later Senior Judge of the Supreme Court, of the State of Louisiana, Pronounced at the Request of the Bar of New-Orleans* 11 (New-Orleans, J. B. Steel 1847).

on the way the Digest was put together, just as there were other sources for various individual articles. It is a truly original work.

It is important to remember the background of the two codifiers. Moreau Lislet and Brown were educated, socially prominent, politically engaged, and influential individuals, who were evidently given a great deal of discretion in drafting the Digest, simply reporting to a revision committee. They both had close connections with the Territorial legislature. Their social background meant that they never doubted that they knew what was needed in the new code by virtue of their knowledge of the Territory and their significant engagement with its institutions, politics, and economy. They did not consider themselves necessarily constrained by a narrow sense of legal positivism. Instead, they will have considered themselves to be legal "technocrats," resolving problems in the law by drawing on their expertise to create a code that would serve the Territory. They will have thought that what was wanted was an effective modern code, and the best example of one was that of France. In 1823 the Committee for the Revision of the Civil Code stated that the code was "hastily compiled." It also stated that there had not been time for a close study of the existing law; but indeed one wonders if Brown and Moreau really believed in 1806-1807 that such a detailed examination was necessary. Their technocratic approach worked, and the Committee in 1823 also described the Digest as a success, because its rules were "concise, and in general easily understood," and had "been read by the people," thus enabling "them to avoid disputes, on the subjects embraced by its provisions, that without them, would have led to endless litigation."[182]

---

182. Livingston, Moreau Lislet & Derbigny, 'Preliminary Report', *supra* note 40, at XCIII.

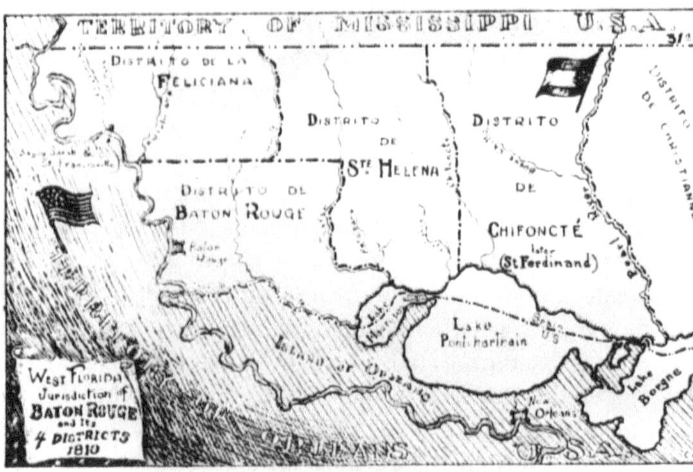

West Florida Map, 1810

CHAPTER 7

BITTER LEGACY

Spanish Colonial Policies and the Tradition of Extra-legal Violence in Louisiana's Florida Parishes

Samuel Hyde Jr.

On a steamy August morning in the summer of 1804, hundreds of armed men concentrated near the Spanish fort at Baton Rouge. Palpable tension filled the air as the men, angry and agitated in varying degrees, streamed into the small river town from the expansive districts that comprised what was then known as Spanish West Florida. The region, which today is known as the Florida parishes of Louisiana, included the territory within the "toe" of Louisiana between the Pearl and Mississippi rivers, bordered on the north by the Mississippi territory and on the south by lakes Pontchartrain and Maurepas. The discontent evident among the overwhelmingly Anglo-Saxon Protestant mob of men proved a curiosity to observers across the border in American controlled territory. The crowd had gathered not to express grievances against the Spanish government but instead to visibly *support* it!

The men arriving that sultry morning had travelled to Baton Rouge in reaction to an abortive rising against the Spanish colonial government known as the Kemper Rebellion. Though unsuccessful, the Kemper rising revealed the deep fissures and factions that plagued a region crawling with foreign agents, and rife with intrigue, occasioned by its dubious territorial identity. It also highlighted a singularly defining characteristic of the people in the area, specifically their fiercely independent nature and intense proclivity toward personal and collective violence.

The Spanish period in West Florida is often considered more from the perspective of what was not done rather than from what results did occur. Scholars traditionally have attributed the sources of the troubled history characterizing the Florida parishes to instability originating in the Civil War era that continued into the early twentieth century. Less revealed, though profoundly relevant, are the precedents set during the Spanish era that directly contributed to the chronic instability, if not chaos, of later generations. This study presents evidence suggesting that the extraordinary levels of collective and interpersonal violence that plague the region into the modern era originated in policies and jurisprudence established in the Spanish period.[1]

Through the course of its history, West Florida endured an extraordinarily complex and convoluted pattern of development. Among the curious aspects of growth, the region endured governance by every major European power that intruded into the North American wilderness. Successive French, British, and Spanish overlords paved the way for an armed insurrection and the creation of the West Florida Republic in advance of the region's forcible annexation by the United States. The resulting social and legal turmoil produced by the parade of competing governments is difficult to overstate. Suffice it to say that the conflicting land grants awarded by each governing power alone contributed mightily to the chaotic conditions that consumed the region in the late nineteenth and early twentieth century.

The initial French period offered little realistic infrastructure development and essentially no efforts to introduce a legal system in a territory where one observer declared "the influence

---

1. For studies detailing the enduring pattern of violence that plagued the region see William Bankston & David Allen, 'Rural Social Areas and Patterns of Homicide: An Analysis of Lethal Violence in Louisiana', 45 Rural Soc. 223, 223-37 (1980); John V. Baiamonte, Jr., *Spirit of Vengeance: Nativism and Louisiana Justice, 1921-1924* (1986); Hodding Carter, 'Not Much of a Man if He Hadn't', *in* Southern Legacy 48-63 (1950); Samuel C. Hyde, Jr., *Pistols and Politics: The Dilemma of Democracy in Louisiana's Florida Parishes, 1810-1899* (1996).

of the law is scarcely felt." West Florida became a British territory in 1763 as part of the treaty concluding the Seven Years War. Incipient English efforts to develop the region and establish a presence in the lower Mississippi Valley were cut short in September 1779 when Bernardo de Gálvez led an expedition that captured all British posts along the lower Mississippi and placed the region under Spanish control.[2]

Compared to their arrival in nearby New Orleans, Spanish ascendancy in West Florida resembled a clandestine maneuver. Following the brief and failed effort at governance performed by the initial Spanish governor at New Orleans, Antonio de Ulloa, Spanish power arrived in force in August 1769 under the determined leadership of General Alejandro O'Reilly. At the head of more than 2000 troops, O'Reilly skillfully neutralized resistance to Spanish ascendancy among the resident French population, executing the ring leaders and sending others to imprisonment at Morro Castle in Havana, effectively establishing firm and determined governance.

Gálvez's arrival in West Florida a decade later served as merely an initial step in his successful bid to drive the British from the Floridas. Following the capture of a British post at Bayou Manchac along with the larger British fort at Baton Rouge, Gálvez concentrated on the main prize of the expedition Pensacola, with the added inducement of securing Mobile on the way. Accordingly, from the outset Spanish authority in that portion of West Florida that would later become Louisiana's Florida parishes remained limited. And, despite its prized location along the Mississippi River, the region would continue to serve as an afterthought to Spanish policy planners. As Gálvez focused on Pensacola, British sympathizers staged a briefly successful rising at Natchez, which had been relin-

---

2. VI *Official Letter Books of W.C.C. Claiborne, 1801-1816*, at 161-62 (Dunbar Rowland ed., 1917); Robin F. A. Fabel, *The Economy of British West Florida, 1763-1783* (1988); Robin F. A. Fabel, 'Boom in the Bayous: Land Speculation and Town Planning in the Florida Parishes Under British Rule', *in A Fierce and Fractious Frontier: The Curious Development of Louisiana's Florida Parishes, 1699-2000*, at 44-57 (Samuel C. Hyde ed., 2004) [hereinafter Fabel, *Boom in the Bayous*]; King Robinson, 'Sustaining the Glory: Spain's Melting Pot Army in the Lower Mississippi Valley, 1779-1781', 1 Se. La. Rev. 5-23 (2008).

quished to the Spanish as part of the negotiations concluding the surrender at Baton Rouge. In contrast to O'Reilly's harsh treatment of the rebels at New Orleans, Gálvez sought to establish Spanish authority through accommodation rather than intimidation. The rebels at Natchez were spared the "iron fist" of Spanish rule, a decision which set the tone for Spanish governance of West Florida.[3]

The very terms of the treaty confirming Spanish authority in West Florida advanced the ambiguous nature of their rule. More significant, the fact that the Spanish accepted such uncertainties suggested that problems would undoubtedly soon arise. The treaty ceding the territory to Spain did so without confirming the territorial borders. The failure to establish firm boundaries, especially to the north, reflected Spain's interest in the territory primarily as a buffer to contain American expansionism. Vicente Folch, Spanish governor at Pensacola, insisted that its proximity to New Orleans, extensive contact with the American frontier, and control of the mouths of key waterways demanded that "West Florida must be considered an object of greatest importance to Spain, just as the American government is certain to eventually endeavor to acquire it at almost any cost or risk." Despite such warnings, the policies Spanish government would adopt once their authority was established would aggravate an increasingly troubled state of affairs.[4]

In the fall of 1795 the Treaty of San Lorenzo (Pickney's Treaty) established the thirty-first parallel as the northern boundary of West Florida. American desire to secure the entire east bank of the Mississippi River and the ever growing numbers of adventurers from Kentucky and Tennessee traversing the great river lent credence to Spain's acceptance of the contracted border. With the exception of the region in immedi-

---

3. Robinson, *supra* note 2, at 5-23; Pa. Evening Post, & Daily Advertiser, June 6, 1783; John W. Caughey, 'The Natchez Rebellion of 1781 and Its Aftermath', XVI La. Hist. Q. 57-83 (Jan. 1933).
4. Isaac J. Cox, *The West Florida Controversy, 1798-1813: A Study in American Diplomacy* 16-17 (1918); 29, II Balance, & Columbian Repository (Hudson, N.Y.), July 19, 1803, at 227; *David Narrett, Adventurism and Empire: The Struggle for Mastery in the Louisiana-Florida Borderlands, 1762-1803*, at 111 (2015).

ate proximity to the Mississippi River, the bulk of the territory extending east to the Pearl River remained woefully under populated. Like the British before them, the Spanish encouraged immigration among their countrymen enjoying some success, especially among Canary Islanders, who established small yet viable communities along the lower Amite and Tickfaw rivers. The pressure created by the burgeoning populations of the surrounding American controlled territory nonetheless encouraged the Spanish to consider the ever increasing numbers of Anglo-Protestant "Caintucks" as less desirable, yet necessary, inhabitants to advance Spanish control of the region.[5]

Hoping to also tap into the migration of disaffected British loyalists from the east coast seeking a home in territory not controlled by the Americans, the Spanish offered generous land grants as an added inducement. The possibility of populating the territory with people on poor terms with the United States mitigated the distaste for Anglo-Protestant settlers. In exchange for a generous grant of land, often in parcels of 800 arpents or roughly 640 acres, the settlers were required only to pledge loyalty to the Spanish Crown and embrace Catholicism, or at least avoid openly practicing their Protestant faith. Offered a substantial amount of tax free land, few found it difficult to embrace in word what they may quickly ignore in practice. Through such an arrangement Spain had opened her territorial doors to an influx of settlers gaining access through subterfuge. In essence, Spain now based her fortunes in West Florida on scores of individuals harboring at best suspect loyalty whose newfound wealth had been largely obtained through deceit.[6]

---

5. Fabel, *Boom in the Bayous*, *supra* note 2, at 44-57; Gilbert Din, 'Proposals and Plans for Colonization in Spanish Louisiana, 1787-1790', 11 La. Hist. 197, 197-213 (1970); Gilbert Din, 'The Canary Islander Settlements of Spanish Louisiana: An Overview', 27 La. Hist. 353, 353-73 (1986); Stanley C. Arthur, *The Story of the West Florida Rebellion* 25 (1935).
6. Din, *Proposals and Plans for Colonization in Spanish Louisiana, 1787-1790*, *supra* note 5, at 197-98, 201; Alvin L. Bertrand, *The Many Louisianas: Rural Social Areas and Cultural Islands* (1955); H.M. Brackenridge, *Views of Louisiana: Together with a Journal of a Voyage Up the Missouri River*, in 1811, at 281 (1814); Arthur, *supra* note 5, at 16.

Spanish policy encouraged the settlers to reside on their land and cultivate as much as they could. Yet from the outset Spanish land distribution policies sowed the seeds for future discontent. In their haste to encourage settlement, the Spanish offered grants that conflicted with or overlapped earlier British grants, which the Spanish had promised to honor. Making matters even worse, both the Spanish and British land grants were almost always vague and confusing. Illustrative of the imprecision inherent in the British titles is a 1776 grant along the Amite River:

> Elihu Bay receives all that tract of land situated on the east side of the River Amit [sic] about four miles back from said river upon a creek called the Three Creeks butting and bounding southwesterly unto land surveyed out to Joseph Blackwell and on all other sides by vacant land.

An 1804 Spanish grant similarly proclaimed that "Luke Collins claims four hundred superficial arpents nine leagues up the east bank of the Tickfaw River, bounded on one side by William George and by public land on the other two."[7]

With no background check on new arrivals, the region quickly became a magnet for army deserters and other desperadoes eager to claim the free land and/or prey upon others who did. The virtual absence of entertainment or any source of amusement rendered military service along the Gulf Coast a breeding ground for disaffection. Troops unfortunate enough to

---

7. Letter from William Ogilvy to My Dear Sir, (Nov. 29, 1805) (on file with the Daniel Hicky Papers, Louisiana and Lower Mississippi Valley Collection, Louisiana State University) [hereinafter LLMVC]; William Wilton Map of Landholdings in British West Florida, 1774, made for Governor Peter Chester (on file with the Donald Sharp Collection, Center for Southeast Louisiana Studies, Southeastern Louisiana University) [hereinafter CSLS]; Petition of John McDonogh to the Honorable District Judge of the State of Louisiana, Holding Sessions in the Parish of Orleans in Said State, concerns disputed land claims in West Florida (on file with the West Florida Collection, Box 3, folder 1, CSLS); 'Documents Covering a Royal Land Grant and Other Transactions on the Mississippi and Amite Rivers During the English Rule', XII La. Hist. Q. 638 (Henry Dart ed., 1929); John H. Napier III, Lower Pearl River's Piney Woods: Its Land and People 31 (1985); News Dig. (Amite City), Aug. 7, 1975.

be assigned to the garrisons from Pensacola to Baton Rouge complained of uninhabitable barracks and miserable sanitary facilities that in many cases emitted a "stench sufficient to knock a man down." Such conditions were augmented by an ever present fear of the native tribes. Reports of atrocities committed by the tribes surrounding the outposts of West Florida, including the Choctaw and fierce Tunicas, kept British soldiers in a constant state of unease. A 1764 British expedition up the Mississippi River headed by Major Arthur Loftus suffered 37 desertions from approximately 340 men before they even made contact with native warriors south of Natchez. Loftus blamed his poor showing partly on "the great desertions we had." French reports reflected similar numbers of desertions among troops stationed in the area. Following the abortive French rising against Spanish ascendancy at New Orleans, 130 French soldiers were reported to have deserted and taken refuge in West Florida.[8]

With colonial resources stretched beyond capacity, Spain lacked both the ability and will to discourage fugitives from locating in West Florida. Spanish policy nonetheless reflected something far more foreboding for the future stability of the territory. Concerned more about American encroachment upon their far more lucrative territories to the west, Spanish officials seemed more interested in quantity rather than quality. Spanish efforts to attract industrious and disgruntled former British loyalists as well as other anti-American Anglo-Protestant settlers worked hand-in-glove with their tolerance of varying degrees of fugitives. The presumed loyalty secured from the more industrious settlers through liberal land grants was matched by the protective shield Spanish tolerance offered rogue elements. The creation of community, based on such

---

8. Letter from Hugh Davis to David Holmes (Sept. 25, 1810) (on file with the Governor David Holmes Territorial Administration Papers, Mississippi Department of Archives and History) [hereinafter MDAH]; Robert R. Rea, 'Military Deserters from British West Florida', 9 La. Hist. 123, 123-37 (1968); James Peacock, 'Historical and Statistical Sketches of Louisiana', XI De Bow's Rev. 265 (1851); Thomas D. Clark, 'The Piney Woods and the Cutting Edge of the Lingering Southern Frontier', *in Mississippi's Piney Woods: A Human Perspective* 64 (Noel Polk ed., 1986).

unlikely neighbors, could work only if an effective legal system was put in place capable of efficiently protecting productive residents *and* enforcing respect for the law among the more desperate. The bold gamble to create a loyal population among such diverse elements was doomed to failure before it began.[9]

Nothing about Spanish ascendancy in West Florida suggested they were engaged in a noble experiment to improve the character of some through intermingling with more productive and purposeful others. Instead, blind self-interest revealed Spanish governance as flawed and unimaginative. The Spanish relied on alcaldes, magistrates who conducted both judicial and administrative functions, to offer a visible presence of their authority. In 1805 approximately 200 Spanish troops manned the fort at Baton Rouge and a small garrison of no more than two dozen soldiers remained stationed at the twin river towns of Bayou Sara and St. Francisville in the Feliciana District north of Baton Rouge. Outside of an occasional posting of a handful of men at the river port of Springfield in the lower St. Helena District to the east, no troops were present to sustain Spanish authority in the remaining expansive Chifoncte' District, later St. Ferdinand, that stretched between the Tangipahoa and Pearl rivers.[10]

With only three garrisons of any substance in the vast 300-mile expanse between Baton Rouge and Pensacola, criminal

---

9. Proclamation to the Inhabitants of the District of New Feliciana (July 1, 1810) on file with the Philip Hicky Letter Book, Hicky Family Papers, LLMVC); Sets of Orders Signed by Charles de Grand-Pré Concerning Opposition to Admission of Deserters and Bandits to Spanish Territory (Apr. 29, 1805) (on file with the Philip Hicky Letter Book, Hicky Family Papers, LLMVC); Letter from Edw. Randolph to David Holmes (Feb. 5, 1811) (on file with the Holmes Territorial Administration Papers, MDAH).

10. Regulations To Be Observed by the Syndics and Alcalds, of the Jurisdiction of Baton Rouge, Signed by Vicente Folch (Oct. 30, 1804) (on file with the West Florida Republic Collection, CSLS); Resolution of the Undersigned Delegates of the District of Baton Rouge (Sept. 4, 1810) (on file with the Philip Hicky Letter Book, Hicky Family Papers, LLMVC); 'William C.C. Claiborne to James Madison, March 26, 1805', *in* 6 *State Department Territorial Papers*, Orleans Series, 1764-1813, January 1–June 21, 1805 (1958); Cox, *supra* note 4, at 153-54; Copy of Map of Spanish West Florida (1810) (on file with the West Florida Revolt Collection, CSLS).

activity thrived. Marauders, including newly arriving deserters from the American army also seeking safe haven in the territory, were free to raid with impunity. Moreover, the absence of a visible Spanish presence diminished any claims of loyalty expected among the residents. Instead, whether intentional or merely the product of an overstretched empire, Spanish neglect contributed to the emergence of a fiercely independent people whose self-reliance extended to personal, and frequently violent, resolution of perceived injustices and grievances.[11]

In such a potentially volatile situation weak leadership could be catastrophic. In command at Baton Rouge as the situation came to a head in 1804 was Don Carlos de Grand-Pre'. French by birth and regularly accused of pro-French sympathies, de Grand-Pré was generally well regarded by pro-Spanish residents despite the claims of duplicity. Others regarded him far differently. Among the regional residents who were not considered friends to the Spanish commandant were the notorious Kemper brothers: Reuben, Nathan, and Samuel. Since their arrival in the area, the Kempers had endured some failed business ventures along with some property disputes. In June 1804 Alexander Stirling, the local alcalde, sought to evict one of the Kempers from a piece of property provoking a series of incidents that eventually resulted in the local militia chasing the Kempers and a small gang of followers across the border into the Mississippi Territory.[12]

Through the summer of 1804 the Kempers, at the head of thirty to forty followers, launched a series of raids into West Florida from their base just across the border in the Mississippi

---

11. Letter from Hugh Davis to David Holmes, *supra* note 8; Letter from Joseph Kennedy to the Convention of the State of West Florida (Nov. 3, 1810) (on file with the Documents and Papers Concerning Transactions During Civil Commotions in West Florida, 1799-1827, container no. 15, reel 4, West Florida Collection, Library of Congress); Cox, *supra* note 4, at 153-55; Arthur, *supra* note 5, at 29. For an explanation of the character of the people residing in the region and their historic tendency for violent resolution of grievances, see Hyde, *supra* note 1, at chs. 1, 5, 6.

12. Cox, *supra* note 4, at 152-54; Andrew McMichael, 'The Kemper "Rebellion": Filibustering and Resident Anglo American Loyalty in Spanish West Florida', 43 La. Hist. 133, 147-48 (2002).

Territory near Pinckneyville. The gang burned some homes, including the attempted arson of the home of alcalde and captain of the militia Vicente Pintado, intimidated Spanish loyalists, and stole property including slaves. The Kempers claimed to have the authority of territorial governor William C. C. Claiborne behind their efforts. In early August the gang took their troublemaking to a new level by launching a political rebellion. On August 7 Nathan and Samuel Kemper crossed the border with thirty followers and captured Pintado, along with two other militia captains, and successfully torched Pintado's house and gin. Carrying a blue and white striped flag with two white stars on a field of blue, the rebels marched on Baton Rouge initiating the Kemper Rebellion.[13]

As they advanced, the rebels posted a proclamation urging West Floridians to "throw off the galling yoke of tyranny and become freemen by declaring ourselves a free and independent people, and by supporting with our lives and property that declaration." The rebels camped near the fort at Baton Rouge exchanging a few shots with the defenders who dared not venture from their garrison and awaited reinforcement from supporters who never came. On August 9 the rebels withdrew to Bayou Sara before withdrawing into the Mississippi territory utterly dismayed that their actions had failed to provoke any semblance of a popular rising from the people of West Florida.[14]

Instead of joining the revolt, hundreds of local men flocked to Baton Rouge in support of the Spanish. Others maneuvered to cut off the raiders and report on suspicious activities. Governor Folch, who upon hearing of the potential for trouble along the Mississippi, authorized the construction of a road between Mobile and Baton Rouge, hurried from Pensacola with a force of 150 men. By the time he arrived in September the rebels had long dispersed. Folch nonetheless remained in the area a few weeks to monitor the situation and make a show of Spanish strength. Before he departed, lingering concerns encouraged Folch to issue a series of directives designed to

---

13. Cox, *supra* note 4, at 155-56; Arthur, *supra* note 5, at 26.
14. Copy of the Proclamation, Charleston Courier, Sept. 2, 1804; McMichael, *supra* note 12, at 154-55.

"protect innocence against the attacks of calumny . . . and to punish the wicked."[15]

Despite such forthright efforts to suppress seditious elements and encourage loyalty to Spain among the people, the indecision and timidity that characterized Grand Pre's later years as commandant at Baton Rouge would be dramatically amplified by his successor. In the spring of 1807 another French born officer in the Spanish service assumed command at Baton Rouge. Carlos Dehault DeLassus had enjoyed a variety of postings amid Spain's holdings in North America including service as lieutenant governor of the upper Louisiana territory prior to the Louisiana Purchase. Almost immediately upon assuming command at Baton Rouge, DeLassus commenced practices that would doom Spanish authority in West Florida and further a troubling pattern for the region's future development.[16]

The neglect that characterized Spanish governance at Baton Rouge in the years prior to his arrival proved immediately apparent to DeLassus. Unimpressed by the small river town itself, the new commandant was dismayed by the condition of the fort. Despite some efforts at repair, the fort, the very symbol of Spanish power on the lower Mississippi, was utterly dilapidated and suggestive of the condition of Spanish affairs in the territory. Aside from a handful of soldiers at St. Francisville, the little more than two dozen troops stationed at the fort were all that remained available to DeLassus; Folch at Pensacola remained a long distance away. Leary of antagonizing any of

---

15. Letter from M. Moore to David Holmes (Oct. 1, 1810) (on file with the Holmes Territorial Administration Papers, MDAH) (noting power of pro-Spanish supporters); Letter from William Cooper to Vicente Folch (Sept. 12, 1810) (on file with the Papeles de Cuba, Legajo 1568 B, letter no. 982, Library of Congress, West Florida Collection, CSLS); St. Helena Volunteer Militia in Spanish Service, (1805) (on file with the Papeles de Cuba, Legajo 142B, folios 144-46, West Florida Collection, CSLS); Regulations to be Observed by the Syndics and Alcalds, of the Jurisdiction of Baton Rouge (Oct. 30, 1804) (on file with the West Florida Republic Collection, CSLS); Cox, *supra* note 4, at 157-58.

16. Cox, *supra* note 4, at 325; William C. Davis, *The Rogue Republic: How Would Be Patriots Waged the Shortest Revolution in American History* 118-19 (2011).

the myriad of factions that swirled about him in his new assignment, DeLassus bided his time. He neglected to advance some decrees initiated but not yet enacted by his predecessor Grand Pre and failed to enforce the collection of debts due the government particularly regarding state sanctioned land surveys. Of greatest concern to those supporting order and the need to ensure public safety, DeLassus proved inept at directing his own garrison troops whose officers soon reached a state of near revolt against his botched leadership. In short, DeLassus did virtually nothing, and in the absence of firm leadership residents of varying stripes began to take matters into their own hands. Spanish neglect allowed for the flowering of notions of independent minded action and a warped impression of individual rights as necessary attributes for survival among many residents.[17]

Rather than decisive action that would have at least galvanized support among one faction or the other DeLassus practiced accommodation, if not cooperation, with the most dangerous faction challenging his authority. Beyond those who longed for a revival of French or British authority, if for no other reason than to protect their land claims, as well as the deserters and desperadoes who favored no authority whatsoever, three distinct factions jockeyed for influence. The American faction included disgruntled settlers who were disappointed that the region had not been included in the Louisiana Purchase of 1803. The pro-Spanish faction preferred things to remain as they were. This group wanted to secure their Spanish land grants but also enjoyed the hands-off manner of Spanish governance in opposition to the obligations of citizenship, such as voting and jury service, certain to come with American control. The final faction may best be regarded as "Independents." This group saw in the possibility of creating an independent nation from Baton

---

17. *'Proceedings of the First Convention of West Florida'*, entry July 27, 1810, *in The Territorial Papers of the United States* 9:893-95 (Clarence E. Carter ed., 1934-62); Journal of the West Florida Convention and Legislature (July 26-29 & Sept. 22, 1810), and Convention of Florida to His Excellency Governor David Holmes (Sept. 22, 1810) (on file with the West Florida Collection, container 14, reel no. 4, Library of Congress); Cox, *supra* note 4, at 369-71; Davis, *supra* note 16, at 122, 161-64.

Rouge to Pensacola opportunity for self-aggrandizement free of the demands of American citizenship amid better security than what could be provided by Spain. Confirming the chaos that the uncertainties of Spanish governance had provoked in West Florida, Governor William C. C. Claiborne, of the neighboring Orleans Territory advised the American government, "the people of Florida will be assailed by a host of intriguers. There will perhaps be a French party and an English party, and a party who would wish to set up for themselves!"[18]

By the summer of 1810, events in Europe offered a subterfuge for actions that could exploit DeLassus' neglect. Napoléon Bonaparte's incursion into Spain and usurpation of the Spanish throne provided the pretext for direct action. Proclaiming their loyalty to the Spanish king Ferdinand VII, a group of Feliciana planters gathered and called for a "convention" to be created to support the Spanish officials should their official capacities be compromised by the French actions. Perhaps to no one's surprise, this independence of action quickly progressed further. In late July anonymous broadsides, signed "A Friend of the People," were found posted about the Feliciana District. The broadside declared "the time has come for us to look out for ourselves," and called upon the Convention to declare independence. Rather than seek to identify and punish such treasonous actions, DeLassus sought accommodation.

> When I learned of the movements there existed, tending to cause a revolt in this city, I did not doubt for a moment the loyalty of those who have never ceased giving proofs of said

18. Letter from William C.C. Claiborne to William Wykoff (June 14, 1810), *in Official Letter Books of W.C.C. Claiborne, 1801-1816*, at 5:31-4 (Dunbar Rowland ed., 1917); Letter from Harry Toulmin to David Holmes (Aug. 19, 1810) (on file with the Governor David Holmes Territorial Administration Papers, Doc. No. 1075, MDAH); Letter from Hugh Davis to Holmes (Sept. 25, 1810) (on file with the Governor David Holmes Territorial Administration Papers, Doc. No. 1097, MDAH); Proclamation to the Inhabitants of the District of New Feliciana, *supra* note 9; Letter from Frederick Kimball to Dear Friends (Mar. 5, 1811) (on file with the Kimball Letters, LLMVC); Letter from Kimball to Dear Sir (Dec. 9, 1810) (on file with the Kimball Letters, LLMVC); Samuel C. Hyde, Jr., 'Consolidating the Revolution: Factionalism and Finesse in the West Florida Revolt, 1810', 51 La. Hist. 265-67 (2010).

> loyalty since the very moment they took the oath pledging to defend the Spanish flag.

DeLassus further called upon his "loyal" subjects to "declare and give full information" as to "who is author of the filthy writings."[19]

As the Convention methodically usurped authority under the guise of support for Spain, even offering to authorize a salary for DeLassus, the intentions of their anti-Spanish supporters began to emerge. An August 13, 1810, letter from eighteen respected residents of St. Francisville to their Convention representatives proclaimed,

> you are the true representatives of the people, we consider you empowered to act independent of any other authority whatever if that authority refuses to adopt or sanction such measures as you may conceive necessary for our future welfare and respectability. And we pledge ourselves to support you in whatsoever you may do that shall have a tendency to promote the desirable objects of your delegation.

Twelve days later the increasingly emboldened Convention took matters to the next level. In a letter to the Convention dated August 25, 1810, a clearly frustrated DeLassus rejected their request to provide a full accounting of all arms and forces in the area and their suggestion that Fulwar Skipwith, a recent arrival in West Florida who had not pledged loyalty to Spain, be named general of the militia. Increasing calls for independence emerged in Bayou Sara and in the adjoining village of St. Francisville where hostility to the Spanish was now barely concealed. The Spanish commandant at Bayou Sara, Thomas Estevan, begged DeLassus to send him a boat so that he and his command of "four unhappy soldiers" could flee if the enmity for Spain flared into open revolt. Shepherd Brown, alcalde in

---

19. Letter from Carlos DeLassus to Don's Thos. Lilly, Juan Johnson, Juan Leonard, Philip Hicky, and Juan Mills (July 30, 1810) (on file with the West Florida Rebellion Papers, LLMVC); Letter from Harry Toulmin to David Holmes (Aug. 19, 1810) (on file with the Holmes Territorial Administration Papers, MDAH); Davis, *supra* note 16, at 158.

the St. Helena district further east, reported on growing tension in the area advising DeLassus that he no longer trusted his militia officers.[20]

In the face of mounting evidence that a revolt was coming, DeLassus continued to procrastinate. Other than penning a couple of letters to known Spanish supporters inquiring of conditions in their areas, his only forthright action was to host a series of dinner parties in honor of the Convention. Ostensibly hosted to celebrate loyalty to Spain, the gatherings outraged his officers and conclusively revealed Spanish authority as weak and ineffective. With the intimidation of government seemingly complete, on September 22, 1810, the Convention unanimously declared that "Carlos Dehault Delassus be divested of all authority as governor of this jurisdiction and that the colonel commandant of the militia be subject to the orders of this convention only." As icing on the cake of humiliation and defeat, a woefully tardy appeal for aid from DeLassus to Folch fell into enemy hands when a rebel patrol intercepted the courier. With Spanish duplicity revealed, shortly before sunrise the following morning rebels stormed the fort at Baton Rouge, and following a brief firefight that left two Spanish dead and five wounded, raised the Lone Star flag initiating the short lived Republic of West Florida, the original Lone Star state. In proclaiming the Republic, the rebels revealed their understanding that legal authority can be intimidated and that violent resolution of grievances is an effective solution to perceived injustice—a legacy of Spanish governance that would have profound implications for future generations in southeast Louisiana.[21]

---

20. Proclamation to the Inhabitants of the District of New Feliciana, *supra* note 9; Letter from Carlos DeLassus to Don's Thos. Lilly, Juan Johnson, Juan Leonard, Philip Hicky, and Juan Mills, *supra* note 19; Letter from the Inhabitants of St. Francisville to Their Representatives Assembled at St. John's Plains (Aug. 13, 1810) (on file with the West Florida Rebellion Papers, LLMVC); Letter from DeLassus to the House of Representatives (Aug. 25, 1810) (on file with the West Florida Rebellion Papers, LLMVC); Cox, *supra* note 4, at 371-74.

21. Letter from John Johnson, William Barrow, John Mills, and John Rhea to Philip Hicky, George Mather, Richard Deval, and Thomas Lilly (July 3, 1810)

Spanish policies and jurisprudence including land grant regulations and loosely enumerated title surveys, toleration of suspect residents including known deserters from multiple armies, lack of resources, especially troops, to enforce the necessary mechanisms of governance, and timid, if not ineffective, leadership doomed their authority in West Florida. Land policies that sought to curry loyalty through large grants that frequently overlapped existing French or British grants contributed directly to a number of vicious family feuds in the late nineteenth century. Permitting lawless elements to assume residency necessarily advanced social instability and the absence of resources to enforce legal authority set a precedent for ignoring or resisting the rule of law among many multi-generational resident families in the region. Worst of all, the absence of a forthright commandant willing to take risks to enforce the law signaled that legally constituted authority can be cowed just as the violent overthrow of the government demonstrated armed resistance to authority could be an effective means for resolving grievances.

In the 100 years following the West Florida Revolt of 1810, Louisiana's Florida parishes suffered some of the highest rural homicide rates recorded in American history. The violence included large scale family feuds that co-opted the legal system and rendered the system of justice impotent. As context, in the same period the great Hatfield-McCoy feud witnessed twelve murders in a twelve-year period with at least some of the perpetrators brought to justice, the Florida parishes witnessed 133 feud related murders with few of the criminals ever successfully prosecuted. The violence, much of it occurring over the ruins of a collapsed legal system, also included mass race riots, union busting, and a precursor to what we know today as ethnic cleansing in addition to scores of bushwhackings and other murders. In an effort to explain the seemingly

---

(on file with the Hicky Family Papers, LLMVC); Proclamation to the Inhabitants of the District of New Feliciana, *supra* note 9; Journal of the Convention and Legislature of West Florida, 1810 (Sept. 22, 1810) (on file with the West Florida Collection, container no. 14, reel no. 4, Library of Congress); Letter from Philemon Thomas to John Rhea (Sept. 24, 1810) (on file with the West Florida Rebellion Papers, LLMVC); Cox, *supra* note 4, at 370-71.

endless chaos that prevailed in the Florida parishes, the New Orleans *Picayune* described the residents as peculiar people "exceedingly jealous of what they deem their rights, and it was mainly through their misconception of what those rights really were that the troubles originated." In a scathing 1909 demand for the establishment of order in the region, the same paper offered a list of reasons the region should be a model of progress, adding "these would seem to be highly civilizing instruments and influences, yet cowardly assassination and savage human slaughter are as rife there as when the country was densely covered with pine forests and modern development was unknown." The *Picayune* noted if the majority of people were not peaceable "it would be the duty of state authorities to go into that region with sufficient force and subdue it savage people into a condition of civilization and order. What then is the matter?" Grimly answering its own queries the newspaper bemoaned the region's future.

> Even if the lawless element is in the minority it is able to so terrorize the balance of the community to such a degree, that the bloody outlaws work their will while everybody submits. As to the courts apparently they punish none of the worst criminals, if indeed they ever get possession of them, but the defaults of the criminal courts are wholly chargeable to the juries.[22]

Even today the region groans under the burden of its past toleration for violent resolution of perceived grievances. In 1996 the Federal Bureau of Investigation released criminal statistics confirming the United States status at the forefront of violence among industrialized nations. The South led in rates of violent crime among the various regions of the nation contributing inordinately to the national homicide rate of 7.4 per 100,000 deaths. Louisiana led the nation with a rate of 17.5 per 100,000 deaths which contrasted sharply with last place South

---

22. Daily Picayune, Apr. 12, 1899, Feb. 28, 1909. For a comprehensive explanation of the chaotic circumstances characterizing the Florida parishes in the late nineteenth century, see Hyde, Jr., *supra* note 1, chs. 5, 6.

Dakota's 1.2 per 100,000. Federal Bureau of Investigation statistical reports for 2012 confirmed Louisiana's leadership in national homicide rates at 10.8 per 100,000 deaths over second ranked South Carolina at 6.8. When broken down by parish in state reports to the FBI, the Florida parishes continue as leaders in rural homicide in the Bayou State. Statistical analysis included in the 2013 Louisiana Supreme Court Annual Report further identify the Twenty-First and Twenty-Second Judicial Districts, both located in the Florida parishes, as state leaders in per capita criminal cases filed in rural districts. Despite a dramatically changed economic and political landscape, the Florida parishes continue to manifest a grim commitment to an enduring tradition of violent resolution of grievances.[23]

Scholarly explanations for this enduring pattern of behavior have traditionally assigned blame to lessons internalized by regional residents during a brutal period of Civil War and Reconstruction. Following the fall of the Confederate bastion at Port Hudson in the summer of 1863, the War entered a new level of savagery highlighted by guerrilla operations and vicious reprisals. Reconstruction witnessed the rise to ascendance of terroristic organizations such as the Ku Klux Klan and Knights of the White Camellia who employed collective violence to effectively overthrow the Reconstruction government. The brutality of the Civil War and Reconstruction did provide additional lessons in the effectiveness of violence and reinforced the belief that legal authority can be cowed. The sixteen years of instability from secession to redemption nonetheless proved but a reinforcement of traditions dating back to antecedents originating in the years preceding American annexation. A period where legal authority failed the law abiding and residents routinely resorted to personal and collec-

---

23. FBI homicide statistics reprinted in Fox Butterfield, 'Why the South's Homicide Rate Is So High', N.Y. Times, July 26, 1998; Fed. Bureau of Investigation, Uniform Crime Report (2012, 2015); La. Comm'n on Law Enf't, Louisiana Index Crimes Reported to the FBI Through the Louisiana Uniform Crime Report (2006, 2007); Ctr. for Disease Control, Louisiana Homicide Death Rate, 1999-2014; Ctr. for Disease Control, Louisiana Life Expectancy Report (2015); Supreme Court of La. of the Judicial Council of the Supreme Court, Annual Report 44-47 (2013); Times-Picayune, Sept. 27, 2016.

tive violence to right perceived injustices even to the point of overthrowing the government. The chronic social instability, along with armed insurrections such as the Kemper Rising and West Florida Revolt, resulted from policies and practices first evident in the Spanish era. A proper understanding of the troubled history of Louisiana's Florida parishes accordingly demands consideration of precedents that originated in the Spanish period whose legacies remain evident to this day.

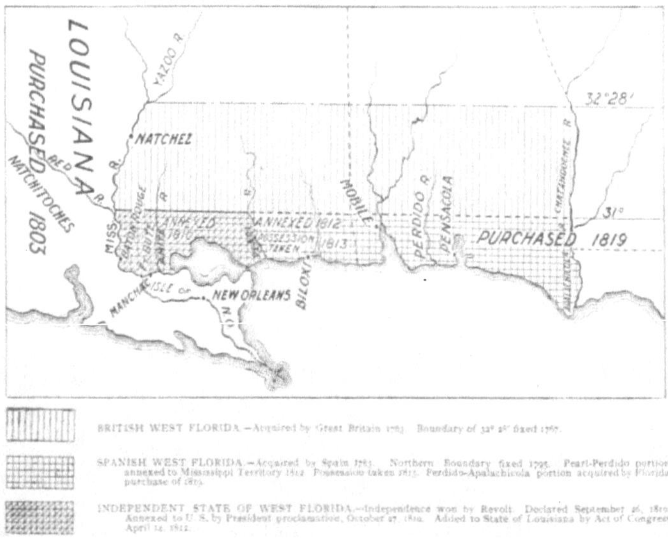

Map showing piecemeal reduction of Spanish territorial control in West Florida, 1803
(Henry E. Chambers, *West Florida and its Relation to the Historical Cartography of the United States* (1898)

CHAPTER 8

THE SUPREME COURT, FLORIDA LAND CLAIMS, AND SPANISH COLONIAL LAW

M.C. Mirow

INTRODUCTION

After Florida became a U.S. territory in 1821, Congress established commissions to determine private land ownership in the territory.[1] A series of federal laws on this subject followed until the mid-nineteenth century. Commissioners and the decisions of territorial courts, such as the Superior Court of East Florida, determined many claims. Some large claims were appealed to the Supreme Court of the United States where Spanish colonial law, more properly "*derecho indiano*" as used in this Chapter, was employed to decide questions of title to land.[2] With the bulk of these appeals in the 1830s and 1840s, the Supreme Court was the final arbiter in approximately sixty cases of titles to land in Florida. The stakes were high. Disputed grants often exceeded 10,000 acres and some claims exceeded one million acres. The largest successful claim was for 1,200,000 acres, approximately the size of the state

1. Louise Biles Hill, 'Introduction', *in* 1 *Spanish Land Grants in Florida* i-lvii (Florida Works Progress Administration ed. 1940).
2. For a brief discussion of the terms "Spanish colonial law" and "*derecho indiano*," see M.C. Mirow, 'Pre-Constitutional Law and Constitutions: Spanish Colonial Law and the Constitution of Cádiz', 12 Wash. U. Glob. Stud. L. Rev. 317 (2013).

of Rhode Island. Two larger claims for 1,850,000 and 12,000,000 acres were denied. The Supreme Court confirmed grants totaling nearly two million acres.[3] These cases have received very sparse or no treatment in the standard histories of the Court during this period.[4]

This study focuses on the way the Supreme Court dealt with these cases with special attention to its use of *derecho indiano*, an early and unusual example of the Court's necessary use of foreign law. It examines the Court's sources, skill, limitations, and biases when addressing complex issues of land title under a foreign legal system. Some lawyers developed a level of expertise in these matters and were consulted in such cases. Although focusing on the Supreme Court, this contribution notes that the records of lower courts and claims commissions are promising and neglected sources for studying the development of comparative law and legal methodologies in U.S. tribunals.

Part II of this Chapter describes the applicable treaty provision, the commissions established by statute, and the Supreme Court's jurisdiction in these cases. Part III analyzes the cases

---

3. These cases are listed in the Appendix. While most cases of Florida land claims before the Supreme Court worked their way up through the levels of the commissioner or the Superior Court of the Territory, some cases were not filed before these lower levels and not reflected in Spanish Land Grants in Florida, *supra* note 1, or the excellent database of claims found in *Spanish Land Grants*, Fla. Memory: St. Libr. & Archives Fla., https://www.floridamemory.com/collections/spanishlandgrants/. Studies assessing the number and extent of grants confirmed or the total amount of land in question subject to confirmation in Florida should survey these cases in addition to the published compilations of the work of the Florida land commissions. *See, e.g.*, Paul E. Hoffman, *Florida's Frontiers* 240, 245 n.7, 253, 270-72, 292-93 (2002). Using footnotes in the Appendix, I have attempted to find the related files for claimants before commissioners in the Spanish Land Grants database and match them to the related Supreme Court case.

4. David P. Currie, *The Constitution in the Supreme Court: The First Hundred Years 1789-1888*, at 277-81 (1985); Felix Frankfurter & James M. Landis, *The Business of the Supreme Court: A Study in the Federal Judicial System* (1928); Robert G. McCloskey, *The American Supreme Court* 53-59 (2000); Bernard Schwartz, *A History of the Supreme Court* 32-104 (1993); Carl B. Swisher, *The Taney Period 1836-64*, at 18, 750-1754 (1974); 1 Charles Warren, *The Supreme Court in United States History* 781-85 (1926); G. Edward White, *The Marshall Court and Cultural Change 1815-1835*, at 897 (1988).

determined by the Supreme Court, and Part IV delves into the Court's use of *derecho indiano* to decide claims to land.

THE ADAMS-ONÍS TREATY AND FLORIDA LAND CLAIMS

After Spanish control of Florida for nearly three hundred years, the transfer of the region to the United States was accomplished by the Adams-Onís Treaty of 1819.[5] Spain's monarch ceded:

> to the United States, in full property and sovereignty, all the territories which belong to him, situated to the Eastward of the Mississippi, known by the name of East and West Florida. The adjacent Islands dependent on said Provinces, all public lots and squares, vacant Lands, public Edifices, Fortifications, Barracks and other Buildings, which are not private property, Archives and Documents, which relate directly to the property and sovereignty of said Provinces, are included in this Article.[6]

Inhabitants of Florida who wanted to leave were permitted to sell and to transport their property without duty.[7] Those who stayed would become citizens of the United States.[8] Claims to property were specifically provided for in Article 8 that divided Spanish grants into two groups, those made before January 24, 1818, and those made after this date. Grants after January 24, 1818, the date cession to the United States was first proposed, were of no effect. Grants before this date were valid under the same conditions

---

5. The Treaty was signed in Washington on Feb. 22, 1819, ratified by Spain on Oct. 24, 1820, and entered into force on Feb. 22, 1821. In addition to ceding Florida to the United States, the Treaty established the United States' western border under the Louisiana Purchase and the relinquishment of its claim to Texas. Treaty of Amity, Settlement, and Limits, Between the United States of America and His Catholic Majesty (Adams-Onís Treaty), U.S.-Spain, art. 8, Feb. 22, 1819, 8 Stat. 252 [hereinafter Adams-Onís Treaty].

6. *Id.* art. 2.

7. *Id.* art. 5.

8. *Id.* art. 6.

required under Spanish law; conditions tied to grants had to be satisfied within the period specified in the grant from the time of the treaty.[9] Diplomatic crisis was averted when three massive Spanish grants made after the date, but predated to appear within the compass of the treaty, were cancelled.[10]

The treaty gave a mechanism to resolve claims by those who had interests held from Spain. The United States obligated itself to pay claims up to a total of five million dollars through a commission of three commissioners appointed by the President. The commission was to sit in Washington within three years of the treaty.[11] The commission was to decide claims "according to the principles of Justice, the Laws of Nations, and the stipulations of the Treaty between to the Parties of 27th October 1795."[12] The treaty also required that grants were to be recognized as valid if they were valid under Spanish law. This activity was taken up by commissions created under various Acts to determine the validity of land claims in East Florida.

Private lands under Spanish grants continued to be privately held and not part of the lands ceded directly to the United States in the Treaty. It was estimated that the territory contained approximately thirty million acres with three million acres

---

9. Adams-Onís Treaty, *supra* note 5, art. 8 states:

> All the grants of land made before the 24th of January 1818 by His Catholic Majesty or by his lawful authorities in the said Territories ceded by His Majesty to the United States, shall be ratified and confirmed to the persons in possession of the lands, to the same extent that the same grants would be valid if the Territories had remained under the Dominion of His Catholic Majesty. But the owners in possession of such lands, who by reason of the recent circumstances of the Spanish Nation and the Revolutions in Europe, have been prevented from fulfilling all the conditions of their grants, shall complete them within the terms limited in the same respectively, from the date of this Treaty; in default of which the said grants shall be null and void—all grants made since the said 24th of January 1818, when the first proposal on the part of His Catholic Majesty, for the cession of the Floridas was made, are hereby declared and agreed to be null and void.

10. George C. Whatley & Sylvia Cook, 'The East Florida Claims Commission: A Study in Frustration', 50 Fla. Hist. Q. 40 (1971).
11. Adams-Onís Treaty, *supra* note 5, art. 11.
12. *Id.*

granted to individuals as private property.[13] Unresolved private claims were the main obstacle to selling public lands, and their resolution became a priority in establishing U.S. control of the territory.[14] Some mechanism was needed to carve out these privately held lands from all the public lands that passed from the Spanish crown to the United States. This was accomplished through an array of institutions created under federal law. The general structure of the statutory scheme was to allocate smaller claims, those under 1000 or 3500 acres depending on the date, to commissions whose reports would be accepted by act of Congress to validate claims determined to be valid by the commissions. Larger claims and unresolved claims at the commission level went to territorial courts with final appeal to the Supreme Court of the United States.[15] Thus large claims and claims where there was not a final determination on the merits often wound up before the Supreme Court. This was not a novel situation for the United States that had to determine private land claims in Georgia and after the Louisiana Purchase in areas including Orleans, the district of Louisiana, and Missouri and Arkansas.[16]

Commission Established for Florida Land Claims: The Act of 1822

Federal legislation established the first commission in 1822. The act required the President to appoint three commissioners to adjudicate claims for West Florida in Pensacola and for East

---

13. United States v. Percheman, 32 U.S. 51, 89 (1833).

14. Hoffman, *supra* note 3, at 292-93. Spanish land grants had a lasting effect on property titles in Florida. Joe Knetsch, *The Impact of Spanish Land-Grants on the Development of Florida and the South Eastern United States*, FIG (2002), https://www.fig.net/resources/proceedings/fig_proceedings/fig_2002/HS3/HS3_knetsch.pdf.

15. Glenn Boggs, 'Florida Land Titles and British, Not Just Spanish, Origins', 81 (3) Fla. Bar. J. 26 (July-Aug. 2007) [hereinafter Boggs, *Florida Land Titles*]. Even some British grants from 1763 to 1783 could be caught up in this process if they had been confirmed by Spanish authorities and were thus arguably valid under Spanish law. *Id.* at 28-30.

16. United States v. Arredondo, 31 U.S. 691, 708, 718, 725 (1832).

Florida in St. Augustine.[17] A secretary to the commission who had to be familiar with Spanish was to record the proceedings of the commission and the reasons for the commission's admission or rejection of claims.[18] A surveyor and deputies were also to be appointed to survey and to record plats.[19] The session in St. Augustine was to run until the end of June, 1823, when the commission would forward its work to the Secretary of the Treasury for submission to Congress.[20] Claims dated before January 24, 1818, and not rejected by the treaty were to be submitted to the commission for determination. Claims based on British and Spanish grants were to be forwarded to the Treasury.[21] The Act empowered the commission to confirm claims based on the records and to determine if conditions placed on the grants had been performed. Confirmation of a claim released it from the United States' assertion of an interest in the property. The commission was granted jurisdiction over claims up to 1000 acres; claims exceeding this size were to be reported to the Treasury for determination by Congress.[22]

The Act of 1822 was amended the following year to apply its provisions exclusively to claims in West Florida.[23] Under the amendment of 1823, the President was to appoint three new commissioners for East Florida who would conduct their adjudication under the provisions of the Act of 1822.[24] This amendment raised the maximum claim before the commission to 3500 acres and loosened the evidentiary requirements for "actual settlers," an operative term in the legislation, to establish their claim.[25] The

---

17. An Act of ascertaining claims and titles to land within the territory of Florida, May 8, 1822, 3 Stat. 709, ch. 129, § 1 (1822); Hill, *supra* note 1, at xxxii-xxxvii (East Florida).
18. 3 Stat. 712-714, ch. 129, § 2 (1822).
19. 3 Stat. 718, ch. 129, § 6 (1822).
20. 3 Stat. 716-717, ch. 129, § 3 (1822).
21. 3 Stat. 717, ch. 129, § 4 (1822).
22. 3 Stat. 718, ch. 129, § 5 (1822).
23. An Act amending, and supplementary to, the "Act for ascertaining claims and titles to land in the territory of Florida," 3 Stat. 754, ch. 29, § 1 (1823); Hill, *supra* note 1, at xxxvii-xxxviii.
24. 3 Stat. 754-755, ch. 29, § 1 (1823); Hill, *supra* note 1, at xxxiv-xliv (East Florida).
25. 3 Stat. 755, ch. 29, § 2 (1823).

commissioners might seek legal opinions from the district attorney.[26] Claims were to be filed before December 1, 1823, or were barred.[27] A second amendment extended the date for filing claims to September 1, 1824.[28] The requirements for documents to assert a claim were loosened and the term "actual settler" was defined to include only those people who cultivated or occupied the land.[29]

Subsequent amendments extended the time to file claims and restructured institutions and schemes for settling claims. For example, on March 3, 1825, Congress extended the sessions of the commission to continue until January 1, 1826, with additional time to file claims.[30] The Act also created new keepers of public archives for East and West Florida who were charged with maintaining property records, translating them, and providing copies or translations to parties.[31] An Act in 1827 required that the commission deliver all its records to a newly created register and receiver for East Florida who would accept future claims, determine them, and report his activities to the Treasury for confirmation by Congress.[32] Thus, the commission was replaced with a register. This Act also delineated the procedure for creating surveys, claimants' certificates, and patents for the land.[33] Additionally, it stated the way claims larger than 3500 acres were to be surveyed and reserved from public sale pending their resolution.[34]

---

26. *Id.* § 4.
27. *Id.* § 5. The amendment also called for the appointment of surveyor for the territory of Florida and the creation of land offices in East and West Florida to dispose of surveyed public lands. 3 Stat. 755-756, ch. 29, §§ 7-10 (1823).
28. An Act to extend the time limited for the settlement of private land claims in the territory of Florida, Feb. 28, 1824, 4 Stat. 7, ch. 25, § 6 (1824).
29. *Id.* § 3.
30. An Act to extend the time for the settlement of private land claims in the territory of Florida, 4 Stat. 125, ch. 83, §§ 2-3 (1825).
31. 4 Stat. 126, ch. 83, §§ 9-12 (1825).
32. 4 Stat. 202 and 203, ch. 9, §§ 4-5 (1827).
33. 4 Stat. 203, ch. 9, §§ 7-8 (1827).
34. 4 Stat. 204, ch. 9, § 12 (1827).

Further Congressional Action

A number of claims could not be satisfactorily resolved through the mechanisms provided for in these acts, and in 1828, Congress addressed this situation with new legislation.[35] It stated that claims that were not "finally decided," larger than the tracts within the jurisdiction of the commission, and larger than the tracts confirmed by the Act of 1822 were to be decided by judges of the territorial courts under the similar act for lands for claimants in Missouri.[36] It also provided a summary method of confirming grants up to one square league (approximately 4400 acres) of land within a claim with the claimant releasing the excess amount.[37] The Act also importantly gave a method for resolving claims over 3500 acres. These claims were to go to the judge of the superior court of the district and were to be resolved the same way claims in Missouri were handled under the legislation for Missouri.[38] Appeals were to the Supreme Court.[39] Claims

---

35. 4 Stat. 284, ch. 70 (1828).
36. Section 6 of the Act of 1828 states that:

> all claims to land within the territory of Florida, embraced by the treaty, which shall not be finally decided and settled under the previous provisions of the same law, containing a greater quantity of land than the commissioners were authorised to decide, and above the amount confirmed by the act, and which have not been reported and adjudicated by the judge of the superior court of the district within which the land lies, upon the petition of the claimant, according to the forms, rules regulations, conditions, restrictions and limitations prescribed to the district judge, and claimants in Missouri, by the act of the 26th May 1824.

Either party, the United States or the claimant, was granted an appeal to the Supreme Court. 4 Stat. 285, ch. 70, §§ 7, 9.

Denial of a claim by the commission or by the register was not a final action that deprived the territorial court jurisdiction over the claim. United States v. Percheman, 32 U.S. 51, 95 (1833).

37. An Act supplementary to the several acts providing for the settlement and confirmation of private land claims in Florida, 4 Stat. 284, ch. 70, §§ 1-2 (1828); Hill, *supra* note 1, at xliv-li.
38. 4 Stat. 285, ch. 70, § 6 (1828).
39. *Id.* §§ 7, 9.

were to be barred if not filed within one year from the passage of the act, May 23, 1828.[40]

Congress hoped Florida land claims would be resolved by 1830. An Act of that year confirmed claims determined by the register and referred pending claims to the system established in the Act of 1828. It also explained the method for employing the square league settlement option and extending the deadline for using it.[41] On winding up its activities, the register was required to deliver its records to the keeper of the public archives.[42] Claims not falling under the provision of the Act for smaller grants were barred if not filed with the Superior Court before May 26, 1831.[43] A final act on this subject, in 1832, clarified the issuing of patents to heirs or others in the regular chain of title from the original claimant.[44]

Thus, instead of meeting in Washington as mentioned in the treaty, commissions were created in St. Augustine in East Florida and in Pensacola for West Florida. After his arrival in East Florida in 1822 as attorney general for the territory, Alexander Hamilton, a Columbia graduate and second son of the Federalist and eponymous Broadway hit, assessed the problems and complexity of land holding in the region. Faced with in his estimation 1200 Spanish claims and 500 British claims, including many fraudulent claims, Hamilton requested the creation of the new land commission for East Florida established by Congress on March 3, 1823. He, David Floyd, and William W. Blair were appointed the first commissioners.[45]

---

40. 4 Stat. 286, ch. 70, § 12 (1828).
41. An Act to provide for the final settlement of land claims in Florida, May 26, 1830, 4 Stat. 405, ch. 106, §§ 1-4, 7 (1830).
42. 4 Stat. 406, ch. 106, § 5 (1830).
43. United States v. Marvin, 44 U.S. 620, 622-24 (1845) (claim filed by Marvin in 1843 was barred by the Act of 1830). Similarly, appeals from the Superior Court had to be brought to the Supreme Court within four months of the decision. Villabolos v. United States, 47 U.S. 81, 89-91 (1848).
44. An Act to direct the manner of issuing patents on confirmed land claims in the territory of Florida, Jan. 23, 1832, 4 Stat. 496, ch. 10, § 1 (1832).
45. Whatley & Cook, *supra* note 10, at 41-42.

Validity of the grants in the United States required their validity under Spanish law.[46] This meant that the commissioners had to consider what Spanish law would apply to the claims presented. The construction of the applicable rules of *derecho indiano* was no easy task even for highly trained lawyers of the Spanish colonial empire.[47] Precisely how the commissioners accomplished this difficult task remains to be studied.[48] It appears that the commissioners focused on a provision from the *Recopilación de las Leyes de Indias* (1680) in which the governor was empowered to assign lands to settlers who would cultivate, reside on and settle grants of different sizes dependent upon the social class of the grantee.[49] Substantive rules of law related to claims were also drawn from "royal orders made with particular reference to Florida, the decrees and regulations of the local governors, and the customs and usages of the local administrations."[50]

While the rules of application governing the substance of property claims were a significant hurdle for the commission, disagreement over the procedural aspects of how to conduct the adjudication of claims led Hamilton to refuse to deliberate in claims, although he continued to attend the sessions. He claimed that the commission failed to examine and to apply Spanish law and to consult original documents. Hamilton tendered his resignation to President Monroe on January 23, 1824, but it was not accepted. He continued to complain of the commission's lack of established procedure, substantive rules, and systematic record keeping. He asserted that the other commissioners acted in favor of one claimant, John H. McIntosh, almost as counsel for the claimant, and asserted that under Spanish colonial law governors had nowhere near the comprehensive power to grant "fee simple" interests in land and in such quantities as asserted by the other

---

46. Adams-Onís Treaty, *supra* note 5, art. 8.
47. M.C. Mirow, *Latin American Law: A History of Private Law and Institutions in Spanish America* 11-94 (2004).
48. Hill, *supra* note 1, at liii-lviii (summarizing reasons for not confirming grants).
49. Whatley & Cook, *supra* note 10, at 44 (citing *Recopilación de las Leyes de Indias*, Lib. 12, Tit. 3 (1680)).
50. Whatley & Cook, *supra* note 10, at 45.

members of the commission.[51] Furthermore, the documents upon which claims could be determined were in disarray, and obtaining adequate translations for the commission was an additional obstacle to substantive determinations.[52]

Nonetheless, after the first two years of operation by the beginning of January 1826, the commission had taken action on over 780 claims. Of these, approximately 470 had been confirmed. An additional approximately 530 claims awaited determination. At the same time, the committee on public lands sent a report to the House of Representatives describing the work of the East Florida commission as unsatisfactory, and requested a different method for the resolution of claims. This led to the new register of public lands for East Florida, but this new office did little to alleviate the problem, and many claims wound up before the Supreme Court of the United States.[53]

In 1860, another act attempted to provide a final adjustment of Florida claims that had been rejected at some point but not finally resolved.[54] At least one case was resolved favorably for the

---

51. *Id.* at 45-47. Referring to the *Recopilación* as the "Codes of India" and citing to a royal order from 1813, he wrote:

> It is evident, from the extract taken from the Codes of India [Book 4, Title 12], through all the royal orders and official correspondence, to the change of the Intendancy of Florida, in 1817, the Intendant of the island of Cuba, that the Governors possessed a very circumscribed and limited authority.

Id. at 47 (citing Letter from Hamilton to Crawford (Mar. 31, 1824), *in* III *American State Papers, Public Land* 767 (Washington, Duff Green 1834)). This was most likely the same John H. McIntosh who was a Patriot leader in the Patriot War in 1812, see M.C. Mirow, 'The Patriot Constitution and International Constitution-Making', 21 Tex. Rev. L. & Pol. (forthcoming).

52. Whatley & Cook, *supra* note 10, at 48-50. For the eventual migration of these documents to the Library of Congress, see M.C. Mirow, 'Law in East Florida 1783-1821', 55 Am. J. Leg. Hist. 89, 90-91 (2015). It appears many documents related to real property were transported to Cuba. Diplomatic and even military efforts to obtain them were unsuccessful. Glenn Boggs, 'The Case of Florida's Missing Real Estate Records', 77 (9) Fla. Bar J. 10, 10-17 (Oct. 2003).

53. Whatley & Cook, *supra* note 10, at 51-52.

54. Act of June 22, 1860, 12 Stat. 85, 87, ch. 188, sec. 11 (extended by Act of June 10, 1872, 17 Stat. 378, ch. 421).

petitioners under this act in 1887.[55] Other cases, from the early twentieth century, generally did not recognize the interests asserted by the petitioners under Spanish grants. In 1901, Chief Justice Fuller writing for the Court, invalidated the claim of the heirs of Jesse Fish, a notable figure in nineteenth-century Florida, to the island of Anastasia. Fish's heirs had not asserted their claim in a timely fashion under any of the federal acts and were barred.[56] Similarly, in 1906, under the Act of 1860, Justice Holmes found fraud in a petition for 1,850,000 acres and determined that the claim was not valid.[57] By the 1920s, two claims under Spanish grants were barred by adverse possession and laches.[58]

FLORIDA LANDS IN THE SUPREME COURT

A wide variety of cases concerning Florida lands under the Adams-Onís Treaty and the congressional acts establishing commissions to determine claims found their way to the Supreme Court. Core aspects of the treaty were interpreted to determine the jurisdiction of the Court in particular cases, and Spanish colonial law was applied to ascertain the validity of claims under Spanish, and therefore under U.S. law. Spanish law was consulted to determine the authority of grantors, usually governors, as agents of the Spanish crown and to determine the validity and nature of conditional clauses attached to Spanish grants that may or may not have been fulfilled by grantees. Cases were usually brought by the grantees or their heirs. Some claimants had amassed several parcels through speculation and sought the Court's confirmation of the validity of their title. For example,

---

55. United States v. De Morant, 123 U.S. 335, 335-45 (1887); United States v. De Morant, 124 U.S. 647, 647-48 (1887).
56. Mitchell v. Furman, 180 U.S. 402, 439-40 (1901).
57. United States v. Delcour, 203 U.S. 408, 425-29 (1906).
58. Del Pozo v. Wilson Cypress Co., 269 U.S. 82, 84-90 (1925); Sanchez v. Deering, 270 U.S. 277, 228-30 (1926).

Moses Levi had purchased tracts totaling 65,000 acres, which were confirmed by the Court.[59]

Apart from claims where the nature and origin of documents were in issue, there were four major categories of cases: treaty interpretation, the power of governors to make grants, the performance of conditions attached to grants, and the validity of grants of land beyond the Indian boundary of 1763. These are discussed in order.

Self-Executing Treaties in U.S. Law

These cases have been recognized mostly for their development of the law of treaties and the development of the doctrine of self-executing treaties in U.S. law.[60] Their interpretation and refinement of U.S. law of treaties have little to do with *derecho indiano. Foster & Elam v. Neilson* is the canonical case in U.S. international law that established this unusual doctrine of self-executing treaties.[61] The court was faced with the following language:

> All the grants of land made before the 24th of January 1818 by His Catholic Majesty or by his lawful authorities in the said Territories ceded by His Majesty to the United States, shall be ratified and confirmed to the persons in possession of the lands, to the same extent that the same grants would be valid if the Territories had remained under the Dominion of His Catholic Majesty.[62]

---

59. United States v. Levi, 33 U.S. 479, 482 (1834). Levi was a Sephardic Jew who arrived in East Florida in 1818 and planned a Florida settlement for European Jews. This effort was not successful, and he purchased African slaves for labor. He was the father of attorney, planter, and Florida politician David Levy Yulee. Daniel L. Schafer, 'U.S. Territory and State', *in The History of Florida* 227 (Michael Gannon ed., 2013).
60. Ernest F. Dibble, *Joseph M. White: Anti-Jacksonian Floridian* 119-29 (2003).
61. 27 U.S. 253 (1829).
62. Adams-Onís Treaty, *supra* note 5, art. 8; Foster & Elam v. Neilsen, 27 U.S. 253, 310 (1829).

Determining on one hand that the words in the treaty were words of contract rather than legislation, the Court noted that further legislative action was required for the language to be enforceable in a domestic court. On the other hand, treaty language that spoke directly to tribunals could be rules of judicial application without intervening legislative action and was, therefore, self-executing.[63]

While this doctrine has become a mainstay of U.S. international law and treaty interpretation, substantially reworked in 2008 in *Medellín v. Texas*, the Supreme Court reduced its application significantly in the years immediately following *Foster & Elam* in the context of Florida land claims.[64] The same language found not to be self-executing in *Foster & Elam* was found to have direct application to the petitioner's claim in 1832 when Don Fernando de la Maza Arredondo's award of nearly 290,000 acres in the Superior Court of the Eastern District of Florida was challenged in the Supreme Court.[65] Justice Baldwin focused on the subsequent legislation as removing the defect in *Foster & Elam* because Congress treated the grants as having been confirmed and gave this congressional action due regard as a rule to be respected by the courts.[66] Furthermore, in perhaps the most interesting passages related to the self-executory nature of the treaty, Baldwin interpreted the treaty in light of Spain's intent and made specific reference to the differences in the original English and original Spanish texts of the treaty.[67] The English text used the future tense related to confirming Spanish grants; the Spanish texts used both the past and present tense for the same idea in the treaty. Baldwin concluded that the obstacles of *Foster & Elam* were not present in this case:

---

63. Mark Weston Janis, *International Law* 89-91 (6th ed. 2012).
64. *See* Carlos Manuel Vázquez, 'Treaties as Law of the Land: The Supremacy Clause and the Judicial Enforcement of Treaties', 122 Harv. L. Rev. 599, 621-67 (2008).
65. United States v. Arredondo, 31 U.S. 691, 734-42 (1832). For Fernando de la Maza Arredondo and his son, also Fernando, see M.C. Mirow, 'The Constitution of Cádiz in Florida', Fla. J. Int'l L. 271, 292-93, 296-98, 308 (2012).
66. *Arredondo*, 31 U.S. at 735.
67. *Id.* at 736-42.

> We consider that the grants were confirmed and annulled respectively—simultaneously with the ratification and confirmation of the treaty, and that when the territory was ceded, the United States had no right in any of the lands embraced in the confirmed grants.[68]

Justice Thompson dissented from the majority's determination of self-execution. He found it unthinkable to reject the plain English text that would require legislative action to confirm grants in favor of the Spanish text yielding a self-executory treaty provision on this question, especially when the United States had been relying on the English version for over ten years.[69] Even within the ambit of treaty interpretation, the Supreme Court was confronted with different legal systems and terminology. Other aspects of the Florida land grants presented deeper questions of Spanish law.

The Power of Spanish Governors To Grant Land

Grants were valid to the extent that they were valid under Spanish law. If the governor exceeded his authority in making a grant, it was void; thus, the Supreme Court had to determine the appropriate scope of governors' power to grant land. At least one Spanish lawyer, José Ugarte, asserted in 1829 that the power of Spanish governors was unlimited. Because, in practice, a governor might suspend the implementation of a royal order or send it back for additional instructions based on local conditions, Ugarte argued that the governor had absolute power. Referring to the well-known and oft-debated Spanish colonial response to a royal order of "I obey but do not execute," Ugarte surmised that governors of East Florida "acted with absolute power, and without intervention of any other authority."[70] Not everyone

---

68. *Id.* at 742.
69. *Id.* at 750-56.
70. T. Frederick Davis, 'Pioneer Florida: An Interpretation of Spanish Law and Land Titles', 44 Fla. Hist. Q. 113, 114-15 (1945). Ugarte's opinion was

agreed with Ugarte's conclusions, and the commissioners and the Supreme Court necessarily explored the scope of Spanish governors' power to grant land as it related to the validity of grants.[71]

In 1834, Chief Justice Marshall examined the authority of and limits imposed on Spanish governors to grant lands.[72] His opinion confirmed in part a grant of 16,000 acres to George Clarke who sought to construct a saw mill on the St. Johns River.[73] Using Joseph M. White's book on Spanish land law and *Clark's Land Law*, Marshall traced nearly one hundred years of Spanish legislative changes related to governors' powers to grant land in East and West Florida.[74] By examining the Spanish provisions and the royal practice of apparently always confirming grants by governors, Marshall's research in these sources overcame the position of the United States that the governor did not have the authority to make the grant in dispute.[75]

Questions of geographic jurisdiction of governors might arise when the United States argued to invalidate grants by stating that the governor was acting beyond the geographical scope of his authority. For example, to such a claim in *Mitchel* and despite the boundaries created by the British, the Court closely examined the historical practice of Governor Folch and Governor-General of Louisiana Gálvez to determine that the lands in question were within West Florida and subject to a valid confirmation of

---

published in the *Florida Herald* on July 8, 1835, in the midst of the Supreme Court's most active period for Florida land claims. *Id.* at 114.

71. Hill, *supra* note 1, at xxvi.

72. United States v. Clarke, 33 U.S. 436, 448-64 (1834); *see also* Mirow, *supra* note 47, at 235-36 (describing the colonial practice of "I obey but do not execute").

73. *Clarke*, 33 U.S. at 436-37, 468-69.

74. *Id.* at 452-53. These works are Joseph M. White, *A New Collection of Laws, Charters and Local Ordinances of the Governments of Great Britain, France and Spain, Relating to the Concessions of Land in Their Respective Colonies* (Lawbook Exchange facsimile ed. with introduction by Agustín Parise, 2010) (1839), https://archive.org/details/anewcollectionl01rogoog, and Matthew St. Clair Clarke, *Laws of the United States, Resolutions of Congress under the Confederation, Treaties, Proclamations, Spanish Regulations, and other Documents Respecting the Public Lands* (Washington, D.C., 1828).

75. *Clarke*, 33 U.S. at 457-59.

Governor Folch.[76] Similarly, grants in the region to the west of the Perdido River led to debates concerning the power of Spain to make such grants in this contested area.[77]

Conditions and Their Performance

With the exception of grants made to individuals for their services to the crown, grants in the Floridas were often made with conditions attached to them. These conditions were either expressed through royal legislation or in the grants themselves. The royal provision found in the *Recopilación* of 1680 that was to serve as a guide to commissions and courts interpreting Spanish land claims in Florida made absolute ownership in lands conditional upon the grantee "having made on them their residence and place of labor, and resided in those townships four years," a requirement that the lands would be farmed and improved.[78] Other grants were made with specific conditions. For example, the grant in *United States v. Arredondo* required that the grantee establish 200 Spanish families on the land and that such establishment should begin within three years of the date of the grant.[79] Conditions for settlement by a number of families were often attached to large grants.

Courts placed these conditions into their familiar, common-law, framework. Justice Baldwin stated of these conditions, "there can be no doubt that they are *subsequent*, the grant is in full property in fee, an interest vested on its execution which could only be divested by the breach or non-performance of the

---

76. Mitchel v. United States, 34 U.S. 711, 738-39 (1835).

77. De La Croix v. Chamberlain, 25 U.S. 599 (1827); Foster & Elam v. Neilsen, 27 U.S. 253 (1829); Garcia v. Lee, 37 U.S. 511 (1838); Pollard's Heirs v. Kibbe, 39 U.S. 353, 368-422 (1840) (Baldwin J., concurring); *see also* Seán Patrick Donlan, 'Entangled Up in Red, White and Blue: Spanish West Florida and the American Territory of Orleans, 1803-1810', *in Entanglements in Legal History: Conceptual Approaches* 213-50 (Thomas Duve ed., 2014).

78. *Recopilación de las Leyes de Indias*, Lib. 12, Tit. 4 (1680), *quoted in* Whatley & Cook, *supra* note 10, at 44.

79. United States v. Arredondo, 31 U.S. 691, 745 (1832).

conditions."[80] Translating the restrictions employed in the Spanish grants to common law property concepts, the grantees obtained fee simples subject to a condition subsequent, and the common law courts thought of them this way.

In *Arredondo*, the first case considering the effect of these conditions, Baldwin was satisfied that the settlement of families on the land had commenced within the required time on the facts, but meeting the condition of 200 families on the land was another question.[81] On this second question, Baldwin turned to the doctrine of impossibility of performance based on the land now lying within the United States. To require the settling of 200 Spanish families on the property was now impossible and would work a forfeiture: "[T]he performance of this condition had become impossible by the act of the grantors; the transfer of the territory, the change of government manners, habits, customs, laws, religion, and all the social and political relations of society and of life."[82] Although a strict application of the common law might yield a different result, Baldwin found for Arredondo. He stated:

> The proceeding is in equity according to its established rules our decree must be in conformity with the principles of justice, which would in such a case as this not only forbid a decree of forfeiture but impel us to give a final decree in favor of the title conferred by the grant.[83]

Not all claimants could avail themselves of impossibility. For example, in 1815, Elizabeth Wiggins was granted 300 acres to farm. The grant was conditioned upon her taking possession and cultivating the land within six months of the grant and upon a continued occupation and cultivation for ten years.[84] Although the ten-year period was not closely adhered to when improvements had been made and when the disrupted nature of the region

---

80. *Id.*
81. *Id.* at 745-46 (1832). Justice Thompson, dissenting, found there was little activity to establish possession or settlement. *Id.* at 758-59.
82. *Id.* at 746.
83. *Id.*
84. United States v. Wiggins, 39 U.S. 334, 334-35, 349, 351 (1840).

was considered, Justice Catron found that Wiggins had not fulfilled the conditions imposed on the grant and wrote:

> [As] Mrs. Wiggins, however, never cultivated, or occupied the land claimed, she took no interest under the rule, or any exception made to it; and it is free from doubt, had Spain continued to govern the country, no title could have been made to her; nor can any be claimed from the United States, as successors to the rights and obligations of Spain.[85]

A common form of conditional grant was for a tract of land on a water course to build a water saw mill.[86] Such grants became prevalent after 1793 as part of an aggressive land policy to increase settlement.[87] These grants were usually for five square miles of land to supply the necessary timber and were conditioned on the construction of an operational mill to saw wood. In one case, the Court had to determine whether the interest transferred in the five square mile tract was a conditional grant or merely a license to remove timber. Resolving the issue in favor of the claimant, the Court found that the mill was constructed and in operation, fulfilling the condition.[88] All subsequent cases viewed such grants as conditional grants of land, usually for 16,000 acres, based on the condition of constructing a mill. Where the petition and grant mentioned a mill, but did not make the grant conditional upon construction of the mill, the Court might interpret the grant as an absolute grant without condition.[89] Furthermore, where a mill was mentioned in the grant but the grant was supported by services to the crown or for earlier losses by the grantee, the construction of a mill was not a condition of the grant.[90] The construction of a mill, which was subsequently destroyed within one or two years, was sufficient to satisfy the

85. *Id.* at 351-52.
86. Hill, *supra* note 1, at xxvi-xxvii.
87. Hoffman, *supra* note 3, at 244-45.
88. United States v. Richard, 33 U.S. 470, 470-71 (1834).
89. United States v. Segui, 35 U.S. 306, 306-07 (1836).
90. United States v. Rodman, 40 U.S. 130, 138-39 (1841); United States v. Hanson, 41 U.S. 196, 199 (1842).

condition and grant absolute title in the grantee.[91] And various acts or successive constructions and destructions of several mills over the period from 1819 to 1829 led in one case to satisfaction of the condition through the application of "performance of the condition *cy pres*."[92]

In the mid-1830s, Justice Wayne began to issue opinions for the Court on these cases, and he appeared to be more demanding when considering the performance of a condition to build a mill. In *Kingsley*, he found that no attempts to build a mill had been undertaken until 1835 and rejected the claimant's assertions of impossibility by stating "there was no more danger after the appellee petitioned for the land, than there had been before and at the time of his application."[93] He also noted that similar claimants had, in fact, been able to construct their mills.[94] For the same reasons, Justice Wayne denied William Mill's heirs their claim for lands for a saw mill despite their claiming that delays in constructing the mill were due to "threats to their persons and property, by hostile Indians, negroes and marauders."[95] The Court denied several subsequent claims for lands granted for the construction of a mill based on non-performance of the condition.[96]

Other grants merely required possession within six months. If the lands were not placed in actual possession by then, the grant was not valid.[97] Thus, in all cases with valid conditions, the Court closely analyzed the factual bases for the satisfaction of the conditions associated with the grant. The juridical leap from a conditional grant under Spanish law to a conditional grant in common law was not too great for the Court to take,

---

91. United States v. Seton, 35 U.S. 309, 311 (1836).
92. United States v. Sibbald, 35 U.S. 315, 323 (1836).
93. United States v. Kingsley, 37 U.S. 476, 484 (1838).
94. *Id.* at 486.
95. United States v. Mill's Heirs, 37 U.S. 215, 216 (1838).
96. United States v. Burgevin, 38 U.S. 85, 85-86 (1839); United States v. Drummond, 38 U.S. 84, 84 (1839); United States v. Delespine, 40 U.S. 319, 333 (1841).
97. O'Hara v. United States, 40 U.S. 275, 279 (1841) (The Court wrote, "We hear nothing of the memorialist, or of any other attempt to settle the land, from the spring of 1804 until 1819." *Id.* at 282.).

and conditions in Spanish grants were transposed into similar conditions under common law which were then scrutinized for their performance.

Lands Granted in Indian Territory

Spanish grants to individuals might also be challenged by the United States through an assertion that the grant was for land that was the property of indigenous peoples under Spanish law.[98] Thus, arguments were propounded that the British line of 1763 between British and Indian territory continued to be in effect after Spain assumed the territory in 1783 and grants west of this line were ineffective.[99] The tacit recognition of this boundary by Spain after it retook the territory in 1783 provided a possible justification for the United States to invalidate claims by grantees from Spain. A trilogy of cases in the Supreme Court—*Arredondo, Mitchel, and Fernandez*—addressed the variety of situations in which claims of lands in Indian territory were challenged by the United States.

In *Arredondo*, the Supreme Court confirmed a grant of more than 289,000 acres with the Indian town of Alachua serving as the center of the grant.[100] The United States argued,

> The land in controversy was, at the time of the grant, within the Indian boundary established by the government of Great Britain during its occupancy of the Floridas, and subsequently acknowledged by the government of Spain; and was therefore not subject to be disposed of by the subordinate officers of the crown.[101]

---

98. United States v. Arredondo, 31 U.S. 691, 701-02 (1832).
99. *Id.* at 705 (arguments of counsel for the United States).
100. *Id.* at 749. The case was given over to lengthy oral argument on March 2-7, 1832, and was watched carefully by the public and President Jackson who disapproved of the Court's conclusion that the claim was valid and who later lectured Justice Baldwin in person about it. 1 Charles Warren, *The Supreme Court in United States History* 782-84 (1926).
101. *Arredondo*, 31 U.S. at 705 (argument of United States).

To overcome the objection that the lands were within the Indian boundary, the Court relied on an official sentence by the Spanish intendant based on a judicial inquest that the lands in question had been abandoned by the Indians and, through abandonment, had rejoined the royal domain again subject to alienation by the crown. This determination of abandonment by Spanish judicial authority was taken by the Court as a factual question that was *res judicata* by a foreign tribunal and would not be re-examined.[102] Thus, where Indians had abandoned the land and the abandonment was judicially recognized by Spain before the grant, the land returned to the royal domain and could then be effectively granted by the crown. Not all lands granted by the Spanish crown from beyond the Indian boundary could be cured by a judicial finding of abandonment.

In *Mitchel*, the claimant sought confirmation of 1,200,000 acres purchased from John Forbes, the Indian trader and principal of Panton, Leslie & Co.[103] These lands were also beyond the Indian boundary, but Forbes's claim was based originally on deeds from Indians in satisfaction of business debts owed his firm. The United States objected to the validity of these deeds: "The Indian deeds to Panton Leslie & Co. did not, either in themselves, or with the confirmation thereof by governor Folch, convey to the grantees therein named, any legal right to the land in question."[104] Justice Baldwin relied on several factor to find that the grant, although within the territory beyond the Indian boundary, was valid. He found that the grants by the Indians and their subsequent confirmation by governor Folch were not gratuitous actions but were undertaken to compensate Panton

---

102. *Id.* at 747-48.
103. Mitchel v. United States 34 U.S. 711 (1835); *see* Blake A. Watson, 'Buying West Florida From the Indians: The Forbes Purchase and Mitchel v. United States (1835)', 9 F.I.U. L. Rev. 361-90 (2014). For Panton Leslie and Co., see William S. Coker & Thomas D. Watson, *Indian Traders of the Southeastern Spanish Borderlands: Panton, Leslie & Company and John Forbes & Company, 1783-1847* (1986). White published his argument in the case and the Superior Court record and briefs exceeded 700 pages. Dibble, *supra* note 60, at 128 n.34, 129 n.37. He published similar arguments in several of these cases. *Id.* at 183-92.
104. *Mitchel*, 34 U.S. at 720.

Leslie for business losses and to reward it for its services to the Spanish crown. The grants and confirmation were made with the highest level of formality and documentation, and both Indians and Spain recognized Panton Leslie as a private holder of the lands. The Court set out its understanding of possession and occupation of land by Indians under the British and noted that there were many instances in which Indians at public councils granted lands to purchasers and that the participation of royal officials indicated license from the crown.[105] Justice Baldwin found that Indians' right to lands was even greater under Spain:

> But Spain did not consider the Indian right to be that of mere occupancy and perpetual possession, but a right of property in the lands they held under the guarantee of treaties, which were so highly respected, that in the establishment of a military post by royal order, the site thereof was either purchased from the Indians or occupied with their permission, as that of St Mark's [the fort within the grant in question].[106]

Thus, the Indians held the land. And they validly granted it with royal license to Panton Leslie:

> In the present case the Indian sale has been confirmed with more than usual solemnity and publicity; it has been done at the public council and convention of the Indians conformably to treaties, to which the king was a party, and which the United States adopted, and the grant was known to both parties to the treaty of cession.[107]

Mitchel, as the purchaser from Forbes of Panton Leslie, had valid title to the 1,200,000 with the exception of the fort of St. Mark's and its appurtenant lands.[108] The confirmation by Spain and the treaty provision made all the difference in this case to distinguish it from the general rule established in *Johnson v. M'Intosh*, a rule that was widely accepted by then. Without the

105. *Id.* at 726-29, 746-47.
106. *Id.* at 752.
107. *Id.* at 759.
108. *Id.* at 761-63.

additional elements of the Spanish acceptance of the grant and the treaty provision, the grant would have failed.[109]

In *Fernandez*, the United States argued that a portion of a grant within the Indian boundary was invalid because the Spanish governor lacked power to grant such land. *Arredondo* had resolved this issue by accepting that similar lands in question had been abandoned by the Indians. And *Mitchel* was easily distinguished because the first grant was made by the Indians to the claimants. *Fernandez* presented the most difficult case; a grant of lands within the Indian boundary that had never been officially decreed to be part of the royal domain.[110] Justice Baldwin rapidly dispatched the objection citing Chief Justice Marshall's famous decision in *Johnson v. M'Intosh*:

> This subject was so fully and ably considered in Johnson v. M'Intosh, that we have only to refer to the language of the court to show that every European government claimed and exercised the right of granting lands, while in occupation of the Indians.[111]

The court affirmed the superior court's confirmation of the entire grant of 16,000 acres.[112] By confirming the private property interests based on Spanish grants, the Court bolstered U.S. rights over indigenous lands as the successor in interest to Spain's sovereign powers. Losing a little over a million acres to private claimants not only served to demonstrate that the U.S. was serious about complying with its treaty obligation but also was preferable to calling Spanish sovereignty and authority into question. Questioning Spanish sovereignty over indigenous lands was tantamount to questioning U.S. sovereignty over them. These cases were decided just as the Indian Removal Act was implemented and illustrated a consistent logic in U.S. approaches to Indian land.[113] These three important cases dealing with

---

109. Watson, *supra* note 103, at 361, 362, 378-79, 388-89.
110. United States v. Fernandez, 35 U.S. 303, 304 (1836).
111. *Id.*
112. *Id.* at 304-05.
113. Dibble, *supra* note 60, at 84; Tim Alan Garrison, *The Legal Ideology of Removal: The Southern Judiciary and the Sovereignty of Native American*

Florida land in Indian territory confirmed the claim of the individual Spanish grantees in territory beyond the line of demarcation between British, then Spanish, sovereignty and Indian control. These were minor losses in the U.S. battle to gain control of all Indian lands.

DERECHO INDIANO IN THE SUPREME COURT

The Supreme Court constructed the applicable rules of *derecho indiano* from a variety of sources and read Spanish documents related to claims in light of this body of law. Materials collected, translated, and published by Joseph M. White were frequently cited by the Court. In a few instances, the Constitution of Cádiz was cited to describe the power of the governor to make grants at particular moments in the Spanish colonial history of Florida.

Records and Traditional Sources of Derecho Indiano

The records presented to the Supreme Court on appeal usually contained English translations of the applicable Spanish documents such as the petitions of the grantees, certified copies of the governors' decrees ordering a survey, and the survey itself.[114] Differences in the practices of keeping records related to land and the validity of certified copies as evidence of grants were often resolved with reference to Spanish law and colonial practice.[115] In some cases, litigants undertook extensive searches for related documents. For example, in *Mitchel v. United States*,

---

Nations (2002); Blake A. Watson, *Buying America from the Indians: Johnson v. McIntosh and the History of Native Land Rights* 320-22 (2012); Watson, *supra* note 103, at 374.

114. *See, e.g.*, United States v. Arredondo, 31 U.S. 691, 691-96 (1832).

115. United States v. Percheman, 32 U.S. 51, 84-85 (1833); United States. v. Wiggins, 39 U.S. 334, 337-39, 345-48 (1840).

the United States requested delays in trial for years as it attempted to gather records from Madrid and Havana.[116]

From the early 1830s, attorneys and judges extensively used *White's Collection of Land Laws* as an important source for English translations of Spanish legislation.[117] The author of this work, Joseph M. White, became the pre-eminent practitioner of Florida land claims. From Kentucky, White studied law at the College of William and Mary for parts of 1817 and 1818, and was admitted to the Virginia and Kentucky bars in 1818. In 1822, he was appointed to the Florida Legislative Council and later took on various positions of government within Florida including the Secretary to the Land Commission of West Florida and later Land Commissioner. Within the context of Florida politics, White became an enemy of Richard Keith Call who later was the Governor of Florida. Their professional rivalry lasted decades with Call often arguing opposite White and losing at the Supreme Court. White was elected the Florida Delegate to Congress six times from 1825 to 1837 where he advocated strenuously and successfully for roads, other internal improvements, and military installations. He also ensured the passage of land laws affecting Florida, especially the Act of 1828 described earlier. He was a consistent winner for his clients before the Supreme Court.[118] His wife, Ellen Adair White, also known as "Mrs. Florida White" in Washington to distinguish her from another Mrs. White from another state, was better known than her husband. She was an important socialite and "southern belle" in Washington society.[119] White died in St. Louis, Missouri, in 1839.[120]

The origin of White's important collection of translated materials was the passage of the Act of 1828 and the Attorney General's opinion that a correct translation of Spanish and French ordinances was needed to settle land claims. White, as a commissioner for Florida land claims, was assigned the task, and his

---

116. Mitchel v. United States, 34 U.S. 711, 723 (1835).
117. *See, e.g.*, *Percheman*, 32 U.S. at 62 (Taney's argument), 78 (White's argument); United States v. Clarke, 33 U.S. 436, 452 (1834); *Mitchel*, 34 U.S. at 740-43; White, *supra* note 74.
118. Dibble, *supra* note 60, at 8, 9, 12, 17-30, 103-37.
119. *Id.* at 139-57.
120. *Id.* at 163.

manuscript was given to the State Department. Congress was informed by the President of this on February 11, 1829.[121]

In 1839, White published a commercial edition of these materials as *A New Collection of Laws, Charters and Local Ordinances of the Governments of Great Britain, France, and Spain Relating to the Concessions of Land*.[122] This was often referred to as White's *New Recopilation*.[123] It was *the* book for use in such cases. With approximately 1500 pages in two volumes, the work contained all the basic sources one would need in translation into English. It included extracts from the *Siete Partidas*, the *Teatro de Legislación*, the *Recopilación* of 1680, and the *Novísima Recopilación* of Spanish (Castilian) law of 1805. It contained various important ordinances and decrees, and even an essay on the Adams-Onís treaty.

Attorneys and judges might also make direct reference to the fundamental source of *derecho indiano*, the *Recopilación de las Leyes de Indias*, often referred to in the U.S. materials as the *Recopilación de las Indias*. For example, in 1841, the United States and the claimants referred to various laws in the *Recopilación* to determine the perimeter of lands transferred with a fort, and the Court accepted these materials to determine that a line established at 1500 *varas* around the fort defined the property that was included with the United States' possession of the military installation. Similarly, in the same case, numerous provisions of the *Recopilación* along with references to White's *New Recopilation* were cited to establish the nature of Spain's claim to land and its treatment of Indian lands.[124]

This did not exclude other sources. For example, to explain better the power of Spanish governors to grant land, White offered the Court translated portions of Juan Solórzano Pereira's *Política Indiana* while correctly assuring the court that

---

121. United States v. Wiggins, 39 U.S. 334, 351 (1840); Dibble, *supra* note 60, at 157.
122. White, *supra* note 74.
123. *See, e.g.*, O'Hara v. United States., 40 U.S. 275, 277, 278, 282 (1841); United States v. Delespine's Heirs, 40 U.S. 226, 227 (1841); United States v. Rodman, 40 U.S. 130, 137 (1841).
124. Mitchel v. United States, 40 U.S. 52, 58, 60, 69, 70, 72 (1841).

"This author is one of the most celebrated of the Spanish commentators."[125]

In addition to general legislation, royal orders gave the governor power to make grants under specific situations and for specific services to the crown. For example, affirming the validity of Juan Percheman's claim to 2000 acres, Chief Justice Marshall examined closely a Royal Order of March 29, 1815, from the minister of the Indies granting land to Spaniards who repelled the U.S. and Patriot invasions in 1812 and 1813.[126] Marshall noted that the Royal Order singled out Percheman as one of a handful of individuals to be rewarded for their actions and interpreted the Order not to limit the discretion of the governor in granting land under its provisions.[127]

Spanish customs, usages, and practices were occasionally averred by claimant but these were usually unsuccessful. For example, in 1839, Moses Levy hoped to have his survey reformed in light of the Spanish custom of excluding water and marshes from the acreage of a grant. The court was unpersuaded by the existence of the custom and noted that a new survey would be a new grant and invalid because it would be made after January 24, 1818, the date provided in the treaty.[128] Zephaniah Kingsley unsuccessfully put forth a Spanish custom of non-reversion to the crown of land for the non-performance of a condition to build a mill. The court responded that a release of a condition had to be granted by the crown in the same way the condition was imposed.[129]

---

125. United States v. Percheman, 32 U.S. 51, 82 (1833) (White's argument). For Solórzano Pereira, see M.C. Mirow, 'Juan Solórzano Pereira', *in Great Christian Jurists in Spanish History* (Rafael Domingo & Javier Martinez-Torron eds., forthcoming), and Ditlev Tamm, 'De Indiarum iure', *in The Formation and Transmission of Western Legal Culture: 150 Books that Made the Law in the Age of Printing* 182-84 (Serge Dauchy et al. eds., 2016).
126. *Percheman*, 32 U.S. at 95-96. For the invasion, see James G. Cusick, *The Other War of 1812: The Patriot War and the American Invasion of Spanish East Florida* (2007).
127. *Percheman*, 32 U.S. at 97-98.
128. United States v. Levy, 38 U.S. 81, 82-83 (1839).
129. United States v. Kingsley, 37 U.S. 476, 486-87 (1838).

The Constitution of Cádiz

Many petitions and concessions for land were made in Florida when the region was under the Constitutional Monarchy of the Constitution of Cádiz from October 17, 1812, to August 9, 1814, and again from May 4, 1820, to July 10, 1821.[130] The governor continued to have the power to make effective grants under the Constitution and these changes did not affect such concessions of land. The Constitution of Cádiz and its institutions, as late constitutional manifestations of *derecho indiano,* appear in the records of grants.[131] For example, one document in the claim by Delespine's heirs, affirmed by the Court for over 10,000 acres, was dated June 13, 1821, and noted that those signing a certificate, Francisco Fatio and Juan Huertas, were "members of this illustrious constitutional council."[132]

In another case, the power of the provincial deputation of Cuba to grant lands under the Constitution and a Royal Order of January 4, 1813, issued by a decree of the Cortes of Cádiz was called into question by the United States as it sought to invalidate a grant of more than 92,000 acres. The United States argued that the grantee did not receive the final copy of his grant until June 30, 1814, and because all acts of the Cortes, including the Royal Order giving the provincial deputation the power to grant lands, were declared null and void by the King on May 4, 1814, then the underlying Royal Order upon which the grant was based no longer existed.[133] Therefore, the grant was invalid. The United States argued, "How could he receive his title in form, or perfect his grant, under a system which was totally annulled?"[134] Because the grant failed for other reasons, Justice Catron did not

---

130. M.C. Mirow, *'The Constitution of Cádiz in Florida'*, 24 Fla. J. Int'l L. 280, 303, 326 (2012).

131. Arguing for the United States in *Delespine*, Attorney General Gilpin provided information about the Constitution, the Cortes, and the application of its decrees to public lands in Florida. United States v. Delespine, 40 U.S. 319, 323-24 (1841).

132. United States v. Delespine's Heirs, 40 U.S. 226, 230 (1841).

133. *Delespine*, 40 U.S. at 325-26, 333-34.

134. *Id.* at 325.

have to decide the issue of the power of the provincial deputation and assumed that the grant was issued by proper authority.[135]

The Constitution of Cádiz was ingeniously yet unsuccessfully deployed to revive a claim by the Duke of Alagon to 12,000,000 acres, the largest single Florida land grant litigated before the Supreme Court.[136] This grant, along with two others, were specifically excepted from confirmation in negotiations of the Adams-Onís Treaty and were the main reason for setting the cut-off date for confirmation of grants at January 24, 1818. The Duke's grant dated from February 6, 1818.[137] These grants were made subsequent to the initiation of negotiations for the treaty and would have transferred substantially all of Spain's public lands into private hands essentially exempting them from the transfer of property to the United States. When the United States objected, Spain agreed to a date that would make the grants invalid, stated in negotiations that they were invalid, and agreed to annul the grants. In return, the grants themselves would not be named in the language of the treaty so that the Spanish crown was not embarrassed at its attempt to circumvent the main purpose of the treaty.[138]

Counsel for the Duke argued that the grants were made during the period when the King had absolute power and was not restrained from granting lands. Nonetheless, at the time of ratifying the treaty, the King was substantially limited by the provisions of the Constitution of Cádiz as a constitutional monarch deriving his powers only from the provisions of the Constitution. The Duke's counsel cited and translated Art. 172, section 10, of the Constitution this way, stating that the King:

> Shall not take the property of any person or corporation, nor hinder nor impede the free possession, use, and benefit thereof, and if at any time it shall be necessary for an object of acknowledged public utility to take the property of an individual, nevertheless it shall not be done unless he be at the same

---

135. *Id.* at 330.
136. Doe v. Braden, 57 U.S. 635, 635 (1853).
137. *Id.* (Mayer's argument). The other grants were to the Count of Puñonrostro and Don Pedro de Vargas. *Id.* at 651 (Cushing's argument).
138. *Id.* at 654-55.

> time indemnified, and a fair equivalent be given him upon a sufficient inquiry made by fit and proper men.[139]

Although the King annulled the grant, there was no finding of public utility and no compensation paid to the Duke. Furthermore, citing other provisions of the Constitution, Mayer correctly argued that determinations of eminent domain under the Constitution properly belonged in the legislative power exercised by the Cortes and King as holders of national sovereignty. Another provision of the Constitution required the nation to maintain and protect the right to property among other rights.[140] Mayer, arguing for the Duke, asserted, "We deny that even the king and cortes, in combined legislative action, or under any title of power, could have annulled the grant."[141]

It was a clever argument, but it did not carry water. Justice Taney noted that written ratifications of the treaty by the King of Spain acknowledged that both sides agreed that the three grants were annulled. This understanding and the cut-off date of the treaty itself invalidated the grant.[142] Furthermore, Taney refused to entertain arguments based on the limitation of the King under the Constitution of Cádiz; the question was, in his view, nonjusticiable by the Court. He wrote, "But these are political questions and not judicial. They belong exclusively to the political department of the government."[143] The Duke was not entitled to the 12,000,000 acres, about one-third of the present land of Florida.

The Court employed a range of sources to construct the applicable rule of law under *derecho indiano*. Most sources were found in translation in the works of Joseph M. White. Other sources, such as royal orders applicable to perhaps one or just a few grants were consulted as needed and as raised by counsel. Even Spain's short-lived Constitution of Cádiz found a place in the Court's jurisprudence and was cleverly yet unsuccessfully invoked as late as 1853 in the Supreme Court.

---

139. *Id.* at 646 (Mayer's argument citing Const. (Spain) of 1812, art. 172, § 10).
140. *Id.* at 647 (Mayer's argument citing Const. (Spain) of 1812, art. 4).
141. *Id.* at 648 (Mayer's argument).
142. *Id.* at 655-57.
143. *Id.* at 657.

The Supreme Court Applies Derecho Indiano

The Supreme Court was also limited by is reliance on English translations and edited selections of Spanish legislation. And the Court was well aware of the difference between Spanish law and its own common law. The nature of Spanish colonial law, its reliance on the will of the Spanish crown, and its various sources with different names were captured well by Justice Baldwin the in first East Florida land claim before the Supreme Court.[144] Similarly, arguing for the validity of Juan Percheman's claim to 2000 acres, White emphasized the difference between the law of colonial Spain and nineteenth-century common law to the Court this way:

> As well might we judge the life of Pythagoras by the law of the New Testament, or the philosophy of Zoroaster by that of Newton, as subject the administration of a Spanish governor to the test of *magna carta*, the bill of rights, the *habeas corpus* act, or the principles of American constitutional law.[145]

Lawyers and the Court had a sense of the difference in legal sources and methods between Spain and the United States and attempted to exploit these differences for the benefit of their clients. Even when Spanish provisions were known, litigants attempted to place them into a context of legal disorder, colonial lawlessness, and poor enforcement. In 1833, White argued to the Court,

---

144. United States v. Arredondo, 31 U.S. 691, 714 (1832).

> The laws of an absolute monarch are not its legislative acts—they are the will and pleasure of the monarch expressed in various ways—if expressed in *any*, it is a law; there is no other law making, law repealing power—call it by whatever name—a royal order—an ordinance—a cedula—a decree of council—or an act of an authorised officer—if made or promulgated by the king, by his content or authority, it becomes as to the persons or subject matter to which it relates, a law of the kingdom. It is emphatically so in Spain and all its dominions.

145. United States v. Percheman, 32 U.S. 51, 77 (1833).

> Even the laws of the Indies, obscure, perplexed, and sometimes even unintelligible, as they are hardly reached across the ocean; and the decline of the Spanish, like that of the Roman empire, was marked by absolutism of the distant prefects.[146]

Such moments of dissonance between two legal systems call out for comparison, as in White's quotations above, and perhaps for the development of comparative methods themselves.[147] Despite the recognition of the complexity of *derecho indiano,* the Supreme Court approached Spanish sources with the assumption that its legal skill and training were sufficient to apply foreign law as needed to resolve the case presented to it.

Several key cases employed *derecho indiano* to determine the nature of documents accepted by the legal system as valid proof of a claim, the power of the governor to make different kinds of grants, and the performance required to satisfy conditions in grants. Once these aspects were settled in the jurisprudence of the court, most of the remaining cases turned on the quality of the survey and its correspondence to the governor's grant or concession.[148] For example, new surveys might be ordered in conformity with valid grants.[149]

A recurring issue was grants that were allocated amongst several parcels by surveyors or claimants after the grant. Attempts to take other tracts or substitute tracts after the deadline provided by the treaty of January 24, 1818, led to the nullity of the new tracts and claimants sometimes obtained confirmation of only a portion of the total grant.[150] Before this date, surveyors were given significant discretion in assigning lands to conces-

---

146. *Id.* (White's argument).

147. M.C. Mirow, 'Foreign Law and the Birth of Comparative Law', *in* 2 *Ratio Decidendi: Guiding Principles of Judicial Decisions: Foreign Law* 229-36 (Serge Dauchy, W. Hamilton Bryson & M.C. Mirow eds., 2010).

148. *See, e.g.*, United States v. Hernandez, 33 U.S. 485, 486 (1834).

149. *See, e.g.*, United States v. Huertas, 34 U.S. 171,171-73 (1835).

150. *See, e.g.*, United States v. Huertas, 33 U.S. 488, 489-91 (1834); United States v. Breward, 41 U.S. 143, 146-48 (1842); Sibbald v. United States., 43 U.S. 455, 455-57 (1844) (Petition to substitute public lands after January 24, 1818, for those in the original concession denied); Chaires v. United States, 44 U.S. 611, 611-20 (1845) (Petition to clarify and grant other lands after January 24, 1818, when surveyor refused to act dismissed).

sions based on claimants' petitions, and even single grants of a certain amount might be divided into separate tracts totaling the amount granted.[151] At times and against the objection of the United States, the Court permitted actions subsequent to the governor's concession, such as surveys, to occur after the treaty deadline and still provide good title to the claimant.[152] Where broad discretion was given to the surveyor to select the land to compensate the grantee for services to the crown, a survey after the date of January 24, 1818, was effective.[153] Nonetheless, where the surveyor did not have authority to change the location of the grant or to split the concession into distinct parcels, such actions did not create valid interests in the claimant.[154] In *Villalobos,* Justice Catron wrote:

> From the long experience this court has had in the investigation of Spanish titles, as claimed in Florida, as well as from the practice in regard to which the witnesses depose, we are of opinion, that the Surveyor-General had no authority to change the location of the grant, and to split up the surveys, as was done in this instance.[155]

Similarly, the Court upheld grants of several tracts when they could be readily identified, and a survey conducted after the cut-off date was acceptable.[156] The Court might even specify the call of the survey in great detail to confirm a grant lacking a survey, as it did for 38,000 acres to the heirs of Fernando de la Maza Arredondo in 1839.[157] The survey must had been made by the official surveyor. In *United States v. Hanson*, the claimant sought to have the United State recognize his claim to 16,000 acres

---

151. United States v. Sibbald, 35 U.S. 315, 323-24 (1836).
152. *See, e.g.*, United States v. Clarke, 34 U.S. 168, 168-69 (1835); United States v. Levy, 38 U.S. 81, 82-83 (1839).
153. United States v. Clarke, 41 U.S. 228, 232-33 (1842); United States v. Acosta, 42 U.S. 24, 26-27 (1843).
154. Villalobos v. United States, 51 U.S. 541, 555-56 (1850).
155. *Id.* at 555.
156. United States. v. Low, 41 U.S. 162, 166-68 (1842).
157. United States v. Arredondo, 38 U.S. 88, 88 (1839); United States v. Arredondo, 38 U.S. 113, 133-35 (1839).

based on a private survey. The Court found this defect readily curable by ordering a survey consistent with the concession.[158]

Grants might fail because they were not specific enough to be identified by a survey. Thus, a grant of 50,000 acres to Augustin Buyck could not be confirmed by the Court because the locality of the grant could not be ascertained when only the phrase "at Musquito" was employed.[159] This doctrine was applied to invalidate large grants, such as the claim by Pedro Miranda to more than 368,000 acres along the "waters of Hillsborough and Tampa bays."[160] Relying on a passage from *White's New Recopilation*, Justice Wayne assured the parties that his decision was based on an application of the Spanish, and not the common law.[161]

These cases required a significant level of expertise in Spanish grants, legal sources, and *derecho indiano*. It is not surprising to find a handful of individuals specializing in these claims. Joseph M. White, author of the leading compilation and translation of applicable sources, was active in representing individuals and had already established a good reputation in the field by the early 1830s. White's rival was Richard Call who had challenged White to a duel in 1825 and served as opposing counsel to White

---

158. United States v. Hanson, 41 U.S. 196, 199-202 (1842).
159. Buyck v. United States, 40 U.S. 215, 222-25 (1841).
160. United States v. Miranda, 41 U.S. 153, 157 (1842).
161. *Buyck*, 40 U.S. at 224-25.

> It is proper for us to remark, that in coming to our conclusion upon this point, we have not been influenced by any of the English common-law rules, which make grants void for uncertainty.... We apply to the case, the laws and ordinances of the government under which the claim originated; and that rule which must be of universal application in the construction of grants, which is essential to their validity, that the thing granted should be so described as to be capable of being distinguished from other things of the same kind, or be capable of being ascertained by extraneous testimony.

Similarly, O'Hara v. United States, 40 U.S. 275, 279 (1841) ("[t]he place called Nassau" too indefinite when "Nassau" was unknown); United States v. Forbes's Heirs, 40 U.S. 173, 180-81 (1841) (the "district of Nassau River" too indefinite); United States v. Lawton, 46 U.S. 10, 25-29 (1847) ("at the place called Dunn's lake on the river St. John's" too indefinite). The Superior Court also lacked the power to locate lands to satisfy a grant from public lands. United States v. Delespine, 40 U.S. 319, 334-35 (1841).

in thirteen of the Florida land claim cases before the Supreme Court of the United States from 1832 to 1835. Blake Watson has captured the overlapping interest on the small group of attorneys who could handle these complex cases before the Supreme Court.[162]

These were technical cases relying on Spanish documents and Spanish laws, not all of which were translated. This led to a small number of trained, repeat players who litigated these claims; experts in *derecho indiano* were sought-after lawyers for petitioners. The United State was usually represented by the Attorney General at the time. For example, Joseph M. White represented seventeen petitioners in the first twenty Supreme Court cases from 1832 to 1836. Individual justices on the Supreme Court appeared also to have developed specific expertise so that their knowledge could be used in cases addressing Florida land claims. Justice Marshall wrote thirteen of the opinions studied; Justices Wayne and Catron wrote twelve opinions each; and Justice Baldwin wrote seven opinions.

---

162. Watson, *supra* note 103, at 372-73. Summarizing the various interests and conflicts of lawyers in *Mitchel v. United States*, Watson writes:

> To recap, during the *Mitchel* litigation the claimants suing the United States were represented by a former federal land commissioner (White), who was currently employed by the United States in other land grant disputes, and the United States Attorney General (Berrien), who otherwise supervised litigation for the federal government. The attorneys for the United States included Richard Call, the Tallahassee Land Office Receiver who had previously challenged White to a duel, and William Wirt, the father-in-law of Judge Thomas Randall [of the Superior Court of the Middle District of the Territory of Florida where the claim was initially filed—note by M.C. Mirow]. In addition to being married to the daughter of one of the lawyers representing the United States, Judge Randall was a friend of Call and had previously traveled to Cuba—on behalf of the government—to retrieve documents relevant to the validity of the Forbes Purchase!

Id. at 373-74. Furthermore, Joseph M. White later served as a trustee of the company that sold parcels from the land confirmed in the case. Dibble, *supra* note 60, at 162.

CONCLUSION

After Florida's transfer to the United States in 1821 under the Adams-Onís Treaty, Congress appointed commissioners to determine the validity of private land claims arising from the Spanish period. These commissions adjudicated smaller claims that were later confirmed by Congress. The methods, sources, and particularly the use of *derecho indiano* in these commissions await study by legal historians investigating the application of Spanish colonial law in U.S. fora. Larger or unresolved claims were assigned to the territorial courts with appeal by right to the Supreme Court of the United States. The Court heard approximately sixty cases on Florida land claims between 1829 and 1926.

Supreme Court cases dealing with Florida land claims raised a number of legal issues. The nature and application of the Adams-Onís Treaty were examined and re-examined as the Court developed its doctrine of self-executing treaties. In this light, the Court turned to the official text in Spanish in addition to the official English text. Its consultation of and reliance on this non-English text are noteworthy examples of the Court employing comparative methods across the different legal cultures touching these grants.

Derecho indiano came into play when the Court had to determine the validity of grants under Spanish law. It employed this body of law to examine grants of land in Indian Territory, the power of Spanish officials to make effective grants, and the satisfaction by grantees of conditions imposed on the grants. These complex legal sources were presented to the Court through a small cast of lawyers including Joseph M. White and his law partner Richard Henry Wilde, who had gained expertise in this area of law.[163] Similarly, Justices Marshall, Baldwin, Wayne, and Catron appear to have developed facility with the *derecho indiano* applicable to Florida land grants and authored the lion's share of opinions in these cases.

---

163. Dibble, *supra* note 60, at 49. Born in Dublin, Ireland, Wilde was admitted to the Georgia bar in 1809 and served as the state's Attorney-General from 1811 to 1813. *Id.* at 151.

The Court took Spanish law and Spanish documents seriously in determining title to large tracts of land under its jurisdiction. The Court made reasonable efforts to understand and to apply *derecho indiano* to resolve petitioners' claims and appears to have dealt fairly with petitioners, although different justices brought approaches that may have been more favorable (Justice Baldwin) or less favorable (Justice Wayne) to claimants under Spanish grants. Of the cases studied here, thirty-three affirmed the grants to petitioners and twenty-two denied the validity of the grants. Others have noted the seriousness with which the Court addressed these cases in light of the treaty obligations imposed on the United States.[164] Florida land claims before the Supreme Court provide a fascinating window into the sources and arguments used by attorneys and justices in the Court, an unexpected forum for the application and interpretation of *derecho indiano*.

---

164. Watson, *supra* note 103, at 377.

APPENDIX

CASES CONSULTED FOR THIS STUDY[165]

Case Name	Year	Citation	Justice	Attorneys	Grant[166]	Confirmed
De La Croiz v. Chamberlain	1827	25 U.S. 599	Trimble	Plaintiff: Livingston Defendant: Owen	not specified	no
Foster & Elam v. Neilson	1829	27 U.S. 232	Marshall	Defendant: Jones Plaintiffs in error: Coxe & Webster	40,000 arpents	no
United States v. Arredondo[167]	1832	31 U.S. 691	Baldwin	U.S.: Call, Wirt, Taney, AG Appellees: White, Berrein & Webster	289,000	yes
United States v. Percheman[168]	1833	32 U.S. 51	Marshall	U.S.: Taney, AG Appellee: White	2000	yes
United States v. Clarke[169]	1834	33 U.S. 436	Marshall	U.S.: Call Appellee: Berrein & Wilde	16,000	8000 confirmed

165. This list supplements and expands upon the list of cases provided in Boggs, *Florida Land Titles*, supra note 15, at 31; see also Dibble, supra note 60, at 173-81 (a list of cases argued by Joseph M. White).
166. In acres unless otherwise indicated.
167. *Spanish Land Grants, Arredondo & Son, F.M.—Confirmed, Fla.* Memory: St. Libr. & Archives Fla., https://www.floridamemory.com/items/show/232480 (last visited Apr. 12, 2017) [hereinafter cited by claimant and link].
168. *Percheman, John—Confirmed*, https://www.floridamemory.com/items/show/232846.
169. *Clarke, George J.F.—Confirmed*, https://www.floridamemory.com/items/show/232573.

Case Name	Year	Citation	Justice	Attorneys	Grant	Confirmed
United States v. Richard[170]	1834	33 U.S. 470	Marshall	U.S.: Call Appellee: White	14,400	yes
United States v. Huertas[171]	1834	33 U.S. 475	Marshall	U.S.: Call Appellee: White	10,000	yes
United States v. Gomez[172]	1834	33 U.S. 477	Marshall	U.S.: Call Appellee: White	12,000	yes
United States v. Levi[173]	1834	33 U.S. 479	Marshall	U.S.: Call Appellee: White	65,000	yes
United States v. Younge[174]	1834	33 U.S. 484	Marshall	U.S.: Call Appellee: White	5,000	yes
United States v. Fleming[175]	1834	33 U.S. 478	Marshall	U.S.: Call Appellee: White	20,000	yes

170. *Richard, Francis—Confirmed*, https://www.floridamemory.com/items/show/232871.
171. *Huertas, Antonio—Confirmed*, https://www.floridamemory.com/items/show/232735.
172. *Gomez, Eusibio M.—Confirmed*, https://www.floridamemory.com/items/show/232674.
173. *Levi, Moses E.—Confirmed*, https://www.floridamemory.com/items/show/232763.
174. Yonge, Philip R.—Confirmed, https://www.floridamemory.com/items/show/232992.
175. *Fleming, Geo—Confirmed*, https://www.floridamemory.com/items/show/232645.

Case Name	Year	Citation	Justice	Attorneys	Grant	Confirmed
United States v. Hernandez[176]	1834	33 U.S. 485	Marshall	U.S.: Call Appellee: White	20,000	yes
United States v. Huertas[177]	1834	33 U.S. 488	Marshall	U.S.: Call Appellee: White	6000 confirmed; 4000 denied	
United States v. Fatio [178]	1834	33 U.S. 492	Marshall	U.S.: Call Appellee: White	10,000	yes
United States v. Gibson [179]	1834	33 U.S. 494	Marshall	U.S.: Call Appellee: White	10,760	yes
United States v. Clarke [180]	1835	34 U.S. 168	Marshall	U.S.: Call Appellee: Wilde	22,000	yes
United States v. Huertas [181]	1835	34 U.S. 171	Marshall	U.S.: Call Appellee: Wilde & White	15,000	yes

176. *Hernandez, Joseph M.—Confirmed*, https://www.floridamemory.com/items/show/232712.
177. *Huertas, John—Confirmed*, https://www.floridamemory.com/items/show/232736.
178. *Fatio, Francis P.—Confirmed*, https://www.floridamemory.com/items/show/232629.
179. *Fleming, Sophia/Gibson, William—Confirmed*, https://www.floridamemory.com/items/show/232648.
180. *Clarke, George, J.F.—Confirmed*, https://www.floridamemory.com/items/show/232573.
181. *Huertas, Antonio—Confirmed*, https://www.floridamemory.com/items/show/232735.

Case Name	Year	Citation	Justice	Attorneys	Grant	Confirmed
Mitchel v. United States[182]	1835	34 U.S. 711	Baldwin	U.S.: Butler, AG, & Call Appellants: White & Berrien	1,200,000	yes
United States v. Segui[183]	1836	35 U.S. 306	Baldwin	U.S.: Butler, AG Appellee: White	16,000	yes
United States v. Chaires	1836	35 U.S. 308	Baldwin	U.S.: Butler, AG Appellees: White	20,000	yes
United States v. Seton[184]	1836	35 U.S. 309	Baldwin	U.S.: Butler, AG Appellee: White	16,000	yes
United States v. Sibbald[185]	1836	35 U.S. 313	Baldwin	U.S.: Butler, AG Appellee: White	16,000	yes
United States v. Fernandez[186]	1836	35 U.S. 393	Baldwin	U.S.: Butler, AG Appellees: White	16,000	yes

182. *John Forbes & Co.—Confirmed*, https://www.floridamemory.com/items/show/232654.
183. *Segui, Bernardo—Confirmed*, https://www.floridamemory.com/items/show/232908.
184. *Seton, Charles—Confirmed*, https://www.floridamemory.com/items/show/232911.
185. *Sibbald, Charles F.—Confirmed*, https://www.floridamemory.com/items/show/232917.
186. *Fernandez, Domingo—Confirmed*, https://www.floridamemory.com/items/show/232635.

Case Name	Year	Citation	Justice	Attorneys	Grant	Confirmed
United States v. Mills[187]	1838	37 U.S. 215	Wayne	U.S.: Butler, AG Appellee: none appeared	16,000? (mill)	no
United States v. Kingsley[188]	1838	37 U.S. 476	Wayne	U.S.: Butler, AG Appellee: none appeared	16,000	no
Garcia v. Lee	1838	37 U.S. 511	Taney	Defendant: Jones Plaintiff in error: M'Caleb, Southard	10,000 arpents	no
United States v. Delespine's Heirs[189]	1838	37 U.S. 654	Wayne	U.S.: Butler Appellee: none named	43,000	yes
United States v. Levy	1839	38 U.S. 81	Wayne	U.S.: Grundy, AG Appellee: none named	not specified	reform of survey denied
United States v. Drummond	1839	38 U.S. 84	Wayne	U.S.: Grundy, AG Appellee: none named	26,000	no

187. *Mills, William—Unconfirmed*, https://www.floridamemory.com/items/show/233196.
188. *Kingsley, Zephaniah—Unconfirmed*, https://www.floridamemory.com/items/show/233161.
189. *Delespine, Joseph—Confirmed*, https://www.floridamemory.com/items/show/232594.

Case Name	Year	Citation	Justice	Attorneys	Grant	Confirmed
United States v. Burgevin	1839	38 U.S. 85	Wayne	U.S.: Grundy, AG Appellee: Dent & Coxe	5 sq. miles	no
United States v. Arredondo's Heirs[190]	1839	38 U.S. 88	Wayne	none named	15,000	yes
United States v. Arredondo	1839	38 U.S. 133	Wayne	U.S.: Grundy, AG Appellees: none named	38,000	yes
United States v. Wiggins[191]	1840	39 U.S. 334	Baldwin	U.S.: Gilpin, AG & Dent Appellee: Downing	300	yes
Pollard's Heirs v. Kibbe	1840	39 U.S. 353	Thompson	Plaintiffs in error: Test & Webster Appellee: Key	not specified	
United States v. Waterman's Heirs[192]	1840	39 U.S. 478	Baldwin	U.S.: Gipin, AG Appellees: none named	16,000	yes

190. *Arredondo, Sr., F.M.—Confirmed*, https://www.floridamemory.com/items/show/232483.
191. *Wiggins, Elizabeth—Confirmed*, https://www.floridamemory.com/items/show/233394.
192. W*aterman, Eleazer—Confirmed*, https://www.floridamemory.com/items/show/232972.

Case Name	Year	Citation	Justice	Attorneys	Grant	Confirmed
Mitchel v. United States	1841	40 U.S. 52	Wayne	U.S.: Gilpin, AG Appellants: Ogden & Webster (printed argument for appellants by the late Joseph M. White)	1500 varas	yes
United States v. Rodman[193]	1841	40 U.S. 130	Wayne	U.S.: Gilpin, AG Appellee: Downing	16,000	yes
United States v. Forbes' Heirs[194]	1841	40 U.S. 173	Catron	U.S.: Gilpin, AG Appellees: Downing	10,000	no
Buyck v. United States	1841	40 U.S. 215	Wayne	U.S.: Gilpin, AG Appellant: Downing	50,000	no
United States v. Delespine's Heirs	1841	40 U.S. 226	Wayne	U.S.: Gilpin, AG Appellees: Downing	10,240	yes

193. *McHardy, Robert—Confirmed*, https://www.floridamemory.com/items/show/232797.
194. *Forbes, John—Confirmed*, https://www.floridamemory.com/items/show/232653.

Case Name	Year	Citation	Justice	Attorneys	Grant	Confirmed
O'Hara v. United States[195]	1841	40 U.S. 275	Wayne	U.S.: Gilpin, AG Appellants: Downing	15,000	no
United States v. Delespine[196]	1841	40 U.S. 319	Catron	U.S.: Gilpin, AG Appellee: Downing	92,160	no
United States v. Breward[197]	1842	41 U.S. 143	Catron	U.S.: Legaré, AG Appellee: Wilde	not specified	13,000 confirmed; 3000 not confirmed
United States v. Miranda	1842	41 U.S. 153	Wayne	U.S.: Duvall & Legaré, AG Appellees: Garr & Ogden	368,000	no
United States v. Low[198]	1842	41 U.S. 162	Catron	U.S.: Legaré, AG Appellees: Berrien & Wilde	16,000	yes
United States v. Hanson[199]	1842	41 U.S. 196	Catron	U.S.: Legaré, AG Appellees: none appeared	16,000	yes

195. *O$Hara* [sic], *Daniel—Unconfirmed*, https://www.floridamemory.com/items/show/233221.
196. *Delespine, Joseph—Unconfirmed*, https://www.floridamemory.com/items/show/233059.
197. *Breward, John—Confirmed*, https://www.floridamemory.com/items/show/232529.
198. *Lowe, John W.—Confirmed*, https://www.floridamemory.com/items/show/232777.
199. *Hanson, John M. et al.—Confirmed*, https://www.floridamemory.com/items/show/232697.

Case Name	Year	Citation	Justice	Attorneys	Grant	Confirmed
United States v. Clarke[200]	1842	41 U.S. 228	Catron	U.S.: Legaré, AG Appellee: none named	15,000	yes
United States v. Acosta[201]	1843	42 U.S. 24	Catron	U.S.: Legaré, AG Appellee: none named	8000	yes
Sibbald v. United States[202]	1844	43 U.S. 455	Story	none named	not specified	petition of other lands denied
Chaires v. United States	1845	44 U.S. 611	Catron	U.S.: Nelson, AG Appellants: Berrien	20,000	no
United States v. Marvin	1845	44 U.S. 620	Catron	U.S.: Nelson, AG Defendant in error: Marvin	7000	no
United States v. Lawton	1847	46 U.S. 10	Catron	U.S.: Mason, AG Appellee: Yulee	23,040	no

200. *Atkinson, George—Confirmed*, https://www.floridamemory.com/items/show/232485.
201. *Acosta, Domingo—Confirmed*, https://www.floridamemory.com/items/show/232464.
202. *Sobbald, Charles F.—Confirmed*, https://www.floridamemory.com/items/show/232917.

Case Name	Year	Citation	Justice	Attorneys	Grant	Confirmed
Villabolos v. United States[203]	1848	47 U.S. 81	Taney	U.S.: Mason, AG, Clifford AG Appellants: Yulee	not specified	no
Villalobos v. United States	1850	51 U.S. 541	Catron	U.S.: Crittenden, AG Appellants: Yulee & Berrien	16,000	no
Doe v. Braden	1853	57 U.S. 635	Taney	U.S.: Cushing, AG Plaintiff in error: Mayer & Johnson	12,000,000	no
United States. v. De Morant	1887	123 U.S. 335	Bradley	U.S.: Janks, SG Appellees: MacVigh, Line & Winter-steen	1600 arpents	yes
United States v. De Morant	1888	124 U.S. 647	Bradley	Movant: Lines no opposition	not specified	motion granted

203. Scrivener's error for "Villalobos." I thank Tom Baker for discussing this issue with me.

Case Name	Year	Citation	Justice	Attorneys	Grant	Confirmed
Mitchell v. Furman	1901	180 U.S. 402	Fuller	Appellants: Dewhurst Appellees: Fleming, Bisbee, Rhinehart & Fleming	10,000 (Anastasia Island)	no
United States v. Dalcour	1906	203 U.S. 408	Holmes	U.S. - Hoyt, SG, & Howard Appellees: Blount, Hatfield, Dewhurst & Blount, Jr.	1,850,000	no
Del Pozo v. Wilson Cypress Co.	1925	269 U.S. 82	Van Devanter	Appellee: Clark & Cooper Appellants: Dewhust, Jones & Jones	5500	no
Sanchez v. Deering	1926	270 U.S. 227	McReynolds	Appellee: Hudson Appellants: Dewhurst	175 (Key Biscayne)	no

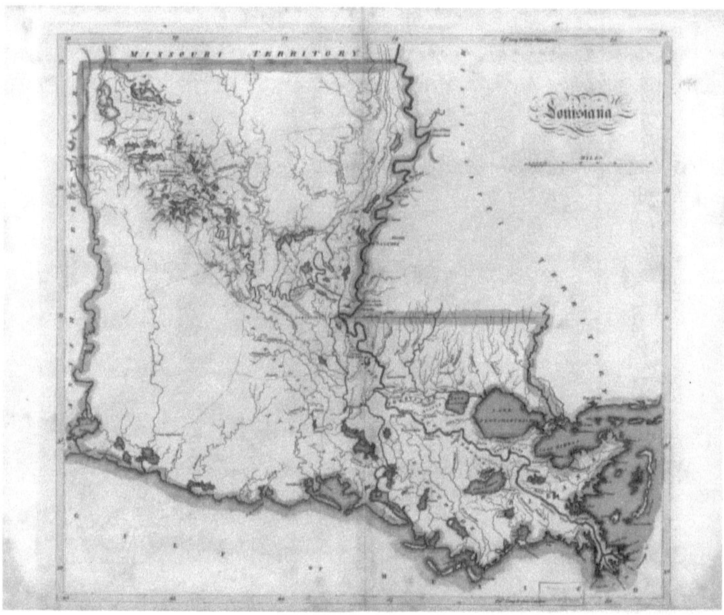

Louisiana
Map by Matthew Carey, 1814

CHAPTER 9

ARTICULATION OF FOLK LAW IN THE LORE OF PLACE

Legend as Expression of Sense of Place and Folk Justice in Louisiana's Neutral Strip[1]

Keagan LeJeune

"There's a place in Winn Parish called Coochie Brake," J. Maxwell Kelley told C. Renée Harvison when she interviewed him in 1990.[2] The former mayor of Winnfield, Louisiana, Kelley visited often with people, and he knew the stories circulating about that legendary swampy wood, a cypress brake running more than 700 acres and sitting roughly fifteen miles south and west of Winnfield. A wide range of local legends describe the otherworldly trees and strange rocks and profusion of fauna rumored to be found in Coochie Brake. Some claim the world's largest tupelo gum was discovered there in 1913;[3] some claim a high hill in the Brake called Robber's Roost stood for years as "a great

---

1. Earlier versions of portions of this essay appear in 'Western Louisiana's Neutral Strip: Its History, People, and Legends', *Folklife in Louisiana: Louisiana Living Traditions* (2015) at http://www.louisianafolklife.org/LT/Articles_Essays/NSLeJeune1.html#page1 and *Legendary Louisiana Outlaws: The Villains and Heroes of Folk Justice* (2016) [hereinafter LeJeune, *Legendary Louisiana Outlaws*].

2. J. Maxwell Kelley, 'Lying Horse Rock', in *Swapping Stories* 233 (Carl Lindahl, et al. eds., 1997) [hereinafter, Kelley].

3. Lonnie White, Assistant District Forester, Letter to State Forester Mixon, (March 16, 1955), State Library of Louisiana, 'Coochie Brake' vertical file; Eck H. Bozeman, 'Coochie Brake: A Most Unusual Spot in Winn Parish', 9.3 North La. Historical Association Newsletter 14 (April 1969).

vantage point" for bandits watching "travelers along the old wagon trail or [for] the law";[4] and some, like Maxwell Kelley, claim a certain part of Coochie Brake is "voodooed, whereby anyone who goes near it, something bad happens to them or a member of their family."[5]

Kelley explained to Harvison that Coochie Brake "was kind of the hideout for the West and Kimbrell clan, the night riders."[6] The gang's "territory was like Vidalia, Louisiana, all the way to the Texas Line. They used to call it No Man's Land in Sabine Parish, Zwolle, that area."[7] The outlaw gang preyed upon travelers moving along the area's early roads. "You see, in southern Winn Parish, the connecting link between Natchez Trace and the El Camino Real comes through Winn Parish. It's called the Harrisonburg Road," Kelley told Harvison.[8] The outlaws

> "really ravaged that road for many, many years.... There's a rock there called Lying Horse Rock that's shaped like a horse lying down on its side. The old tale goes that that's where they buried their gold.... We've had some say that old so-and-so died because he got too close to Lying Horse Rock."[9]

Such legends are typical of Coochie Brake,[10] and while these stories convey a degree of historical information, their remarkable or supernatural elements likely earn the disdain of the

---

4. Wanda Cornelius, 'El Camino Real Was Scene of Thievery', *Alexandria Daily Town Talk*, March 5, 1972.
5. Kelley, *supra* note 2, 233.
6. *Id.*
7. *Id.*, 232.
8. *Id.*, 233.
9. *Id.*, 232.
10. Harley Bozeman (1891-1971) served in the Louisiana House of Representatives and acted as the area's local historian. He related his own story about Coochie Brake. In 1937, Bozeman and Dudley D. Lang, former parish representative, visited the mysterious woods in order to purchase a tract of land. The guide who brought them to Lying Horse Rock (and sat on the rock) died the following day. Bozeman claimed after that trip he never returned to the spot. See Wanda Cornelius, 'Superstition Hovers Over Lying Horse Rock', *Town Talk* (Alexandria-Pineville), March 1, 1970.

historian and the skepticism of the general reader. However, the folklorist recognizes the legend's anti-historical components as floating elements belonging to a "stock of themes and motifs in constant circulation among the peoples of the world."[11] These reoccurring structural components should be regarded, then, not as extraneous or fictitious, but as the very fabric of the deep-seated truths behind such stories.[12] The stories attached to Coochie Brake and Lying Horse Rock are no different. These detailed localized legends contain familiar structural components and widespread folkloric themes and motifs that connect to Neutral Strip residents' deep sense of place.

Sense of place can be understood as the close relationship people form with the physical landscape which unfolds as "a thick layer of history, memory, association, and attachment that builds up in a location as a result of our experiences in it."[13] This essay seeks to examine Neutral Strip residents' sense of place expressed through the region's preponderance of outlaw legends, which almost without exception connect to the region's brief

---

11. Richard M. Dorson, *Folklore: Selected Essays* 159 (1972). Dorson explains "in general usage the word '*legend*' implies an exaggerated and colorful account of an event", but for scholars, legends are traditional oral narratives set in the real world and containing an element of truth. *Id.*

12. For an overview of debate surrounding the definition of 'legend', see Timothy R. Tangherlini, '"It Happened Not Too Far from Here ...": A Survey of Legend Theory and Characterization' 49.4 Western Folklore 371 (Oct. 1990). Tangherlini offers this definition: "Legend, typically, is a short (mono-) episodic, traditional, highly ecotypified, historicized narrative performed in a conversational mode, reflecting on a psychological level a symbolic representation of folk belief and collective experiences and serving as a reaffirmation of commonly held values of the group to whose tradition it belongs." *Id.*, 385. For the presence of truth and belief at the core of legend's definition, see Linda Dégh, 'The Landscape and Climate of Legend', in *Legend and Belief: Dialectics of a Folklore Genre* 311-400 (2001).

13. Kent Ryden, *Mapping the Invisible Landscape: Folklore, Writing, and the Sense of Place* 38 (1993), 38. Ryden contends 'descriptions of regional folklore coincide closely with the notion of sense of place formulated by humanistic geographers: the strong sense of rootedness in a location, of identification with (and self-identification in terms of) that location, of membership in a unified place-based community, and of a common world view as a result of a common geographical experience are all key elements in the formation of the local understanding of geographical meaning.' *Id.*, 59.

historical stint as an official buffer. The scope of this essay narrows its comments to The West and Kimbrel Clan (the group many consider the region's most notorious outlaw band) and to the legendary connection tellers envision between this group and the historical moment that defines the Neutral Strip. Furthermore, this essay considers how residents transform the region's past by linking the West and Kimbrell Clan to the present landscape of Coochie Brake. In the way of evidence, the essay recounts portions of the Coochie Brake and West and Kimbrell legends, theorizes about the outlaw figure as a commentary of folk law, and examines the role of *place* in key portions of these narratives.[14] Making this argument first necessitates unfolding some of the Coochie Brake place-name legend.

Nearly fifty years ago, Eck Bozeman claimed that from 1767 until 1803 the area was home to a Spanish fort known as Fort Coutier.[15] Current oral tradition still holds "the Spanish used the massive stone hill as a fortification and to cache deposits of gold brought from Texas."[16] Legend says Spanish officials, seeing the locale's massive and mysterious rock formations, intentionally established the fort at this location locale and employed the "labyrinth full of underground passages and tunnels"[17] to conceal "great quantities of gold and silver bullion from Mexico" before the treasure was transported by mule to "Post de Concordia (Vidalia)" and then loaded onto ships sailing "up the Mississippi River."[18] Then, Spain's authority in the region vanished.

According to locals, when Spanish Louisiana shifted suddenly to France and then to America, the abrupt transfer prevented Fort Courtier's Spanish owners from being "able to

---

14. For a humanistic geographer's discussion of 'place' and 'sense of place', see Yi-Fu Tuan, *Topophilia: A Study of Environmental Perceptions, Attitudes, and Values* (1974) [hereinafter Tuan, *Topophilia*] and *Space and Place: The Perspective of Experience* (1977).
15. Bozeman, *supra* note 10.
16. Bruce Shultz, 'Winn's Coochie Brake—A History All Its own', *Town Talk* (Alexandria-Pineville), August 19, 1979.
17. Robyn Jones, 'Interesting Tidbits Add Flavor to CenLA', *Town Talk* (Alexandria-Pineville), February 17, 1991 [hereinafter Jones].
18. Wanda Cornelius, 'Legend of Coochie Brake—Is It Truth or Myth?', *Winn Parish Enterprise*, February 27, 1969.

move out all the gold and silver bullion from the tunnels." Faced with immediate evacuation and not wanting the area's new owners to claim Spain's imperial wealth, the soldiers "sealed" the entrances or "rolled rock boulders in and around them until the treasure laden tunnels were hidden."[19] When American soldiers took possession of the fort, not only did they find no gold, they evidently also wrestled with the name Courtier. Legend says these English-speaking soldiers took Fort Coutier and "interpreted it as 'coochie.'"[20] Rumors of Fort Coutier/Fort Coochie's hidden Spanish gold still circulate in the region and locals share several stories about people searching for treasure. However, local legend also suggests those who look for this treasure instead find a hexed, "voodooed" landscape cursed because of this Spanish gold.

As recently as 1999, Darryle K. Lacour claimed that while "researching the history of this area" he learned a monk directed "the storage and safekeeping of that gold and silver."[21] According to Robyn Jones, a newspaper writer gathering "interesting tidbits" about Central Louisiana, "the 'mad Spanish monk' hoarded" these "treasures of gold and silver" while he, "his personal servant and several Mexican workers lived" in the "wilderness area ... on Beech Creek near Coochie Brake."[22] Lacour referred to the legend as one of "a monk, murder and mystery," which seems apt. Eventually the monk becomes "mad" with greed, and variants of the legend claim by the monk's command, his "workers would kill the Mexican drivers and their burros and steal the loot."[23] In fact, a few variants of the story even have the monk treating "the drivers to a sumptuous dinner with a menu that included delicious dishes which unfortunately contained poison," and some versions explain the monk "cooked the deadly feast for his [own] workers and they all died."[24] With

---

19. *Id.*
20. Jones, *supra* note 17.
21. Darryle K. Lacour, 'An Adventure in Coochie Brake in North Louisiana', *Town Talk* (Alexandria-Pineville), December 7, 1999 [hereinafter Lacour].
22. Jones, *supra* note 17.
23. *Id.*
24. Lacour, *supra* note 21.

the workers murdered, the monk "loaded up all the gold and silver and buried it by one of the creeks near the Fort."[25]

While the legend's narrative contains an obvious amount of remarkable details that may cause tellers to dismiss the story, the narrative's attachment to the physical landscape and the tangible place name of Coochie Brake help it to endure. Some place names are created "as the result of a real or imagined (i.e., believed to have happened but not historical) event of the past" and sometimes a meaningless name develops an "explanatory story which...tries to give meaning to ... a name."[26] However, the attachment of a legend to a place name can make it seem historical. There is some speculation that a fort was in the region, but there is no historical evidence that it was located in the Brake or was named Fort Coutier. Several linguistic scholars, as a point of fact, explain *Coochie*'s origin is not Spanish, but American Indian. *Coochie* likely derives from the Choctaw word *kũska(k)* meaning *reed.*[27] Thus, the legend circulating around the name seems to be an explanation of a "meaningless" term rather than a narrative resulting from portions of the historical record. This invention might once again prove uninteresting to those seeking definitive historical evidence, but the worth of the legend may be less a record of the past than a reflection of how locals relate to that past. Legend scholar Bill Ellis contends, "Legendry should be seen more dynamically as a threefold interplay, with the ongoing social history of the place engaging with the culture's definition of the supernatural and with the ways we emotionally respond to the world we live in."[28] Place-name legends, I argue, operate as a more condensed expression of this interplay.

---

25. Jones, *supra* note 17.
26. W.F.H. Nicolaisen, 'Place -Name Legends: An Onomastic Mythology', 87.2 Folklore 146, 150 (1976). Elsewhere, Nicolaisen writes that "[s]ince the name is attached to such and such a place," he explains, "the past must have been the way the story tells it." 'Names and Narratives', J. Am. Folklore 259, 266 (1984). Once on the map, the place-name legend gains veracity, that link to the past solidified, made truer, in a way.
27. William Alexander Read, 'Louisiana Place-Names of Indian Origin', *in* 14.2 *University Bulletin Louisiana State University* 27-28 (February 1927).
28. Bill Ellis, 'The Haunted Asian Landscape of Lafcadio Hearn', in *Putting the Supernatural in Its Place* 196 (Jeannie Banks Thomas, ed., 2015). Ellis explains

Louisiana folklorist Frank de Caro, American Folklore Society Fellow and Professor Emeritus of Louisiana State University, claims people see legend "as a kind of alternative history."[29] What does this "'maybe' quality to the 'history'" afford? In legend, "we are freed ... to enjoy an easier, preferable version of the past...one which may require not belief but willing suspension of disbelief, so that the past can, in part, be imagined." Certainly, local legends can maintain local stories and family histories that otherwise may have been forgotten,[30] but more importantly, rather than strictly record and reflect the past, these legends likely mean to comment on the past.[31] Linda Dégh describes this function as filtered through the specific qualities of a place-name legend, which ties together the historical, remarkable, and localized environment: place-name legends "provide not so much ironclad details from the historical record

---

that we "socially construct the space around us.... We experience place not just in terms of sensory impulses, but also as the most recent unfolding of the sport's ongoing history" and follows with a brief explanation of this process. *Id.*, 196-197.

29. Frank de Caro, 'Legends, Local Identity, and a New Orleans Cookbook', 9 La. Folklore Miscellany 23-31 (2009), in *Folklife in Louisiana: Louisiana Living Traditions* (2015) at http://www.louisianafolklife.org/LT/Articles_Essays/LFMcookbook.html. De Caro explains that legend appears "more fragmented (and hence more easily come to terms with) and more fun than conventional history." As such, legend offers "an alternative way of talking about the past" and "shaping the past" and a primary role in developing what de Caro terms a "l*ore of place," which I define as people's perceptions about the cultural essence of a locale, an essence formed over time and likely best expressed in local traditions, like familiar stories.* For a discussion of 'the lore of place,' see Frank de Caro, 'New Orleans, Folk Ideas, and the Lore of Place', 7 La. Folklore Miscellany 68-80 (1992).

30. There has been a great deal of discussion about the power of narrative and storytelling. One example is the work psychologists have done on the idea of narrative transport—how narrative transports speaker and audience into the world of the story, which can often engender a deep empathetic capacity in both. See, for instance, Richard Bauman, *Story, Performance, and Event: Contextual Studies of Oral Narrative* (1986).

31. Ronald Baker, 'The Role of Folk Legends in Place-Name Research', 85.338 J. Am. Folklore 367-374 (October–December 1972). Baker argues place-name legends serve as reminders of a past—sometimes positive, sometimes negative, sometimes acting as "wish fulfillment," sometimes "providing catharsis," and often revealing "something about the humor, beliefs, prejudices, and values of the people who applied the names." *Id.*, 368.

nor a direct depiction of the area's landscape, but more so the artistic reflection of both."[32] This point connects to the manner in which place-name legend transports the past to the present—its linking the past to the present landscape. For residents, Coochie Brake's localized environment stands as a symbolic piece of the wild physical landscape.[33] Locals know it and its rumored mysterious qualities and otherworldly reputation. This strangeness makes Coochie Brake especially noteworthy and a more symbolic or psychically resonant locus than the region's broader landscape.

"At the center of the classic legend," legend scholar Carl Lindahl claims, "is the overlapping of two worlds, an intersection of the everyday and the supernatural."[34] That seems to describe Coochie Brake. Its topography, its terrain, its giant trees and strange rocks, its unusual tunnels, its ostentatious display of a rugged natural world—all of it marks Coochie Brake as a different place where the "intersection of the everyday and the supernatural" is ever-present.[35] Scholar Jeannie Banks Thomas describes these types of places as "weird spaces" and argues this type of "strange or uncanny" place stands as "a repository and a trigger for memory, desires, and cultural concerns" because as a "weird" locale, it allows for "the subversion of norms…feelings of transformation and difference."[36] In this regard, the legend of

---

32. Linda Dégh, 'Importance of Collecting Place-Name Legends in Indiana', 1.2 *Indiana Names* 34 (Fall 1970).
33. For a discussion of wilderness as a symbolic place, see Tuan, *Topophilia*, *supra* note 14, 63-64, 109-112, 113-115.
34. Carl Lindahl, 'Psychic Ambiguity at the Legend Core', 23 J. Folklore Research 1, 2 (1986).
35. For a discussion of this role, see Charles Stewart, 'Dreams of Treasure: Temporality, Historicization, and the Unconscious', 3.4 Anthropological Theory 481 (2003).
36. Jeannie Banks Thomas, 'Introduction', in *Putting the Supernatural in Its Place* 20 (Jeannie Banks Thomas, ed., 2015). Thomas explains that "weird space" connects to Edward Soja's description of 'third space'. She writes, "First space is material, mappable space.... Second space is how we conceive of space.... Third space is how we actually understand space; it's how we 'practice' place." *Id.*, 20. Thomas argues *weird spaces* allow us to be in two places at once: "We are still in and of this world, but ... simultaneously in another, more ethereal, space." *Id.*, 21. This openness marks the space as a transformative space.

Coochie Brake may be an avenue to interpret the population's active creation of the landscape existing as an official neutral zone.

The Neutral Strip region draws its name from the area's brief stint as an official buffer zone between Spain and the United States following the Louisiana Purchase. When the United States purchased the territory from France, Spain and the United States argued over the boundary south of Natchitoches.[37] In lieu of an armed clash, the nations removed all troops from the disputed area until boundaries could be determined. Historian J.V. Haggard defines the region as east of the Sabine River; west of the Calcasieu River, Kisatchie Bayou, and Arroyo Hondo; south until the Gulf of Mexico; and north until the 32nd parallel of north latitude. While diplomatic negotiations moved laboriously forward, squatters, fugitive slaves, filibusters, smugglers, and even outlaws used the Neutral Ground as a haven. Soon the region became known as a no man's land where residents in the region often faced criminals alone and without governmental aid.[38]

The region's historical status during this time not only serves as the region's namesake but also as a mental reference point for many of its residents, but in truth, the region existed as a buffer zone before its official status. Spain considered the region key in stemming American expansion and saw western Louisiana as an important buffer between American settlements in the South and the prized lands of Texas and Mexico.[39] However, due to the expense and difficulty of fortifying it, the region was left comparatively unprotected and unsupported by Spanish troops. Thus, Spain employed American Indian tribes as useful tools in

---

37. The 1819 Adams-Onís Treaty established the Sabine River as the western boundary and officially ended the Neutral Strip. See J. Villasana Haggard, 'The Neutral Ground between Louisiana and Texas, 1806-1821', 28.4 La. Hist. Q 1001-1128 (1945) [hereinafter, Haggard, *The Neutral Ground*]. Haggard claims confusion about the boundaries derived from the region's long history, even before Spanish rule during the 1790s and 1800s, as a contested area with unclear boundaries. *Id.*, 1009-1010. Moreover, to a large degree Spain governed the region with a blind eye, allowing squatters and all manner of self-directed settlers, such as American Indians who lost lands during the French-Indian War, to settle there in order to thwart American expansion. *Id.*, 1002-1004, 1010-1011, 1019, 1021-1023.

38. *Id.*, 1045-1047, 1049, 1050-1051.

39. *Id.*, 1018-1019.

slowing American settlement by encouraging several groups of Southern American Indians to settle in the region if these groups promised to deter American expansion.[40] For instance, as early as the 1780s, members of the Alabama and Coushatta tribes settled in eastern Texas and western Louisiana, which was under Spanish control. Offered land by Spain, the Coushatta tribe clustered into a cultural island in response to perceived threats to its cultural independence.[41] The Coushatta people are one of several Neutral Strip populations who engaged in a settlement strategy of intentional separation in an effort to avoid assimilation by other groups and to maintain cultural identity.[42]

---

40. *Id.*, 1010.

41. Linda Langley, Claude Oubre, and Jay Precht, 'Louisa Williams Robinson, Her Daughters and Granddaughters: Recognizing the Contributions of Three Generations of Coushatta Women', La .Cultural Vistas 26-27 (Winter 2009-10) and Edwin Adams Davis, *Louisiana: A Narrative History* 299 (1971).

42. See H.F. "Pete" Gregory, 'Native Americans in the Neutral Strip', in *NSU Folklife Festival Booklet* 5-6, (2004). The region's remoteness and long history as a border allowed for many groups to carry out a strategy that preserved cultural practices through isolation. To avoid contact with Europeans and avoid war, bands of Koasati or Coushatta, for instance, left their ancestral homes in Tennessee for Alabama, Georgia, Mississippi, Florida, Texas, and, of course, Louisiana. By 1861 at least 250 Coushatta migrated to the Calcasieu River, and in the 1880s, another group of approximately 300 Coushatta settled at Bayou Blue. At Bayou Blue, the Coushatta preserved a culture rich in traditional arts and crafts and preserved their ancestral language, which is still spoken by tribal members.

In 'Louisiana Indians in the 21st Century' in *Folklife in Louisiana: Louisiana's Living Traditions* (2013), anthropologist Dayna Bowker Lee contends that during the region's official status as a neutral buffer, a band of Choctaw also moved into the region and merged with the Ebarb community, many residents of which trace their ancestors to Spanish soldiers who manned the Los Adaes Presidio and refused to return to interior Spain when the presidio closed in 1773. Scholars also note that as late as 1997 some residents still spoke a unique, archaic Spanish filled with Nahuatl Indian and French loanwords. In Ebarb, Zwolle, Los Adaes, Robeline, Spanish Lake, and other areas in the Neutral Strip, colonial Spanish influence remains a part of the culture, such as folk practices with roots in Spanish Catholicism and those exhibiting Indo-Hispanic ties. Some of the region's lore also connects to the Spanish influence over the region. Several variants of the La Llorona legend have been collected in the region. La Llorona, known as "The Weeping Woman" or "The Woman in White," is a ghostly woman wailing over the loss of her children because of the harm done to her by the man she loves. La Llorona is a widespread legend in Hispanic culture and indicative of the region's Spanish cultural features.

While some of these early groups, like the Coushatta, held official land grants, many settlers in the region simply squatted on land that was considered unclaimed since it was unfenced.[43] The region held a great deal of available land because of delayed settlement in the region,[44] and even though these squatters held no *official* rights to the land, they held strong beliefs that a tract of land was theirs by right of having settled it and remaining on it for several generations. Moreover, while these squatters in the region often fenced their small gardens or patches of corn or peas surrounding their homes, wooded grazing land was often left unfenced. Though unfenced, this grazing land, however, was understood to be the property of certain families. To complicate this, settlers let cattle and hogs range free, which often caused disputes over stray animals violating grazing rights, and as in other regions, feuds among families often served as a means of settling gross infringements of property and grazing rights.[45] This strong sense of entrenched but unofficial boundaries fills the region with a history of property disputes, and in turn, fills the region's lore with a corpus of stories concerning fights and feuds and various other extralegal endeavors.[46]

Illustrations of this can be found in the region's earliest economic endeavors. During the colonial period, specifically due

---

43. Thad Sitton and C.E. Hunt, *Big Thicket People* 3-4 (2008).

44. Steven Smith, *A Good Home for a Poor Man: Fort Polk and Vernon Parish, 1800–1940* (1999). Smith claims "settlement was delayed by the political maneuvering and intrigue of European nations.... Legal settlement, including the establishment of legitimate government, religion, and the development of towns, roads, and industries was thwarted." *Id.*, 42.

45. Samuel C. Hyde, Jr., 'Feuding Is Our Means of Societal Regulation: Elusive Stability in Southeastern Louisiana's Piney Woods, 1877-1910', 48.2 La. Hist. 133-155 (2007). Perhaps the region's most famous feud is the Conner feud involving the Conners, Smiths, and Lowes of Scrappin' Valley, Texas, which borders the Neutral Strip and is often associated with The Neutral Strip's history. The fight began over grazing rights.

46. One event often recounted is the story of 'The Rawhide Fight', which occurred in the 1850s. Legend says the fight occurred over a schoolhouse in Walnut Hill, Louisiana, near present-day Leesville. While some versions of the legend say a young man who did not want to attend school burned the building down, other versions hint that the burning of the school and subsequent fight were more about disagreements over who would run the school and the outsiders who might attend it.

to Spanish commercial policy, smuggling and black-market trade flourished in the region, and these extralegal activities became a mainstay even of those enterprises officially sanctioned to operate and trade in the Neutral Strip. For example, despite official Spanish policy prohibiting trade with Louisiana, a thriving smuggling operation existed between Spanish troops stationed at Nacogdoches and French troops at Natchitoches, and a portion of this was overseen by the sanctioned trading outposts in the region.[47] Due to the agreement's removal of troops, robbery also plagued the region's early trade. In fact, highwaymen along roadways became such an impediment to all sanctioned dealers, the region developed a reputation as a haven for outlaws. One victim of the area's bandits in a petition to the U.S. government claimed the region had been so overrun with bands of desperate men that "the damned Neutral Ground is cursed of the Devil."[48] During the region's existence as an official buffer, cattle rustling also reached such extremes occupants petitioned Spanish and American authorities to intervene, but when those petitions failed, some communities formed brutal vigilance committees, an early example of communal response in administering extralegal justice.[49]

---

47. J. Villasana Haggard, 'The House of Barr and Davenport', 49 Southwestern Hist. Q. 66-88 (July 1945-April 1946). [hereinafter Haggard, The House of Barr and Davenport]. Haggard explains, "Spain had restricted and prohibited commercial intercourse with Louisiana, but the urgent need that often developed for supplies compelled frontier authorities to amend all prohibitory legislation whenever necessity dictated such a course. Spanish commercial policy gave rise to a highly profitable smuggling trade for which the Neutral Ground served as an ideal base." *Id.*, 70. See also Ralph Lee Woodward, Jr., 'Spanish Commercial Policy in Louisiana, 1763-1803', 44.2 La. Hist. 133-164 (Spring 2003).

48. Haggard, *The House of Barr and Davenport*, *supra* note 47, 1064. Pages 1059-1069 provide an overview.

49. Early residents of the Neutral Strip often relied on family members and close-knit neighbors for protection and survival, forming an extended network of partnership. Through the years, patches of residents banded together to provide their small communities with schoolhouses, churches, and even a means of self-rule and self-defense, such as masonic lodges, which on occasion acted as policing forces. For decades no outside system could unseat this rule of family, neighbor, and clan.

Concepts of the justice inherent in extralegal activities also shape personal narratives. For instance, similar to "Gone to Texas" (G.T.T.) stories found in the sagas of pioneering Texas families, family stories in the Neutral Strip often describe an ancestor's early settlement in the region, but set during the region's *neutral* status, these stories frequently involve the pioneering ancestor fleeing to Louisiana's No Man's Land in order to avoid punishment in his or her native region. As in G.T.T. tales, these details may be pure fabrication, but as Texas social historian Mody Boatright explains, they have "a relation to social context and reflect a social value."[50] In the Neutral Strip, these narratives seem to promote the population's value of self-reliance and communal regulation superseding that of an outside agency. Of course, a great deal of this family folklore also circles around to outlaws and buried treasure, which are more traditional narratives.

Many local legends claim several early residents of the region were displaced members of Jean Lafitte's crews[51] or members or supporters of John Murrell's large outlaw gang, the Mystic Clan. These members identified themselves through signs and secret handshakes and marked their homes with black locust trees and Spanish Dagger plants.[52] Place names in the region, like Black Locust Hill, connect to these enduring legends. Residents

---

50. Mody Boatright, 'The Family Saga as a Form of Folklore' in *Mody Boatright, Folklorist: A Collection of Essays* 124 (Ernest B. Speck, ed., 1973).

51. Tom Watson, 'Early Exploration and Settlement of the Lower Calcasieu Watershed', in *Gateway to the Gulf* (2002). Legend says these men settled in the region once Lafitte was removed from New Orleans and established a series of contact points within the region. Cast in legend as they are, these early locals, rumored to be ex-pirates employed by the notorious smuggler and his contacts like the Bowie brothers, possessed legendary tenacity, toughness, and a dangerous reputation.

52. Mabell R. Kadlecek and Marion C. Bullard, *Louisiana's Kisatchie Hills: History Tradition, Folklore* 517-524 (1994). John Murrell goes by many names (the Great Western Land Pirate, the Reverend Devil, the Terror of the Natchez Trace, the Leader of the Mystic Clan) and many spellings (Murrell, Murel, Murrel). Local lore has it that Murrell used a network of fellow bandits collectively known as the Mystic Clan to rob people along the Natchez Trace and the El Camino Real, and legends claim that this network of outlaws extended into the Neutral Strip.

along the Sabine River and along the historical route of the El Camino Real also share many stories about Spanish gold and silver being lost as it was transported along these routes and local families' experiences searching for this treasure.[53] No doubt reflecting local historical awareness of the region's status as Spanish possession, local lore also holds many legends about lost Spanish mines.[54] In fact, Haggard points out that these rumors drew some of the earliest residents to the Neutral Strip.[55]

As one can see, there are historical and cultural reasons the Coochie Brake place-name legend involves a lost gold mine and Spain,[56] but in truth, this kernel narrative of a lost mine is attached to various locales and contains elements common in a widespread cycle of stories about Spanish mines, which may indicate the presence of the legend's connections to sociological

---

53. These roads became infamous to locals, and a great deal of the stories in the Neutral Strip detail travelers falling prey to highwaymen and bandits. Even inns and boarding houses along the roads could be dangerous. Several legends circulate about treacherous innkeepers renting a room to a forlorn and exhausted traveler only to murder him in his sleep and steal his possessions. The best example of this is the Yokum Inn named after the infamous Yokum Gang, the Parkers' Halfway House, and subject of this essay, the West and Kimbrell gang who posed as law-abiding citizens but were actually a gang of robbers who waylaid boarders at the Kimbrell farm.

54. There are several other personal accounts of locals finding gold and silver in the hills of central Louisiana or along the rivers. One example can be found in J. Frank Dobie, *Legends of Texas, Vol. 1: Lost Mines and Buried Treasure* (1992), which includes legends of a Spanish silver mine near the Sabine or Red River. In addition, in DeRidder and Merryville, residents tell of a lost Spanish silver mine and a small tight-knit group of men who discovered it. These men disappeared into the woods periodically to return with bags of minted silver dollars, but kept the location a secret until each of the men died.

55. Haggard, *The Neutral Ground*, *supra* note 37, 1002-1003.

56. The region also experienced small mineral discoveries which likely reinforced the legend. For instance, in 1887 assayers of the United States Mint in New Orleans received "a cigar box full" of dirt and rock from Barce, Louisiana, a place relatively speaking not too far from Coochie Brake. A legend about a site roughly forty-five miles away also concerns lost gold. See John L Doughy, 'The Hub Lake Gold: An Analysis of a Legend', 15 *La. Folklife J. (December* 1991), available at www.louisianafolklife.org/LT/Articles_Essays/LFJhublake.html.

reasons.[57] Specifically, Robert Myers argues the "Lost Louisiana Mine is an American legend about buried Spanish treasure that has been sought since the Victorian era," with a core narrative claiming "a Spanish expedition concealed a rich gold mine in the wilderness of Spain's Luisiana colony."[58] Myers is one of many scholars connecting the legend of lost Spanish gold imbuing the land with a curse to The Black Legend cycle, which was promulgated by a deeply anti-Spanish bias in Europe and North America in order to demonize Spanish empire-building.[59] The essays in this collection alone offer substantial evidence of the anti-Spanish sentiment circulating after the transition of the Louisiana colony, in particular concerning the regime's governance of its colonial possessions and its approach to the rule of law. In the Neutral Strip, this ire focused on Spain's encouragement of settlement by Southern American Indians, its policies' involvement with smuggling, and its inability to rid the

57. Paul Harden, 'Buried Treasure Tales', *El Defensor Chieftain* (Socorro, NM), Saturday, March 3, 2012. This article about legendary Spanish gold in New Mexico argues miners in New Mexico "were not so honorable, being located far from Mexico City" and "to avoid discovery by the Spanish soldiers at Santa Fe, the miners would often hide their riches in caves or bury them near some recognizable landmark for later recovery." One of the tales he discusses involves a Spanish monk who uses caverns and tunnels to hide mined gold from Spanish soldiers. Harden references the legend as the story of the Lost Padre Mine.

58. Robert A. Myers, "'Lost Louisiana Mine', in *Encyclopedia of Arkansas History and Culture*, at http://www.encyclopediaofarkansas.net/encyclopedia/entry-detail.aspx?entryID=8415 <accessed 13 January 2013>. Myers explains in Arkansas the legend, based initially on early reports by Lieutenant Governor Francisco Bouligny in 1778 and other Spanish territory officials, was spread by "nineteenth-century stock promotions" and pulp-fiction writers.

59. The papers of this collection discuss this idea in detail. For instance, in 'Sounding the Retreat: The Exit of Spanish Law in Early Louisiana,' Vernon Valentine Palmer directs readers to David J. Weber, 'The Spanish Legacy in North America and the Historical Imagination' 23 Western Hist. Q (1992) and Thomas Ingersoll, *Mammon and Manon in Early New Orleans: The First Slave Society in the Deep South 1718-1819* 153-154 (1999). It is interesting to note that Weber begins his article describing the architectural remnants embodying Spanish rule, such as adobe buildings and stone forts. These forts become tangible reminders of Spanish expansion into the New World, and in legend, their ruins remain cursed because of the Spanish empire's rumored brutality, avarice, and fanaticism.

region of outlaws, despite various military attempts to purge the region of this element.[60]

In legend, this ire takes the form of a narrative directly tying Spain's influence to the land's status as being perpetually cursed. Spain's thirst for gold (and by extension its policies concerning trade and law) and its emissary (a monk mad with greed) not only bury their ill-gotten gains in the tunnels of Coochie Brake, but curse the land itself by doing so, perpetually affecting those who travel to the Brake, specifically to Lying Horse Rock. The narrative makes that link and does so in a memorable way. However, the most potent expression of the land's twistedness resulting from Spain's governance rests in Coochie Brake and Lying Horse Rock then being tied to outlaws, as Kelley does when he links Coochie Brake to the West and Kimbrell Clan.[61]

From the 1840s to the 1860s, John West and Laws Kimbrell led a gang of outlaws who robbed and murdered countless victims. These two prosperous men organized residents into a clan operating by secret signs and special passwords. Most members existed as part of an outer ring and a few select members, all well-regarded citizens, formed an inner circle, which even included the local constable and West himself, who served as a Methodist church deacon and was elected justice of the peace for one Winn Parish ward. The outer ring enforced law and order in a region reeling from pre–Civil War chaos and post–Civil War poverty; the inner circle, endowing the gang with its legendary reputation, waylaid unsuspecting travelers and terrorized uncooperative residents. The gang exerted supreme authority until local citizens, eventually organized by Dan Dean and James O. Maybin, brought West, Kimbrell, and the entire gang to justice.

Following the 1819 Adams-Onís Treaty, many residents of western Louisiana looked to vigilance committees for protection

---

60. Haggard, *The Neutral Ground*, *supra* note 37, 1062-1063.

61. Many of the stories that describe the events surrounding the West and Kimbrell Clan were collected by Richard Briley and put into his *Nightriders: Inside Story of the West and Kimbrell Clan* (1968). Jack Peebles published his *The Legend of the Nightriders* (2005) which seeks to develop the legend using archival material unavailable to Briley.

where they considered governmental structures to be inadequate. If necessity dictated it, normal citizens, such as members of a Masonic lodge or faithful members of a church, banded together to operate as the law.[62] That this group turned to an outlaw gang comments on the anxiety residents hold about the difficulties emerging when citizens must take the law into their own hands. In other words, when citizens must confront an existing system of law by stepping outside of it, they understand, even if subconsciously, the danger that reach of law poses. The outlaw folktype stands as an expression of that awareness.

The term *outlaw* means being outside the law. Historically, an outlaw earned this status by committing a crime that warranted being banished by the king or by fleeing and depriving his victims the opportunity for retribution.[63] Outlaw status meant the person was outside the community, outside the shelter of the church, and outside the punishment or protection of the law. The official pronouncement equated the outlaw with a wolf—the outlaw deserved no judge, no trial, and could be killed on sight. In this regard, the outlaw differed significantly from the criminal, who breaks the law but remains within the legal system.[64] The

62. See C.C. Rister, 'Outlaws and Vigilantes of the Southern Plains, 1865–1885', 19.4 Miss. Valley Hist. Rev. 19.4 537-554 (1933); Samuel C. Hyde Jr., 'Feuding Is Our Means of Societal Regulation: Elusive Stability in Southeastern Louisiana's Piney Woods, 1877–1910', 48.2 La. Hist. *133-155* (2007); and Joe Gray Taylor, *Louisiana Reconstructed, 1863–1877* (1974). Co. D, 1st LA Reserves, CSA was the local home guard unit during the war. For a discussion of outlaw violence following the Civil War, see Gilles Vandal, "Property Offenses, Social Tension and Racial Antagonism in Post–Civil War Rural Louisiana', 31.1 J. Social Hist. 136 (1997). Residents' use of Ebenezer Campground near Montgomery, Louisiana, is an excellent example. Ebenezer Campground was a thatched hut/brush arbor meeting place for religious services. Beyond gathering for religious services, folks gathered there to discuss problems and issues and to decide on policing actions when necessary. Maxwell Kelley's version of the legend also connects to this historical development of civil authority when he says, "No one ever expected these people. No one ever knew that it was them that was doing these atrocities. Like I said, they were Masons!"

63. Frank Richard Prassel, *The Great American Outlaw: A Legacy of Fact and Fiction* 3-20 (1993).

64. Carl Ludwig von Bar, 'A History of Continental Criminal Law', 6 *Continental Legal History Series* (1968), and Joan Kent, 'Folk Justice and

outlaw is the representation of law outside the official system. In legend, he roams a lawless land. He lives by a separate code. He's captured by agents outside the law. In nearly every way, the figure embodies the concept of extralegality in the folk imagination, and for this reason, to understand the outlaw, especially as a folktype, we must first understand certain fundamental aspects of law, most specifically the figure's connection to a community's ideas of folk justice.

Alongside society's official code of law—including the components derived from statutory law and case or customary law—exists another channel of unwritten laws known as folk laws. Folk laws are the deep-seated rules of behavior particular to a locale or to a tight-knit group. They are communicated orally or by firsthand experience, and they carry with them punishments meted out by members of the groups who hold them as laws.[65] While an official code of law is codified, fixed, articulated overtly, and administered by institutions and bureaucracies, the folk system of law is oral, dynamic, administered by an entrenched population, and often unarticulated except through folk practices, such as being embedded in folk rituals or customs or communicated through exempla, often in the form of narratives. The outlaw legend stands as the most pronounced and clearly articulated narrative expression of folk law, especially when an entrenched folk law is being supplanted by an introduced official law.[66]

Royal Justice in Early Seventeenth-Century England, A "*Charivari*" in the Midlands,' 8 Midland Hist. 70–85 (1983).

65. Notions of folk law can be quite complicated, and many scholars have addressed how unwritten laws interact with written laws, especially in times of conquest and colonization. For this discussion and for a definition of folk law, see *Folk Law: Essays in the Theory and Practice of Lex Non Scripta* (Alison Dundes Renteln and Alan Dundes, eds., 1994). See also Rupert B. Vance and Waller Wynne, 'Folk Rationalizations in the "Unwritten Law"' 39 Am. J. Sociology 483-492 (1934). In Vance and Wynne's article, "folk" means anything outside of or contrary to the state.

66. I explore this concept in LeJeune, *Legendary Louisiana Outlaws*, *supra* note 1. Outlaws take on one of two basic forms—the outlaw and the outlaw-hero. The outlaw breaks a law, thus earning the status of an outsider. The outlaw-hero (or social bandit) breaks a law for the good of the folk, thus earning the status of a noble defender operating beyond the limits of the law.

In his 1989 book *Criminals as Heroes: Structure, Power and Identity*, Paul Kooistra argues the outlaw embodies "a sense of justice based upon kinship and community rather than one based upon impersonal, bureaucratic procedures established by the state."[67] In his work on Irish outlaws, Ray Cashman contends "outlaw lore ... sets traditional morality in direct conflict with that of the state" and the outlaw "provides a kind of cultural script that advocated a moral system alternative to, and higher than, official law."[68] Jean Laffite offers a pertinent example for this discussion. In legend, perhaps most obviously in relation to the social history of New Orleans, Laffite becomes a representation of the entrenched population's anxiety about and ultimate resolution with the shifting legal code introduced through America's purchase of Louisiana.[69] While Laffite's legendary exploits did reach western Louisiana, the West and Kimbrell clan makes a more definitive statement about the Neutral Strip's lingering effects on the population's sense of place because, unlike Laffite's legend, key portions of the West and Kimbrell legend connect directly to the region's history as a buffer.

Though nearly all of the West and Kimbrell legend demonstrates the social and psychological function of the outlaw folktype, for clarity and effect this essay limits its discussion to the gang's rise and fall. First, outlaws in legend often possess similar traits and their narratives follow predictable arcs.[70] One typical feature is the outlaw in legend is driven to a life of crime, often committing a first crime as an act of retaliation against an oppressive force or as an act of desperation after being marred, sometimes physically, by the system in power

---

67. Paul Kooistra, *Criminals as Heroes: Structure, Power and Identity* 11 (1989).
68. Ray Cashman, 'The Heroic Outlaw in Irish Folklore and Popular Literature', 111.2 Folklore 209 (October 2000).
69. Keagan LeJeune, 'The Prince of the Pirates: Jean Laffite, 1776–1823' in LeJeune, *Legendary Louisiana Outlaws*, *supra* note 1, 16-42.
70. Richard Meyer, 'The Outlaw' 17 J. of the Folklore Institute 94-124 (1980); Eric Hobsbawm, *Primitive Rebels: Studies in Archaic Forms of Social Movement in the 19th and 20th Centuries* 13-29 (1965) and *Bandits* (1969); Carl Lindahl, 'Outlaws and Other Medieval Heroes', 53.3 Southern Folklore 139-256 (1996); and Graham Seal, *Outlaw Heroes in Myth and History* (2011).

and thus made unfit and perpetually *outside* the community. Dispossessed of his status and cast out, the outlaw often must flee to a region beyond the control of law—the outskirts, the woods, the caves, the swamps.

According to legend, John West began an outlaw's life by joining William Quantrill's band of Civil War deserters and even developed a friendship with Jesse and Frank James.[71] While West's connection to Quantrill and James cannot be verified, the broad details of the narrative follow the Neutral Strip's post-war history since the region did experience a surge of rural outlaw gangs consisting of Confederate veterans.[72] In addition, the legend contains other explanations more specifically tied to place. According to some versions, the West and Kimbrell Clan leaders, especially Dan Kimbrell, learned the outlaw trade from the notorious John Murrell.[73] In fact, nearly all outlaw legends in the Neutral Strip, even those set much later than the 1820s and 30s, connect to this famous southern outlaw. This seems to prove residents' desire to link the region's reputation as a rugged, rough place to that defining historical moment when Murrell capitalized on the region's lack of stability following its neutrality.

However, the most salient detail from the legend that ties the West and Kimbrell outlaws to the landscape's neutral status exists in a portion of the story involving "voodooed" Coochie Brake. In some versions of the local legend, "Elbert Weston, now calling himself John West," and Laws Kimbrell formed a "volunteer organization ... to act as a police force" to protect Winn Parish, which "had always been poor" but was now "defeated, overrun with carpetbaggers and even poorer." Their noble plans, however, changed during one hunting trip "in the nearby swamp" when "the two young men decided to rest on a rock formation shaped like a side-lying horse. A dark mood came over them as they talked into the night. At daylight they realized they had been on that rock all

71. Briley, *supra* note 61, 4. Local legends also have it that Jesse James and his gang frequented Louisiana, and on some occasions, the James Gang even turned to West for a place to hide.

72. In 'Property Offenses', Vandal elaborates on the propensity of Confederate veterans to be in Louisiana's rural outlaw gangs. *Supra* note 62, 135-136. In fact, he specifically discusses the West and Kimbrell gang. *Id.*, note 36.

73. Briley, *supra* note 61, 3.

night." West and Kimbrell "had entered the Brake full of spirit" but would leave "feeling victimized by all of the events outside their control—the poverty, the war, and the chaos—and were determined to take back the life that was owed to them. Coochie Brake had changed the men forever." The following night, West and Kimbrell kill their first victim.[74]

These origins of the West and Kimbrell Clan represent the outlaws of the region and the residents' suspicious and independent natures grown from settling an area overrun with outlaws. The legend conveys the tendency to employ the land as a metaphorical scapegoat for the region's history, specifically tying the region's most notorious outlaw band to a place cursed by the buried treasure left by Spain's occupation of the region and that country's symbol-laden emissary—a "mad monk" made brutal and greedy by a lust for New Spain's gold. In the way the monk poisons his own workers, Spain's governance poisons its own possession, or that's what legend would have us embrace.

Like the rise of the West and Kimbrell gang, the gang's fall is equally resonant. Aided by members of a community, the outlaw in legend for a time outwits the law, avoids capture, and escapes punishment, which demonstrates the limits of the official system of justice and the power of the folk; however, the outlaw never lasts. Living outside the law comes with a heavy price. Once the community's tolerance and perhaps even celebration of violence and outlawry end, the outlaw is brought to justice, but not by the power and might of the official legal system. According to official records, outside officers of the law failed on several occasions to bring the West and Kimbrell Clan to justice; for instance, when a visiting marshal sought to arrest the Kimbrells for suspected murder of a Freedmen's Bureau Payroll officer, the local population refused to give him aid for they saw him as a further intrusion by outsiders in local affairs.[75]

---

74. Charles Bobuck, *This Is Also for Readers... The Wax and Wane of Charles Bobuck*, publisher Charles Bobuck, Itunes, 34-35.

75. In his official report Brevet Brigadier General Samuel Thomas describes the incident in this manner: "April 27th, 1866—Bt. Major James Cromie, Natchitoches, reports Usan Tennace was killed about 5 miles from Natchitoches by Samuel Newman Lawson & William Kimball of Winn Parish. Inquest held and warrants issued for arrests of accused. On June 30/66 Major Cromie reports

Over the course of their reign of terror, the gang's crimes escalated from run-of-the-mill highway robbery and horse stealing to murder. Many of the gang's early crimes preyed on outsiders, such as wealthy New Orleans cotton buyers, northern timber speculators, and other "carpetbaggers" and "damn-Yankees," but later they turned to dispatching disloyal gang members, robbing defiant locals, and even murdering women and children. These very violent crimes made the inner circle of the gang unredeemable in the eyes of local people and necessitated the end of this malfunctioning "home guard." Here, the West and Kimbrell legend is a complex expression of the locals' feelings about submitting to home guard authority for protection and of the citizens' roles in dismantling the guard when it was found to be corrupt. Because these feelings exist, the legend of the West and Kimbrell Clan follows the pattern typical to outlaw legends, which is even though the official agents of the law can't bring the outlaw to justice, the folk can. The outlaw in legend is inevitably betrayed by a compatriot and brought to justice by the everyday people. The end of the West and Kimbrell Clan follows this same pattern.

The local population, however, did eventually form a posse to bring down West once he and his clansmen accosted a local family on Easter Sunday. Led by Dan Dean and James O. Maybin, the local population finally rallied and ended the gang, some accounts even describing the crucial role young men attending the local school played in supporting Dan Dean when the older townsfolk were too timid to come forward. On that Easter Sunday, West watched his power vanish at the hands of the people. He asked to speak, and when the crowd refused, he asked to pray, but that plea, too, was rejected. Eventually, a shotgun went off, and West was killed. The fall of the West and Kimbrell Clan becomes a statement about the folk's role in the development of law and order. The West and Kimbrell Clan offered protection from outsiders and thwarted those who sought

---

accused have evaded arrest and defy civil and military authorities. At the end of the year these parties were reported as living near Harrisonburg in Winn Parish, unmolested by Civil Authorities" (March 9, 1867), in 'Records Relating to Murders and Outrages,' *Miscellaneous Reports and Lists Relating to Murders and Outrages*, Bureau of Refugees, Freedmen and Abandoned Lands, 1865–1869 (National Archives Microfilm M1027, Roll 34, March 1867–November 1868).

to challenge the entrenched civil system, but through their zeal, power, and secrecy, the clan returned something more dangerous—unchecked power of corrupt insiders who abide by no law. The fall of the West and Kimbrell clan restates the citizenry's unending role in maintaining peace and order.

When the stories of outlaws are misunderstood, they appear merely as morbid glorifications of violence or as shortsighted cheers for anarchy. But understood with proper historical and cultural context, an outlaw legend can reveal a great deal about the people and the historical moment which produced the figure. Like many legends, the story of the West-Kimbrell Clan builds from historical fact and symbolic invention. The outlaw group was a product of social disintegration, a disintegration made even more severe by the town's proximity to the Neutral Strip and its history of banditry and highwaymen. Yet, this legend does more. While an outlaw legend acts as a monument to and commentary on the past, connected to a specific locale, it also acts as a representation of a people within a place. Its details arise from the local environment, emerging to express the deep-seated experiences people have shared with each other and their landscape. The outlaw's clothes, his name, his weapon of choice—nearly every facet of his being embodies the locals and their home, and in that way, each telling of the legend becomes a statement about a group's common world view arising from not only their common historical experience but also their shared geographical experience. Thus, the place-name legend of Coochie Brake becomes a touchstone of regional lore, for its narrative of a lost Spanish mine, a landscape perpetually affected by this history, and that cursed landscape spawning outlaws exemplifies the region's entrenched historical awareness and the role of that awareness in creating the people's sense of place. At the core of this sense of place is the residents' entrenched beliefs about the importance of autonomy and self-reliance, the acceptance of self-generated codes superseding imposed codes of law, and the role of individuals and tight-knit social circles as internally generated agents of folk justice.

INDEX

www.ingramcontent.com/pod-product-compliance
Lightning Source LLC
LaVergne TN
LVHW091525200926
848483LV00002B/306